A SUCCESSION OF DAYS

'Days that are over'.
The POMMERN approaching Dover

A
SUCCESSION
OF
DAYS

by

ALEX A. HURST

Comprising two volumes — DOWN TO THE SEA concerning the author's days at sea in both sail and steam, and IN DURANCE VILE, which relates his experiences and those of his colleagues in a German raider, in a couple of German prison ships and then as a prisoner-of-war in Japan, with much additional anecdote and comment in both volumes.

A Square One Publication

MCMXCII

Other books by Alex. A. Hurst

Ghosts on the Sea-Line
The Call of High Canvas
The Music of Five Oceans
The Sailing School Ships
Square-Riggers — The Final Epoch, 1921 – 1958
Arthur Briscoe — Marine Artist
Thomas Somerscales — Marine Artist
Anton Otto Fischer — Marine Artist (Co-author)
The Medley of Mast and Sail 1 & 2 (Co-author)
The Maritime History of the World (Co-author)

First published in 1992 by
Square One Publications
Saga House, Sansome Place
Worcester, England

British Library Cataloguing in Publication Data

Hurst, Alex A.
 Succession of Days
 I. Title
940.54

ISBN 1-872017-63-0

Typeset by Avon Dataset, Bidford on Avon, in Times 10 on 13pt and
Printed in England by Biddles Ltd, Guildford

CONTENTS

LIST OF ILLUSTRATIONS

FOREWORD AND ACKNOWLEDGEMENTS

No two people describe the same events in the same way or with the same slant or emphasis as, indeed, it is well-known that a newspaper report of an event which one has attended seldom bears much resemblance to one's own recollections and impressions of it. At least there should be a common, recognizable thread to such accounts as Martin Boyle's and my own, even if he and I, and our respective books, are separated by the breadth of the Atlantic. I refer to his book on p. 316 and, in the same way as the late Jocelyn Baines' book *In Deep* (p. 311), spurred me to put pen to paper and write a string of nautical books, Boyle's book has provided me with the necessary stimulus and now, after so many years, this book has at last been retrieved from my desk and presented for public consumption. Its publication coincides, I believe, with a period in which the Japanese are engaged in examining their national soul.

Inevitably, the text is largely autobiographical. The first volume, 'Down to the Sea' is mainly anecdotal and, if the second volume, 'In Durance Vile', lacks a certain emphasis almost peculiar to myself, it is because I have consciously played down the problems and difficulties which accrued from the keeping of a diary. These loomed much larger in my life than might be supposed from the text, but I believe that greater discussion of this subject would have been both repetitive and boring. In any case, I brought these matters on myself quite voluntarily and they did not apply to the vast majority of my fellows.

The second part of the Epilogue sets out to restore certain balances by including items of contemporary historical fact which are seldom appreciated in the West on the one hand, and by presenting a view of the Japanese and how they might have been treated at the conclusion of the war on the other. I believe that this latter point of view is not without its merit, even if those, whose experiences were so much harsher, will find it abhorrent, quite apart from those who paid lip-service to the Japanese War Crimes Tribunals: a subject on which my own opinions have *not* been altered by the passage of time.

Once read, it will now be appreciated why these volumes were so long in their gestation, and thus why some of the pictures were passed to the author so many years ago by people or organisations no longer in being. Thus Plate 20 was supplied by the now-defunct Burntisland Shipbuilding Co: Plates 12, 17, 19, 26/29 and 44 came from my old friend, Captain Fred. C. Poyser, now long departed, who was then running the Nautical Photo Agency: The Frontispiece and Plate No. 14 came from the late Dr. P. Ransome-Wallis and Plates 10/11 from Central Press Photos Ltd. before the last war.

I take this opportunity of thanking the Imperial War Museum for their co-operation in obtaining Plates 33/37, 39/41 and 43 and last, but by no means least, my grateful thanks go to Caroline Sills for producing the cover design and the sketches comprising Plates 25 and 30/32. Apart from one which I can no longer trace, the other plates derived from photographs which I took myself at various times.

Alex. A. Hurst

VOLUME ONE

DOWN TO THE SEA

"Yet when I am dust my penman may not know
Those water-trampling ships which made me glow,
But think my wonder mad and fail to find
Their glory even dimly from my mind,
And yet they made me. Not alone the ships
But men hard-palmed from tallying on to whips
....."

(*Biography*, John Masefield.)

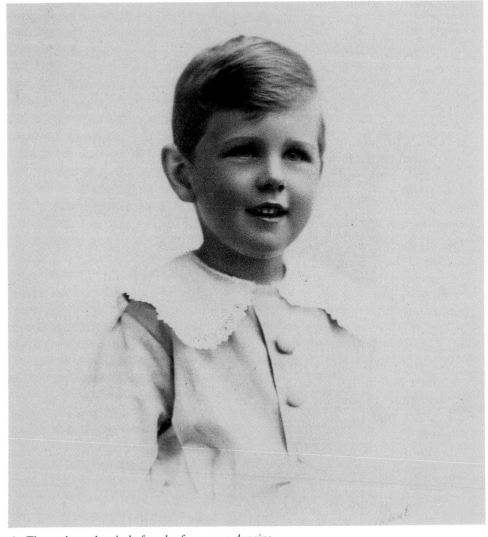

1. The author, shortly before he foreswore dancing.

I

A SAGA STEMS FROM A SWALLOWED STUD

Few people can pinpoint those acts or occasions which determined the course of their future destinies, since they are seldom obvious at the time and are often difficult to determine in retrospect.

Just before my third birthday, my parents moved to a very rural area in Kent. I was an only child and there were but few others of my generation scattered over a wide area. One family, in a manor house, did make an effort to assemble such as there were for dancing classes, to the first of which I was sent in my push chair in charge of my nurse. It was an optimistic venture, though no-one had foreseen what would happen. I was paired with a horrid little girl with a spotty face whom I disliked on sight and, at the end of the first dance, the small boys were instructed to kiss their partners. All did so, except myself — which did not go unnoticed. I was then told to rectify the omission, but refused. This led to various strict admonitions from my elders and a clear command to kiss my partner who, finally realising that she, alone, remained unkissed, evidently felt slighted and started to scream. Finding myself under increased pressure, I followed suit and the upshot was that I was removed and taken home, never to go to a dancing class again in my whole life. Whether the classes continued I have no idea but, partly as a result of this social gaffe, I was sent to boarding school as soon as it became practicable at the tender age of six.

Naturally enough, I was immediately homesick and, being quite the youngest boy in the school, soon found it necessary to assert myself in some manner to gain a modicum of status; so, to this end, boasted in the dormitory that I could balance my front collar stud on the tip of my tongue. This claim is totally lost on my grand-children and their peers, who know nothing of the horror of the Eton collar, but in those days front and back studs were almost the staff of life, and I was promptly challenged to fulfil my boast. Needless to say, I failed miserably and swallowed the stud. Granted that it was finally recovered by the matron and placed in her 'museum': its pristine gilt now turned a sombre black by my gastric juices, but, nevertheless, in my failure lay my triumph,

1

2. Pre-school days, before swallowing his stud, wearing a smock. The author has never worn anything nearly so comfortable since.

since no other boy in the school had ever done such a thing before. I had not only made my mark but, unwittingly, determined my destiny.

It was quite by chance that, within a week, when playing stump cricket, I had swung a stump and accidentally knocked out the front teeth of one of the older boys. The fact that he was so unpopular with his fellows that he found himself bound to play with the smaller fry had never occurred to me but, at all events, the fact of knocking out the hated Acton's teeth, coupled with the incident of the stud, cemented my position in the school. The fury of the other boy's parents (they were his second teeth), touched me not at all.

The school used to walk across fields, long since covered with bungalows, to swim off a beach more or less opposite the Needles, at the entrance to the Solent, where we used to watch the great Atlantic liners of the day on their passages — the *Mauretania, Aquitania, Berengaria, Olympic, Albert Ballin, Leviathan*, and the like. These, with the occasional seaplanes passing overhead, formed the great spare time interest of the majority of my school-fellows. Thus, when a couple of square-rigged sailing ships appeared in the Solent, one after collision and both very distant, the incidents of the stud and the teeth having made me dimly conscious that it paid to be different, I announced my interest in *them*.

Of course, I knew nothing whatever about such vessels other than what little I could glean from the current *Wonder Book of Ships*, which was little enough, and my declared interest was shared by no-one else. No doubt it would have died quickly enough but for the fact that my father, when unwell, had been lent some magazines on the subject, which I devoured avidly during the ensuing holidays, and which made me realize that sailing ships were to be seen in Gravesend Reach, which was only five minutes walk from the shops patronised by my parents, since Gravesend was the town used for shopping by our village.

From then on I had a virtually one-track mind. It was not long before I knew all about the sailing ships which were still in trade and, more by luck than good judgement, made a number of contacts amongst men who were unbelievably kind and who enabled me to spend most of my holidays on tugs on the river, often towing big square-rigged ships out to sea as they made sail. Moreover, I was given the run of the largest privately-owned maritime library in the world and, with such similar and unique opportunities, there was no turning back.

It is undeniable that the sea has cast some sort of a lure over men ever since the most distant reaches of history, if for different reasons. Some, of course, followed a family tradition: others were fired by adventure stories read in their youth; yet more were ensnared by the so-called Romance of the Sea, and few ever found that deep satisfaction which they expected, having small realization of the enormous death toll by disease or accident down the years, of the appalling food and conditions which were common to the majority of ships, or even, in past ages, of the vast numbers of men captured and set to the thwarts of Algerine or other galleys. Yet, even to many of those who were alive to those things, there was still woven about them an unbreakable spell from which there was no escape.

For my part, I was under few illusions. I was going aboard the ships and knew their conditions very well, whilst I had often sampled the unappetizing food, which was little better in the average steam vessel, but all such considerations were transcended by the sailing ship herself since, for all her defections, I believed, and still believe, that man has seldom produced anything more beautiful or which demanded such skills when working with or against the elements. Man has, it is true, produced great cathedrals, palaces, mausoleums and other edifices of unsurpassed beauty which have, in many cases, survived down the centuries, but the sailing ship had movement, and changed visually almost with every scend and pitch. Probably no other waterway in the world saw such a multiplicity of shipping in those days as Gravesend Reach, when each

3. The PONAPE *in the Barrow Deep, making 10 knots with the tow-rope in a bight. Inward-bound colliers are passing on the right.*

and every vessel had her own character, but so far as I was concerned the modern motorships and steamers played very much second fiddle to the big deep-water sailing ships and the coasting schooners.

My parents allowed me a freedom in my holidays which was almost unparalleled in my generation, probably because they did not know what else to do with me and were thankful that I could make my own amusements. When still very young I was often away in tugs or coasting schooners for days at a time, sometimes visiting Antwerp, Emden, Delfzyl and other Continental ports.

However, although totally co-operative in allowing me to pursue my hobby, they were adamant that I should not go to sea. No member of the family had ever done so since Nelson's time. My father averred, with much truth, that I only wanted to go to sea to be in sailing ships and added, with equal truth, that they could not last many more years. My tongue firmly in my cheek, I denied this, although in truth neither passenger nor cargo screw-propelled vessels had anything like the same appeal to me. Privately I considered that a few good years in sail were worth a lifetime of commuting to a City office and that, if and when the sailing ship did become extinct, I would aim for research or

4

whale-marking vessels, which carried neither cargo nor passengers but which did spend a lot of time at sea.

Nevertheless, before I left school, strings had been pulled and, almost before I had realized what had happened, I *was* in a City office, as a Management Trainee, but with indescribable folly I was initially placed in charge of the "Captains' Room" to look after the business of the collier masters serving most of the Thames gas and power stations. Often just arriving in the office on time, if a little bleary-eyed, I would be greeted by one of the captains with: — *"You should have been with me this morning, Mr. Hurst. We passed a four-masted barque running through the Barrow Deep under six topsails behind her tug with the line in a bight, and making about ten knots"*. *"Yes"*, I would reply, *"she passed you just to the east of the Mouse, but after we dropped her off the Sunk she had everything set and she was making about fourteen!"* The wind taken out of his sails, the captain would gape in astonishment, but such a day was sheer hell. Lack of sleep apart, I felt like a wild bird in a cage in that office, because in spirit I was aboard that lofty ship as she raced across the North Sea for the Skaw. There were many such occasions although, during the working week, I was constrained to go out with the ships only when they left in the evenings.

I had been in the tug towing that same ship, the *Ponape*, through the night about a year previously when we had dropped her and run ahead to haul in the 120 fathoms of tow line, and then waited for her to come up to get the towing bill signed. I had suddenly been aware of the odd creak. There was no moon, but every star was shining brilliantly as I suddenly became aware of a few becoming obsured as the sails passed across them, and there she was! Under every stitch of canvas, with no sound but the faintest lapping of her bow wave and the odd creaking of a block. There was nothing of the pulsating vibration of the steamship. I knew well enough that this was a rare and almost magical moment with the four-master sailing so silently under the stars, but it was another nail in the coffin of the City office and, at the same time, another stage in the saga that started with the swallowed stud.

A major crisis in my mind occurred one day when the office stopped work for its afternoon tea early in the summer. One fairly senior man suddenly turned to me and asked, rather patronisingly I thought:- *"You're taking your holiday soon, aren't you, Mr. Hurst?"* (Christian names were never used in those days). I replied that I was. *"Are you going away?"* he queried. Of course, I might have been going with my family, but on a wage of 25 or 35 shillings per week — I forget which rate I was on at that time — I was the lowest paid person in the office. At that time only the directors ever went abroad, and then only to Le Touquet or La Zoute, just across the Channel. There were no such things as packaged holidays and Imperial Airways were, to all intents and purposes, patronised only by the very rich or the very important. Visits to Spain or the Mediterranean were beyond imagination. Very senior managers might go to Torquay and, as the grade and salary range diminished, people went away, if they went at all, to places nearer London, the lowest echelons treating themselves to a day away at, say, Ramsgate, if they were lucky.

I replied that I was going to the Åland Islands. One could have heard a pin drop. After a stunned silence, I was bombarded with questions by everyone present. *"Where were the Åland Islands?"* I explained that they lay, roughly, between Stockholm and Åbo on the Finnish coast, at the southern end of the Gulf of Bothnia. I might as well have saved my breath. They had never heard of the Gulf of Bothnia nor of Åbo, and had only the haziest idea where Stockholm really was. *"But how will you get there?"* I pointed out that Mr. Angus, in the Export Department, was agent for various Scandinavian tramps carrying coke from Beckton Gasworks to Copenhagen, and that I was going in such a Danish vessel for half a crown a day. (In the event, a very old vessel, she was slow, taking four days instead of three, and thus costing me ten shillings!)

"Had I a passport?" The intelligence that I had one created another silence, since few, if any, of them had ever seen one. *"Can you speak the language?"* When I answered that I could not, it was apparent that they not only thought me mad but that they would never see me again. So the catechism went on. A few of the men had, it is true, made cheap holiday passages aboard the firm's colliers, mainly to the north-east coast coal staithes, but none had ever considered a trip abroad.

So far from being flattered, I was appalled. All were considerably older than I, and had caught the same train to and from their homes, and joined the same pasty-faced crowd to walk between their stations and their office, day in and year out, and it was all they would ever know. The world was a vast tome that their circumscribed lives would never allow them to open and examine.

It had emerged that my ultimate goal was Mariehamn, the home port of most of the surviving deep-sea sailing ships. They had never heard of the place, and it passed over their heads. When I finally arrived there, to pay three shillings and fourpence *per diem* for a room with a marvellous view over the islands, full board and the hire of a boat during my stay with half the world's surviving big sailing ships in the harbour, I have little doubt that a blackened front stud in the matron's museum stirred on its base, for it was but another stage in the natural progression which it started.

On my return, only just on time as it turned out, since my ship had been hove to for thirty-six hours in a gale in the North Sea, I was greeted as though I was some long-lost explorer returning. I found this terrifying, believing that, sooner or later, I too would succumb to their environment. I had expended five pounds on travel and about another five pounds on photography. Within a month I had recouped all this expenditure by the publication of some of the photographs, thereby achieving what was, in effect, a free holiday, in which I had also been to Stockholm and Malmö.

Nevertheless, if that trip had hardened my desire to go to sea in sail, it had equally hardened my attitude to the City and to the narrow outlook of those who worked therein. Then two things happened almost simultaneously. My parents, and others, had constantly been pointing out to me that my ambitions were out of perspective and that I judged ships and the sea too much from books and an armchair. Seeing ships in and around ports was, they averred, very different from, say, being off Cape Horn in one. In a sense, this was true, but I knew it was only half the story.

However, one day there came into the Captains' Room an old, rather grizzled man, who was master of a ship we had on charter. I had long since divided the masters into two groups: those who had been in sail and those who had not (I suspect to the resentment of the latter!), and normally talked or took coffee with the former. As usual, I had turned the conversation on to this subject when this captain, who was rather deaf and had been listening with his hand aiding his ear, suddenly began to speak in a quiet, modulated tone and, although obviously not a literate man, combined a marvellous poetry with his rather rough expression and phrasing. He had, it seemed, been in various sailing ships but, after speaking of a North Country barque in which he had served his time, he turned to the *Sam Mendel*, an old iron wool clipper by that time hauling manganese ore, in which he had been second mate, but he spoke from his soul, almost as though in a trance, recapturing all the high moments which most men would have long forgotten or, most likely, never have noticed at all. He described the spray in the moonlight: the light on the sails in different conditions as the dawn rose; the sounds of the wind in the rigging and, indeed, the very motion of the ship and her relationship with the sea. Had it been recorded and transcribed it would have been one of the major pieces of sea literature. This was not just a fine seaman relating his experiences, but one who had found something much rarer, namely: a true personal affinity with the sea and his ships.

I had read many books of reminiscences, many of them interesting enough, but only in a handful had I sensed that very affinity of ship, self and elements. The reason is self-evident. It is innate, and can never be acquired as, indeed, one is born with good hands for a horse but, if not,

7

will never have them. A young boy may have this affinity before he has acquired proficiency in seamanship, yet the most proficient seaman may never know it. This captain held his audience spell-bound, including the Shipping Director (who had entered the room) and the other masters, whether he was describing gale, calm or any other condition, for he presented the sea and his ship in a light that they had never known before and I, for my part, knew that my own perspective was not so awry as my family maintained. Within days I was summoned to the presence of one of the Directors who professed himself more than pleased with my progress, but said that I was several years younger than the other trainees who had all been to university, and that perhaps I had been engaged too young. This being the case, I might either remain where I was for a year on my present salary (on which I could barely live!), or I might take a year's unpaid leave until my age had, as it were, caught up. What an escape route! I opted for the latter alternative without a moment's hesitation and returned home that evening cock-a-hoop. My father was clearly furious. *"Are you going to hang about here for a year, then?"*, he asked: his face as black as thunder. I replied that that was the last thing I wished to do. I might hitch-hike to China perhaps, but what I would really like to do would be to spend the year making a voyage to Australia and back in a Cape Horner. All the old arguments were advanced against me. Finally, weakening a little, he said that, were I to go to sea, I should go as apprentice in a British merchant ship or, better still, enter the navy. I pointed out that I was too old for normal naval entry and that, in any case, the tax-payer could not afford to keep the ships at sea. I had no stomach for swinging at anchor at Malta or anywhere else. As to going as apprentice in a British ship, I reminded him that my leave was for a mere year — not four years.

Relationships at home became very strained. Finally an uncle, always a good friend to me and whose influence had obtained my job in the City, produced some good sense. *"Let him go,"* he said, *"Either it will make him or break him. If it breaks him, you will hear no more of it. If it makes him, it is what he should have been doing all along."*

The die was cast. Equipped with a fully furnished sea chest I finally left for Finland, again in a coke vessel. By this time there were few enough deep-sea sailing ships in trade. There had been no British ship for several years and the Germans were closed to foreign nationals. Apart from a couple of sail-training vessels in Sweden, the choice was confined to a Finnish vessel, hailing from the Åland Islands, and I, knowing all the ships except one at first-hand, had opted for that same *Ponape* which I admired above all the others. If my feet were beating to the time of a jig as I crossed the North Sea, I had no doubt that that discoloured front stud was doing something similar for, if it had taken twelve or thirteen years, the end of the first revolution of the wheel of destiny, inadvertently set in motion that evening in the school dormitory, had been reached and, of course, all the burden of this book which follows stemmed from that same event as a natural consequence.

~~~~~~

II

THE SPELL OF THE SAILS

Today there are vast ferries of some 30,000 tons and over operating between Stockholm, the Åland Archipelago and Finland, but in the 1930s they were small and rather beautiful little steamers, one of which arrived at Mariehamn, my first destination, at about 1.0 o'clock in the morning. Most of those disembarking merely had hand luggage and, with them, I went ashore with my sea-bag. Only when the ship had backed away from the wharf and was out in the harbour, turning prior to proceeding to Finland, did I realize that my sea-chest had not been landed. There was no time to think back to the office-workers' question:- "*Do you speak the language?*" I fell back on the usual recourse of my countryman and shouted as loudly as I could in the only language I knew — English — on the premise that the louder my shout the more likely I was to be understood! Perhaps by luck I was standing under a lamp-post and was recognized by the second mate of the steamer, to whom I had been talking and who knew my plans. To my relief, the steamer came alongside again and disgorged the precious chest.

However, when I reported to the owner's office later in the morning, I was met with the depressing news that the *Ponape* had just been sold for scrapping. There were only five big ships in the harbour, and two more (excluding the *Ponape*), on the mainland at Nystad. One, the *Pommern*, which I should have chosen, had a full crew. I opted for the one vessel I had never seen — the *Moshulu*, which was the biggest sailing ship afloat and which was at Nystad.

Luckily Mariehamn was still a cheap place to stay, as I had some days to wait before the company's tug was leaving for Nystad, during which I accompanied her on several occasions as she towed several of the ships out to sea. When I finally arrived at Nystad and steamed up the harbour there to see the *Moshulu* for the first time, she seemed immense, although actually only marginally bigger than some of the vessels I had seen in the past week. This was partly because her spars were painted white, which enhanced her size, and because she was lying just ahead of

11

the barque *Penang* and the 4-masted barque *Ponape*, which were both a good deal smaller, making the *Moshulu* seem larger by contrast.

In a sense I was luckier than many first-voyagers in sail because, although I could not speak the language (despite having learnt the main elements of the ship in Swedish, which was the language in use*), I knew myself competent to steer and could probably have passed a Board of Trade *viva voce* seamanship examination several years previously, had I had the sea-time and been of the age required to do so. Moreover, unlike many young men whose first sight of a sailing ship was when they joined her, I was fully prepared for the foc's'le, for the food, for the primitive form of 'heads' and even for the more menial work.

Nevertheless, mine was hardly an auspicious beginning, as the first morning we were bending sail: our spars towering above the countryside and being the only barrier to an unbelievably cold wind which came unbroken from the Arctic tundras. It is both impossible and unsafe to wear gloves aloft, and the steel spars and rigging were too painful to clasp. Apart from the galley, to which we were barred, there was no heat in the ship.

There are no tides in the Baltic, although the water level varies slightly and seasonally with the atmospheric pressure but, with unbelievable folly, this great ship, the largest ever to visit the port, had been topped up with an extra 500 tons of ballast. One night of high gale we suspected that she was firmly aground, as she neither surged nor moved at all. Sure enough, when we came to sail and the tug passed her line, she would not move. We set some sails: we passed breast lines to a small island abeam to try to warp her off with the ship's capstans, and all the time the tug *Johanna* hauled. This went on for day after day, with the weather getting colder and colder. The *Johanna* was a small wooden vessel which burnt local logs for bunkers, and her power was negligible. We foresaw being frozen in for the winter (as had happened to another of the company's ships, the *Archibald Russell*, in Sundsvall a few years previously). I, in particular, was filled with apprehension for, by this time, the other vessels had all left on the long haul south to Australia.

Finally, we had to discharge the extra ballast, haul the ship off, and then re-stow it. The crew were already at odds with the master and owner (who was aboard), having demanded a better tug from Helsingfors, and also having complained about the food, for which one man had been dismissed the ship. She was not a happy vessel that voyage, but a forum for much factional ill-will throughout the passage: Finns against Swedes, the crew against the master, and so on.

---

* After the First World War the Åland Islands, although linguistically and anthropologically Swedish, were ceded to Finland. (Like Finland, they had previously been brought under Russian domination by the Treaty of Frederikshamn in 1815).

We finally sailed during a gale but, although we had only a few rags of sail set, went rushing down the harbour so that the miserable *Johanna* could not get round our bow for a turn. The sails were run down and the anchors let go on the run but, as the ship swung head to wind, she again grounded, and all the warping started again. It was a miserable start. Bitterly cold throughout, Nystad or, as the Finns termed it, Uusikaupunkki (and only Finnish was spoken there) was a small place which offered nothing in the evenings save a cinema once a week, and the ship offered even less.

On the second day out, when we were passing down past the islands of Gotland and Öland, I was sent aloft to do a job on one of the royals: the topmost sails some 180 feet above the deck. I had often been aloft and height had no terror for me, but I had never been on a royal yard *at sea*. In port, the yard is down on its lifts but, when the sail is set, it is hoisted and is above the ratlines — the steps up the rigging — necessitating climbing up the wire stay to reach the yard. I was (and am) a heavy man, and initially this did not come easily, as I at first slipped back more than I won.

However, once on the yard, I never had more trouble in that respect and the view which met my eyes was stupendous. The sun was out: it was temporarily milder; there was just over an acre of our own gleaming canvas below me and, all over the 550 square miles of sunlit sea within the bounds of my horizons, a veritable armada of barquentines and schooners of various sorts kept us company, whilst a firewood barque, bound the other way, was going about on our port beam. Not a single steamer was in sight and, as we slowly overhauled this fleet, I realized, with more prescience than I knew, that such a sight would seldom be seen again.

I could have stayed there all day, drinking it all in, but my watchmates, employed on the other two royals, saw nothing of it. At all events, it meant nothing to them and passed them by. For my part, it was indelibly printed on my memory.

It soon got cold again, and we were constantly anchoring and getting under way in an effort to beat up to Copenhagen where we were to dry-dock. Once, temporarily with a good wind, we were going knot for knot with the steamer *Royston*, whose master had spoken from his heart in the Captain's Room some six months previously. I was sure that he never took his eyes off us, probably marvelling at the very size of our ship and height of our masting, and wished I could communicate with him.

It is idle to pretend that life in a sailing ship is a bed of roses any more than any other form of human activity, and many discovered more thorns than blossoms. We were working every week-end initially and, after leaving Copenhagen, made a magnificent run down to the Skaw with another four-masted barque in company, passing every steamer in sight. Next morning, with both sailing ships lying becalmed, they all chugged past us again in solemn procession, and then we were bottled up in the Skaggerrak for nearly ten days with unremitting headwinds in a succession of gales. We were constantly battling with frozen canvas, often in snow squalls, and watches below were broken by the need to wear ship every few hours. (Because the extra ballast had been badly re-stowed, the ship was out of trim and would not stay.*) Sometimes we saw the other, white four-master on the opposite tack. Nobody had had more than an hour and half below at a stretch for days on end and, when I relieved the lookout one night on a foc's'le head lashed with icy sprays, I was thoroughly demoralised, tired, hungry and beginning to wonder why I was there.

The man I had relieved had pointed out a white light he had already reported on the port bow, which I assumed to be the stern light of a steamer. We were storming along, close-hauled, under six topsails and foresail under an unrelieved murk of flying cloud punctuated by squalls of snow and sleet. Suddenly there was a break in the cloud and the moon came out, casting a golden path across the heaving expanse of dark sea and catching the heads of the square-sails in ghostly light. Almost simultaneously, we came up with the light ahead, which proved to be the other four-master which was immediately silhouetted on the moonlit sea, rolling and wallowing with some of her sails blown out, and only her spanker and fore and mizzen lower topsails set, whilst her hands were visible aloft on the main lower topsail, which was presumably split. In an instant we were past her, our bow wave creaming to leeward, almost as if in triumph at passing our rival. The effect of the moon, the straining canvas, the hapless square-rigger dropping astern and even the whipping sprays suddenly rendered the whole scene into one of the high moments of life. Conrad wrote:- *"For a true expression of dishevelled wildness there is nothing like a sailing ship in a gale in the bright moonlight of a high latitude."* This was just such an expression. I wondered how on earth I could have been feeling so demoralised so short a time before, for now my blood seemed to be coursing in sheer exhilaration. Such moments are not given to the steamer man nor to the longshoreman.

Nevertheless, it was a hard outward passage, the ship being caught badly aback off Scotland when the helmsman was thrown over the wheel, and then old Aeolus threw all the gales in his bag of winds at us. One morning the ship was running under foresail and three lower topsails, almost the ultimate reduction in sail for a ship of the *Moshulu's*

---

* That is, being trimmed too much by the head, she would not pass head to wind when tacking. Wearing is a more arduous operation, entailing turning before the wind before coming up on the other tack, thereby losing ground.

4. Full storm and bright sunlight — the MOSHULU.

type, in full storm but in bright sunlight. After my breakfast, it being my watch below, I climbed out to the end of the bowsprit and sat there, watching the ship coming at me. And what a sight it was! *"Beauty in hardest action: beauty indeed"* as Masefield wrote. The sight mesmerised me until the mate appeared in the eyes of the ship and called out to ask what I was doing there. I shouted back that I was watching the ship coming at me. He, a man of long experience in sail, shook his head and ambled away, muttering (in Swedish) *"Crazy Englishman."* It was not that the novelty had worn off for him, since I verily believe that, excellent seaman as he was, he saw nothing beyond his job. He was not born with that 'affinity' that the collier master possessed ....

Next morning the wind had dropped a little and the master gave the order to set all sail. There was no cloud in the sky either then or for days afterwards but, before the first sail to be set, the main upper topsail, was fully hoisted, the ship lay right down before a wind of monumental intensity. For the rest of the day, there was little sense of reality. Initially, the ship had heeled over beyond her maximum clinometer reading of 62 degrees and, before long, when all hands were still struggling to take in that upper topsail again, an ominous rumbling told us that the ballast was shifting. By now the ship was listing to some 75 degrees, with the lee lower yardarms, which were checked right in, dipping in the sea, although she was high in the water. The ship steered amidships and, when all hands bar the master and helmsmen were aloft, the steering wires carried away. Fortunately the master saw it happen and, rushing aft, managed to screw down the quadrant and bring the auxiliary wheel aft into play.

It was by then impossible to stand on deck and, indeed, three men were injured: one very badly. Men had to claw their way along the weather rail by their hands. The sea was flattened by the intense wind (later shown to be well over 110 m.p.h.) but a solid spume was blown across the face of the sea to a height of over forty feet, rendering it difficult to see from one end of the ship to the other. Sails were constantly blowing out of their gaskets and having to be virtually marled down with extra line. Climbing aloft was extremely difficult, since all sense of balance was lost in that wind. Working on the yards at that unnatural angle of incline posed equal problems. Going alow or aloft, a man was flattened against the shrouds and ratlines whilst, if he opened his mouth to windward, he seemed to be filled with hot air — for it was a warm wind — like a hot air balloon.

Every movement was an effort, yet there was simply no time to feel exhaustion. Lesser ships could not have carried so much sail as we had set, but to touch any of it then would have been courting disaster.

The Finnish ships were always under-manned and now, with only eight men in each of two watches, of which half were on their first voyage, three were injured and four at the auxiliary wheel. After eight hours, a split appeared in the weather side of the foresail. Somehow, as if by telepathy, the rest of us converged on its gear. It was almost impossible to give or to hear orders, but it was resolved to take in just the weather side. In six hours this was accomplished after a fashion. That was the measure of that gale which I record, not because it was such an exceptional circumstance, but because it was a demonstration of men and ship against the elements at their worst, in which a crew, already much divided, worked as a solid team in unbelievable conditions. We had lost canvas and a small amount of rigging. I saw, for instance, a royal buntline, one of the longest ropes in the ship, become washed from its pin and, taken by the wind, stream out horizontally from near the mast-head until, as the whipping came adrift, the whole two hundred feet and more of it disintegrated in a flash. If the master had not seen the steering wires part, I should not be writing this book now. All day the ship had been fighting for her life: a ship which many would have said was an anachronism in her generation yet, as we subsequently discovered, a brand new, large German steamer had foundered not so far from us, and the peerless *Queen Mary* had suffered a good deal of damage in the same gale.

No-one can look back and pretend he enjoyed such a day, even if, in retrospect, it provided him with cherished memories and a sense of achievement, but the point is that each and every man was freshly tempered, almost as steel is tempered, by such experience and, having had it, displayed a better sense of perspective when he came to grips with adversities and hardships in later life. This may have been a very exceptional day, yet it was but an extreme example of the lessons constantly learnt in sail, not least of which, in large, undermanned ships, was self-sufficiency.

In the Trade Winds, one would suppose that a lofty sailing ship, her canvas etched in sunlight and shadow, heeling through the blue seas with flying fish skimming around her and, often enough, with dolphin, bonito or albacore playing ahead of her bow wave, would catch at the most unperceptive imagination. Almost better is the sight as she ploughs through the moonlight, under a star-studded sky, and there are all those marvellous transitions of light before dawn as the darkness lightens. In addition, one is struck by the incredible peace of the ship for, heeling steadily and, often enough, nearly steering herself, she is almost utterly silent, only the lap of the bow wave being heard forward and, occasionally, the creak of the wheel aft, punctuated only at intervals by the ship's bells making the hours. Watches are reduced to three or four men and, even when making some fourteen knots, especially outward bound in the North-east Trade, the ship presents an aura of beauty *par excellence.*

There was, too, the pleasant warmth and, for my own part, I was ever a potential worshipper of the sun. Yet, to my amazement, my shipmates did not see things in the same light at all. At the outset of the voyage, in all the bad weather, most of the first-voyagers had not been allowed to stand a wheel alone, but only to assist at the lee wheel when two men were necessary. I had stood my wheel throughout and, even in the wildest and bitterest weather, had found it the most satisfying occupation. It was as though the ship was, literally, mine, and although a vessel like the *Moshulu,* which steered amidships, was not so satisfactory to steer as one with her wheel aft, the primitive screw gear might still be likened to the tiller of a small boat, enabling the helmsman to 'feel' the ship in a manner that was impossible with the telemotor gear of a steamer. Certainly the operation required judgement and a certain foresight, anticipating the movement of the ship in the seas, and I had supposed that it was an art that anyone could have acquired with practice.

Nothing could have been further from the truth. Some men never became good helmsman, though most became reasonably competent. This was, essentially, dependent on whether a man had that affinity with both the ship and the sea. It was surprising how very few men possessed this or even the desire to have it. At first, in the cold weather of the Baltic, the ship's work (as distinct from working the ship herself) had been the soulless job of chipping the anchor cables which were flaked along the decks for the purpose. Then, the ship being in ballast, the main job outward bound was down the hold, chipping and scraping the rust from the interior of the shell plating. This can hardly fall within anyone's ambition yet, to my sheer amazement, nearly all my watch-mates preferred this to standing their trick at the wheel in all the glory of her tropic passage, and were only too pleased for me to take their places. Often (for the Finns did not keep normal European watches), I was five hours at a time steering the ship, revelling in all the beauty of the scene, the curving canvas, the warmth of the sun and the glitter of the sea. In truth, a ship in the trades generally needed little enough attention.

There were occasions when the helmsman's position was no sinecure. Certainly the best helmsman shone, mainly down in the Southern Ocean, when the ship was running dead before a hard gale and big following sea, for it was then that steering was the most difficult. But no ship is properly balanced in her sail plan under all conditions, and there were occasions when it was physically impossible for one man to hold the wheel, and when she was griping. That is, when, with too much canvas aft, she was fighting to come up into the wind, with the result that the

5. *Fair wind and Weather — the* POMMERN.

wheel (and rudder) were turned to leeward, the latter acting as a brake on the hull. There were times when if, say, headsails were coming in with the wind forward of the beam, it was essential that the man at the wheel did not let the ship luff (*i.e.* come up into the wind) since, if he did, the men forward could be swept overboard. In such conditions the helmsman was utterly alone, whether steering aft or amidships: his shipmates and the very ship itself relying on him implicitly.

The wheel was never relieved while sail was coming in, or the ship was being worked in any way. Once, down in the Westerlies in another four-masted barque in which the wheel was right aft, there were two helmsmen when I relieved the weather man. I told the mate that the ship was griping badly. The wind was rising fast. The gaff topsail and the odd staysail were taken in. Then the mizzen topgallantsails. By this time it was blowing really hard and the master decided to call all hands to reduce sail more drastically. He asked if I could hold the ship while the lee man was sent to turn out the other watch. I replied that I could, but that man was diverted and never returned. The ship was now racing through the seas with an immense pressure on the rudder transmitted to the wheel, and I was utterly alone, right aft, yet by then unable to win a single spoke. It was all I could do to prevent the wheel running back. Had it done so, the ship could have come up into the wind and, possibly, all aback, with fearful consequences to herself and the men aloft. The binnacle lights had gone out and, having lowered my sou'wester, I was steering solely by the feel of the wind on my neck. Yet there was little I could do as the effect of the steadily increasing wind more than counter-balanced the reduction in sail and when, after just over five hours, I was finally relieved, it was all I could do to stagger to my bunk and roll into it, oilskins and all, just as I was!

There were occasions in certain ships, which I happily never experienced, when a ship got pooped and the helmsmen were washed away or when, by their own incompetence, they let the ship fall off and broach to, lying in the trough of the big seas. Probably most such instances are never known, for this is the stuff of being 'posted as missing'. Nevertheless, in most ships, when steering was of such supreme importance, only specified men were allowed to take the wheel, with good reason. Indeed, in one ship we were sailing at night into an anchorage, relatively crowded with anchored sailing ships. A square-rigger was normally steered by quarter points (though a good helmsman hardly used the compass at all). On this occasion I was roused from my watch below, on the master's instructions, to bring the ship in. At first he gave me courses in degrees, but then said:- "*You know what I want.*" and merely advised me of what I could not see on the lee side. It was an exercise in precision and close navigation seldom seen in such ships, and

6. *Two big square-riggers in company — the* OLIVEBANK *seen from the* POMMERN.

later there was some muttering by the watch on deck at the time that I should have been sent for rather than any of them. The master presumably thought that none of them could have done it. Oddly, I had probably not spoken half a dozen words to him previously, nor he to me, since I had signed on months before.

Later, I was called out in my watch below in that ship to relieve the wheel in a full gale with a long, following sea, much to my fury at the time, but we did run with drier decks and, in retrospect, a certain sense of pride was inescapable. There is not much in common between steering a ship and riding a horse, but the fact is that few people ride really well, but those who do find themselves in perfect *rapport* with their mount, and the two work and think as one. So it is with a good helmsman and his charge. I was perfectly in tune with that ship and, as I believe, she with me. It was almost as if we were one, and to me both she, and every other sailing ship in which I served, had a personality and character all her own. Most men regarded such an opinion as being sheer nonsense. Yet I have known others who could step aboard a ship in dock and divine her character infallibly. Even sister ships could be quite different: one being invariably a happy and easy vessel: the other being brutish, unhappy (whoever her master and whatever her crew) and, often enough, a killer.

I am sure that the old collier master was one of those who understood this. Many men have achieved what is described as a sixth sense at sea, being better able to anticipate the weather, their position in fog, and much else, but although experience clearly played a major part in this, the fact was that most men were merely doing their job, whilst a small minority were, literally, part and parcel with their element. A man may be lucky enough to strike a *rapport* with his ships, and I speak particularly of sailing ships and not of the modern mammoth self-propelled behemoths, but the ship cannot be separated from her medium — the sea and the winds which drive her. A man is either in sympathy with the whole elemental forces of wind, weather, sea and ship, vibrating to the same tune, or else he never truly catches the music as long as he lives, even if competent as a sailor. If I stress this point, which is doubtless as incomprehensible to modern seamen as to landsmen, it is because the two classes of men not only have different expectations from life, but also because subsequent events in this book will demonstrate that the true philosophy taught by the sailing ship, the self-sufficiency and indeed the expectations which it engendered, were often sadly lacking in other vessels during those days of its ultimate decline.

On the whole the *Moshulu* did not have a bad passage during her homeward voyage, though the long haul to Cape Horn far south in the Southern Ocean, and mostly in the latitude of the Horn itself, inevitably

7. *Flooding decks on the way to Cape Horn.*

produced the gales so traditional to the area. There was a night when the ship was labouring in huge, long seas which ran unbroken from horizon to horizon and then on and on, never stopped by land, all round the bottom of the Southern Hemisphere. No other sea can produce such long, awe-inspiring or magnificent seas with such vast distances between their crests. The ship now having a low freeboard, each sea spilled several hundred tons of ice-cold water over our decks as it passed. Once wet, one remained wet. For my own part, I had lost all feeling in my feet, and maintained this condition for many winters to come.

All hands were wrestling with an upper topsail one night in full gale. It was ballooning out in great semi-frozen bulges on which we could make little impression as we tore our finger nails below their quicks, clawing at the recalcitrant canvas with hands suppurating from sea-water cuts which were scarcely improved by the day work of scraping teakwork with caustic soda. Had such sails been sewn with perforations, not only would they have provided the ship with better speed, but they would have been easier to furl, yet few ships adopted this principle, such was the innate conservatism which characterised the whole age of sail, not only in this matter but in many others.

No man enjoys such experience even if, in retrospect, he feels a certain pride in accomplishment. It was pitch black, only the blown crests of the seas and the ship's bow wave surging a-lee providing any contrast in the murk of the night, while a touch of southerly in the wind brought intense cold from the Antarctic. Then, in another of those magical moments as previously recorded in the Skaggerrak, the sky cleared momentarily and the moon shone forth, illuminating the foresail and lower topsails in arches of golden light with weird shadows of the rigging arching across the swelling canvas: passing another great band of heaving gold over the long, relentless seas, and displaying such a scene of elemental wildness under the very cathedral of Heaven that one might suppose the pagan gods of old to be indulging in some drunken revel. The change of scene was short enough in all conscience for, within minutes, it was snowing and we could scarcely see the deck below us. Yet, against all the odds, the sail was conquered almost at once. Somehow, that sudden vista of the straining ship and sails against a background which might be likened to the very forces of creation in all their power, yet in a wild harmony and all illumined by the moon, had had some subconscious effect on the men on that yard though, oddly, not one of my shipmates would admit to it making any difference nor even to being in any way impressed by the sight. For my own part, those few instants, together with many more of the same sort in one condition of weather or another, often with all the changing shades and lights in the hollows of the sea, have remained as clear in my memory as though they occurred only yesterday, and demonstrated to me the sheer insignificance of the human race.

In those years most of the crews disliked the life in sail. So far as it concerned the majority, who were Finns or Ålannings, it was a means to an end, since they needed time in sail to obtain their tickets and they accepted it philosophically enough. Only very few went back. Yet the life was such that it called for, and generally received, a team-work *par excellence* even from men who loathed it. This was the difference between sail and steam. A steamer man might have no strong views either way about his life, but in sail a man either loved it or he loathed it, and the latter was not seen again after the voyage end unless he needed the sea time as a means to an end. Yet, to all, it taught a sense of perspective and self-reliance. Of course, there was always the 'bad egg': the man who did not fit in either because he did not pull his weight, because he stole or because he was filthy. There were ways of dealing with such men, and they were, in any case, the exceptions. They exist in every walk of life.

I was perhaps fortunate to be promoted half way through my first voyage, thereby missing some of the worst jobs aboard. The junior men had to wash the dishes after meals and clean the foc's'les. Perhaps coming on watch at 7.0 p.m., they might first of all be involved in

8. *The* MOSHULU *arriving in the Mersey — then the largest sailing vessel afloat.
Her high masting and low freeboard will be noted, despite having consumed three
months stores and water. (The bulwarks were some 5 feet high).*

working the ship, taking in or setting sail, or bracing the yards. By the time they were finished, the galley would have been long locked, and they were faced with the task of cleaning hideously greasy plates and dishes with ice-cold sea water. Such men were called upon to clear the antiquated form of heads, or to clean the pig-styes. When the decks were full of water with the pigs, often enough, almost hysterical and panic-stricken, this often involved wrestling with the squealing animals in the scuppers, into which they slipped as they lost their footing, and trying to manhandle them bodily back into their styes. Such work was a far cry from the romance of swelling sails in the imagination of many of those who joined these ships, often mesmerised by the books of a popular sea-writer who only gave one side of the story. It is broadly true to say that a man who made one voyage never became involved in true 'sailor' work, apart from joining in the actual working of the ship, and many never had much understanding of what was really happening at all or, at all events, not until near the end of the voyage. Some, who made a passage from Australia to England, where they left the ship, were only three or four months in their ships altogether, during which they were mainly employed on the most menial tasks when the ship was not being worked, yet today, after more than half a century, they strut about as though they were the veriest salts and would hail their old captains while they were still alive (men to whom they had never spoken when aboard) as though they were their oldest friends! One, who went straight from his ship to the care of a psychiatrist in a mental home, now passes himself off as being a real old sailing ship man with all the knowledge which that implies, and there are others of the same ilk!

There is no doubt that, for all her imperfections, the sailing ship was a marvellous school for character training. Whether, by that date, the seamanship which she taught was worth the time it took to acquire is doubtful, but to those who found themselves in harmony with her sailing, she provided some *je ne sais quoi* which stood by them all their lives, for they gained a sense of perspective and self-sufficiency, and an appreciation of all the sights and sounds of the ocean, together with the very run of the sea, which coalesced into indelible memories and experiences. Yet, undeniably, there were times when every man aboard wondered why he was there and when he was miserable. The high days were beyond all description. To some the bad outweighed the good, but to others the good outweighed the bad. That was the measure of it.

After my first voyage it was clear enough to me and even to my family that the sea was the proper place for me, although I did return briefly to the hated City office as a matter of good form and to save everybody's face. The deep sea sailing ships were all by then on their way to Australia, so I joined a big four-masted schooner which was to be the

9. *The Author at the wheel of the* WESTWARD

10. *The* WESTWARD in the Channel.

parent ship for an Antarctic expedition. At that time I had a great yearning to visit the Antarctic, and the ship promised quite a lot, for she was first to cruise with passengers, ending with a round the world voyage, during which some of us would be transferred to the expedition ship. In the event the whole affair was a financial disaster and the main aims were never achieved but, before we ever went to sea, the vessel was completely re-rigged in the West India Dock. The master would not engage anyone for the expedition who had not been in sail. Both the main crew and the riggers we had aboard were almost all older men who had been in clippers or in the last great surge of square-rig and, under their tuition, I learnt more of practical seamanship than was possible in any voyage.

The master, John Stenhouse, had taken over command of the *Aurora* in Shackleton's expedition and had sailed her back to New Zealand after rigging a jury rudder, whilst the mate was Frank Worsley, master of the *Endurance* on that same expedition, when she was wholly crushed in the ice and when they had made the historic trip to Elephant Island. He had been with Shackleton in the boat voyage thence to South Georgia, which still stands as an epic, especially in those latitudes, after which they had scaled the South Georgian mountains — the first men ever to do so — and came down to Stromness to obtain help for the men left on Elephant Island. The second mate, Dawes, also held the Polar medal, and these three men were, in some sort, 'sailors of fortune', undertaking expeditions and all sorts of other interesting ventures. When forced to leave the ship, I resolved to follow their star and, indeed, was going to sail a barquentine to Haifa with them if the war had not rendered the venture impossible. Stenhouse, a big bull of a man, was killed in the Red Sea a few years later, though I did see Worsley, then retired, often enough after the war. The bos'n, who left before we sailed, was a marvellous old fellow, who had not only been bos'n of the *Discovery* when Stenhouse was her master, but had been in an array of clippers and other vessels from the 1880s onwards. The schooner, the *Westward*, was a converted merchantman, but did not perform well, and in any case I found a vessel of her rig much more unsatisfactory than a square-rigger.

The owner, who was backing the scheme to a large degree, was H.K. Hales, who had become known for presenting the Atlantic Blue Riband trophy. The ship was not quite ready when she had to leave for the first part of her cruise, to Plymouth, over Easter. The spilling lines were not rigged on the immense lower boom-sails and, off the Start, we were caught in an electric storm with these vast sails ballooning clear over the side as we vainly tried to take them in. As the lightning illumined the scene that night, with rain lashing down, I was aware of Hales running up and down the deck with a raincoat over his pyjamas, wringing his

11. The WESTWARD, an unlucky and unhandy vessel, making her number off St. Catherine's Point.

hands, till Stenhouse finally could bear it no longer and sent him below!

The ship would not stay in the perpetual head-winds we encountered, due to the drag of the propeller, nor could her auxiliary engine be coaxed to function. Finally she had to turn back when *en route* to the Canary Islands, by which time the passengers had overstayed their leaves and the bars had run dry. They were utterly miserable, especially as the weather was mainly cold and beastly. Finally, the engineers did get the engine to work on a fine, calm day, and the passengers, by then completely demoralised, showed glimmerings of hope. I was at the wheel and smelt burning, so I called to Worsley, whose watch it was, and it was found that the exhaust, led through the jigger mast, was scorching the spanker gear! The engine was then abandoned!

Finally we came up to the Needles in a gale, under double reefed lowers. We took the pilot aboard but he, finding no engine beneath him, and learning that the master proposed to make a running gybe round the Calshot Spit lightship, turned literally green, and he, too, was sent below. Again, I was at the wheel. To make a running gybe in that weather was no light matter and, as we approached the lightship, the new bos'n, an Australian of the worst possible type, who, in some sort of unholy league with the steward, had managed to retain some store of liquor (both being drunk for much of the time), attempted to assault me and drag me from the wheel at the crucial moment. Stenhouse was there, took him by the scruff of the neck and, dragging him the length of the long shelter deck, flung him down to the fore-deck as though a mere bundle. He ran his ship in an older style! No rats ever abandoned a sinking ship more quickly than our passengers once we did come to anchor!

I was soon away again and managed to stay in sailing ships of different sorts until just before the Second World War started, except for a brief period when, between two such ships, I joined a large trans-Atlantic liner. The shortest voyage was a disaster. I learnt of a harbour racing yacht, next in size below the big 'J' class, which was to be delivered to Genoa, calling at various ports on the way, and the crew returning home overland, which I thought might be fun, so I obtained a berth.

Named the *Black Swan*, she had formerly been the famous *Brynhild* but, not being built for sea work, she had been well rigged down as a ketch for the passage. The master was an old square-rigger captain named Lawrence, who had never sailed with an engine in his life: the mate was a professional yachtsman, and there was, besides myself, a trainee police officer, one other and a man who was alleged to understand the engine.

Our first shock came when we cleared the Nab Tower in fairly calm weather, for the ketch lay right over and proceeded to Havre at eleven knots but, the two professional yachtsmen apart, we were all intolerably sick, since the motion, with an outside ballast keel, was quite outside our experience. After arriving at Havre in short order, a large crowd assembled to watch so large a racing yacht warp into the yacht basin, for which purpose the engine was brought into play. When the master, using an engine room telegraph for the first time in his life, expected to achieve a touch astern, the craft leapt forward at full speed! She was swinging hard, as she had plenty of helm at that moment, whereupon her bowsprit slashed savagely into the match-boarding of one of the gipsy caravans quartered on the quay.

The French crowd were delighted and broke into exultant cheering, though their patent delight was not caused by our puerile effort but by the victim of the accident since, with her wall torn away, the mistress of the vehicle was exposed in close communion with a bucket, and seemed to be marooned with her throne since the door connecting with the other section of the caravan had become jammed and frustrated her panic-stricken efforts to avoid the public view! How the lady extricated herself from her dilemma we never knew, since we were too concerned with extricating ourselves from our own position.

Whose fault it was I cannot say, but the master and motorman were permamently irreconciled. Since the latter had to take the blame, he was paid off and the master shipped a Frenchman in his place, believing that, because my French had been adequate to cope with buying stores and so forth, he could take his orders from me. After a few hilarious days in port, the man joined just before we left, and it was not until we were outside the breakwaters that I discovered that I could not understand a word he said, whilst he, for his part, either could not, or would not, understand me. It proved that he was a Breton who spoke a dialect quite beyond my knowledge of the Gallic tongue. The man was sufficiently quick-witted to appreciate the position and in that instant transformed himself into a passenger and, wearing a smug smile on his face, never attempted to do a hand's turn that morning.

It was a fine enough day, but with a freshening wind, and we were bowling along, heeled well over, at over eleven knots, with, let it be said to our shame, all save the mate and the Breton being again vilely sick. This was particularly galling since the Breton, whom we already regarded with feelings of dislike and near-loathing, was evidently enjoying himself thoroughly! We flew past the Casquets in grand style, but the wind was increasing rapidly with a vicious scream in it. The sky was overcast by then and contained the threat of more wind to come, whilst the barometer was falling unnaturally fast.

By the time that we were off Guernsey, conditions were becoming really bad and the little ship, quite out of her intended element, was making very heavy weather of it, straining a lot and taking heavy water aboard. It was clear that, once we turned to the south'ard, we should receive a bad battering as things were and, with the promised deterioration in the weather, really bad damage might be expected with both wind and sea on the bow.

In the circumstances, it was only prudent to run for the English coast for shelter until the weather moderated, so we ran her off until the wind was fine on the starboard quarter, scudding before a violent squall with very restricted visibility. The rain blew over, but by now we were in full gale and dared not take in any sail lest we incur damage. We had all lashed ourselves about the wheel, for her deck, under water for most of the time, was really dangerous and, in any case, she was lacking bulwarks, providing a real risk of going overboard. Perhaps we had underestimated the portents and should have hove to at the outset, but it was too late to think about that. There was nothing left except to run and to make the best of it, and we were resigned to doing that, sprays sweeping right over us. No-one felt sick any more, nor could we say at what point that unpleasant sensation ceased. Perhaps the situation left no room for such weakness.

The Breton had the smirk off his face by then, but we were all as one in appreciation of the scene which opened before us as we raced into a wild sea which appeared to stretch but a short distance ahead of our diving bowsprit, yet which had no visible horizon, since the flung spray had all the effect of solid rain. Water was cascading over and off the deck in a constant mill-race and, although the horizon would have been little more than a couple of miles with so low a freeboard, the weather conditions on the one hand and the steep sea which had built up in the comparatively shallow Channel waters on the other, created a scene beyond the scope of normal imagination because the little ketch, flung forward by the wind and shuddering against the seas, had an air of unreality as though flying endlessly from nowhere into nothing, amidst the crashing cacophany of the fiendish orchestration of elemental fury. That is the effect of so limited a horizon.

Then, in the mid-afternoon, we saw a dark shadow in the grey and white smother of water on the starboard bow and, in less time than it takes to tell, perceived that a big tanker, flying light and rolling abominably, was crossing right across our bow. It was too late to worry about the Rule of the Road. There was nothing we could do, since any deviation from our course would have courted certain doom, while I doubt if that great ship ever saw us at all nor, had she done so, was there time to take avoiding action. Not only did our world seem small enough to us, but to her we could have been little more than an additional flurry of foam smoking through the spray-splashed seas. We could have had little of our hull visible, if any at all, as we seemed to be running through the seas, rather than over them, like a diving petrel, and the little sail we had set had little chance of being distinguished in that confusion of waters.

We were probably all tensed as we drove closer, her great bulk passing slowly ahead as we seemed to be hurling ourselves at certain disaster. At the moment of greatest crisis I heard the Breton, his face taut and every muscle tense, cry: *"Mon Dieu!"* so loudly that I caught the words and experienced a transient flash of satisfaction that I had understood something that he had said, though whether he uttered them in supplication or as an imprecation I have no idea!

The whole affair could not have taken more than a minute since we first sighted her, though it seemed that her stern could never clear our bow We watched, fascinated, as her propeller, half out of the water, threshed at what seemed to be a miserable speed. We were so close that, in other circumstances, we could have thrown a heaving line aboard when our helmsman dared a little helm and took her down a fraction, balancing the doom of dismasting against the certainty of collision and, almost before we could believe the impossible, we were diving under her stern to look up and read her name and port of registry — Bremen — before we were away on her quarter and smashing on into the murk.

If, as is most likely, we took away her log and log-line, that would have been the only indication to that German tanker that anything untoward had occurred. Certainly no power on earth could have altered the situation of the two vessels in that weather and in so short a time.

Still we ran on: diving, shuddering and flinging the seas apart whilst they, in turn, flung themselves over us. The wind seemed fiercer and we watched the seams of our sails with apprehension, but they held and, in the failing light, we picked up the coast on the starboard bow yet, within a minute, so close had we approached before we saw it at all, it was on the port bow as well. There was no time to pause and consider but, fortunately, the topography was too well known to admit any mistaking it and we recognised Berry Head. We knew that we had been making great speed for so small a craft and it was clear that, running the sixty five odd miles since we had turned before the wind, we had been making a good 13 knots. Despite our fine lines, the nature of the seas made this an outstanding performance.

There was no time for congratulations on that score, since we were sailing at the same speed straight on to a singularly uninviting coast. Course had to be altered. To have made for the Dart would have involved a suicidal gybe and Tor Bay was our only hope. The helm was put down, though we never attempted to man the sheets, since we could

12. The EMPRESS OF BRITAIN.

have won nothing and, once round, being slacked off, they would ease the strain.

So, in the grey twilight, she came round in the trough of a sea which promptly crashed green and solidly over the decks and us. No-one ever knew the sequence of events in that moment, for the noise was intolerable: there was the sound of the flogging of rent canvas, sounds of splintering and others which were as unfamiliar as they were ominous. For a moment, once we could take breath after being cleared from the sea, we were half-stunned. Still gasping, soaked utterly and aware of being subjected to great bodily stress as the sea tried to wrest us from our lashings, we saw that the mizzen mast was trailing over the side to leeward: that the mainmast was sprung and the sail badly split and flogging, while the one headsail that had been set was flying in ragged tatters that were lashing themselves to pieces. Next, and belatedly, we saw that the main skylight was smashed and that we were shipping heavy water down it with every sea! If there was any consolation, it was that the ketch now rode more easily, and we cast ourselves off our lashings and did what we could for the skylight, cut away the mizzen and repaired the various ravages as well as we were able. It was not for another twelve hours, a sorry sight, that we limped out of that Channel storm into Brixham after lying to for most of the night under the lee of the headland.

I left her there, as it was going to take too long to effect repairs and I believe that she was finally shipped out to Genoa on the deck of a steamer. Going from one extreme to another, I then joined a great Atlantic liner — the *Empress of Britain* — simply because her voyages were short and thus enabled me to keep an eye open for a sailing ship. What a contrast! When a quarter-master went sick, the bos'n had to ask the huge crew of so-called A.B.s: *"Can anyone steer?"* Few could.

34

13. Known as 'Armstrong's Patent', this form of windlass for raising the anchor was very slow and real hard labour. Note the deck-cargo of 'split' wood — virtually fire-wood.

14. The POMMERN, the author's last sailing ship, coming up to the land.

When he wanted two men to paint over the side, where the anchor had fouled the white hull, he had to ask: *"Who can rig a stage?"* — something the veriest tyro should have known. There was no form of sailor work in that vessel and, indeed, little real work at all. The vast crew was mainly to cope with the 42 odd lifeboats in the event of disaster. Three men never saw the sea at all, as they swept the working alleyway, down in the bowels of the ship, from forward aft, then back from aft forward, day in and day out. There were two gardeners on the crew list ....

Certainly we broke the record for the Northern passage outward bound one trip, while the *Queen Mary* captured the Blue Riband on the New York route: the last part of our voyage being in thick fog when we sometimes swung off course abruptly to avoid the occasional iceberg.

We came home over the Grand Banks in brilliant sunshine with icebergs and growlers all over the face of the sea, glistening and glinting as if in a scene from fairyland. Then we saw what we had passed through at well over 20 knots so few days before but, before we could reflect, we were back in fog which we held till the Fastnet light and ... only just failed to beat our own eastward record. Had that ship not met a fearful fate in the war, there is little doubt that she would have been the subject of a major peace-time disaster sooner or later. Three of her masters had already cracked under the strain. The prudence demanded by the sea can only be ignored or over-ridden by mail schedules for so long. It was before the days of radar.

That vessel was utterly removed from the sailing ship and, for all her high feeding standards and sacrosanct watches below, it was a stultifying form of life which to me seemed to have no soul. Even the sea itself seemed to be remote, with so high a freeboard. Other ships at that period have no place in this book, though I have a soft spot for a small, wooden 'onker' barque in which I voyaged to the Baltic. These craft were known as 'onkers' because they were all equipped with a windmill pump, the noise of which was said to make a sound like '*onk-urr — onk-urr*', and in those days were engaged in carrying the off-cuts from the Baltic timber mills to London and elsewhere for use in cheap furniture and packing cases. A big ship, with a deck cargo of cut timber, has it well levelled off and usually covered with tarpaulins, but in these craft the short lengths were loose and protected merely by baulks built up about the bulwarks, making work on deck awkward when loaded. A friend of mine was in a very small barque of this type which lost her deck load in bad weather, but they went out on to it and managed to get most of it back aboard: a remarkable feat! Much lighter to work than the big deep-watermen, if more often anchoring and making sail in restricted waters, these craft were pleasant enough in the summer time.

Fortunately, I was soon able to join another 4-masted barque. Nevertheless, the deep-sea sailing ship generally had no radio and for months we were cut off from the world at sea, whilst such news as percolated through to small outports in Australia all seemed very remote. We had heard, for instance, nothing of Munich. Yet, when we had finally towed up the Humber and hauled into dock at Hull, we noticed paravanes piled ready on the quay. The curtain was about to ring down on the end of an era.

~~~~~

15. The 'onker barquentine' FRIDEBORG, built as a composite barque for the China trade in 1866. Note her windmill pump and, again, her deck-cargo.

III

IN WAR PAINT

Aruba, in the Dutch West Indies, has little to offer a visiting seaman, despite the efforts made by the industrious Dutch to provide an aura of domesticity. No animals are native to the island in which cactus is the most common vegetation, and it lacks not only oil, but even its own supply of water. Its *raison d'être* lies in its oil refineries, which are situated there because the Venezuelan ports on the mainland have insufficient depth of water to admit larger ships: the oil being ferried to Aruba by a fleet of small 'mosquito' tankers.

I had joined a tanker, the *Cheyenne*, purely because I had some five weeks to wait for another sailing ship, and the voyage would have filled in a little sea-time during the interval. Again, I found it a stultifying existence, and mention Aruba simply to record an incident in a bar at this time, at the end of August, 1939. While there, two Germans entered. They came from a German tanker, flying the flag of convenience of Panama, which was employed in transporting fresh water to the port. Ordering his drink, one of them held it up towards us, saying;- *"All good friends! Nicht?"* whereupon I answered;- *"What about your Hitler?"* His friend clearly understood the exchange and flung his untouched glass on the floor, smashing it, while breaking into an excited torrent of German which we did not understand. Seeing our bewilderment, the first German cut in:- *"He says that Hitler is no good for the German people. We, who travel to other countries, know the truth."* It was not the first time I had heard such an opinion from a German, but they were voices in the wilderness.

As we sailed, with over 10,000 tons of aviation spirit, we were ordered into Port o' Spain, on Trinidad: war being imminent. There we were told to paint our funnel and upperworks grey, and given a route home. We were also told that it was impossible to give us a gun, but were advised that, in the event of encountering a submarine we should, if possible, inject steam into the tops of our tanks and set the tank pumps in action.

39

The theory, never actually tested at that time, was that the steam would condense and fall to the bottom of the tanks and, in so doing, form some sort of blanket which would prevent an explosion.

There were other tankers in the port with us and, one by one, we left: the *Clea* keeping company with us for the first twelve hours. Then we heard of the declaration of war and were promptly issued with gas masks. The white paint was duly turned to grey and the 'idlers' — the carpenter, bos'n and officers' peggy — were put in the watches to increase the lookouts. The mate produced a revised roster for wheel and lookouts to this end but, as it entailed a man standing on lookout for three hours on end, I produced a different one, which meant that no-one spent more than two hours at either wheel or lookout. The men thought this better, and the mate also agreed that it was more efficient, so it was adopted. I considered that a man would not be keeping a good lookout in a third hour.

When we approached the Irish coast, we already knew that the *Inverliffey* and another of our company's ships, the *Kennebec*, had already been sunk, apart from those which had become head-line news, like the *Athenia*. On successive days we heard the S.O.S. messages of the tankers *British Influence* and *Regent Tiger* which were both caught by a U-boat in almost identical positions in the very area through which we, a slower vessel, had been ordered to pass. The following day we were proceeding in a fairly calm sea with a big swell under low cloud when we passed a four-masted barque in the late morning — the Swedish *Abraham Rydberg* which I knew well. Years later her master became one of my best friends, and he told me how his wife, whom he had aboard, had said:- *"I pray for that tanker."*

Her prayer made no odds. As we reached the fatal area a submarine surfaced and started firing. We put her astern, increased to full speed while sending out distress calls on the radio and, simultaneously, injected steam into the tanks and set the pumps in operation, albeit with little confidence that it would have any effect. Then, with a crash out of all proportion to the damage done, a round from the U-boat smashed into the galley, right aft. The submarine was gaining fast. I observed a steward cowering *under* a mess-room table, though how he supposed that that would help him if the cargo of aviation spirit exploded was difficult to understand! However, realizing the hopelessness of the situation, and our distress signals having been sent out and acknowledged, the master decided to stop and abandon ship. The boats were launched easily enough, despite the third mate who was in a state of panic and shouting incessant inane orders, but it was clear that the crew had but the haziest idea of anything to do with boats. A Swedish sailor was using the steering oar to row, and the mate soon told me to row

16. *Painting the* CHEYENNE *grey for war.*

17. *The* CHEYENNE *in peace-time colours (her funnel was red).*

stroke, as I was the only man in the boat who could maintain a steady rhythm. The boats were quickly filling with water, apparently not having been set in the water to tighten up for years, and those not rowing were set to baling. Indeed, we had to abandon two oars very quickly to allow more baling.

Still on the surface, the U-boat approached the *Cheyenne* and fired two torpedoes into her. She broke in half just forward of the bridge; the foc's'le head coming to rest on the monkey island, above the bridge, before she broke into two halves: the bow pointing straight up into the air and the after part well down by the head. *Mirabile dictu*, the steam trick worked better than anyone could have supposed, for there was no fire. (It was not long before ships were being sunk without warning, when this tactic was impossible.)

The U-boat then came over to the boats, gave our master the course and distance to the Irish coast and asked if we had everything we wanted — tobacco, food, cigarettes, food, etc. On being assured that we had, he said that he believed a neutral ship called the *Colon* was about sixteen miles away and that he would go and request her to pick us up. In the meantime we should follow him. As soon as he was gone, the mate ordered the mast to be stepped and the sail set. The third mate, throughout, had been sitting aft in a state of prostration. The mate tried to cover for him by saying he was sick (a few were being sick with the motion of the small boat).

To my amazement, I discovered that I was the only man in my boat who knew how to get ours under sail. Of course, in the sailing ships, usually at anchorage ports, we had used our boats a lot, but it spoke little for the 'Lifeboat Efficiency Certificates' issued by the (then) Board of Trade in the calm and peace of one dock or another. The only other man who had been in sail was the bos'n, an old and fascinating man with long walrus moustaches, but he had rescued and was tending his pet canaries which represented his sole concern at that juncture. Most men seemed to be labouring under some hazy idea that the sail was a dipping lug, whereas it was a standing lug, and all they seemed capable of doing was getting turns in the halyard and backstays, and even the jib about the lug. It was a wonder that none of them went overboard. Finally, I got both sails set, and the mate ordered the tack to be bowsed down to the mast. No-one save myself even knew what the tack was! I made it fast to a cleat on the weather gunwale, at which the mate himself protested. I said we were sailing by the wind and that that was how it should be, which led to an argument until the third mate, finally coming to, said that I was right. We then sailed on for a couple of hours, gaining rapidly on the other boat, since the second mate had no idea how to sail it and was keeping her luffing, whilst his men were not properly disposed in her.

42

On this occasion, and on many more I witnessed as the war progressed, the steamship seaman showed himself to be woefully lacking. Thus the difference between the words 'seaman' and 'sailor'. The open seams were still pouring in water and two bailers had been dropped overboard. Several men started grumbling at the prospect of spending the night in the boat, and I was not thanked when I said that we might be several nights before we reached the coast!

The U-boat then returned, said that the neutral ship was not coming and that he was going over to sink the two halves of our wreck (presumably to prevent possible salvage) and that, having done so, he would give us all a hot drink and then tow us in to the Irish coast providing we undertook to show no lights after dark. Indeed, as we learnt subsequently, he had done no less for the *British Influence's* crew and, when one of the *Regent Tiger's* boats had got caught in blazing oil on the surface of the sea, he had gone in with his conning tower barely awash to take them off. As he spoke, a few of us noticed smoke on the horizon when we rose on the top of the swells. Clearly the Germans, who were all staring at us, had not noticed this. Of course, the horizon from a boat is very close — barely two miles at most.

While they were on the surface firing at the *Cheyenne*, the smoke we had seen materialized into two British destroyers, which started firing across us. The U-boat crash-dived and we, some way away, were nearly blown out of the water by the depth charges dropped on her as the destroyers arrived on the scene. By now dusk had fallen and, shortly afterwards, a fine Norwegian freighter, the *Ida Bakke*, which had been ordered to pick us up as the destroyers passed her, arrived and took us and our boats aboard. Needless to say, many of the men jumped for the Jacob's ladder when the boat was in the troughs, and it was lucky that none crushed their feet.

In an effort to sink the two parts of the wreck, the destroyers were now firing at them. Her two parts were a mile or so apart, by now, and there was aviation spirit all over the surface of the seas between them. Due to her number of watertight compartments, it is hard to sink a tanker, and the destroyers did not succeed, but now she did catch fire. The effect was fantastic. The base of the fire was, perhaps, now two miles long. It reflected off the low cloud back to the oily sea and in every direction. The whole world seemed blood red, as though the very day of Ragnarök had come. Even aboard the *Ida Bakke*, and after we had dropped the actual fire below the horizon, everything was still reflecting red. The *Abraham Rydberg* could not have made much progress in those conditions, but I now know that she was out of range of these fantastic reflections and did not, in fact, know what had happened. The American charts were still registering our wreck as a hazard many months later.

The Norwegians had made preparations for us and promptly fed us a good meal, after which most of our crew went down to the hold where refrigerated hold dunnage had been spread as bedding. Mollerström (the Swede) and I, who by then had quite a smattering of Swedish, were able to talk with the Norwegians, with whom we spent a most convivial evening, aided by several bottles of rum which had been obtained, or purloined, from her Chief Officer. At the end of that session, we were given a comfortable two-berth cabin, much to the envy of our shipmates when they discovered the following morning! The *Ida Bakke*, a 17-knot vessel, arrived off the Fastnet lighthouse early the next day and we were transferred to the Courtmacsherry lifeboat which took us aboard and towed our boats into Baltimore. It was an idyllic autumn morning, with marvellous colours on the mountains and a scenario worthy of any travel brochure. The inhabitants of the fishing village were nothing if not hospitable, each cottage taking in a couple of men and giving them a good breakfast, after which the hospitality turned to the form of large quantities of Irish whisky. Many men were hopelessly drunk before breakfast time. We had a very strong impression that the people there were well acquainted with the U-boat and her crew and, indeed, many U-boats found succour on the coast of Eire during the ensuing hostilities. Eire was, of course, neutral, and did not give Britain the use of Queenstown harbour, condemning all her convoys to pass north about round Malin Head at the North of Ulster once the Germans had occupied France.*

Finally a coach appeared to take us to Cork, but it was a slow journey, due to the calls of nature caused by the excessive liquid refreshment and, every few miles, a message was relayed from the back of the coach to the captain:- *"The carpenter wants to pump ship."* Oddly, this man was able to make his way to the front and out of the coach, but on each occasion had to be retrieved and manhandled back from the various hedges into which he had collapsed, and somehow passed back to his seat in the rear of the vehicle. It never occurred to anyone to make him sit in the front. Much time was lost over this and, consequently, it was late when we reached Cork, where it was only possible to provide us with tickets and a minimal amount of money for our various journeys home.

Although the *Cheyenne* had not been a modern tanker, and was fairly primitive in her accommodation, I had realized that, as modern tankers generally provided much better conditions, often with two men to a reasonably furnished cabin, such a ship might give me an opportunity to study the theoretical aspects of my forthcoming second mate's examination and to this end joined the *Regent Panther* which was far ahead of her times in this respect.

* Yet, oddly, The Irish in England had, and still have, a vote in British elections.

44

Outward bound to Trinidad, initially in convoy, we saw the changes wrought by the war: the vast array of vessels swinging off Southend, which we joined, waiting for one convoy or another. As we passed through the Downs, there was one solitary wreck on the Goodwin Sands: Brocklebank's *Mahratta* which had run aground five days previously, partly as a result of the congestion of shipping and partly because the coastwise lights were extinguished — a very different situation to that which obtained next time we passed that way whilst, off Deal, was a veritable armada of over two hundred neutral vessels waiting to pass through the contraband control. The *Regent Panther* was equipped with paravanes and a 4.0″ and 12 pounder gun on a platform at the after end of the poop.

There had been some dummy gun-drills before we left under an ex-marine, who had been seconded to the ship, but it turned out that he was useless and he was replaced by another who proved to be better. However, when a practice was carried out with live ammunition, the gun-platform rose and fell with the shock, and the damage done to the accommodation at the after end of the ship was so great, bringing down doors, smashing lavatory pans and so forth, that the gun was never fired again while I was in the ship. As for the paravanes, their davits had been wrongly placed and were useless, so they were unrigged and ignored until we came back to Avonmouth at the end of the trip.

Sleeping in beds with vi-spring mattresses, as opposed to bunks with "donkeys' breakfasts", the privacy of two-berth cabins, and the better food and bathrooms was all a far cry from the sailing ships, but the life was boring in the extreme; the men had insufficient to do and never worked together as a team, with the result that they tended to dream up all sorts of complaints against each other and against the ship. Tankers are clean vessels, their cargo never being seen at all, and this was as good a one as any afloat in that era. They have the disadvantage, of course, that they are seldom long in port and are often berthed at inconvenient and remote locations.

After loading in Trinidad, we proceeded north to Halifax, N.S. for convoy. One morning we were sun-bathing on the deck in glorious weather in the Gulf Stream. That evening the temperature was dropping rapidly with blue-grey clouds ahead. Then there was a series of flashes of mauve lightning — a strange and striking phenomenon — which was promptly followed by sleet which, in a rising wind and plummeting temperature, soon turned to snow as we came into the bottom of the Labrador Current and approached the latitude of Cape Hatteras. Soon, we were not only iced right up in blinding snow — a swift and traumatic change of temperature — but, reduced to half speed, smashing into a gale of well over 100 m.p.h. Again, the sea was flattened but, as usual in such conditions, there was a solid spume some forty feet high which froze as it was swirled to leeward by the wind. Decks were invisible as seas crashed over them and broke into cascades of spray on the tank tops, and a man had to fight his way along the flying bridge. One can stay at sea for a lifetime and never encounter such a force of wind. This was the second time I had experienced one but, whereas that in the *Moshulu* had been a warm wind, this was a freezing one. It often occurred to me to wonder how that great sailing ship would have fared, on her beam ends and frozen up in such conditions. As for the tanker, she simply ploughed through it, at reduced speed. Yet an astonishing incident occurred just before dusk.

Perhaps the most beautiful craft ever built were the two-masted fishing schooners out of Gloucester (Mass.) and adjacent ports which fished for cod on the Grand Banks or for mackerel on George's. Few vessels carried a greater press of sail for their size, were more staunch or more beautiful to see. Just before dusk, as the snow eased momentarily, we sighted one of these craft on our starboard bow. Listing well over, she was reefed right down and frozen up with great icicles half the height of her masts. It would have been impossible to start a sheet or anything else. She was travelling so fast that she appeared to be flying through the surface of the blown spume which rendered her hull and booms wholly invisible. Passing ahead of us, and presumably running off George's for shelter, she had run too long or else the wind had increased so quickly (as it had) that she had no chance to lie to and ride it out. Now, apparently sailing into eternity, she vanished into the murk almost in a flash. What happened to her, we never knew. If she came under the land in such conditions, I believe there was no way of stopping her short of cutting away her gear. The epic stories of the sailing of the Banks schooners are legion, but I never heard of any to compare with the wild flight of this vessel at a speed I should not wish to guess, and so iced up that only her wheel could be worked.

Scarcely had she gone than a steam trawler appeared in her wake, entirely iced-up, like some fancy Christmas cake, and passed across our bow on the same course as the schooner, which must have swung close by her just previously like a flying wraith.

The weather remained cold. A variety of ships were with us in Bedford Basin, above Halifax, including the *Empress of Britain*, now looking only half her peace-time size in her grey paint. As our convoy formed up outside the harbour, two or three schooners — the Canadian equivalent of the Gloucestermen — came out under all sail to their big fishermen's topsails, flirting with the morning sun in all the height of their masting, and in stark contrast with that craft we had seen in the grip of the Storm Gods off Hatteras. The outward-bound convoy had called for little

18. Winter-time in the North Atlantic — the REGENT PANTHER.

comment but now, after four hours forming up, the thirty merchantmen, in eight columns, got under weigh with the battleship *Warspite* in
the centre and two destroyers weaving ahead for the first twenty-four
hours, after which they returned. There was no doubt that convoys
presented some splendid sights never seen in peace-time, and the first
night out, in a relatively calm sea, the variety of ships was silhouetted on
the sea which reflected all the colours of the setting sun. That sort of
condition did not last long. The weather deteriorated and soon the
convoy was in full gale. The seas of the Atlantic are shorter and steeper
than those in the Southern Ocean and, on the Grand Banks, they are
steeper still. The *Warspite*, which left us the following day, was simply
burrowing into the sea, throwing up enormous sprays all over her fore
part, whilst we and the other tankers were streaming seas over the well
decks. Some ships were making very heavy weather of it. A United
Molasses tanker astern of us was rolling most vilely, but the Commodore's
vessel, the *San Fabian*, was almost as steady as a rock, creating quite an
illusion. The fact was that she had a far from modern appearance and
looked to be some 12,000 tons at the most, but in fact was one of the
largest tankers then afloat, with a deadweight of about 19,000 tons. She
apparently had an incredibly deep draft.

The scene made a contrast with the small armada seen so peacefully
silhouetted against the sunset so short a time before. Now it was seldom
that more than three of four vessels could be seen at all, and those that

were visible were either rearing their bows heavenwards or pitching so that only their sterns were visible over the seas. Sometimes a ship in the next column would only be showing her masts and, occasionally, her funnel. There was an unutterable grandeur in the sight of a whole convoy smashing into all the fury of an Atlantic gale, sometimes in bright moonlight, the crests of the seas whipping off in smoking plumes of spray before they crashed aboard the labouring ships. Zig-zagging was temporarily abandoned, and several ships were to lose the convoy altogether. Few men realize what their own ship looks like from without in different conditions.

I recalled a glorious trade wind day when passing St. Helena in a four-masted barque, with another of our own sort in company. The wind was right aft, and the other ship was rolling tremendously (the one condition when sailing ships do roll!), and we then realized that we must be (and, indeed, were) behaving in a similar fashion. The other ship always looks worse! So, although we were pitching, scending and screwing this way and that, and our decks were a mass of broken water, the sight of the *other* ships was quite awe-inspiring. Sometimes, between flurries of snow, signal flags stood bright against the blue-grey clouds reflecting on the seas. Such scenes incorporated a wild splendour which seemed to purify a man's soul till he began to understand the very elements of creation. No doubt the great sailing convoys of past eras, particularly in the Napoleonic Wars, presented some of the finest sights ever beheld at sea, but there was something spell-binding about these freighters in high gale and the steep seas of the North Atlantic: conditions which were common enough and often repeated.

After discharging in Avonmouth, we joined a small convoy as a lead ship in Milford Haven and, on the second night out, in bad visibility, a mast-head light and two sidelights were suddenly switched on close ahead of us. We swung hard a-starboard and, as we did so, ships' navigation lights were all around us. The first ship passed so close to our foc's'le head that one might believe that collision was only averted because the two vessels were rolling in opposite directions but, within seconds, ships of both convoys were heading in all sorts of directions trying to avoid one collision only to find themselves in imminent danger of another. It may seem incredible that two convoys, on opposite courses, should have been allowed to meet head on but, not long afterwards, in another ship, I found myself in a similar predicament. That night we lost the convoy, though managed to pick it up again the next day. Two ships never saw it again.

The voyage was the same round. As we came up past Tobago, glorious to see in its variety of greens in the sunlight, an island schooner came out with a big deck-load. Many of the Grand Bank schooners had been sold, as they became older, to the Caribbean, and they had set the standard for the local schooners which had much in common with them.

This one beat out and, when she was on our beam, swung round and matched our twelve knots, knot for knot, all the way to the Serpent's Mouth, where we stopped for the examination vessel. By the time that we reached the anchorage, off Port o' Spain, she was tied up with all her sails nicely furled. There were still many of these craft in those waters, although now any that are left are cut right down and have diesels, but the locality, the climate, and the form of these vessels probably provided the most perfect and pleasurable sailing of any craft in all the world.

Christmas was spent off Port o' Spain pleasantly enough, well provided with fruit from the bum-boats. It was gloriously hot and the ports were all open. My cabin-mate entered our cabin to find a black hand hauling its owner through our cabin port, clearly with felonious intent. He let the heavy deadlight drop, without a moment's hesitation. There was a yell, heard all over the ship, followed by a swiftly departing bum-boat, and our cabin gave the impression of having been sprayed with blood under pressure!

Once again bound to Halifax and roughly where we had seen the schooner on the previous voyage, in the middle of the night the wheelhouse was suddenly flooded with a brilliant light, which I could see also on both sides of the ship. Darting to the door, I was just in time to see the tail of a meteorite which had crashed into the sea. It seemed incredibly close, but was probably a mile or two away. Oddly, although the odds against such an occurrence are astronomically high despite the innumerable ships which have sailed through the ages, it is seldom considered that some of those which have gone missing could have been struck by a large meteorite.

Weather apart, for it was another winter crossing of the Western Ocean, the convoy made its passage without incident. On arrival off the Western Approaches, two days were lost, literally steaming first north, then south, awaiting our escorting destroyers which had evidently been weather-bound: two potentially very vulnerable days. Three other ships and our vessel were detached to proceed up Channel to the Thames, with one destroyer. The weather moderated and, indeed, we came up Channel in January, 1940, in a glassy calm in unbroken sunlight and, at night, brilliant moonlight though it was bitterly cold — the coldest winter in England within living memory. Initially in two columns, we finally formed into one, led by the Canadian Pacific *Beaverburn*, with us astern of her and ahead of the New Zealand Shipping Company's *Rotorua* and, astern of her, the Dutch tanker *Ondina** which was still in peace-time

* Actually, she had only been built in 1939 for the Royal Dutch Shell Co. At the end of 1942 she signally distinguished herself in the South Indian Ocean when, in company with

49

paint and whose white upperworks shone like a beacon in the moonlight. This vessel had lagged all across the Atlantic in the main convoy.

Officers and men nearly all became very jumpy. The sea was a mass of flotsam, easily visible at night, though it was impossible to determine what might be a mine until it was too late. Then there was a thick haze and, steaming by some flag buoys, still in line ahead, there were more nerves aboard our ship until the *Beaverburn* swung right round to starboard, realizing, just in time, that she was leading us straight into a British minefield!

As we slowed for the pilot, we were alongside a big Dutch vessel which we had heard the previous day had been in a serious collision. Her port side was rent wide open from the bow, displaying a mass of twisted steel while, nearby, was anchored the *Teakwood* with all her midship section smashed up: presumably the other ship involved. So we passed on through the Downs but — what a change since we had last passed that way! And how sobering the sight! The *Mahratta*, now with her back broken, was still there, but the channel was littered with wrecks: the pilot constantly referring to a sheaf of hand-written notes. Here the funnel and a mast of the *Dunbar Castle* stuck up out of the sea: there a stern; two more masts with derricks still topped up close by, elsewhere a ship sitting on an even keel with a signal hoist still fluttering, and, indeed, there seemed to be wrecks everywhere: victims of the magnetic mines which had taken such a high toll when first introduced in those three intervening months. Moreover, where there were not wrecks, there was every likelihood of the mines themselves, despite the small armada of sweepers which were busy operating both there and right along the estuary.

I had concluded that I needed little enough study to pass my forthcoming examination and that a tanker was poor experience. The sailing ships had offered little practical cargo-work other than bagged grain and timber, and a tanker offered none. I therefore thought it more sensible to finish my time in a vessel which would give me a greater

---

the virtually unarmed British minesweeper *Bengal*, they were attacked by two Japanese armed merchant cruisers, the *Hokuku Maru* and *Aikoku Maru*. The *Ondina* sank the former with her 4-inch gun! Subsequently, after being abandoned, her crew were machine-gunned in the water and in their boats, but the survivors later re-boarded the tanker and, independently, both allied ships made port.

There were many instances, particularly of Japanese submarines, wantonly machine-gunning sunken ships crews: sometimes taking them aboard and shooting them; once — and this was not unique — as in the case of the Japanese cruiser *Tone*, decapitating many survivors of the *Behar* on her decks. Such atrocities were normally accompanied by laughter while being filmed by cameras. It would seem that extermination of survivors was a Japanese policy, but reference should be made to the Epilogue of this book in this context.

knowledge of cargo-handling and ports generally, and signed off the ship on arrival.

I got home with great difficulty. My parents' house was cut off from the outside world by nine-foot snow drifts on the main road which was impassable. My mother and I did make one expedition to London to see a show and, had Jack Hulbert and Cicely Courtneidge appreciated our journey, I feel sure we should have been given the best box in the theatre, gratis! Apart from that, I made one large shopping expedition for my parents, shod in snow shoes and dragging a toboggan. On the way back, I saw something move in the hedge at the verge of a field and, taking off my glove, put down my hand, whereupon a tiny field-mouse ran straight into it and started nibbling, attracted by its comparative warmth. I put it in my pocket and took it home where, whether or not out of gratitude for being saved certain death by cold or starvation, it behaved as though perfectly domesticated and was a friendly little creature with no fear at all. (My parents returned it to its habitat when the snow finally cleared.) A quantity of frost-bitten apples were set in a shed with its door left open, and this attracted multitudes of birds of all species, which feasted on the apples (for they, too, were starving) and sheltered in the shed between times. That was the measure of it. Pipes were frozen and it was no sort of leave, so I soon set about finding another ship.

The Shipping Federation arranged for me to join Shaw, Savill's *Tamaroa*, which involved a wait of five days. When I went to sign on, I found they had bungled things and there was no berth. I left them in no uncertainty about my displeasure, and was offered a choice of two vessels: one of Constantine's tramps, which I turned down flat, and a vessel named the *Chelsea*, which I did not know. Asking where she was bound, I was told probably to the Plate, but possibly to Cuba for sugar. I decided to take her and, having passed the doctor, actually had the pen in my hand to sign the Crew Register when I happened to say to her second mate, who was standing by me: *"Is she going down to B.A?"* (Buenos Aires) *"so far as you know?"* He, not having been primed by the Federation, replied that he thought they were bound for Halifax, to the consternation of the Federation men. I handed back the pen and walked out, never to set foot in a Shipping Federation office again. It turned out that I was followed by half the potential crew!

I then got myself a berth in another, older Shaw, Savill vessel, the *Raranga*, a twin-screw coal-burner of nearly 8,000 tons gross which had been built in the previous war. Unfortunately, she had been badly loaded (for we had a full general cargo for New Zealand) and was very tender. That is to say that the weights had been wrongly stowed, so that her centre of gravity was too high. Once we reached Dover we started to roll. Not a normal roll, but a long, slow one through an enormous arc and, at the end of each and every one, she stopped, as though wondering whether to come back or to roll right on and over. It was not only disconcerting, but extremely tiring, since one was sub-consciously bracing and flexing muscles whether on deck or in one's bunk. She never stopped until we reached the Sambro Channel and entered the Caribbean, when conditions were flat calm with a twelve knot breeze right aft, which matched our speed and meant that there was no apparent wind at all. It was incredibly hot. For my part, I enjoy any temperature the sun can throw at me, but the stokehold became an inferno. Ventilators were quite useless. Both stokers and trimmers were being sent up on deck on the ash hoist, unconscious. The steam pressure was dropping. Others of them laid up, sick, and were not malingering. It was then felt that the deck crowd should go below and assist. Fortunately this did not come about, since I know of nothing created by man which more resembles Hell than a ship's stokehold. I thought, somewhat ruefully, that had the war not come about I would be under sail and far removed from such a situation!

Then, in the heat haze on the horizon, we discerned the shape of a warship about three points forward of our port beam. Immediately afterwards, a tanker was sighted heading for her. The Master of our ship and the Chief Officer had both been in our sister ship, the *Tairoa*, which had been sunk by the pocket battleship *Graf Spee*, being ultimately rescued from the *Altmark* with her other prisoners but, when aboard the pocket battleship, they had signed a paper undertaking not to return to sea during the war. Both men were exceptionally jumpy, and at once assumed that we were witnessing a German supply ship about to refuel the 'German' warship. It was too hazy to see much detail of either ship, but it then became apparent that the tanker was light, and unlikely to be carrying any fuel.

The warship then got under weigh and headed for us. We altered course, but she was gaining fast and, as we changed course again, she followed suit. By now it was apparent that the pursuing vessel was a destroyer and therefore unlikely to be German in those waters. Nevertheless, although she did not fire, she made no signal nor gave any form of identification. Considering that she was acting in a most suspicious manner, the master then told the radio officer to send out an S.O.S. with our position, which he did. When the destroyer was almost alongside us she broke out the Stars and Stripes and started to morse, asking our name and destination after which she sheered off: a four-funnelled vessel with a fair turn of speed. The captain was, not unnaturally, furious, since he had been obliged to break wireless silence and broadcast our position to the world.

Only the previous week we had picked up the distress signals of the

British steamer *Southgate* in the Mona Passage, which added that she was being chased by a submarine. This, too, had turned out to be an American and, like ours, her signal was subsequently cancelled. Within an hour or so of the departure of the destroyer, a big American flying boat came to inspect us and, in the afternoon, we saw the traces of a submarine very close indeed. The sea was still like a mirror, and a trail of exhaust fumes were moving across the surface. There were a number of similar scares to other British ships at this time and, although it cannot be denied that the Americans were bending their neutrality to the uttermost and gave the British much useful information, they also gave some of their ships nasty moments.

It is not the intention of these chapters to emulate a travelogue, and I shall generally make no references to places unless they had a bearing on some facet of life at sea which is not generally appreciated, and shall therefore omit any description of the Panama Canal, perhaps the most fascinating of all man-made channels, or of the beauties of New Zealand, and much else.

Few ships were free of those who became drunk in port and a coal-burner, with her rather tough 'black gang', was often worse than most. It was easy for the most sober and unassuming person to become involved in a fight on returning to his ship and I, for my part, always carried a knuckle-duster in my pocket. I had procured the original one in Belfast, when in a four-masted barque and when one of our number, a young, inoffensive Finn aged only 15, was so badly beaten up when returning from the Seamen's Mission that he could barely crawl back aboard and, indeed, had to be paid off the ship due to his injuries. At that time there were gangs roaming the area about the York Dock whose favourite weapon was a sock filled with broken glass, which marked a man for life.

After this incident, the ship's company generally rendez-voused somewhere and returned to the ship in a body. Everyone knows that Ulster is touched with a madness, nominally in the name of religion, but a crew of Finns should hardly have been a target for any faction. Nevertheless, we were set upon by a gang of thugs one night. Not only were they outnumbered, but my knuckle-duster, brass with knobs on the knuckles, was brought into immediate play and the man it hit went down so fast and so hard that the others took flight. I replaced it, in due course, with a lighter, aluminium model, which I never had occasion to use in the event, though I should never have had the slightest compunction about doing so had the need arisen.

The *Raranga* saw quite a number of fights, generally between two men rather than general melées, both at sea and in port. I recall the chief steward with his face blown up to almost twice its normal size after being attacked by the second mate, though nobody witnessed the incident. It may be thought that a ship had reached a pretty pass when the officers were indulging in this sort of thing but, after the war, when viewing a Shaw, Savill publicity film about their latest liner (and flagship), there was this self-same second mate as her captain and fleet commodore!

The *Raranga's* carpenter was attracted to the bottle in port, though the effects on him were normally of a more soporific order. One evening in Wellington the ship was to take fresh water, being by then well advanced in her lading, which included the largest cargo of frozen meat ever carried to England. Discovering the carpenter to be so drunk as to be utterly incapable, and not wishing to get him into trouble by drawing attention to the fact, the water man, who clearly had some experience of such ships, used his own initiative and, having pumped in the amount ordered, went ashore. It was not until the next day that it was found that he had inserted his hose, not into the tank inlet pipe, but into one of the pipes used to lower thermometers to take the temperatures of the refrigerated holds, and that the cargo already loaded there was now encased in ice! It need hardly be said that this situation caused as much delay as it did ill-will from the company.

We had resumed our dreadful rolling outward bound from Panama all across the Pacific and now, homeward bound, the ship met filthy weather, head on, for days on end. Awning stanchions were bent back to crazy angles, ladders were carried away, a boat smashed, and there was other damage but, by the time we reached Panama, we had almost bare bunkers and were hardly able to get through the Canal to Christobal, where we bunkered. We were advised not to go ashore to Colon, across the ferry, because there was an election in progress and it might be dangerous. Anything was better than being aboard a ship coaling, so a few of us *did* go, to find that a large sector of the town had burnt down since our previous visit, leaving over 20,000 families homeless and living in U.S. army tents. There was a strange atmosphere of quiet, save only for some loud-speaker vans bearing pictures of candidates, the physiognomy of each looking to be more criminal than the last. The American Canal Zone police, unusually, had their batons and revolvers out of their holsters.

The Germans had broken through the Maginot Line and were driving the allied armies back fast. Consequently the exchange rate was so low (50 cents instead of $4.80 to the pound) that we could not bring ourselves to change any money and were about to return to the ship when we became aware that the street was emptied. We dived into a doorway just before a machine gun started firing. Then there was silence. After a short time we emerged, to see a crowd about a figure slumped on the ground, so lost no time in getting back. However, the jungle came almost to the coaling station, and we started to walk through it, finding wild mangoes and plantains to which we helped ourselves liberally. It was a splendid place, a mass of luxurious greens and exotic colours with splendid butterflies, and we could have spent long there had we not espied a large, venomous-looking bluish creature with long hairy legs of the tarantula variety regarding us malevolently, and appearing to be poised to pounce. We beat our second hasty retreat of the day and when, in the early evening, the ship steamed away past Colon, we heard a good deal of firing going on. The election was evidently going splendidly!

We went to Bermuda to pick up a convoy and, 22 ships strong, proceeded. There were some fine vessels with us, including another of our Company's fleet — the *Zealandic*. Suddenly she hoisted a flag signal which was read as:- *"Please accept apologies. Slim."*

Perplexed, the third mate referred it to the master, who said:- *"That's all right. He promised to have lunch with me the other day and never turned up. Hoist 'Accept apologies'."* Then, after a few minutes' thought, he told the third mate to hoist:- *"Do not make unnecessary signals"*. As this was hoisted, it was realized that the original signal was not for us at all. Going a bit red in the face, our master said:- *"I'll get that ZEALANDIC yet!"*

Our convoy joined up with one from Halifax, doubling its size, though two ships, the Norwegian tanker *Hilda Knudsen* and a British tanker, both bound for France, were ordered back to Bermuda. There were in the convoy a number of French vessels which, unlike those of other nations, were dazzle-painted in the fashion of the previous war: some of them done very well as it was often difficult to determine how they were heading. The war news was depressing in the extreme as the British army was evacuated from Dunkirk and French capitulation was clearly imminent. At nightfall one day the convoy was intact. By dawn the French ships were gone, having fled to Martinique where they remained for the duration .... It is probably true to say that the French nation was almost equally divided in its loyalties.

Outward bound again, leading a column in the convoy between the *Manchester Progress* and the *Clan Murdoch*, we had barely passed Malin Head when the tramp *Boma*, laden with coal, was torpedoed and sunk after a U-boat's periscope had been sighted by most of the ships in the convoy, which was quickly in utter disarray as each ship took independent avoiding action. Shortly after the convoy dispersed, we took avoiding action from a large steamer which appeared out of a squall, and again thought ourselves to be pursued, as the ship resembled a raider then operating, but she turned out to be a (then) neutral Japanese. Nevertheless two of our former convoy, the *Koranton* and *British Fame*, were sunk after dispersal, the first by a raider and the second, off the Azores, by a submarine.

We bunkered in Durban where, having friends, I had a splendid time. The bunker station on the Bluff was alongside the whaling station, which I found interesting, but there was the usual filth which attends coaling, the worse on this occasion as a strong, warm wind spread the dust everywhere. Indeed, we had as much coal as food for lunch! The bunkers were trimmed by Bantu coalies who worked at the station until they had accumulated enough money to buy a cow or other suitable dowry for a wife. Each wore a metal disc with a number on his wrist, and all were checked at the end of each shift, as in the past it had been no uncommon thing for some of these men to be buried in the coal and their corpses to be dug out *en voyage*. In fact, only three years previously, one was missed at the end of a shift in the *Port Sydney*, whereupon the bunkers had to be dug out and discharged until they found the body: an operation which took three days.

When coaling was complete, the ship was just casting off her final moorings when a swarm of locusts descended, causing chaos. Each about four inches long and substantially built, few of us had ever realized just how thick such a swarm is. The air seemed to be solid. One could scarcely keep one's eyes open at all as they bumped into them continually and even into an open mouth. The swarm was so thick that it was virtually impossible for those on the bridge to see forward or aft, let alone the tug. Seldom could any ship have presented such a shambles leaving her wharf. Large numbers of locusts were still aboard days later, but by then comatose. We could not resume normal working until a couple of miles offshore.

The ship encountered very heavy weather *en route* to Australia and presented one of the few occasions when I heard *"All hands on deck"* called in a steamer. The forward fall block of one of the boats had carried away, leaving it hanging in its flying gripes. Three ribs had been smashed and we had to get it inboard. (Boats were swung out, in readiness, during the war.) Here was the difference between sail and steam. The men had no idea how to pull in unison and made a mountain out of a simple job. We suffered a good deal of damage, and one porthole in a foc's'le, over which the deadlight had not been screwed down properly, smashed, flooding one of the seamen's bunks. He at once went to the mate to complain!! The mate turned to me and asked how often I had been flooded in sail (he himself was well used to it) and the man got short shrift.

Indeed, many men were enabled to sign on as A.B.s with no knowledge whatever. Although the majority of the country threw itself into the war effort, including most of that vociferous lobby which had preached appeasement before war was declared, there was a minority of what was termed 'Army dodgers' who had turned to the sea as being a 'safer' war-time occupation. Most joined as seamen, but a few of the more intelligent became radio officers. They made a great mistake, since the death toll in the Merchant Service was, *pro rata*, higher than in the armed services for the greater part of the war, but when one considers that most ships only had three men in a watch, it accounted for much of the appalling seamanship so often exhibited in British ships in those years. The previous voyage, a man had been sent into the chains with a hand lead as we came into Panama. He had no idea what to do, and was quickly replaced (by the man who complained about the broken port.) He cast the lead in very amateurish way and, with the thirteen fathom mark still inboard, called:- "*No bottom.*" The pilot nearly doubled up with laughter, to the embarrassment of the master and mate.

Similarly, one such man asked me one day which of our rafts I thought the best. Like most vessels, we had some on the shrouds, which could be lowered easily, but other, more substantial, ones actually on deck. I said I thought the latter, to which he replied that one would never get them overboard. I replied that, at worst, they would float off. He nearly screamed at me:- "*But they're lashed down!*". In a sailing ship, no man moved without his sheath knife on his belt. These men did not possess one .... In the light of some of their behaviour, particularly in ports, it was perhaps as well.

Later, in the *Dalhousie*, when she was almost discharged in Port Said and the crew saw bombs stowed in the lower part of each hold, I heard men of this sort exclaiming, in horror, that they would never have signed on if they had known about this item of cargo ....

In Melbourne, which I was visiting for the first time, I had a free day and, taking a tram into the town, first embarked for a sight-seeing trip on the River Yarra. This was spoilt by the fact that it was the day of the Melbourne Cup — a horse race — the prospects of which not only monopolised the tannoy system, but also the conversation of everyone else aboard. In the afternoon I went to a film — *Gone with the Wind* — and then, after some shopping, saw an excellent performance of *The Mikado* in a theatre.

As it was a fine evening and the theatre had been a little hot, I resolved to walk back to Victoria Dock. I did not take the same route as the tram in the morning, but it never occurred to me to query my direction. In any case, I have a good bump of locality. On the way, having eaten nothing since breakfast, I began to feel hungry, so decided to call in at a delicatessen shop which was slightly off my route to buy a couple of mutton birds for my supper. To this end, I turned to the left and then into a very narrow street leading off to the right, which all seemed familiar enough, and duly bought my mutton birds. (Having only the most rudimentary ideas about cooking, I chose them because they will cook in their own fat!)

After retracing my steps to the previous road, in due course I reached the ship, where I cooked my supper. It was only when I was half-way through it that I was disconcerted to realise that, never having been in Melbourne before, I could not possibly have known of the existence of the delicatessen shop or of its location, let alone that it would still be open at eleven o'clock at night! Such instances of *déjà vu* pose large questions ....

There was a consignment of china stowed in our 'tween decks, and this was believed to have been the origin of a colony of rats. They multiplied at an unbelievable rate. At night, they were running all over the decks, up the rigging and along the derricks. The man in the crow's nest was once startled when he was joined by one. We had streamed our paravanes through Bass Straits (where an American ship, the *City of Rayville*, which had been in port with us and, of course, had no paravanes, was sunk at the same time), and we would see them in the moonlight running down the wires and even onto the paravanes themselves, sometimes being washed away. All ports insist on protection against rats and rat-guards are secured on the mooring ropes to prevent them coming aboard, but never on the gangway or accommodation ladders. I have not only seen rats board ships up the gangway, but have seen them swimming both ashore and out to a ship in broad daylight, climbing up the anchor cable. Yet, writing with a certain experience of rats, I have never seen such infestation, or so quickly, as in that ship.

She was lucky. In the Great Australian Bight, homeward bound, she again struck very hard weather and had to limp into Fremantle for boiler repairs. We had hardly arrived before we heard that the *Port Brisbane* and our sister ship *Maimoa*, which had both been on the coast with us, had both been sunk by a raider (the *Pinguin*) and their crews taken prisoner: the *Maimoa* having taken our route and being just where we should have been had we not had boiler trouble.

In the light of what will be related in due course of the captain of the *Patella* in Japan, it may be worth retailing an incident which occurred aboard the *Raranga* this voyage. There was in the crew an elderly and rather staid old greaser. His wife and home were in Wapping, in London's dockland, and he had a grown-up family. He was probably past retiring age, since few older men gave their right age when signing on, and was a short, stocky man with a grizzled, grey moustache, who habitually wore a close-fitting beret, like a skull-cap, and a grey choker round the neck of his dungaree jacket, with a short, nose-warmer pipe stuck in his mouth, whether aboard or ashore. He kept much to himself, but was what was termed a 'steady man', standing by the ship voyage

19. The RARANGA

after voyage and invariably conducting himself quietly enough in port. One would have presumed that such ambition as he may ever have possessed had been extinguished by endless years wielding his grease gun in the bowels of his ships, even in all the sun and splendour of Sydney Harbour.

There he fell in love with a whore — madly in love. Little is known of her, and the presumption is that she, probably one of the raddled remnants which haunted that rather tough waterfront*, found him acutely distasteful but he resolved to desert and join her, letting two of his pals into his secret in order that they might assist in getting his gear ashore unnoticed. Unfortunately for him, the master had not seen fit to inform him that we were to shift out to anchorage on the very evening that he had planned his exodus, which was thus foiled. Only his two friends knew anything about it but, after we sailed, he started to act oddly: going below to grease in his free watch: climbing into the wrong bunk, often in the wrong foc's'le, and so on. After we left Fremantle, by which time he had become withdrawn with a faraway look in his eyes, he would belabor the engineer on watch with his grease gun when told he was working in his watch below.

Finally he was persuaded not to take watches at all but to take it easy. He sat all day on the fore hatch, incessantly sucking at the dottle in his

---

* In the Pyrmont area, above the harbour bridge, it was as well to walk in the middle of the road. Our Chief Radio Operator had gone missing this very trip. Since he left money and other valuables aboard, he did not desert. A smartly dressed man, he was almost certainly robbed and dumped in the harbour.

pipe, staring into space and speaking to no-one. His presence there was disturbing and unnatural, since it seemed that he had utterly detached himself from the ship and, indeed, from life itself. In Durban the master, who had now learnt the story, did everything he could to have him put ashore, but the doctor, a materialist to the core, could find nothing wrong with him and he remained. Rounding the Cape in dirty weather with sprays whipping over him, he remained immobile, apparently seeing nothing nor feeling the wind or sea, as if drenched with some Lethean dew. While we steamed up the African coast, it became, one would suppose, intolerably hot on that hatch for the wind was aft and there was no apparent wind on deck, but still he was there early every morning, and only led to his bunk late in the first watch. Then, as the sea turned aurelian with the setting sun and our wash glistened in a mass of brilliants amidst the widening wake in a dead calm as we approached the anchorage off Freetown, the old *amoreux* suddenly slumped on to his back, dead. His body was taken ashore and an autopsy held, but it found nothing whatever wrong with him. Of course, we all knew why he had died, but such causes do not enter into medical text-books. The old sailors' superstition that a sick man would die as he came under the land was not one generally accepted in steam.

I am fond of animals and, when in a port for any length of time, usually acquired or adopted a cat or kitten, but always ensured that I found it a good home before leaving, since I have always considered that a ship is no proper environment for a pet, let alone in time of war. However, a number of our men bought monkeys from bum-boats. I had no intention of doing so, until I saw a very small one looking miserable in the stern sheets of one boat so, in a sudden impulse of pity, I threw down an old shirt and secured it, together with a large stock of bananas in various stages of ripeness. It was a very young male and, as I quickly discovered, not yet weaned. This might have proved to be a major impediment, but by that time there were about sixty or more monkeys aboard the ship, of various shapes and sizes, and to my joy I found a spider monkey which was in milk and which had no offspring with her.

Her owner was agreeable and, although my grass monkey was a quite different species, she was happy to sit under the windlass, fostering and feeding him until she saw fit to make a trip to the surgery where she purloined and consumed an entire packet of cigarettes, wrapping and all, which proved fatal. But, by that time, mine was starting to take solids. I also found it immediately necessary to bath him, as he was infested. This he hated, and I was so badly bitten in the process that it was all I could do to hold a knife and fork for days! However, I got him clean and, by the end of a week, he was actually enjoying his baths and showing a measure of affection.

Monkeys overshadowed everything else on that homeward passage: everything, that is, except the chronic constipation suffered by the whole ship's company. We had what was said to be the largest cargo of eggs ever carried in a ship, amongst other items. These we had loaded in Newcastle, N.S.W. and, because the ship's food was not of the best, however illicitly, eggs became the staple diet. Steamship men, with too little to do, tend to over-eat as a measure of their boredom, so eggs were eaten for each and every meal, between meals and even taken, boiled, into the crow's nest. This went on for about three months: at the end of which the effects were much as though we had been on a diet of cement so far as our natural functions were concerned. Nevertheless, a mush of banana and raw egg yolk helped to wean my little monkey. Indeed, although immediately appalled to find him unweaned, it proved to be a blessing in disguise, since it is often said that one cannot train a monkey but, by the time we arrived in England, having spent much time with him, I did have him practically house-trained and obedient in many ways. This was in virtue of being able to start so young, much as a dog, if not trained from a very early age as a puppy, will seldom learn true obedience.

The captain was terrified of monkeys, it seemed, and on one occasion was chased out of his day-room by one only to arrive on the bridge to be confronted by two more. He quite panicked! There had been a certain excitement while still in Freetown when one fell overboard, but it swam magnificently, and was finally rescued. One suddenly terrified the lookout by joining him in the nest, on a dark night. All had their own living quarters, like miniature kennels, which were swiftly constructed, but many nevertheless got loose and there was a certain mortality, yet there were still well over three dozen aboard when we finally entered the Mersey. As we had come up into the colder weather of the North Atlantic, I had transformed some old rugger stockings (striped bright blue and yellow!) into a sort of elongated jersey and kept my animal close to the warmth of the fidley bulkhead, by the boiler uptakes.

A number of ships from our convoy were bound in to various Liverpool Docks but, because the knuckle of the Gladstone Dock had been bombed, most had to use the same set of locks and eleven ships of a variety of nationalities were secured, cheek by jowl, in three rows of three and one of two, together with their attendant tugs, in the same basin waiting for the tide to lock in. We were alongside the *Port Caroline*, aboard which was a man who had been in our ship the previous voyage and who had been most disappointed that, passing through Panama, he had had no chance to obtain a monkey. He was quickly recognized, and asked if he now had one. Despite the cold weather with much snow on the ground, he fetched it, while the first man, not wishing to be outdone, fetched his.

We had been with this ship on the Australian coast, and many men knew each other. More monkeys were produced in both ships. Other vessels followed suit. Then they started to escape and were clambering from ship to ship, and all over each. They explored new cabins and foc's'les, climbed ladders and occasionally the rigging. Frantic men were not only calling and swearing in English, Dutch, Norwegian, French and, possibly, other languages but boarding other vessels. There was indescribable confusion as there must have been two or three hundred loose for, once those monkeys still under control saw the others at large, they lost no time in breaking free themselves. I saw the pilot of a Dutch ship trying to fend two monkeys off the anti-aircraft guns on her bridge: a fat cook chasing a spider monkey which had stolen a tit-bit from his galley, and many other minor dramas of the same sort. (I had resolved at the outset to leave my pet where he was, and was thankful I had done so.)

In the meantime, the dock-masters were blowing their whistles and bellowing orders to get the ships moving through the lock. Dock-masters, with great authority, brook no delays or interference, but they could do little in the confusion then reigning, whilst the tuggees, called upon to manoeuvre their charges, were so doubled up and convulsed with laughter at the scene that they could do nothing. Finally, order was restored and I think that most people who started off with a monkey had one at the end of the day, though few had their original animals!

Once ashore, I bought a lead and harness and went shopping with my new friend. Seeing a queue in Lewis's, the big department store, I asked what was at the end of it, to be told *"Bananas"*. Since my stock was exhausted, I promptly joined it and bought a dozen large ones, taking one off the stalk and holding it up, whereupon the monkey scaled my legs and torso from the floor and sat on my shoulder, enjoying it. At this moment the stock of bananas became exhausted, with a long line of Liverpool housewives disappointed behind me and furious to see one being consumed by a diminutive monkey. I sensed the rumblings of fury and, had my immediate movements ever been reported to the *Guinness Book of Records*, there is little doubt that my speed down Lime Street would take pride of athletic place. (Away for so long at a time, one was not aware of the growing shortages in England on arrival.)

The manageress of a small hotel where I usually stayed in Liverpool thought him 'sweet', and allowed me to bring him in for the night, though one or two of the residents did not, unfortunately, share her view ...

Arriving in London, I found that the railway line home (now to Sussex) had been bombed and that it was going to be an awkward journey. Simultaneously an air-raid started. I therefore decided to stay the night in London and booked into the Charing Cross Hotel, which was adjacent. I did *not* inform the receptionist about the monkey, which I had left in a lined box by a guttering fire in the station waiting room, but smuggled him in by a side door. I had, fortunately, had the foresight to buy some small towels (which I subsequently discovered to be nappies, appropriately enough) and, finding no heat in my bedroom, swathed the monkey in these and took him into bed with me. I am probably the only person to have spent the night in a London hotel in bed with a monkey. Next day, I caught a train, which had the heat on under the seats, so I removed the monkey from his box and placed him there, as I was worried about the low temperature. In due course a woman and her little girl got in and sat down. After a bit, the monkey emerged, whereupon the little girl was utterly entranced, but her mother, evidently a foolish woman, proceeded to have hysterics. It proved useless to point out that her presence in the carriage was not having this effect on the monkey, who was obviously far more balanced in his outlook, and that there was no reason for her to behave like this, even when I gave the little animal to her daughter to hold. It was an unhappy journey.

The monkey settled in very well at home. It was well behaved and soon a favourite, despite grim forebodings by my parents. Their house was then approached through a farm yard, with fields containing horses, pigs, sheep and poultry adjacent. The odd thing was that no animal could stand him. If the cows were coming in to be milked, the effect on them was to create a sort of wild west rodeo: horses neighed and even screamed as they galloped to the furthest corner of their paddocks: pigs, sheep, dogs and all other animals behaved in like fashion. If I was a mile or so from the house, I would put him down and tell him to run home, and always knew precisely where he was by the startled sounds of the farm animals on his way. No animal could have attacked him, as all were too terrified, but ... in the evenings he would curl up on my lap with the household Siamese cats which, alone, completely accepted him, and he them. I did not take him back to sea with me.

~~~~~

IV

THE *DALHOUSIE*

It did not take me long to take my ticket, merely attending navigation school to dot my i's and cross my 't's. For this purpose I was staying on Tower Hill, except at week-ends, during the height of the Luftwaffe 'blitz' on the City. Returning one evening, I passed my old city office, with its "Captains' Room", blazing in a mad inferno along with the beautiful Wren church alongside it. Indeed, for one of my *vivas*, after fighting uncontrollable fires all night (for it was the occasion when all the pumps on Tower Pier received a direct hit, cutting off all the water to the fire services), the examiner and I confronted each other with distinctly bleary eyes!

There was a slight *contretemps* at one point, since I was also taking a Sail Endorsement to my ticket, and there was great difficulty in finding anyone to examine me, since none of the regular men had been in sail themselves. This *viva voce* went well enough except for one question, which I record because the principle has a certain bearing on matters which will be mentioned later. Towards the end, I was asked how, if using a hand log, I would haul it in. The point was that, although I thought I knew all about the hand log, I had never actually seen one in use, as all my ships had used patent logs. In fact, a hand log needs three men. One holds a reel of line over his head, to pay out a triangular 'log chip' over the taffrail. The mate on watch gives the signal at the appropriate moment when he is ready to pay out to a third man, who turns over a sand glass and, when the sand has run out, the line is checked and the mark on the line on the taffrail indicates how many knots have run out, thus giving the speed in knots (and, incidentally, the origin of the term 'knots').

Not appreciating the point, I thought it rather a silly question, and answered:- *"Hand over hand, Sir"*. *"Suppose you could not?"* asked the examiner. I said I would call another man, to be met with the same question again. After enrolling a third hypothetical man, and with ebbing confidence, I was still met with the same response so, feeling that there was a limit to this, finally said, tongue in cheek, that I would take the log-line to a capstan. In fact, I had not realized that the line should have been jerked, in order to trip the chip and avoid its pressure against the water when hauling it in. Since it was my only fault, it made no odds and the examiner explained the point to me, but it soon became evident to me that many men simply did not have the necessary practical experience of many matters arising in both their written and oral examinations.

However, the first thing to be done was to find a ship and, at that time, there were very few in the Port of London. In any case, I was looking for a good-class tramp which would carry a variety of cargoes and be likely to visit an equal variety of ports. I was sent down to the Surrey Docks — a fascinating area before the war which I had known well, though now filled in and a housing estate! — to interview the master of a ship called the *Dalhousie**.

The master turned out to be a tubby, rather jolly little Welshman, named Davies, who was enormously impressed by the fact that I had been in sail (though he had not been himself!), and offered me the job of third mate at once. I liked the look of the ship, and accepted, joining within hours.

It was only later that I discovered that Davies had been master of some of the worst type of Welsh tramps running to the River Plate and Black Sea before the war (and these were, perhaps, as bad in every way as any ships afloat), and had retired from the sea some years previously[‡]. He had been overseeing the building of various vessels at the Burntisland yard, and hearing that the *Dalhousie*, which was nearing completion, was to proceed to Vancouver where she was to be finished off internally before loading her first cargo, he had put in for the command. In fact, her managing owner was a Greek, named Nicolaides, who paid wages above the standard rates and ensured that the ship was well-found. I met both him and his partner, an Englishman named Gundry, and liked them both. Their intention was to build up a fleet from this, their first ship.

My first day aboard we were to shift down to the Royal Albert Dock, but the captain had business ashore. He therefore told the mate to take charge and me to take the mate's place on the foc's'le head. Normally

---

* This proved to be a diesel vessel of 9,200 tons deadweight which, ordered before hostilities, had been launced in August, 1940, at a cost of £130,000. Built to peace-time standards, she represented the very latest in British tramp shipping.

‡ Many Welsh ship-masters, especially from the lower strata of tramps, retired when around forty-five. This could not be done from their pay and would not have been possible in the great companies. They had greater overall responsibility and could (and did) indulge in 'fiddles' — see p. 99.

the mate is on the foc's'le head and the second mate aft with the third mate on the bridge with the captain. One would have expected Stacey, the second mate, to have taken charge forward and for me to have taken his place, but this was apparently not to be. The second mate said nothing, but it was evident that he felt slighted. The Captain also said that we should use our own towing wire. I promptly enquired which tugs we were using and, on being told Watkins', which was the company in which I spent so much time as a boy when towing sailing ships and in the river generally, I said that, if we did not use the tug's wire, our wire would be broken by the tug. I knew only too well that the tug-masters hated using a ship's wire and, being extremely proficient in handling their craft, could break any wire without the slightest trouble and had no compunction about doing so. It was an unnecessary meanness. The Captain would not accept my point of view, and doubtless thought I was throwing my weight about rather quickly, while the mate, who was a Canadian, possibly did not entirely believe me.

As we came down the river, our tug was waiting and ready to take us in tow. To my joy, I knew her well and also her skipper, so I removed my cap and waved to him. He, a portly, red-faced figure, recognized me at once and gave me a cheery wave back. I hoped that a spirit of 'Auld Lang Syne' would prevail, but was still a little apprehensive. At all events, we passed down our line to the tug, which made it fast, and we were then hanging off the knuckle of the lock just at tide time with a mass of craft, mainly coasters and barges, crowding the river. Then, at the crucial moment, all his ingrained principles about ships' wires proved too much for my rubicund friend in the tug, and he carried the wire away. I was prepared for this eventuality to some degree, with a heaving line ready, but the men I had were inexperienced and, before we could take up the tug's line, our head had slewed right round.

The pilot was dancing about the bridge like a frenzied dervish and shouting himself hoarse, while the mate was not much better. A sailing barge was forced to go about so peremptorily that she almost collided with a passing collier, starting some sort of chain reaction amongst the passing shipping. I soon got matters straightened out, but it was an early object lesson that, if the *Dalhousie* was a fine modern cargo-ship, she was likely to be run more like one of the more pariah-like pre-war tramps. I did not feel that it became me, as the most junior deck-officer, to say:- *"I told you so."* and neither the master nor mate ever referred to the incident thereafter!

We waited at Southend for convoy and, when we sailed up the East Coast and round Scotland (the English Channel being by now effectively closed to deep-water shipping), we were the commodore ship. Although I possessed a sextant and had practised with it, not having been a formal apprentice I had never had the opportunity to take sights and work out the resulting positions at sea, although I was quite confident of my ability to do so. This was another example of theory without experience in Board of Trade examinations. The first evening at sea, soon after sunset, the master told me to take star sights and fix our position. He himself also took sights simultaneously.

When I had finished, rather more slowly than him, he asked where I put her. I gave the position I had worked out, whereupon he said:- *"You're wrong!"* I was aware of the very senior Commodore of the convoy looking at me as though I was the lowest possible species of marine life and felt rather a fool, immediately going over my working again. Getting the same result, I was able to see the master's working which, I quickly realized, was a position more or less in the middle of France! Taking heart, I waited till the Commodore returned to the wheel-house and pointed this out. Then, comparing our respective figures, it turned out that he had entered one of his tables from the bottom instead of the top and that, when adjusted, his position was the same as mine. Experience proved that this was by no means an unusual incident, and the second mate told me that he had often suffered similar accusations from the Captain. In consequence, I did not regard Capt. Davies with that awe with which junior officers are wont to regard their captains!

Actually, he and I got on very well. He frequently came up on the bridge in the first watch from 8.0 to midnight and we would discuss and argue about all the most unlikely subjects. For instance, culled from some American magazine article, his belief that all Scotsmen were descended from Jews! He usually told the steward to bring him up sandwiches or the like, and also some for me, and there is no question that, for the first few voyages, my evening watches passed pleasantly enough, and I am sure that he enjoyed them as much as I did. Nevertheless, he could be most irritating, especially when we were in convoy. It must be understood that most motor ships have a 'critical speed' which may vary according to the pitch of the propeller. Initially, the ship had a five-bladed one but, because it created too much vibration at the best of times, it was changed for a four-bladed one with a different pitch in the big dry-dock at Esquimault. One could be sure, however, that whatever the speed of the convoy might be, it would invariably be in the middle of one's own ship's 'critical speed', with the result that first of all one had to go rather slower than the convoy speed and drop back, and then increase above the critical speed to catch up again, and perhaps get a bit ahead of station, thereafter repeating these operations almost *ad infinitum*. Naturally, if several diesel ships were in the same column, station-keeping tended to deteriorate.

Often, if I was out on the wing of the bridge, the master would appear in the wheel-house and, seeing us too close (or too far astern) of the ship ahead, would blow down to the engine room and tell them to decrease (or increase, as the case might be) by so many revolutions. Having done that and, as he supposed, put things right, he would go below again, whilst I never knew that he had appeared at all. The next thing I knew was that, having already made the engine revolution adjustment, and the captain having given a similar or even bigger one, we would suddenly be rushing up on the ship ahead, or else dropping astern twice as fast as I had anticipated, which was quite maddening. Finally, I caught him at it, and asked him whether he was taking over the watch. He started blustering, and finally said:- *"No, No! You do as you think best!"* after which I had no more trouble on this score.

The second mate was a nice enough little fellow, who had apparently started life as a pit boy in the Northumbrian coal mines: his advance in life being much to his credit, but he would never stand up to the master and, in consequence, suffered a great deal from this interference with the engine revolutions when he was on watch. This matter of speed adjustment assumed the greater importance when in thick fog, as was often the case on the Grand Banks of Newfoundland, when each ship (except the rear ones in a column) streamed a fog-buoy aft on a line just over two cables long. This was a wooden object, shaped roughly like a crude aeroplane, but with a groove carved out of its middle so that, when towed, it sent up a spurt of water. If in proper station, this spurt of water could be kept just forward of the bridge on one side or the other and, once in position, it was essential to keep it there, however the engineers may have cursed the frequent changes in revolutions entailed. Once it was lost, it was by no means easy to find it again and, in conditions when one could see none of the ships on either side, ahead or astern, navigating in convoy in such conditions was a sheer nightmare. I thought fog-buoys a brilliant innovation and relied on them implicitly.

For some reason, the second mate was quite incapable of keeping station on a fog-buoy. I never failed to hand over to him without the buoy being just where it should have been. Yet he never handed over to the mate with a fog-buoy in view. Sometimes he had simply lost it, sometimes he had run over it and cut it off, and by the time I came on watch again it might or might not have been picked up again. Of course, if in a column with two other diesel ships ahead, both on their critical speeds, there was all the greater need for re-acting quickly, since each ship was tending to alter her speeds the more frequently. It was for this reason that I preferred to keep the buoy on the starboard side, which was the side of the wheelhouse on which the speaking tube to the engine room was situated.

On one occasion, soon after leaving Halifax in a homeward-bound convoy, fog buoys were streamed, not because of fog but due to the low visibility brought about by heavy snow. The danger in such conditions was that one's attention became focussed on the buoy to the exclusion of everything else. A snow flurry had just passed one dark night and the visibility was marginally better when, to my horror, I saw a dark shape right ahead and very close, though I could not determine which way the ship was heading. I found it difficult to believe it could be the ship ahead of us, but in that same instant navigation lights were being switched on all around us and, once again, our convoy was in the position of meeting a large outward-bound one head on.

There is no question but that the master should be called in any emergency. The word 'emergency' may be interpreted in different ways and I had long since concluded that, since he was apparently pathologically incapable of giving a definite order, I would only call him in times of 'dire' emergency! However, there was no doubt whatever that on such an occasion as this he *must* be called and, on requesting his immediate presence, he appeared very quickly. However, he said simply, and very sensibly:- *"You keep her, Mr.Hurst. You've got your eyes."* It was as well that his eyes were not attuned to the darkness since, although I had, in the interim, ported our helm, as he spoke a large, light tanker was rolling down so close to our starboard side that I wondered whether the wings of our respective bridges would clash together. As in the previous instance in the *Raranga*, we rolled in opposite directions, but it was the nearest possible miss.

Because ocean convoys are so much broader than they are deep, the whole affair was over in a very short time. Nevertheless, those few minutes were exceedingly fraught: some ships, in order to avoid collision, giving themselves too much helm, and thereby not only losing all semblance of station, but creating the more confusion for the ships around them. The snow had started again, and few vessels could be seen at any one moment. Shortly after the tanker had wallowed into our wake, I was aware of two ships crossing our bows in opposite directions, roughly at right-angles to our own course, but was loth to reduce speed, since that would have made us the less manoeuverable so, giving a little starboard helm, managed to pass under the stern of both of them, more by luck than good judgement, since questions of Rule of the Road simply had no application at all in such a situation.

Not only did we pass extremely close under the sterns of both these vessels, but it was clear that they themselves only avoided coming into collision by the narrowest of margins. As we approached the space which I hoped would appear between them, Capt. Davies, who was now able to see in the dark, simply clutched at the bridge dodger, saying:- *"Oh! My*

20. *The* DALHOUSIE *on trials. (The Maltese Cross was painted grey in service.)*

God!" but, to his credit, having once given me charge of the situation, he did not interfere at all. Other vessels were not so lucky and did come into collision: two or three having to put back to St. Johns and Halifax to repair their damage. So far as our convoy was concerned, many ships lost contact altogether and, although some were rounded up, others we never saw again. It seemed incredible and, indeed, it was incredible that such a situation should have been allowed to develop.

Perhaps in this context it is worth recalling another incident on a quite different occasion when we were proceeding up the Minches in convoy from Glasgow, heading for Loch Ewe. It was a glorious Sunday morning in early August: the sun casting a golden light over the islands and, with a little rolling cloud and a certain warmth still in the air, it was, in short, one of those days when it was a sheer joy to be alive. In these narrow waters, the convoy was in two long columns, our opposite number in the other column being the Shell tanker *Diloma*.* All the ships were flying barrage balloons from long wires led through sheaves at the foremast heads, and down to a cargo winch. These were to discourage dive-bombers from coming too low, and would be removed by the responsible army unit in Loch Ewe.

I was savouring the scene to the full when I glanced aloft and, to my horror, saw that our balloon wire was entwined with that of the tanker with myriad turns, and that the two vessels were, in effect, joined by these wires. Our decks were cluttered with all sorts of war materials for the armies in North Africa, from heavy lorries to all sorts of other things. A tanker's decks, with her multiplicity of pipes and valves, are never clear. Those aboard her had clearly no idea of the situation, so I rushed for the Aldis lamp and called up their bridge. On receiving an answering flash, I morsed:- *"Your balloon has entangled with mine."* In fact, of course, I had not the slightest idea how those two balloons could have fouled each other and, indeed, have no idea to this day, but my signal placed the onus squarely on him, and he accepted it without question. I then signalled:- *"I will slack away our balloon wire and keep station on you."* As we slacked away, and the tanker hove in her wire and finally got both balloons on her decks, I had edged in as close as I dared to her and, having straightened up, was proceeding on a parallel course, adjusting the engine revolutions as circumstances dictated. Had there been no wind, we could almost have tossed a biscuit on to her decks, so close was the navigation involved. At first I was slightly apprehensive that the *venturi* principle, by which two floating bodies are attracted together when within a critical distance from one another, might take effect but, when it did not do so immediately, felt that it

---

* The *Diloma* was torpedoed and sunk by a U-boat in the North Atlantic six months later.

72

would not happen. The men on the tanker were having a terrible time clearing the wires, passing their deflated balloon round and round our wire, and all my concentration was centred on keeping close station on her, in order to avoid tightening the wire, while standing at the port door of the wheelhouse to be handy for the engine room speaking tube.

I had decided that this was not a 'dire' emergency and that I would not call the captain who, I considered, would be perfectly maddening, and for this reason had used the Aldis lamp in preference to the loud hailer, which would have alerted him. However, by chance, he entered the wheelhouse at that moment and wished me *"Good Morning"*, to which I responded, before he moved out on the starboard wing of the bridge. Then, a few minutes later, as he walked abaft the chartroom, in a voice which reached a screeching crescendo and was more Welsh-accented than usual in his sheer anguish (and he did speak Welsh at home and to his family), he shrieked:- *"My God, Mr. Hurst, do you know how close you are to that other ship?"* I merely replied:- *"Yes, Sir."*, without enlarging in any way and awaiting his next move but, in fact, and it seemed with a note of relief, all he said was:- *"Thank God you know!"* and, as if the sight of such close navigation was altogether too much for him, clattered down the stairs to his day-room again! I do not believe that he knew, to the day he died, that we had been connected to that tanker by our balloon wires!

The Canadian chief mate had left the ship and been replaced by a Mr. Llewellyn, who came from the next Welsh village to Capt. Davies, and who proved to be a man with a monumental lack of imagination, but one who did his job very efficiently so long as everything was going to plan. I suspected that he lacked initiative and, if it was a disappointment to him that he had never risen to command, it was certainly a greater one to his wife, as this was obvious, if unspoken, when she and the other wives stayed aboard the ship in home ports. (Her status in her Welsh village would have been so much the greater as a captain's wife! However, when I once remarked on a man who had taken his ticket with me and who was aiming for a 4th. mate's job, since he thought the loss of pay more than compensated for the lack of responsibility, Mrs. Llewelyn at once said that he was sure her husband was like that, and would much prefer still to be 2nd. mate, which he had been for many years. This was probably true. He was not a good chief mate and had only been engaged in Montreal since we needed a mate and he was ashore there. Indeed, once I became 2nd. mate, I began casting eyes at his job, unofficially taking over from him whenever possible!)

On these occasions there was a good deal of Welsh spoken. Capt. Davies was an ebullient little man, and each voyage our discussions and arguments in the first watch continued very amiably, many of them being continued at meals in the saloon, which were generally rather cheerful. The engineers had their own mess room, and the wireless operators, of whom there was a certain turnover, were generally callow youths who had dodged the army and who usually contributed little.

The *Dalhousie* was well armed defensively for a merchantmen, having a 4″ gun and a Bofors aft: two Oerlikons at the after end of the boat deck, two Hotchkiss on the bridge, a 'Chicago piano' (rockets) on each side of the boat deck and depth charges aft. Although the merchant crews formed the nucleus of the gun crews, we had increased our quota of D.E.M.S.* gunners, loaned by the navy, for whom extra accommodation had been built. On one voyage these men included a London Cockney, named Butteriss, who followed the calling of a 'bookie' in peace-time. No man was ever more out of his element at sea. It was, perhaps, a measure of the wasted effort in war-time that, bound to Cape Town, we sighted the Cape Sable light (off Nova Scotia) outward bound and, when we finally reached Table Bay, this man was almost out of his mind and chafing to get ashore. We then received orders to proceed straight to Calcutta and, when it became apparent to him that we were only going to wait long enough to take bunkers with no shore leave, it was feared that he might turn suicidal.

However, on arrival in Calcutta, since the gunners tended to be rather in the way in port, they were given a good deal of shore leave. Then Butteriss came into his own. Discovering that there was a race course on the Maidan, he attended each race while we were there and not only laid his money according to his knowledge — and remarkably he seemed to be expertly informed on the pedigrees of the horses there — but he advised his fellow gunners how to lay their bets. None of these men had any regrets about Calcutta. Butteriss did both himself and them proud, since all made considerable profits on every bet they laid and it is unlikely that any other body of men out there acquired so much money to spend so quickly. Whilst there is much in the old adage that the cobbler should stick to his last, we were all astounded that a Cockney bookie could achieve such resounding success with horses in Calcutta!

There were always men missing when we came to sail and, because I was large (but the second mate puny), I was generally dispatched to round them up. If there was an American ship near us in the dock, I could be pretty sure of finding them there, cashing in on the comparative riches and the largesse of their seamen. So it was in Madras, where the rickshaw coolies had all taken their rickshaws off the road, after receiving 10 rupee tips and the like from American sailors for pulling them just from the dock-gates to their ships. This resulted in such quick

---

* Defensive Equipment of Merchant Ships.

74

(comparative) affluence for the rickshaw men that they stopped work until they had exhausted their gains, to the fury of the residents who depended on them. (Although they were regarded as being 'Non-U' by the whites in Calcutta, who used horse-drawn *gharries*.)

In Madras I had routed three of our men out of an American vessel and man-handled them along the quay, slightly tipsy, to the *Dalhousie*, which was already singled up prior to sailing. As soon as I had pitched them aboard, somewhat to my surprise they rushed for the bridge and started punching both the pilot and the captain. For this, being gunners subject to naval jurisdiction, they were court-martialled in Colombo, taken out of the ship and, after a period of imprisonment and punishment ashore, were transferred to H.M.S. *Exeter*. This was the last thing they expected. Whether they survived the subsequent Battle of the Java Sea, in which the *Exeter* was sunk, I do not know, though I doubt it.

In Chittagong we had had quite a few men missing when the time came to sail. There was little enough there, at all events near the quay, and for once I was quite flummoxed about where to look for them. Finally I saw a grass structure, rather like a large, old-fashioned beehive and, walking over to it, heard sounds within. It was a brothel of the crudest possible sort, and our men were there. As I dragged them out, a greasy, female form was clinging to each like a leech. I never saw such a disgusting place anywhere else in the world.

On the Indian coast a chameleon had found its way into the saloon, where it performed miracles in catching flies and insects with its tongue. One day, at lunch, we were watching it when the master challenged me to catch it, defying me to do so in terms which left me little option but to try. Much to his and to everybody else's amazement, and even more to my own, I succeeded almost at once and bore the creature down to my cabin where it took up residence for some time until it vanished. However, both because it failed to change colour as dramatically as I had hoped, and because I never succeeded in establishing any sort of *rapport* with the creature, it proved to be a disappointment.

Both Capt. Davies and his wife displayed a very religious, God-fearing stance, and we were thus extremely surprised when a passenger arrived aboard for the short passage across the Bay of Bengal in the form of a half-caste woman who was extremely attractive physically and who shared the captain's day-room. I did not see much of him during my night watches for a week or two after this incident. Whether he supposed that my memory only functioned for as long as that, I can only guess!

Relationships did become a little strained on the last leg of the homeward voyage, when we were in the North Atlantic. It had been a pleasant voyage, in all the splendour of the trade wind seas and with tropic dawns galore, but now the ship was back in all the spite of the North Atlantic winter. Soon after we had left, a ship abeam of us had suddenly and unaccountably altered course and, in so doing, taken the impact of a torpedo aimed at us, to be left settling in the water. Soon afterwards, the convoy had disintegrated in the face of the weather and, with an enormous sea running and in a gale force wind, we found ourselves virtually hove to in a night when visibility was reduced to a minimum. I was still third mate and keeping the first watch. Any form of light, even navigation lights, was banned in war-time but, taking stock of the situation: of the fact that the huge seas and the spray-laden air militated against any possibility of sighting any other vessel which might cross our bows, I switched on the navigation lights.

In due course the master came up on the bridge and, noticing the reflected gleam of one of the side-lights on the blown spume, asked me whether I knew they were on. I replied that I did. He then asked whether I did not know the regulations. Again, I replied that I did but that, in my view, no submarine could hit us in such weather: that a torpedo would be as likely to pass between our mast and funnel as to hit the hull; that I considered our greatest potential danger in the prevailing conditions to be a running tanker, with no vulnerable hatches and no need to heave to, which might be making for the convoy rendez-vous position, and that I had therefore switched on the navigation lights 'for the safety of the ship'. (This latter was a very useful emotive phrase, which it was difficult to gainsay!)

As I knew full well, Davies was not a decisive character and, mumbling:- *"You do as you think best"* (his invariable response when he found himself in disagreement!), he shuffled below again. Much the same exchange took place an hour and a half later and, soon before my watch ended, he re-appeared for a third time and once more raised the subject. I then asked him if he wished to take over the watch, but was again met with:- *"You do as you think best."* When I was relieved by the second mate, I warned him of these conversations and, knowing him to be petrified by the 'Old Man', advised him to keep the lights burning all his watch, pointing out that I had been in tankers and knew that they would not be stopped by such weather as had caused us to heave to. I then wrote up the deck log before going below, noting that the navigation lights had been switched on throughout the watch.

Two and a half hours later the second mate appeared in my cabin to summon me to the bridge, as we had been in collision. (I had not been aware of this, since every time the ship pitched she shuddered.) In fact, Capt. Davies had left the second mate alone until about 2.0 a.m, when he had gone up to the bridge and told him that I had kept the navigation lights burning but, as the moon had now risen (a fact which he had culled from the Nautical Almanac!), there was no need to keep them alight any longer. Actually, the storm wrack was so thick and the night still so pitch-black, with the steep seas still just as big, that it would have made no difference at all to the visibility had fifty moons risen! However, almost predictably, the second mate did as he was bid. Half an hour later a tanker which proved later to be the *Cymbula* laden with benzine and running for the rendez-vous, was sighted almost on top of us and, after first trying to pass under our stern and realizing the impossibility of so doing, with both ships switching on their lights when it was too late, she belatedly tried to cut across our bow which, as she passed, cut deep into her at the fore end of her poop and was itself smashed right back to our collision bulkhead! Heavens knows that 'the seas are wide and far are the ways to their secret places,' and that, if collision with a tanker represented, in my opinion, a greater risk than any submarine that night, the odds against such an occurrrence must still have been astronomical. But .... it happened — about 480 miles south of Reykjavik.

Tankers are virtually unsinkable, and this representative of the Anglo-Saxon fleet was no exception, being in no real trouble. As for the *Dalhousie*, the lower part of our bow was, to all intents and purposes, gone and we were dependent on the collision bulkhead holding for our survival. Our compasses were useless since, the ship being de-gaussed against magnetic mines, the damage to the degaussing wires had completely upset the compass adjustments but, fortunately, the corvette *Fritillery* picked us up after a day or so and escorted us home. The weather remained frightful and she acted as guide, while we did the navigation for both vessels, since her motion was so dreadful to behold (and, I imagine, to endure) that her navigator could obtain no horizon.

Butting into the head seas, we proceeded at reduced speed, lest we overtax the vital bulkhead, and finally rounded the Butt of Lewis to come down the Minches as wind and sea swung to the south'ard. Still we crawled along. As we came up to Barra, the radio bearing was not changing one whit, and it was clear that we were setting ashore there. Then we picked up the light, and the bearing still never changed. There was a conference about what was best to be done: whether to increase speed and risk the bulkhead or to remain as we were (and presumably trust to luck!). The alternatives were the captain's decision but, again, he made none. We each gave our opinion, mine being to increase speed, but I was out-voted. Next morning we were diametrically on the other side of the island, the current having taken us right round it! During the night we had heard the distress calls and seen the rockets of ships from a north-bound convoy which had run ashore on that inhospitable coast. (It was near the scene of the wreck of the *Politician*, immortalised in Compton Mackenzie's *Whisky Galore*.)

21. *Looking down the forepeak at the open sea after collision. Note twisted and fractured metal. The Fore-peak was the repository for ropes and other stores, its after end being the collision bulkhead.*

22. *The damaged bow, seen when moored in fog off the Tail of the Bank.*

We hove to off the Skerryvore lighthouse to signal for a tug in the Clyde since, although our anchors were intact, the force of the collision had wedged them immoveably in their hawse-pipes, rendering their use impossible. The second mate found that he could not read the answering flashes from the light-house so, obviously feeling he was losing face, called me up to the bridge. I could not read them either, whereupon we summoned the mate, who found himself in the same position. Finally we had to call the master to read the answering signals. The reason was that, having each spent so much time morsing to the naval signalmen in the corvette, our speed had increased so markedly that we had temporarily lost the ability to read at the slower, merchant service speed!*

It was the collision which had soured relationships. Or rather, to be more accurate, it was my entry in the deck log. It seldom pays to be right and, lamentably, I had much pressure put upon me by both the master and his crony, the mate, backed by the second mate, to amend my deck-log entry. Considering this to be totally amoral, I refused. The master and second mate feared it might prejudice their position in the event of an enquiry. Stacey, the second mate, said that, were he in my shoes, he would certainly alter it, to which I retorted that, had I been in *his* shoes, I

---

* The navigation school which I attended transmitted morse at an incredibly high speed. At first one sat in sheer, frustrated bewilderment, but was soon able to read it infallibly. Then, immediately prior to the examination, one had to attend another establishment to be 'slowed down' again. It was a good system.

should not have switched off the lights in the first place, unless the master had taken over the watch and entered the log book accordingly. In the event, there were so many such incidents in war-time that there was no enquiry. If I was apparently forgiven, these pressures did leave a certain question mark in my mind about the integrity of both the master and mate.

Stacey was leaving the ship at the end of the voyage, and I wanted his job. I thus felt that this collision had occurred at a particularly unfortunate moment. However, once it was clear that there was to be no enquiry, Capt. Davies' natural ebullience put the incident behind him, and he said I could come as second mate providing that I took a gunnery course and became gunnery officer. I agreed to this, and took a course aboard the *President* on London's Embankment, though did not consider that I was much wiser at the end of it!

I had, of course, been in gun crews in previous ships, but had never felt that guns were my *forte*. For one thing, as soon as the gun went off I became temporarily deaf for several hours! Nor had gun practices ever been attended by much success. In a previous ship we had opened fire on a floating target we constructed aboard after it had been allowed to drift well astern. Unfortunately, as soon as the first round was fired, a pod of whales starting spouting around the target and, although the spout of a whale has little resemblance to the splash of a shell, the exercise was called off, possibly because no-one wished to hit a whale.

After this fiasco in the Atlantic, we found ourselves routed rather far north in the South Pacific through the Tuamotu Archipelago, and were to pass very close to an atoll named Mowane Island soon after dawn. Being listed as uninhabited, it was decided to use it as a target. After the sun rose in golden glory, we sighted Mowane, which might have been lifted off the traditional travel poster: just a small, slightly humped coral atoll boasting a small clump of palm trees and with the deep blue Pacific swell broken into cascades of glittering foam by an outlying reef which apparently marked the outer edge of a small lagoon.

The gun's crew closed up and, at the appropriate distance, the order came to open fire. Being temporarily deafened by the first round did not prevent me from joining in the general astonishment when a figure could be discerned running to the beach and waving his arms. Promptly, the order was given to cease fire, but .... that is the end of the story! Naturally we did not break war-time radio silence, nor was it felt prudent to stop to pick him up. The Germans did occasionally reach the Pacific. The master reported the incident on arrival, but who the man was, how he got there, or whether anybody ever did anything about him I have no idea.

It was most odd that this should have happened, as I remembered well a story told to me by an apprentice in the *Port Chalmers* when she had lain ahead of the *Moshulu* in Port Adelaide — a tale I subsequently checked in the Queensland papers. At the time, he had been in another of the Company's vessels: a coal-burner with a large crew whose master was almost due for retirement. When crossing the Pacific, he took his ship some fifty miles out of her way to get a shore fix and check his chronometers. This was common enough practice in the age of sail, but totally unnecessary in the era of radio. In the event they passed close to Motu One* Island, another uninhabited atoll in the Tuamotu group which was well off normal shipping lanes.

The weather was drizzly with a slight swell. As they approached, a man was seen trying to light a fire and endeavouring to attract their attention — a man who was evidently a castaway. Naturally, word of this soon got round the ship, whose decks were soon crowded with men expecting the man to be rescued, while the mate remarked that he would see to getting a boat away. The master stopped him, saying that to do so would be to delay the ship by five or six hours, possibly losing a tide into port, which was unthinkable. Unthinkable? And to a man who had already diverted his ship's course by some five hours? So the ship passed on, making no sign to the castaway, though a radio message was transmitted to the Governor of Tahiti, who does not seem to have acted upon the intelligence in any way. Although Tahiti is the nearest place of any importance, it is a long way from Motu One. The ship's master took the unusual course of writing up the deck log himself, recording the sighting but adding that there was too great a swell to launch a boat. This was not the opinion of his ship's company.

The story soon leaked out when the ship reached Australia and caused a sensation: it being believed that the man was probably the well-known Australian airman Ulm who had gone missing on a flight over the Pacific a few months previously. (This was in the days of the pioneering aviators.) The controversy was fanned by the fact that this man had gone missing in the past and once, I think in Northern Territory, had been found in extraordinarily good fettle, as a result of which he had achieved a certain publicity — and notoriety — since there had been suspicions in some quarters that it had been a publicity stunt. Whatever the truth of that, it is certain enough that the man on Motu One was not involved in anything of the sort and, once again, the story ends there, since I have no evidence that any effort was ever made to rescue him.

How, it may be asked, could a ship steam by in peace time, even if it involved the loss of days on voyage? No-one can speak for that captain's mind, but the presumption was that he thought that, should he rescue

---

* Pronounced 'Motu Ōny'.

the man, it might lead to awkward questions from his owners as to why he was there at all, not realizing that by ignoring him the publicity attending his action would be all the greater.

To revert to the *Dalhousie*, a ship conceived in peace but baptised in war, her lot had, on the whole, been attended by good fortune. In one outward bound convoy, after forming up, we were proceeding off Malin Head when I took over the watch. We had a new crew. The first helmsman had no idea how to steer, and I sent him packing. The next man was no better, and the third was just as bad. That was my entire watch! Yet they were rated as A.B.s. I demanded that the Old Man disrate them, but he would have none of it. On the whole I did not blame him, remembering an occasion before the war in Southampton when one of the two biggest Royal Mail ships had arrived. Southampton men were seldom called upon to do 'sailor' work, which was normally accomplished in port by shore gangs, but on one occasion a man had been told to do a piece of serving on one of the shrouds. The Staff Captain happened to pass and, observing that the fellow had no idea how to use a serving mallet, caused the bo'sun to give each A.B. a similar job. Most were incapable of doing it, and all were disrated.* What a battle that man had with the Seamen's Union and the Shipping Federation when he reached port! Certainly he lost all the leave due to him in dealing with it, and what the final outcome was I never knew. There was nothing unique about the *Dalhousie's* helmsmen.

There were many such in all manner of ships. Some were army dodgers, but there was, in truth, a shortage of seamen, and all sorts of men were being taken on, some of whom were, at all events initially, positively lethal.

A merchant ship's officer was his own signalman. He was engaged in keeping station, in keeping a look-out, and was responsible for the ship's navigation, so it was a blow when he had to teach a man, with no sea sense whatever, how to steer, especially in the close navigation of a zig-zagging convoy, when they had no idea how much helm to give or how to check the ship on course. The convoy would operate to a zig-zag pattern: each ship changing course on a signal from the synchronised convoy clock in the wheel-house, which buzzed, like an alarm clock, as the big hand reached moveable settings on its rim. But these men did not even understand the compass card ....

I have already recorded the ineptitude displayed by a peace-time crew in the case of the *Cheyenne's* boats, but have omitted the tally of vessels

---

* This is a simple job, which any A.B. should have been capable of doing at that time. The old and well-known rhyme ran:-
  "Worm and parcel with the lay,
  But serve the rope the other way."

whose sinkings I had witnessed subsequently and when boats had sometimes been launched in panic: when one fall was released and not the other with the result that the boat tipped in the swell and upended, often throwing men into the water. It was all too obvious that many of these boats had not been in the water for years and quickly filled, to the greater discomfort of their occupants. (However full of water a lifeboat may be, she will not sink due to her buoyancy tanks but, discomfort apart, she becomes so heavy to row and impossible to sail as to be virtually unmanoeuverable.) The death roll on merchant ships was undeniably heavy and regrettable, much of it being unavoidable, but the truth is that many men were lost by their own ineptitude or by that of their fellows. When, in later years, Lawrence Holt, a Director of the Blue Funnel Line, was engaged in founding the Outward Bound Trust (providing a team of Chinese stewards for the first course of all!), he remarked that he would rather entrust a lifeboat to a sail-trained octogenarian than to a young sea-technician who, while completely trained in the modern way, had never been sprayed with salt water. From my own observation of the abandonment of torpedoed ships, I felt bound to echo his sentiments, with the rider that so many of the 'sea-technicians' were *not* completely trained in the modern way in those years of war.

I was always keen to get our boats in the water and give the men some experience in handling them, but it was not so easy. On one occasion in Sydney, New Brunswick, whither we had arrived for convoy, I persuaded the master that we needed some sand and proposed to fetch some from a sandy beach which was visible ashore. He agreed and, after filling some bags, I proceeded with my real purpose, which was to make for and visit two modern Portuguese schooners which were in the port: vessels with stacked dories on deck and which were engaged in the Banks cod fishery. I further intended to visit a very historic vessel which lay beyond them, then an auxilary barquentine in the role of the U.S. Coast Guard cutter *Bear*. Hardly had I started before I was chased back aboard by a naval picket boat for breaching regulations. How visiting three neutral vessels was detrimental to the national war effort was not clear, nor was my explanation that the men were receiving practice in boat handling acceptable. Maybe that young officer later witnessed such men die for lack of that very experience.

One summer crossing of the Atlantic our convoy was hounded by wolf-packs of submarines. We were routed far to the north by Iceland, and the sun never set when we were within the Arctic Circle. The weather was fair and the convoy large. Many ships were lost. We saw our sister, on the opposite side of the convoy, suddenly explode with a vast geyser of water forward of her bridge, and then settle down to sink.

Our chief engineer, an elderly man who, of course, did not keep watches, came up on the bridge soon after the sinkings started and could not be persuaded to go below at all, developing an almost perpetual tremble in his fear and terror. That voyage broke him, and he never went to sea again. Nor were the ships I have mentioned the whole tale. It was a dreadful convoy. Nor did any ship appear to have any warning. One night towards the end of the passage, in a latitude further south when there was a short period of darkness at night, we were rather too close to the tanker ahead of us when she suddenly exploded. I immediately had our wheel put hard a-port to keep clear, almost running into the next column, but was forced to run from the starboard wing through the wheelhouse to the other end of the bridge, so great was the searing heat from that blazing tanker. I saw some of her crew at her boats, but they were never launched ... They must have roasted where they stood. That fine vessel had been transformed into a vast incinerator in an instant. The sea all about her was ablaze. In the morning light, we found the paint along our starboard side all blistered.

Such sights, and the uncertainty of one's own lot, affected a number of men. Maybe people are made differently. For my part, I took the view that if a bomb or torpedo carried my number, there was nothing I could do about it, and that it was no use worrying. If a belief in predestination was good enough for the ancient Greeks and the Vikings, it was good enough for me, at all events in these circumstances. Life has been a lottery throughout the history of mankind and death or disablement can come without warning out of a summer sky. It is as useless to speculate whether or not the high Gods predetermine each man's doom as it is to avoid crossing a street lest one is cut down by a runaway chariot in one age or by a drunken car driver in another. One can only assume some situations to be more potentially dangerous than others, and leave it at that. In consequence, I could turn into my bunk and lose no sleep. I had tried to instil this sort of philosophy into the Chief Engineer, even quoting the lines of Omar Khayyam:-

> "The Moving Finger writes; and having writ,.
> Moves on: nor all your Piety nor Wit
> Shall lure it back to cancel half a Line,
> Nor all your Tears wash out a Word of it."

Yet I was met by a silent stare from terror-filled eyes which seemed to encapsulate latent madness. There was a stronger element of a lottery when in a beleagured convoy. The next torpedo might hit you, or it might hit the next ship. It was simply a matter of odds, and I was never a betting man. I found dive-bombing far more disturbing since, when such a 'plane was attacking, with the unearthly sound of the 'screechers' on its wings, there was no doubt at all that one was the immediate target. On such occasions most men were too busy on the guns to contemplate consequences and, had they had time to reflect, would often realize that, although such attacks were sometimes successful, more often than not the dive-bombers were insufficiently accurate. In one ship, after our convoy had become dispersed, we were passing the Northern Irish coast one morning with only one other vessel in sight which we thought was the *Brabant*, an unarmed Belgian, about two miles on our beam. Two dive bombers swooped on her time and again, and we could see the splashes of their bombs. She was zig-zagging, but was woefully slow, yet she was never hit once, although a sitting target unable to defend herself, before the Stukas ran out of bombs and ammunition and turned for home. In such circumstances, the situation is infinitely worse, building up anticipation in an apparently hopeless position without being able to take any positive action to occupy the mind. It must have been analogous to facing a firing squad.

One convoy I recall in particular. We had left Sydney, Cape Breton, with 13 other vessels which subsequently merged with the Halifax contingent and, later, with a further section from Bermuda, making 58 ships in all. Five ships returned to Canada after being in collisions whilst three more, also in collision, kept at sea. One, the *Emma Bakke*, returned after losing the convoy and a Greek put back with engine defects. It was mid-summer and again we steered far north with little darkness at night, being mauled by a submarine wolf-pack which sank six ships, damaged two more and hit a ninth — the *Baltara* — which was fortunate because the torpedo did not explode. That evening the Dutch *Maasdam* was sunk and, soon afterwards, there was an unbelievable roar and an enormous sheet of flame, followed by an even greater pall of smoke in which wreckage of the *Malaya II* could be seen flung hundreds of feet into the air. Underneath it there was nothing to be seen: she had utterly disintegrated, thanks to 431 tons of TNT in her cargo. One moment she and her crew were there: the next they were gone. I was astonished, years later, to learn that there were, in fact, six survivors out of her complement of forty five. We were four columns from her, but both the master and I were flung bodily against the wheelhouse bulkhead by the force of the blast.

There were disadvantages about the *Dalhousie*. For one thing, neither the master nor chief steward drank or smoked, with the result that the customs men, particularly in some foreign ports, did not receive the 'back-handers' which they normally expect as their right, and the consequence was that we often had a lot of trouble and unnecessary searching from these men. However, there was never a dull moment aboard, as Capt. Davies had a *penchant* for creating minor crises almost without cessation. There was the occasion when he discovered deep scratch marks on the stairs leading from his day-room to the wheel-house, which led to him accusing everyone who could possibly have used them of responsibility and of having a nail protruding from the bottom of their shoes. With rather bad grace, all had to produce their footwear, with no result except that Davies was becoming more and more excitable. The affair blew over when it was discovered that one pair of shoes *did* have a nail sticking from its bottom, and that that pair belonged to *him*! Incidents of this sort were legion, and he was always thinking up some madcap subject as a topic for debate or general argument. On the whole, it was rather amusing even if, sometimes, one felt that the ship was degenerating into some sort of Fred Karno act. It must be said, however, that he retained a steady calm during the attacks when in convoy although, as subsequent events proved, this might not have been the case had we actually been torpedoed ourselves.

━━━━━

V

A SHIFT OF FORTUNE

Before the *Dalhousie's* last voyage she was a long time in port: first having her bow repaired and then loading rather slowly. I had had quite a good leave, first doing the gunnery course and then going home during the repair period. Loading was a long-drawn out process, mainly because the Glasgow dockers were making their contribution to the war effort by striking throughout the port (except for a vessel loading whisky, whose cargo they worked and, broaching it, made themselves incapably drunk), with the result that we had to be loaded by soldiers who had not the most rudimentary idea of stowage. Nor was ours an easy cargo to stow, as it contained practically everything required by the armies in North Africa, from razor blades to bombs, from tank-landing craft to army vehicles of all sorts, from clothing to cranes (in parts) and a good deal more. We had five hatches and a deep-tank all loading at once and, being on nights, I had to go from hatch to hatch to get each re-stowed. When the army shift changed about midnight, there was scarcely a night when one or more of the soldiers did not fall off the blacked-out accommodation ladder into the icy Clyde, often involving considerable effort and ingenuity to get them out again, particularly on the flood tide when the ship had to be prised off the quay to release them. (I never understood how, in this condition, they invariably got trapped *below* the quay level.)

I was rather glad that Stacey, the previous second mate, had left. The officers were allowed to have their wives aboard in port and Mrs. Davies had much disapproved of Mrs. Stacey, which had often created rather an atmosphere. This young woman was a large blonde of ample propor-tions who might have been attractive had she possessed a modicum of good taste. She was head and shoulders taller than her husband and, when together, she would wear low heels and lean over to one side, as though her cargo had shifted, in a vain effort to conceal the disparity in their heights, thereby making it the more obvious. However, one trip when Mrs. Davies was in the train coming to join the ship in port, this girl had entered the same carriage and spent the entire journey pressing her (superficial) attractions on to a couple of naval ratings. Mrs. Davies had, I am sure, made her disapproval obvious without speaking a word, but she had a great shock when she met her in the saloon and discovered that she was Stacey's wife. Since he was fundamentally a nice little chap, no-one ever told him why his wife was so out of favour, and he remained mystified about it, although her presence upset the tenor of his own life.

On one occasion he had accidentally sat on her sweets, not only ruining them but making the seat of his trousers filthy. In retribution, she rose early next morning, hid all his trousers, and then persuaded the 'Old Man' (who viewed her in a more favourable light than his wife) to go down to her husband's cabin and ask him something. Stacey, trouserless, and being the sort of man he was, found this extremely embarrassing.

That her entertainment became a matter of constant common concern to the Master and myself was also an irritation to Stacey and, unwittingly, caused Lindsey, the 2nd. Radio Operator, to fall into Mrs. Davies' bad books. Our ideas were invariably attractive and Stacey had little option but to fall in with them, whether he wanted to do so or not. So, when I asked her at lunch whether she had ever been to Loch Lomond, she replied that she had always wanted to see it. I, knowing well that Stacey had only the haziest ideas about sailing, immediately suggested that he hire a sailing boat and take her round the Loch. I could see that Stacey was livid at the suggestion but was surprised when Lindsey gave a yelp and jumped in his chair so violently that Mrs. Davies, who sat next to him, was so startled that she upset her soup into her lap. Since the matter was never explained, she treated him with suspicion for ever thereafter. In fact, Stacey had aimed a savage kick at me under the table but, being a short man, had accidentally connected with the Radio Operator! In the event, Stacey 'could not find a sailing boat'(!), but a trip in a launch was enjoyed by them both.

The captain's younger son, Gwynnedd, who was in his early 'teens, was also aboard. He did not wish to accompany his parents ashore, but was felt to be too young to go on his own. One evening, at Mrs. Davies' request, the two junior wirelesss operators agreed to take him with them. In the event, it seems that he took them and that they learned from practical experience far more facets of the 'facts of life' that evening than they had ever dreamed about. Since the boy had once emptied his pockets on my settee and I had observed the contents (which would have given his mother a heart attack), I was not unduly surprised, even in 1941!

Another evening Capt. Davies suddenly said that he would relieve me from keeping ship if I would take Gwynnedd to the cinema. I could think of no valid excuse for not doing so, whereupon Stacey, smarting under my interference over the entertainment of his wife (which had probably caused him to put his hand deeper into his pocket than he intended), felt that the tables had turned, and promptly referred to me as 'Nanny' from then on.

However, he who laughs loudest laughs last. It so happened that we found ourselves next to the Staceys at the booking office and, partly by chance and partly because I retained a better grip on the situation than Stacey, he ended up sitting next to Gwynnedd, who talked to him in a loud whisper throughout the performance, whilst I sat with Mrs. Stacey, who did not seem displeased by the arrangement but at least kept quiet. Stacey himself was most displeased on all counts!

On another occasion, Gwynnedd asked the younger Radio Operator to take him round the dock. On their return, his trousers were inexplicably covered with oil. Mrs. Davies was most annoyed and, I think unjustly, blamed the 'Sparks', who also found himself in her black books. As remarked elsewhere, Life is a Lottery ....

The new third mate, Miller Brown, who had been apprenticed in the Anchor Line, had gone ashore on the death of his father and taken over the family box-making factory. Now he had come back to sea. A pleasant enough fellow, he nevertheless had the demeanour of a frightened rabbit, but we got on very well. His wife was a most attractive and extremely pleasant Scots girl, of whom Mrs. Davies approved as much as she disapproved of Mrs. Stacey. As I, alone, was unmarried, I generally kept the ship at nights, to let the others all go ashore, it being understood that this would be adjusted in foreign ports when the marital encumbrances of the others did not apply.

Some evenings I did go ashore, invariably on my own. At breakfast next morning, Mrs. Davies would enquire how I had enjoyed myself and what I had been doing. This was not in any spirit of inquisitiveness, for she was a very nice woman who was simply being friendly. Indeed, both she and Mrs. Llewellyn were of far greater stature in every way than their respective husbands. On one occasion I reported that I had been to see a performance of *La Bohème* by the Carl Rosa Company, but my account was not such as to move the Welsh party. It had not been a successful performance. Gwen Catley, then at the outset of her career, had hardly managed to throw her voice across the orchestra: the theatre's snow mechanism had misbehaved and dropped snow both during the attic and café scenes and it had, in general, been a disappointing evening.

However, after I had been to *Macbeth* a few evenings later, I gave a glowing report of it. When I said that I had had to study the play as a set book at school, and had loathed it, the captain and mate might have appreciated what I was talking about, but they evidently did not do so. I commented that it was the first time I had seen it performed and that I had thoroughly enjoyed it. Indeed, I told them that it was well acted with a good caste, and that I would like to see it again. At once the two Welsh ladies said that they must all go and, their husbands concurring — not that they ever had much option but to agree with their wives! — it was determined that, if they could obtain tickets, they would go that very evening and indeed, when the time came, they all trooped off to the theatre in very good spirits.

Capt. Davies sat through the first scene in a state of hopeful expectation, encouraged by the witches on the blasted heath, but this condition was soon dashed into the utter desolation of complete boredom. The wives quietened his complaints and he dropped off to sleep. Then, waking, he began to fidget. He checked to see that his cap was still under his seat, but it was gone. They were in one of the front rows of the stalls and the floor sloped steeply towards the orchestra. He became convinced that it had either rolled or been kicked forwards. He then became panic-stricken because he was under strict and standing instructions from his wife that he must *never* put his hat on the floor but always use the cloakroom. Before long his patent agitation communicated itself along the row and made further concealment impossible as more and more people became involved in the search until most of the first eight rows of the stalls were on their feet. The mutterings of discontent behind them began to drown the actors on the stage. The circles craned over curiously, wondering what was afoot. In their excitement, our party had relapsed into their native Welsh and this attracted the attention of other Welsh people in the theatre. Bedlam became almost complete and their unpopularity absolute until it was remembered that the offending cap had been properly placed in the cloakroom all the time. The fact that this information was finally provided by the mate, who had accompanied him in this purpose, demonstrated the speed of that gentleman's intellect very accurately!

It was a matter of complete surprise to me to learn at breakfast the next morning that, despite the fact that I had been aboard all the evening, the whole affair was unquestionably my fault for recommending the play in the first instance. As the two ladies were extremely angry about the affair of the cap, and their husbands were equally furious because the play had been bereft of what they described as 'any George Robey stuff', I received a good deal of reflected ire about it for many moons, even when Glasgow was on the other side of the world. I had clearly committed the most heinous of crimes, and it was interesting to recall that my sin of being right about the navigation lights the previous voyage and declining to alter the log had already been long since forgotten! Certainly it had never entered my head that Davies and Llewellyn, not having been reared on the National Bard, had supposed, because it was the Christmas season, that they were going to see some sort of pantomime!

Llewellyn was a nice enough fellow, but ineffectual and incapable of asserting himself. Indeed, if Brown, the 3rd. mate, or I spoke at all sharply, he would automatically tack the word 'Sir' on his reply, although we were his juniors. He was an excellent navigator, and regarded that science in the light of a hobby*, yet in matters of seamanship he was lacking, though largely, as I believe, because his mind worked so slowly. Insignificant events displayed his character. Once a naval officer came aboard to check our armaments with me and asked if we had everything we wanted. I replied that we had, but Llewellyn, who was present, said that we needed non-magnetic steel helmets. Keeping a straight face, the naval officer asked him why, to be told "To take magnetic bearings". After that the poor man was continually being told, even by the captain, to 'put his helmet on' until the joke was worn threadbare.

When we were long in dry-dock for repairs to our bow, I had observed something move in the general slime at the bottom of the dock. Donning a pair of boots, I went to investigate and discovered a very small kitten, wholly covered in a mixture of paints of different colours, oil and water and almost at its last gasp. Bringing it aboard, I managed to clean it up, after which it followed me everywhere, and even round the dock complex each morning when I went to buy it milk, though I found it a home before we sailed. Then, one day, I observed a black cat coming aboard, so suggested to the mate that I put it ashore. He said "No, it is lucky". In fact, this cat made its home in the galley and became rather dirty.

One day it strolled into the saloon when we were at sea and the master, recalling the kitten, asked if it was mine. I replied that it was the mate's, but that he did not seem to be looking after it very well. Instead of saying it was nothing to do with him, Llewellyn was lost for words, which led to the belief that it *was* his cat, and it was thenceforth known as 'the Mate's cat'. At first he was rather annoyed but, perversely, the animal then took up residence in his cabin, though he seemed to be incapable of ridding himself of it. Finally, when we were casting off from alongside another ship off Port o' Spain, the 'mate's cat' became aware that some Chinamen in the other vessel were gutting fish, whereupon it took a flying leap and was last seen being pursued down its deck by angry

---

* But it was Capt. Davies who introduced me to Johnson's *On Finding the Latitude and Longitude in Cloudy Weather*, which was a great boon in those days when navigation virtually depended on sextant, chronometer and sun.

celestials with a fish in its mouth. By this time the ships were well apart, but jibes about 'not catching any fish himself for his cat': 'the loss of a black cat bringing bad luck', and so forth were only tolerable to the mate in that they tended to replace the helmet joke.

At breakfast one day, when I was not present, Capt. Davies announced that he was going to have the refrigerator moved into the saloon. No-one said anything save the mate, who said, weakly, that it was a good idea. I was furious when told about it but, after Herculean labour by the crew, it was moved up and duly installed. I came in to lunch just as the master remarked to the mate that he was very pleased about it, so I promptly asked if he was going to hang a curtain round it.

Capt: *"Why?"*
Me: *"It looks horrible in here".*
Capt   (sensing trouble): *"I might have it oak-grained to match the panelling".*
Me: *"Are you going to have all the galley pots and pans oak-grained and hung round the walls?"*
Capt: *"What do you mean?"*
Me: *"I mean that the saloon now looks like a kitchen and we might as well either have the galley up here or go and eat in the galley. I have never heard of anything like this."*
Mate   (abjectly): *"It certainly does look a bit like a kitchen round the fridge."*

That was the end of the exchange but, that afternoon, the crew had to move it back again, on the ground that 'it might smell in hot weather'. Such minor incidents demonstrated the total lack of the traditional hierarchy in the ship, but it was all very good humoured and lacking in rancour at that time. Indeed, my cabin became something of a social centre, and the master was as likely to drop in as anybody else.

All through the war the Ministry of Information pumped out propaganda demonstrating the magnificent and splendid efforts by the different services and sections of the community: much of it with great truth. Less publicised were the perpetual muddles brought about by incompetence. I have already cited but two instances of convoys meeting head-on. There were examples of ships being sent to ports which had insufficient water for them to enter: of vessels with heavy items of cargo being sent where there was no means of discharging them; of the young sub-lieutenant in charge of the convoy anchorage of Southend who actually had a very senior master and pilot court-martialled for not carrying out his orders, when he had told them to shift their vessel, only to wish the floor would swallow him when the President asked him whether he had checked the draft of the vessel and realized that, had his order been carried out, she would have been firmly aground! There was the occasion when, for its greater safety from U-boat attack, a Halifax convoy was sent through Cabot Straits to pass west-about Newfoundland and out through the Straits of Belle Isle, during which passage it got caught in fog and icebergs: the resulting collisions between the vessels and between ships and icebergs doing immense damage. The Royal Navy only learnt how to transfer fuel quickly at sea from ship to ship from the methods used by captured German ships but, even in the later stages of the Pacific war, some of the chartered vessels in the fleet train gave shameful performances. This tally was almost endless.

A more minor incident of this sort occurred one evening when we were loading, alongside a single track railway on which, once the shunt had come in, it was impossible to move the relative positions of the railway trucks. Since the manifest merely stated 'war material' for the majority of items, there was no knowing whether they were heavy crane parts or khaki trousers in cardboard boxes. Our deep tank was already loaded with light material of this sort (over a layer of heavy bombs, as in all the hatches) and, when some heavy steel crane components appeared in a truck opposite this tank, I refused to load them, involving a bitter argument with the Sea Transport Officer responsible for the ship. My reasons were that we could not stow such items on top of what we had already loaded on the one hand, and that the deep tank derricks were not strong enough for the weights on the other. Finally, after much acrimony, this truck was taken away, still loaded, with instructions that it was to be brought back and placed abreast No. 2 or No. 3 hatch the next day. We had already loaded other parts of that heavy crane, but we never saw the truck again. Half a crane was useless. If another ship subsequently took it out to Port Said, bearing in mind the confusion in that port when we arrived, the odds against the whole crane ever being assembled must have been astronomical.

The last item to be loaded was a triple-screw Tank Landing Craft in four sections: the after section weighing 120 tons, the fore section 96 tons and the two centre sections 60 tons each, which were bedded on enormous baulks of timber athwart the hatches and lashed down, after which we passed down to the Tail of the Bank to swing for compass adjustment, and then proceeded to sea in convoy. In Glasgow there had been a good deal of trouble about pilferage of some more desirable items of our cargo, but no-one had been apprehended and, at that time, neither the third mate nor I had guessed the truth.

Brown, the new 3rd. mate, would never have displayed cowardice, but he was of a nervy disposition. One night he mistook the wake of a dolphin for that of a torpedo, which was perhaps an understandable mistake. But, as the ship was accompanied by dolphin throughout his watch, the number of torpedoes which he saw became rather monotonous.

So one night, with the ship rolling a good deal, I came on the bridge just before midnight to relieve the watch and first passed into the chartroom to find that a tea-tray, complete with an opened tin of condensed milk, had been flung off a table all over the chart. As navigating officer I was, to say the least, highly displeased and expostulated with the third mate as I went out to relieve him. I did not see Capt. Davies, who was a short man hardly able to see over the bridge dodger. Brown was clearly in a very over-wrought state, for he almost screamed at me, asking how I could worry about condensed milk and charts when the landing craft was likely to go over the side at any moment. Amazed, I asked him what he was talking about. It seemed that the men relieving the wheel, having had to pass under the great timber skids across No. 3 hatch on which the largest section was mounted, had been terrified out of their wits by the noise it made on these skids, and had started the scare.

I knew that Capt. Davies had been somewhat awed by the experience of a Welsh shipmaster friend of his who had put his ship back into the Clyde while we were there — I rather think she was the *Primrose Hill*, though am now uncertain of this. At all events, this vessel had sailed with six large locomotives on her well-decks, three on each side. With the ship rolling heavily in dirty weather, the master had been down to inspect them himself and, satisfied, was mounting a ladder to return to the bridge when the ship suddenly shed three on her starboard roll and then, without hesitation, the other three on her port roll! Rails apart, the ship was undamaged, but he nevertheless returned to port.

By this time I had realized that we were alone on the sea, and learnt that Brown had persuaded the master to run out of the convoy on to a course that would ease the rolling to some degree. Whilst saying that I thought this sheer nonsense and that, to a submarine, with our landing craft sections on deck, we could well look like a 'flat-top' aircraft carrier and appear to be the most desirable U-boat target of all, I became aware of the presence of the master, who cut in by asking me to take a shielded torch and have a look 'without showing a light'.

On the after-deck I found that the 120-ton section was working easily enough through about two or two and a half inches. This seemed to me to be a good safety factor and that the situation might well be dangerous if it were rigid. I reported this and reminded the captain that, having previously sailed in a wooden barque, I knew that the sounds of wood working in a seaway were at first terrifying to anyone who was not used to them. The captain accepted this, although the mate had in the meantime been called while I was carrying out my inspection. He seldom produced a line of thought of his own and, having sailed in Portmadoc schooners in his youth, was pleased enough to back my views. Finally, I managed to chase the third mate below and, when Capt. Davies had also gone below, I altered course. Before long I had resumed our position in the convoy.

I had supposed that that was the end of the matter but, unbeknown to me, the third mate was secretly lobbying the rather receptive ear of Capt. Davies about the danger of the sections of the landing craft taking charge so that, when we finally called into Cape Town for bunkers, orders were given for a gang of workmen to come aboard and to weld large steel sections between the hulls of the landing craft and the deck. I protested about this, fearing too great a rigidity, and worried about the possible weather we might encounter off Cape Agulhas and in the Mozambique Channel. By luck, the weather was in our favour from then on and, when we finally entered the Red Sea we were passed right through the accumulated mass of shipping and through the Suez Canal to Port Said with our cargo for the hard-pressed North African armies, because we were said to be the first vessel to arrive with all four sections of a landing craft intact.

The quays on Port Said were a mass of heterogeneous cargoes from various vessels, and the impression gained was that it would be a miracle if it was ever sorted out. Heavy-lift cranes were at a premium and, although one came and discharged the landing craft, we had other items which it did not lift off, but which were too heavy for our own derricks — such items as workshop lorries. Discharging one night, the Sea Transport Officer told me to get a couple of these vehicles discharged into a barge alongside. I refused point-blank, saying that he should arrange for a floating crane to do it, since the weights involved were far beyond the proof load of the derricks, let alone their safe working loads.*

Finally, fulminating that I was disrupting the war effort and would pay for my attitude when I was reported in the morning, he left to go to the next vessel in the tier, where he apparently made a similar demand. The officer on duty complied with the orders of this rather senior man, whereupon the whole derrick collapsed: the vehicle went right through the barge and to the bottom of the harbour (as did the barge with other items already in it) whilst I understand that one man in the barge was badly injured and another lost. I did not witness this but, when Capt. Davies came aboard, I told him what had occurred and he gave me his full support. In the light of the events on the other ship, it need hardly be said that I heard no more about my quarrel with the Sea Transport

* The original plans for the ship show a jumbo (heavy-lift) derrick at both Nos. 2 and 4 hatches, but they were never installed — possibly due to the wartime shortage of steel.

Officer, who never came aboard us again! It should be recorded, however, that this man was only trying to do his job with the inadequate facilities at his disposal.

One night a couple of engineers came aboard from the shore. They mounted the accommodation ladder quite normally and the Second, a man named Craggs of whom more anon, passed the time with me for a few minutes before saying he was going to turn in. In no way did he seem any the worse for wear. Shortly afterwards I had occasion to go to my cabin and was aware of an intense smell of burning. I traced this quickly to the Second Engineer's cabin which was full of smoke. He was sound asleep on his bunk with his pyjama jacket open, and it, with his bedding, was smouldering fiercely with flames starting at various points. I slapped out the fire on his pyjamas, and quickly picked him up — he was not a big man — and dumped him on No. 4 hatch, after which I fetched out his bedding, beat out the fire and doused it. Then I checked on his cabin generally.

Craggs slept all through this, and was only awakened when the hatch was opened in the morning! He was much mystified about how he had got there or who put him there, and it was some time before I enlightened him! It was that evening when the senior radio operator came aboard, almost in tears with disappointment, for he had bought a packet of 'feelthy postcards' from one of the many hawkers or beggars which clog one's movement in Port Said on the strength of the top one, which was visible. Now he had found that all the rest were blank! It was difficult to summon up one iota of sympathy for him but, in any case, he was perpetually in a state of terror brought on by the war, and at that time trying by every means to get himself certified by a doctor as unfit to continue his job. In the end he succeeded, and was shipped home as a D.B.S.*, presumably spending the rest of the war at his home in Bournemouth, consuming the food brought home in ships manned by men with redder blood than his in their veins.

Perhaps such people as him, as the previous Chief Engineer, and as our gun-layer (whose subsequent conduct appears at the end of this chapter) should be pitied. Perhaps they were born with too vivid imaginations. Nevertheless, so far as I was concerned — and I think that this applied to the vast majority of men — the fear of displaying fear far outweighed its cause. I am sure that all of us were frightened on occasions, but any public display of it involved a loss of face worse than death. In the event, those who made a public display of their nerves were despised by their fellows. Possibly he had some vision of the future, but it is certain that, glad though we were to see the end of him, he would

* Distressed British Seaman

96

have been a far greater nuisance as a prisoner subsequently.

Once we were discharged, we were ordered to take a part cargo of steel pilings from another vessel, with which we were to proceed to Safaga Bay at the head of the Red Sea. This was the time of the great Free French defence of the ridge at Bir Hachim when the German Afrika Korps was almost up to Alexandria, and an effort was being made to construct forward discharging facilities at Safaga. Whilst alongside this ship, I had a nasty surprise. Being very hot, I decided to have a swim so, asking the third mate to have a ladder put over the side for me to get back aboard, I dived in to the harbour. I had hardly started to swim when I saw a tug with a barge alongside turning to deliver it to a ship in the next tier, so moved over out of the way. I saw the tugmaster observe me and then, without reducing speed (as he should have done even had I not been there) he steered straight for me — or rather, so that his barge was heading straight for me.

I had no chance of escaping, but realized that the barge was flat ended. I therefore resolved to turn on my back and to set my feet against the flat bow, allowing myself to be pushed before it with my back hollowed. I had not appreciated that the lighter was swim-headed*, the angle coming just below the waterline, so that my feet slipped down under the hull. Raising my hands, I managed to clutch on to the angle and could see that the whole under-water body of this barge was a mass of sharp barnacles. It seems that the third mate and all those aboard the *Dalhousie* were shouting themselves hoarse at the tugmaster, who took not a blind bit of notice until he was almost at the bank, when he *had* to back off. For my part, I had exhausted my breath long before this and came to the surface half full of water and gasping with my chest horribly lacerated. Had I not been able to hang on, and had passed under the barge (as was obviously intended), I doubt if I should have survived.

People ask why the tug-master did this. Only he could answer that. Perhaps he had some personal or family grudge against the British, but there was an impression that the Egyptians as a whole had no interest in a British victory and that they would just as soon the Germans were in their country, if any foreign nation was to be there at all.

Llewellyn, the mate, was not bound to stand nights on cargo-work, and never offered to do so. It devolved on Brown and myself. When we went ashore we always went to the same place, in a party. It was an establishment where, as one sipped one's drink, a cabaret took place. This always included a turn in which a young woman first came on and performed various acrobatic contortions. These alone precluded any thought that she had any support down her back, though it was obvious

---

* A swim-headed barge has a flat cross-section forward, but is angled so that the top, flat section is over-hanging. It was a type which I associated with the Port of London.

97

that she had nothing of the sort because she was dressed only in an abbreviated G-string and an apology for a bra. Then, while she remained on the stage, which was more like a ring and surrounded on all sides by the clientele of the place, her partner appeared and set three swords by their hilts in sockets in a large block of wood at intervals of rather less then three feet. The tips were fitted with cork or some other blunting medium. Then, after going through the motions of hypnotising the girl, the man laid her across the tips of the swords so that one was under the nape of her neck; one under the small of her back and the last under her ankles. Then, carefully, he removed the sword below her ankles and she remained horizontal. This was not impressive and we felt that, with practice, anyone could do it. Next, again carefully, he removed the sword from the small of her back, and the girl still remained horizontal, while he passed a hoop along from her feet to her neck to demonstrate that there was no hidden suspension. The last sword was not removed, but we were quite sufficiently impressed with the trick as it was — for the girl was no dwarf — and the subject provided a constant argument for debate and discussion.*

In the meantime Capt. Davies had let it be known that this was to be his last voyage at sea and it had become clear to us that he intended to retire in style. Indirectly, this had caused relationships both on the bridge and in the saloon to deteriorate markedly. There had been vast discrepancies between the invoiced and delivered quantities of the ship's stores until thieves fell out and, unaccountably, the master and chief steward came at odds with each other. As previously remarked, there had been pilferage of the cargo in Glasgow, but there was more in Port Said and various other matters to which neither Brown nor I had been able to lend our countenance, and he had already been in touch with the appropriate authority (the S.I.B.). The culminating incident, which created two irreconcilable camps, was when Capt. Davies insisted that Brown and I should have an evening ashore together and see if our combined wits could solve the mystery of the horizontal girl, saying that he was sure Mr. Llewellyn would be happy to keep the ship, at the same time turning to him for confirmation.

One might say 'predictably', for Llewellyn, who was always a jump behind everyone else in any conversation, missed his cue and started to burble that he had intended to go ashore that evening, when he suddenly gave a sharp yelp, having obviously been kicked under the table by the master, whereupon he recovered himself sufficiently and said that of course he would be pleased to stay aboard. Brown and I caught each other's eye, both deeply suspicious, since this was obviously a 'put-up'

---

* I have since seen this trick done when the third sword *was* removed, thus apparently coming into the realm of pure levitation.

job to get us out of the way and, in any case, if not together, we had both seen the trick with the girl on a number of occasions, but we did not see how we could refuse and, that evening, went ashore together. We were so much more concerned with what might be happening aboard that we gave little thought to the cabaret act and, on our return, found a deputation of the crew awaiting our arrival, to be told that, in our absence, the master and mate had sold the greater part of the ship's mooring ropes and had passed them down to an Egyptian in a boat, privily and after dark.* We at once took an inventory of what was left, appreciated how much was gone and, in the morning, I lodged a formal protest with Capt. Davies. He assured me that the ropes were old (which I knew to be untrue) and that he was procuring more new ones.

When we arrived in Safaga Bay, we lay at anchor whilst we discharged the pilings. It was not a place which provided anything ashore, and I asked the master if I could put the boats in the water to tighten them up so that, once tight, I could use them in the evenings and at week-ends to sail about the harbour and out to the dhow channel, thereby not only providing some measure of enjoyment for the crew, but giving them experience in handling them. He said that there was no need and refused, thereupon going ashore with the mate. In his absence, I had everything removed bar their tanks from the boats, lowered them in the water and hung them under the stern. They promptly filled with water. This proved my point and, on his return, he accepted a *fait accompli*. In fact, once they had taken up and were emptied, he did allow their use. What a pity this was not done in more ships as a routine! In the event, the crew enjoyed sailing them, sometimes to view the odd dhows entering or leaving the harbour, and sometimes sailing closer inshore where we could bathe without so much fear of sharks, or try to catch the young sword-fish which skimmed over the surface of the water. Everybody, down to the galley-boy, was enabled to take charge of the sailing of the boats.

Indeed, Llewellyn often took a crowd in one boat when I took the other, but Capt. Davies clearly felt he had lost face over the matter. Since we *did* have to take to the boats in earnest not so long afterwards, it was a good thing they had been in the water. However, there was a phosphate wharf in the harbour and, once the pilings were discharged, we were to go alongside to load a part-cargo for Cape Town. It was a very short wharf and, initially, we had to berth so that the fore-part of the ship was abreast of it, whilst the after part was moored to buoys some distance astern, with a long back-spring to the jetty.

---

* One would not have supposed that Llewellyn's speed of intellect made him an ideal conspirator. I suspect that he was suborned by Capt. Davies simply because he needed someone to help him and not because of the Welsh connection.

I was in charge aft and simply was not left with sufficient moorings for the drifts entailed, so that I had to resort to the expedient of unreeving the derrick runners, which took time, apparently upsetting the pilot. Capt. Davies, obviously well aware of my situation, but presumably to maintain his authority and appease the pilot, took a megaphone and shouted aft, chiding me at the delay. By this time I was boiling with rage at being put in such an intolerable position and not only shouted back the reasons for the delay in full, but my own opinions on his actions in selling the ropes and wires. This silenced the captain who was, I am told, much embarrassed at so public an exposure of his wheeling and dealing before both the pilot and crew. From that time onwards, meals in the saloon were eaten in utter and complete silence!

Calling at Aden for bunkers, I was once more in the same position, with insufficient rope for both tug and buoys, and it was more by luck than good judgement that we avoided falling down on one of the Furness Withy 'Prince' Line vessels with a cargo of ammunition.

After this, I confronted the 'Old Man' and insisted on making an entry of complaint in the Official Log Book. He was now, I think, thoroughly frightened, particularly after the *contre-temps* in Aden. He promised to buy more ropes in Cape Town. Brown had reported the sale of the ropes to the S.I.B. in Port Said and learnt that it had been discovered that the cargo pilferage had been brought home to Capt. Davies, being told in confidence that, were it possible to bring us up to strength there (in Port Said), both Davies and Llewellyn would have been taken out of the ship there and then. As this was not possible, arrangements were to be made for them to be replaced when we arrived at Houston, in Texas. Of course, neither Davies nor Llewellyn had any inkling of this. The captain no longer came on the bridge when either Brown or I was on watch. Brown always relieved the officer on watch during meal times, so was never in the saloon with him, and so far as I was concerned, my conversation with him was confined to saying:- *"This is our position today."* as I pointed to the noon position on the chart each day. Since the mate sat on one side of him at table, and I on the other (Davies sat at the head of it), and since the atmosphere could be cut with a knife, nobody else spoke either! Perhaps fortunately, my ears had completely waxed up, possibly as a result of my experience with the barge in Port Said, so I could not have heard what was said anyway. These were cleared at Cape Town.

After discharging there we took on more bunkers and sailed for Trinidad for yet more bunkers before proceeding to Houston. As we left Table Bay, with the magnificent mountains of the Cape standing against the sunrise, I was still fulminating about the ropes which, needless to say, had *not* been replaced in Cape Town. We were the first vessel to

24. *The Author before the DALHOUSIE's final voyage.*

23. *Boats were griped outboard in war-time for quick lowering, but few were ever put into the water, so that the seams (of wooden ones) were generally wide open!*

take a new Admiralty course but, because the weather was worsening, we kept rather to the south of it. We sighted the masts of another vessel and sheered off, but we could never drop them below the horizon for long, however much we altered course. Then, one day, an apparently neutral Swede with superior speed came very close to us: a vessel with big cases on her well decks. We had not seen the masts on the horizon for two days but felt ourselves to be shadowed. *"Was this Swede the other vessel?"* we wondered.

Capt. Davies temporarily dismissed the whole subject in his anxiety to recover his false teeth, which he had inexplicably dropped down his lavatory pan when shaving and then, not realizing what he had done, pulled the plug. This involved the engineers, though it was some time before anyone understood what he was talking about since, *sans* dentures, he was virtually incomprehensible. Once I learned what had happened, I confess to much secret mirth but when, to my infinite surprise, the engineers managed to recover them by a brilliant piece of plumbing, I joined in the general rejoicing no more than I had commiserated over their loss. We had had to speak about the mysterious ship, but that was all.

Finally, on the tenth day out, we picked up the South-east trade but I daresay that I, having been in the ocean sailing ships, was the only person to recognize the fact. Possibly unbending under their beneficent influence, I went so far as to comment to Capt. Davies that we should hit the Admiralty course for the first time about 11.00 a.m.

Perhaps that was a mistake and he thought that I had forgotten and forgiven. At the time he was amusing himself by painting out his day room, affecting various and variegated colours and, in his natural ebullience (and doubtless encouraged by my earlier remark) had so far forgotten the state of the parties that he had maddened me by calling me up to see what he had done on two separate occasions. I was unimpressed and determined not to be so disturbed again.

In due course that familiar Welsh voice called:- *"Mr. Hurst, just come up here a moment, will you?"* but I remained silent and pretended that I did not hear. Once or twice more he called and then, to my surprise, the alarm bell rang. Still feeling that this was some ruse connected with his painting, I nevertheless dashed up to the bridge. Coincidentally, it was just eleven o'clock.

I was wrong. I should have gone the first time, but it was the old tale of crying 'Wolf' too often. On the horizon a ship was firing. We were heading right for her at that moment, considerably off our course. As she was firing very short, I looked for some common enemy between the ships. At first glance the distant vessel appeared to be a small merchantman and, in that sparkling sea under a tropic sky, the whole affair, whatever it was, had a momentary aura of unreality.

'Momentary' was the operative word. It seemed that that ship had been sighted right ahead and that we had immediately turned away but, realizing that he had started to turn the wrong way to obtain any assistance from the swell, Brown had had the helm put back and then over the other side. The other vessel, which had already revealed herself as a raider by opening fire, was temporarily non-plussed by this (as we subsequently learned), believing that we might be a decoy ship. In less time than it takes to tell I was aft with my four-inch gun's crew and the raider had been brought right astern, almost broadside on to us, whilst she fired salvoes of what turned out to be four 5.9″ guns. I opened fire at maximum range but a return salvo landed right astern of us and I could not see where my round had landed, though was sure it was short. Then another salvo landed close by, two shells landing, one on each side of the gun platform, splashing us with their spray. My gun-layer was a man whom I had considered to the smartest we had had but, like many others, it seemed that he did not maintain his standards in crisis. At this moment he turned to me a face ashen with fear, shouting:- *"It's no good, Sir! They've got our range!"* and, without further ado, this descendant of the bulldog breed had deserted his gun and fled. As I closed up the rest of the crew and gave the next firing order, the bridge telephoned to me to cease fire, but we still continued to run and send out ''RRR-RRR-RRR'' — the raider signal — on the radio. The master had realized that we were only wasting ammunition in trying to deal with a target outside our range.

I sent the hands under cover and repaired to the bridge. By this time we had sustained several hits and were on fire forward. The raider, still maintaining her distance, was signalling us to stop, whilst another vessel was now hovering on the other horizon, making it clear that we were trapped, so Capt. Davies ordered the ensign to be hauled down. Because there was no-one visible on deck, I went to do the job myself while another salvo whined through the air towards us. As I laid hold of the halliards, it landed: one round bursting close behind me on the No. 5 hatch coaming and the shrapnel cutting the halliards from my hand so that I was unable to haul the ensign down, for the working parts were flying over the side from the gaff. Again I repaired to the bridge, where Davies, seeing my right arm to be a mass of blood from what was, in reality, only a very minor spray of shrapnel, lost no time in hoisting *"The way is off my vessel"* in International Code, in order to bring about an end to this 'bloody' engagement as quickly as possible. No-one else, on either side, had received as much as a scratch!

The raider steamed towards us very slowly, still being suspicious of that turn into the swell, and then, revealing herself to be German, ordered us to abandon ship. We had plenty of time to accomplish this, and were lucky as few stricken ships' companies had this advantage.

I knew our position, 22° 24' S. 24° 50' W, almost right in the middle of the South Atlantic, and that if we were left in the boats it would be a long trip before the South-East trade to the coast of Brazil. The weather, which was so balmy on the deck of a ten thousand ton ship, would be chilly next to the water running the swells, and some of our crew were old. While the master was disposing of the secret papers and the mate was still (by that time unnecessarily) organizing the fire-fighting on the fore-deck, I decided that, so far as the immediate future was concerned, the boat journey represented the greatest hazard and accordingly determined that everybody should prepare for it, instructing all hands to wear as much as they could of their warmest clothing and to take as much tobacco and chocolate as they could stow about their persons, their personal papers and nothing else. I warned them that it was not a boat outing, as in Safaga Bay, and that I would not tolerate any suit-cases in my boat, foreseeing that it might be a ticklish matter to rid it of such impedimenta once we were alone with the ocean. I put the ship's chronometer and my sextant in the starboard boat, with a chart and other things, and thanked God that I had insisted on putting it into the water at Safaga against the wishes of the master and mate. Now we reaped the reward.

By this time the *Dalhousie's* engines had turned over for the last time; her charts and secret papers were fathoms deep and she was lying a little off the wind and sea so that her head was canted to bring the weather on the port bow. I had donned my best uniform, thickest jersey and heavy bridge coat by this time and, as we mustered the crew by the boats, I threw a number of suitcases out of mine on to the deck, noticing that they all belonged to engineers and radio officers who should have known better. Then we lowered the boats. Ours was on the weather side and, in the big swell that was running — much bigger when seen from its troughs — it became so difficult to fend the boat off from the ship's side as to be impossible. At all events, when the painter was cast off, the boat sped aft, rising and falling on the swells and scraping the hull all the time. We held our breath as we sank into a trough and swept towards the great bronze propellor, which might have torn the boat apart, as towards an immutable fate, but the swell lifted us just in time and, in the next instant, we were swept clear on to the lee quarter.

The raider was now quite close, calling us up on a lamp and instructing us to go alongside her, so I altered course accordingly. Capt. Davies was sitting aft, next to me, and several of the men were pulling at the oars. I observed the craven gunlayer at one, but he was still shaking like an aspen leaf in such paroxysms of fear that I ordered him away from it, since he was doing more harm than good. All the other men seemed to be in good heart and calm enough. The mate's boat, which had had a good lee with which to leave the ship, was some little way ahead. Suddenly the raider swung round till she was apparently heading straight for us, whereupon the master burst out, in a frenzy, his voice getting progressively shriller:- *"My God! She's going to ram us and leave us to drown!!"* and a good deal more in a similar vein. I could have cheerfully pushed him overboard for providing such a degrading exhibition, scarcely calculated to instil any morale into his crew, and he remained quite deaf when I pointed out what should have been obvious to any practical seaman, namely: that the German was making a lee for the mate's boat to go alongside. I felt bound to speak so that all the men in the boat could hear, since those rowing could not see what was going on and were already looking apprehensive after Davies' outburst. It was not until we had pulled clear and he saw the mate's boat boarding the enemy that he ceased his wail.

So we came alongside, and the test came to see who had sea-sense and who had not when it came to grabbing the Jacob's ladder as the boat rose on the swell. I was holding her in by a boat-rope aft, and the men jumped one by one: the wireless operators, it need hardly be said, in the troughs, despite warnings, so that they were lucky to escape injury. Finally the 'Old Man' went up and then I had to jump for it. I had thought that the Germans would let the boat go, but they must have boarded her subsequently as they had my sextant amongst them later and, when time had gone by and our lives had entered a condition of perpetual want, I sometimes experienced a twinge when I thought of those suit-cases which I had ejected from it, although my conscience told me that I was right at the time and their owners never mentioned them during the years that followed.

We found ourselves on the fore-deck of the raider, her guns still exposed with their camouflage of packing cases lying around them. I was quickly whisked away from the others due to the gory state of my arm — a fact which, in the swift march of events, I had completely forgotten — and was taken to a very clean and impressive little surgery where a doctor removed the shrapnel and suggested, with what I considered to be a warped sense of humour, that I keep the splinters as a memento! During this period, there was a dull explosion as a torpedo was fired into the *Dalhousie* which, I gather, sank stern first. None of us saw her go. I have since seen photographic illustrations in books which purport to be her in her final death throes, with her bow sticking into the air and about to go under, but they were not of the right vessel, since her bow, curved outwards towards its top, was not the one in these pictures.

Soon after the war, Capt. Davies was sent a very badly-reproduced newspaper cutting which did show the vessel, soon after the torpedo had struck her, but I could never trace the original. It made no odds: the ship was gone.

～～～～

VOLUME TWO

IN DURANCE VILE

"The grim recording Angel turns the pages of the book,
And the leaves are thrust behind us past recall,
All the sorrows that we tasted, all the pleasures that we took
In the life we lived together, brothers all."

(Anon.)

25. *A profile of the STIER. Her funnel-shape could be altered, as denoted by the dotted line.*

VI

THE *STIER*

As I was led forward to join the others, I reflected that it was bad enough to be taken prisoner but that, had this occurred the previous voyage, when the *Dalhousie* had been a fairly happy ship, it would not have presented the problems which now faced us. Brown and I were not on speaking terms with the master and mate: the master and chief steward had their own private feud; I had already determined that the gun-layer should be court-martialled for his behaviour when he deserted his gun, and I felt that Capt. Davies' hysterical outburst in the boat had not improved relations with anyone. Despite the kaleidoscopic memories of the past, including stolen ropes, forged disbursement sheets, Glasgow theatres, profanities when berthing in the Red Sea, pilfered cargoes and so much more, it seemed to me that, without prejudice to anything the future might hold, past disagreements must be forgotten while we were captive and that everyone should be persuaded to 'muck in' together as amicably as possible.

I found the officers in one large room and the crew in another, on opposite sides of an alleyway. I never discussed it with any of them before or afterwards, but I think that the crew had no more time for the master and mate than the third mate and I had, so my arrival was a signal for a deputation to appear. I had been keeping the time aboard the *Dalhousie* so that noon by the sun fell at about 11.50 a.m. in order that the ship's position might be determined by lunch time at eight bells, but the raider was keeping zone time. This discrepancy in clocks, taken in conjunction with the time taken in the action and in abandoning ship, had caused our fellows to miss their lunch as the Germans, they had discovered, had already fed. It was requested, therefore, that I make representations to the German captain that they be provided with dinner!

They had just heard the dull boom which marked the *coup de grâce* sending their own ship down to the port of no return: they were prisoners, they had lost their possessions and had no fore-knowledge of their future fate and were, henceforth, to be a source of anxiety to their relatives. All this, and these men wanted their dinner above all things else! I never did decide whether this was an example of heroics or the product of an abysmal lack of imagination! On the whole, I suspect the latter. I recalled, the first day at sea, hearing one of the gunners calling down the companionway to his mate: *"Ted! Ted!! Come upstairs" (sic) "quickly! I can't see any land!"*. This man was a peace-time crane driver on a wharf on London River: his mate had been a night porter on Paddington station for years on end. I do not believe that they possessed one iota of imagination between them but, throughout, they took life exactly as it came and were utterly unflappable and wholly reliable. These characteristics stood them in extremely good stead so long as they were prisoners.

The officers' accommodation consisted of a large room containing a couple of tables and sundry benches, together with a number of double-tiered bunks which were placed round the perimeter and were at right-angles to the bulk-heads. There were a few lockers along the fore bulkhead and these, with a loud speaker, represented the sum total of our furnishings. The men's accommodation was very similar.

We were all faced with an imponderable future and uncertainty is, at the best of times, a bad shipmate. We knew, of course, that a raider would not wish to keep us aboard for any longer than she could help. We neither knew her identity, how long she had been at sea nor whether we were the only prisoners aboard. In due course we did discover some writing on the inside of one of the locker doors, evidently written by a previous occupant, and this, together with certain observations which we made, led us to believe — accurately as it proved — that we were aboard the raider *Stier*, formerly the fruit ship *Cairo* which ran to the Levant in days of peace. This accorded with our general observation of the vessel, allowing for her war-paint. She was quite nice-looking, painted a light grey with a raking bow and a cruiser stern. A long foc's'le head extended somewhat abaft the foremast, and she was flush-decked aft. We had had little opportunity to observe her as we came aboard because she had kept us fine on her bow both before and after we had abandoned ship, and the one feature which implanted itself on everybody's mind was the two lookouts slung in bos'n's chairs at the trucks of her two masts, sweeping the horizons incessantly with powerful binoculars.

During the afternoon, Capt. Davies was sent for and escorted to be interviewed by Capt. Gerlach, the commander of the raider. He was always very secretive about this interview, but did tell us that the Germans were very well informed and had told him, *inter alia*, the names of all the ships which had been in Cape Town with us quite accurately, together with our secret code and sundry other information which the enemy had no business to know. That the Germans knew all about the shipping in Cape Town was hardly surprising, as many Boers had much greater affinity with, and loyalty to, the Germans than to the British, though I found the matter of our recognition code, in particular, hard to swallow. We never heard what Capt. Davies said as his contribution to this interview and could only guess: our opinions hardening later when he was accorded a favour not granted to us or to other captains.

The prison officer, named Petersen, came to see us and, I suppose, did his best in what he could hardly have found a very congenial job. He had been master in the Hamburg Sud-Amerika Line before the war and was more at home in discussing ships and the sea than in trying to interest us in the parlour games which he produced for our recreation. He did bring some chessmen, but I found that none of my colleagues possessed more than the rudiments of the game. (I had always played chess and, having been in the Finnish ships — the Finns playing chess compulsively like the Russians — had acquired some proficiency.)

The food was excellent. We had, I imagine, the same as the crew and on Sundays were served with chicken, then more of a luxury than in the battery age of today. For my part, I liked the German black bread and sauerkraut: the only time I found a meal to be unpalatable being when it consisted of soused herrings. Nor was I in a minority in this. However, the third mate, being a Scot although slightly built, made up for us by eating eighteen without turning a hair!

We had excellent relays of gramophone records through the loud-speaker during the day, particularly at week-ends, and the news in English from Tokyo once a day. This was in August, 1942, when any news meant a great deal. The Japanese had swept through South-East Asia and much of the Pacific in a victorious surge eight months previously: the Allies held nothing in Europe; our armies had been sorely pressed in North Africa when we had been in Egypt short weeks earlier and the Battle of the Atlantic, by our own observation, was hitting the convoys hard. The announcement that a landing had been effected at Dieppe in one of the last news broadcasts we had heard prior to capture had led us to hope that a second front had been created, and it did not enhance our spirits to find that this was far from being he case, let alone to hear the Tokyo reports of the raid.

We were normally allowed on deck once a day for exercise by a companion-way leading up to the foc's'le head, which was our stamping ground. We were supposed to keep moving and not to loiter, but to most of us this presented no difficulty after being confined below and immediately above, as we learned, the forward magazine. The ship was running south; the weather was fine and fresh, and we came to look forward to this part of the day. Even now we could see little of the ship. The guns were camouflaged again, those on the foredeck being concealed behind imitation packing cases in the representation of deck cargo, while the foc's'le head gun fitted into a dummy derrick, of which it seemed a part when viewed from another vessel.

I noted the speed and estimated the courses each day as accurately as possible and, having been in close contact with the Nautical Almanac, was able to make pretty fair estimates of our positions. It was evident that the ship was running down into the Westerlies as fast as she could: perhaps, we thought, because she was alarmed by the effects of our radio signals while we were being chased. It was not till long afterwards that I learnt that Capt. Gerlach wished to run round the Horn into the Pacific, but was refused permission from Germany. In the meantime we ran into very dirty weather. Engine revolutions had been reduced owing to overheated bearings and the ship was pitching heavily and crashing into every big sea which, as we were berthed forward, made our condition extremely disagreeable. It was blowing with hurricane force which reduced the vessel's potential ten knots (at reduced revolutions) to three, and there was no exercise.

On the whole, we were making the best of things. A few of us had constructed a set of Monopoly, which we had played aboard the *Dalhousie,* and this was found to keep the peace for a longer period at a time than anything else. We had no books except a Bible. Capt. Davies had suggested that we read through it by chapters and then discuss them, starting with *Genesis.* This was a very sensible suggestion, however ill it may have come from him, and we did do this two or three times. I think that we were all pulling well together by this time, all feuds and feelings having been shelved, if not forgotten, in order to make life tolerable and to show a united front to the enemy. Engineers rank as officers in merchant ships and, as they vary considerably in variety and outlook, we were a motley collection, taken all round. It was the chief steward, who berthed with the officers, who sowed the seeds of discord however, as he openly sneered at the bible readings and made scornful jests at discussion times. At others he spent much of his time making snide remarks about, or to, the captain. This was quite uncalled for and led to a great quarrel between him and Capt. Davies, whose authority was being defied and sapped to a great extent. Perhaps as a result of some previous dealings, the steward thought that, if they were to hang, they would hang together.

All the same, time passed heavily. A few men engaged our guards, who were friendly enough disposed, in language lessons. I took the view, however, that I was unlikely to derive any benefit from learning the enemy language in the South Atlantic, and I had no intention of giving them the benefit of learning mine. Every day I assiduously maintained a diary, which I had started on the first day of capture, and which commenced with our first contact with the *Stier*.

Our crew, whose accommodation was similar but larger than ours, had been provided with boxing gloves, which they used to quite good effect, although the weather was by now so bad as to put an end to that and almost every other activity, even in our restricted condition. Finally, the motion of the ship became easier and the men who fetched the food from the galley reported that there was land in sight.

My calculations, after ten days, were obviously open to a certain margin of error, particularly after being confined below for several of them, but I had previously stated that we must be somewhere near the Tristan group and, when I questioned these men, reached the conclusion that we were lying off Gough Island. This subsequently proved to be correct. I had passed it more than once, far out, in the sailing ships outward bound to Australia and was roughly familiar with its contours, though it was not easy to see it, as it were, through the eyes of others. We lay there all day, presumably under the lee of the land as the ship was very still and there were sounds of craft alongside. The galley party thought they had seen a U-boat. We were not allowed on deck and were left to ardent speculation. The suggestion that we were to be set ashore there appealed to most of my colleagues, few of whom had any accurate idea of the island's position, and none of whom had ever set eyes on it. They believed in getting ashore at all costs, possibly with more than half an eye cocked towards the magazine below them, taken in conjunction with the very *raison d'être* of our captor.

Personally, I found the idea highly distasteful because not only is the island precipitous and barren, but without human life: in fact, albatross and other sea birds coming ashore to breed represent the only life of any note. It lies in the northern belt of the Westerly Winds — The Roaring Forties — at a point where the ice-limit curves northwards and where, as I knew from experience, the weather would soon be cold, bleak and very thick. It is miles off any trade route in peace or war-time, and chances of survival or rescue would be more than remote. Fortunately, the idea remained nothing more than speculation and apparently did not occur to the Germans!

There were a few Chinese prisoners in the ship, who did most of the laundry work in a space which abutted our accommodation alleyway and was adjacent to the lavatories and wash-room which we used. They had been held back from the crew of a Shell tanker, the *Patella*, which had been sunk previously and we gained a little more information about the raider from them and this, with further facts we learnt during the course of our stay aboard, provided a certain amount of interest about the *Stier*.

Viewed dispassionately, the German surface raiders were amongst the most interesting vessels at sea during the war, and their crews probably lived under as great a strain as anyone. As previously recorded, I had only avoided being captured in the *Raranga* by the *Pinguin* when our boilers had failed. The *Pinguin* later distinguished herself signally by her astounding exploit in rounding up the whaling fleet in the Antarctic, under the ice barrier.

The *Stier* was a smaller vessel of some 4,413 tons and was generally referred to by the Germans as Number 23. She had sailed from Rotterdam on 12 May, 1942, and was shelled by the British 14″ guns at Dover without effect as she passed through the Straits, but when off Cape Griz Nez she suffered a severe M.T.B. attack, two of her four escort being damaged, and she put into Boulogne for a period.

She did not prove to be the most successful of the raiders because, after proceeding down to the area of Fernando Noronha, she only sank two vessels: a British tramp named the *Gemstone* loaded with iron ore and the American tanker *Stanvac Calcutta* in ballast, which had put up a very good fight with her two guns. Then she had re-fuelled from the tanker *Charlotte Schliemann* which had previously broken out of Las Palmas, and she had been in company with raider No. 28, the *Michel*, under the command of Capt. von Ruckteschell who had previously made a successful cruise in the raider *Widder*, sinking ten ships totalling 58,000 tons. The *Michel* was a modern ship and had been on the stocks, under construction, as the Polish *Bielskoi* when the Germans overran Copenhagen and diverted the ship for their own purposes. She had sailed from Flushing in March 1942 to go a-raiding and was well armed with four 5.9″ guns, three 4.1″ and two 40-knot L.S. boats. She had failed to catch the Blue Funnel *Menelaus*, whose master evaded capture at 15 1/2 knots (although a 14-knot vessel) in a number of well-executed and well-planned manoeuvres, despite the presence of one of the *Michel's* torpedo boats which was badly handled. She had sunk a Norwegian, a broken-down Liberty ship some 600 miles south and west of Ascension and a British tramp, putting all the accumulated prisoners aboard the German supply ship *Doggerbank* which, as the British *Speybank*, had previously been captured by the raider *Atlantis*.

After laying mines off Cape Town, she sank four vessels in revolting circumstances about which we heard in great detail when we joined with their survivors in the *Charlotte Schliemann*, which had also re-fuelled the *Michel*.

She and the *Stier* had been steaming in company for nearly a fortnight, mainly some ten miles apart, and they had only parted at 2.0 a.m. on 9 August, six hours before the *Stier* had sighted the *Dalhousie*. It was another hour before she had got into position to attack at 17,000 yards, and it was the *Michel*, turning back to see what was going on after the *Stier* had fired some twenty salvoes at us, which we had sighted on the other horizon. Although we did not see her, the *Michel* came right up to the *Stier* as the *Dalhousie* was sunk. After this they parted again, and the *Michel* sank two more vessels whose crews were transferred to the supply ship *Tannenfels*, of which I shall write again. She re-fuelled from the tanker *Uckermark*, once the notorious *Altmark* of *Graf Spee* and *Cossack* fame, and then, proceeding via the Indian Ocean, she arrived at Batavia after 324 days at sea, sinking four more ships *en route*. There the Germans had every reason to complain of the attitude of their allies *(sic)*, the Japanese: an attitude of which we shall take further note in due course, and she then proceeded to Kobe via Singapore. Ruckteschell, who was a sick man, was relieved by Capt. Gumprich who had been commander of the raider *Thor*, which we saw at close quarters later on, and, after a cruise to the Indian Ocean, she was sunk by an American submarine off Yokohama in October 1943 — the last of the German raiders still afloat.

The foregoing digression may prove to be justified, since we heard a good deal of the *Michel* before very much more time had elapsed.

On the second day of our stay off Gough Island, Capt. Davies was again summoned from us and, on his return, it transpired that we were to be transferred to another vessel which was understood to be an oil tanker. This was no more than we had expected to happen sooner or later, except that we would hardly have expected a tanker, but speculation naturally reached saturation point on receipt of this intelligence. We had no idea of the nationality of the vessel nor, of course, of her destination. On the whole, it was considered that Dakar was the most likely goal; partly because it was the nearest port under Axis control, partly because we doubted if many vessels were trying to beat the Allied blockade back to Europe and, I suppose, partly because we did not want to even consider the possibility of the Far East. In some ways we were sorry to leave the *Stier*, although solely on the grounds that 'The Devil you know is better than the Devil you don't'. At least we were dry, relatively comfortable and well-fed, and were probably living under as good conditions as any prisoner can hope for at sea. We were, however, alive to the implications of going into action when all our sympathies would lie with the *Stier's* adversary, although in practice we were sitting, literally, on the forward magazine. This is the sort of thing which would occur to few men whilst engaged in the heat of an action, though it must loom large in the minds of those who can do nothing but sit and listen. In our case, the situation did not arise.

All our old feuds had been set on one side. Others, it is true, had arisen, but it was now clear to most of us that there was a long road ahead and that a common and united front was an essential requisite to our preservation. In spite of all the squalid events of the *Dalhousie's* last voyage, which extended far beyond the incidents and personalities I have described, there was actually a perfectly good foundation for a state of harmony. The master and I had actually been good friends until his extensive preparations for retirement had torn all loyalties asunder and, during previous voyages, he had often come up on the bridge to spend my watches with me when out of the 'Danger Zones', to our mutual enjoyment. Since our capture I had often weighed in on his behalf in order to establish and maintain a proper sense of order and discipline, as one or two of our members, mainly junior engineers and the chief steward, had been inclined to think that the old order had passed.

It now seemed that Davies and the chief steward were to remain aboard, together with a Capt. Griffiths of the *Gemstone* who was being brought across from the tanker. It appeared that Davies had been told that he could go back to Germany and that he might retain one man, whomsoever he liked, to wash up and act for him and his fellow shipmaster, who was also a Welshman. We never knew why they had this privilege. It is true that they were the only two surviving masters of ships sunk by the *Stier* and it may be that Capt. Gerlach allowed this as a personal favour. On the other hand there were a couple of masters whose ships were sunk by the *Michel* aboard the tanker with Griffiths to whom this principle was *not* extended. It is true that Davies had been captured by the cruiser *Emden* in the First World War. Whether Griffiths had had a similar experience I do not know, though I should hardly have thought that such a reason would account for it. The more we considered matters the more we remembered how reticent Davies had been about his initial interview with Gerlach. No reader will be in any doubt about his lack of integrity. Nor had his outburst in the boat enhanced his reputation or any assessment of his character. Passing information to the enemy is another matter altogether, and an act of which we had no evidence. Yet, if there was not some sort of *quid pro quo*, why were Griffiths and Davies given what most of us regarded as a tremendous favour? What *was* the reason? And, if an innocent one, why was it not disclosed? If there were answers to these questions, we never learnt what they were.

Whether Capt. Davies had been told our ultimate destination or not I do not know. I rather doubt it, but I suspect he knew that we were not going to Dakar and possibly surmised that we should be taken to the Far East*. In any case, if Europe were to be excluded, there was little scope

---

* In his report written after the war, he said that he believed we should be landed in the Argentine. I never heard this put forward and, if so, what was the point of him returning to Germany? In fact, his account was full of errors. Even the bridge glass was all shattered: the radio room put out of action, and so forth.

left outside the tropics which, although they may be nice enough for a visit or for residence, can hardly be held in any estimation by a white man with the prospect of some years of captivity before him. I doubt if anyone believed in a quick end to the war in 1942.

Very rightly and naturally, Capt. Davies did not wish to advertise his good fortune too blatantly, so he first approached Llewellyn, privily, to see whether he would wish to go. The fact of doing the washing up, fetching the food, and so on, was obviously of very minor importance. The opportunity was the over-riding consideration and as the mate was also a Welshman, being a near neighbour of Davies; as their wives were friends, and as he was the next most senior man in the ship's company, besides having been involved with the 'Old Man' in much of his skulduggery, he was the obvious choice. Not believing in the Dakar story, Llewellyn turned it down, fearing the British blockade round Europe! On this the captain completely changed the emphasis of the offer, bringing out the role of servant, and asked the cook, a very good man, if he would like to remain, but he, too, refused. I never asked him his reason afterwards, since he probably assumed that neither I nor anyone else knew that he had had the offer.

By this time Davies was beginning to think that it was not a popular job and, still with a view to the service, he approached the chief steward who had not only been at daggers drawn with him for the greater part of our voyage, but, alone of us all, had baited and annoyed him since capture. Time was short and I can only suppose that the rubicund little mariner panicked. When we came to say 'Good-bye' he spoke to me and told me of it. I gasped. I could not help myself and he saw it. *"Good God, man! Would you have stayed if I had asked you?"* he asked. *"Good Heavens, yes!"* I replied. I had never whole-heartedly subscribed to the Dakar theory and saw little hope of escape if we should go to the Far East. Germany was a different matter. The 'Old Man' was obviously upset, summed the situation up, both past and present, very reasonably, regretting that he had asked the steward and saying, rather plaintively, that he had thought of asking me but, as the mate had refused, he had not thought that I should accept. I suspect that the real trouble was that Llewellyn, in declining, had not given his real reasons and thus created this unfortunate assumption by the master. However his mind may have been working at the time (and it did work slowly), I know that the first mate bitterly repented his decision before he finally died in Japan. As for the steward, we shall see what happened to him.

So we trooped out, said 'Good-bye' and disappeared up the companionway, passing Capt. Griffiths as he came aboard. I never saw them again, though Capt. Davies wrote me a long letter after the war and a very extraordinary tale he had to tell.

26. The STEPHEN HOPKINS *in Table Bay.*

It seems that the *Stier* soon headed north, after passing round the Tristan da Cunha group, but the only ship that she sighted was the 29,000-ton *Pasteur* which was too fast for her to catch. She met the *Michel* again, but this ship left for another rendezvous, whilst the *Stier* was to store from another blockade-runner-cum-store ship, the *Tannenfels*, before keeping an assignment with the *Brake* to take in coal, after which she was to proceed to the Gironde. She found the *Tannenfels* and the two vessels were lying close together in rainy weather some 200 miles north and west of Tristan da Cunha when another ship loomed into sight about two miles off. Accounts of the action vary somewhat and that of Capt. Davies was certainly based on hearsay to a large degree as he and his companions were locked below as soon as it started.

Many of the German crew had been painting over the sides on stages, to smarten up the vessel before her arrival, but as soon as the alarm was given they scrambled back aboard. This was one of the few occasions when a raider did not choose her time for fighting, and she might have done better had she taken no action at all. She opened fire with machine guns, which was a tactical error, but the other vessel, which proved to be the American standard liberty ship *Stephen Hopkins*, was almost trigger-happy and replied at once: her first round hitting the engine room of the *Stier*, doing a great deal of damage and putting all her electrical gear out of action. The next hit the bridge, destroying the radio and firing controls and killing the doctor and several of the officers, while the third went into the forward magazine directly under the two shipmasters but, fortunately for them, it did not explode and merely caught fire.

In due course, when their gaol was filled with acrid smoke, they were moved to another lock-up directly under the foc's'le head gun which they found somewhat traumatic for, by then, with no central control, the raider was firing her guns independently. One of the early rounds from the *Stephen Hopkins* jammed the raider's helm hard a-starboard, so that she could only move in a circle but, as the next cut off the oil supply to the engines, they stopped. The ship still had some way and, as she swung round, Gerlach tried to fire torpedoes but, because his electrical gear was defunct, he was unable to do so. Meantime the *Tannenfels*, which had stood off, was jamming the liberty ship's distress signals. (Some of the *Stephen Hopkins'* survivors have said that the *Tannenfels* was keeping company with the *Stier* in the action and also firing, but the balance of conflicting evidence seems to weigh against this.)

Certain it is that the *Stier's* guns also had very telling effect, smashing into the American ship until the two vessels were caught in a rain squall and lost to sight of each other. The liberty ship had received a direct hit in her starboard boiler and, by then, both vessels were badly a-fire and stopped. Once the squall had passed, the *Stier* re-opened fire but, although the two vessels were relatively close to each other, it is not entirely clear to what degree they could see each other from then on. Certainly a cadet named O'Hara in the American ship, having found his way along the tunnel and up the escape hatch after the order to abandon ship had been given, found the 4-inch gun's crew lying dead and then, although he had never fired such a gun, loaded and fired the remaining five shells single-handed, each scoring a hit but, directly he had done so, he himself was killed by a shell from the raider.

As the *Stephen Hopkins* sank, the raider tried vainly to fight fierce fires aboard caused primarily by leaking oil. The fire control was useless and the hand extinguishers were soon exhausted. The crew were hauling up water from over the side, but this was hopeless and, as the fires were out of control and approaching a store of live torpedoes, they abandoned ship. The *Tannenfels* had now returned. The three prisoners were released from their purgatory beneath the gun, but Capt. Davies had been overcome by smoke and fumes and was half-carried up on deck by Griffiths and Groves, but he fell against a ladder and injured his shoulder. This led to a frozen shoulder and virtual inability to use his arm for the rest of the war. The three of them managed to seize a rubber raft and get over the side while the Germans were leaving the ship as fast as they could. Capt. Davies said that many lost their heads completely and that at least two of her big life-boats were dropped bow first into the water and lost. The *Tannenfels* came as close as she dared to pick up the men struggling in the sea whilst the *Stier* finally blew up, most spectacularly. The two shipmasters derived great satisfaction when they saw that forward gun disintegrate!

Never in the history of time was a four-inch gun used with such effect as that of the *Stephen Hopkins*. That was all the liberty ship had to use and she scored fifteen hits on the far more powerful raider, almost all of which wrought decisive destruction. The *Stier* fired 400 lbs in each broadside of four guns and the American 31 lbs, from her single gun. On paper, the raider had all the advantages: a trained naval crew, fire control, and much else, and it must be admitted that the *Stephen Hopkins* had a great measure of luck in wreaking such havoc with her early rounds. Yet the measure of her luck, in the final analysis, was that, given the destruction of the raider, which must be matched against her own loss, only 15 of her complement of 57 men survived the action and a boat journey of a month to the coast of Brazil. Yet it ranks as one of the epic single ship actions. Whether either ship knew she had sunk the other seems to be doubtful, though each must have known that she had inflicted mortal wounds.

It was strange that, of nine disguised surface raiders sent to sea by the Germans during the Second World War, two should have been lost in duels of mutual destruction. The other was the *Kormoran* which sank the Australian cruiser *Sydney*, which was last sighted steaming over the horizon with her fires gaining. There was a larger flash and she was never seen again.

As for the *Tannenfels*, she already had 300 men and prisoners (mainly from the *Michel*) aboard when the *Stier* sank, and sufficient provisions to last this complement for three weeks. Now she had a further 400 men from the raider and, instead of steaming straight for the Gironde, steered further south for a month due to the signals which might have been picked up, and it was seven more weeks before she reached Bordeaux, by which time, as may be imagined, living conditions were dreadful and everyone was on very short commons.

One of the more peculiar things about our capture was that we had never been searched. Very few of us had anything to find, it is true, but the chief steward had retained not only his camera, with which he had photographed the raider from the boat, but also the mate's revolver which he had purloined from his cabin before we abandoned ship. (For all the Germans knew, we might all have had revolvers!) He had kept these two articles throughout his various vicissitudes, even up to the time of being taken aboard the *Tannenfels*. He was a New Zealander: a heavily built man who, although he neither smoked nor drank, was in very poor condition with a large and flabby waist-line and a pudgy face which ill became his years, for he must have been in his early thirties. As the *Tannenfels* neared home, she stood well in to the Iberian coast in order to keep within the neutrality limits and, when close off Cape Finisterre, our steward went up on deck at night as if to go to the lavatory, laden with a revolver, a camera, a rolls razor and his surplus adiposity which, I gather, had not been reduced much by his recent short rations. With all this, and still wearing shoes, he leaped over the side to strike out for the shore. He was not used to exercise and, apart from anything else, it is difficult to understand what good he supposed his camera would be after being immersed in the sea or why he should want a revolver in a neutral country. But these were academic questions because he was never seen or heard of again. No-one can say for certain, but it seems that his death can be attributed to folly rather than to suicide.

As for the two captains, when the *Tannenfels* finally arrived at Bordeaux they were transported in cattle trucks to Bremerhavn and thence to Stalag Milag Nord, near Bremen. Formerly a corpulent man, Davies went down to six stone. At one point he was put aboard a Red Cross vessel for re-patriation, but then taken off again. He needed a great deal of physiotherapy after the war.*

Leaving the *Stier*, the rest of us were shepherded over the side into a motor-boat. It was dark, with a nearly full moon shining at intervals through a fitful cloud as it moved, slowly and majestically, across the sky to cast a path of shining gold across the deep, oily swells which sent the raider into a long, slow pitch. As we drew away from her we saw, lying ahead, the loom of an oil tanker silhouetted against the moonlight, a line of foam indicating the course of a pipe-line through which the precious fuel was being pumped. The scene was stupendous; the two enemy ships, secretly oiling in one of the least frequented parts of the ocean, sometimes standing well up on the swells, sometimes one or both of them being invisible as we fell into the hollows. The light paint of the *Stier* was catching the moonlight a little while the tanker (although light ship) looked low, gaunt and dark in comparison with only splashes of whiteness where the swells spilt over her well-decks to break into glistening foam. The sky directly overhead was clear but a patch of cloud, caught by the moon, marked the peak of the island. Our recent confinement below lent the spectacle all the greater grandeur, but its enjoyment was tempered by our doubts about the nationality of the tanker and our fear that she might prove to be Japanese, the very thought of which was sheer anathema to us.

All too soon we were alongside, riding up over her rails as we lifted to the long swells sweeping up from the storms of the Southern Ocean; dropping down again until we almost looked to see her bilges in the

---

* Nicholaides, the managing owner of the *Dalhousie*, had collier interests in South Africa and, knowing nothing of the disbursements and troubles surrounding her last voyage, offered Davies a shore job out there, but Mrs. Davies preferred to remain in Morfa Nevin. Miss Seppings, the company's charming secretary, used to stay with them regularly for some years. Davies died in 1966 and his wife about 14 years later.

Stygian gloom of the troughs. Men jumped as the boat started to fall: the wireless operators at various odd moments, but they came to no harm and seemed to bear a charmed life. We came over in two boat-loads but, even when on board, in the shadow of the centre-castle, we could not immediately identify the nationality of her crew, though soon found ourselves being marshalled forward to the foc's'le head.

As we emerged on to the fore-deck we saw, in the silvered moonlight, that our escort was in the uniform of the German Navy, but any sighs of relief which we might have contemplated on this account were quickly stifled when we entered the space under the foc's'le head.

Most tankers have a hatch right forward, giving entry to the one hold in the ship of tanks, and this one was no exception. There was very little light and this in itself made the scene the more *macabre*. All around the hatch, on the main-deck level where we stood, were human bodies. Some were sitting, some lying; a few were white, but most were yellow or brown. Some had had amputations: others appeared to be dying. A Chinaman's face seldom registers hope, but we did not see any in the lascar faces nor yet in those of the white men. There seemed to be little order in the *tableau* save only that there was one narrow passage on each side of the hatch, which was fenced around its edges. Certainly there was no comfort here: only depression in its uttermost.

We approached the hatch and looked down. Officers were berthed in the 'tween deck, the men in the lower hold. The lower hold appeared to be full to over-crowded already. Pallets were spread all over the bottom of it, which, at first glance, seemed to be, literally, a squirming mass of humanity — much of it ill-clad. In the 'tween decks were brown hammocks slung and a few men, not yet turned in and being aware that something out of the normal routine was afoot, peered up out of the gloom. The 'tween decks did not look quite so bad but the whole scene, exaggerated as it was by the meagre lighting, filled us with a sense of utter desolation. The memory of the splendour of the moon-light on the heaving swells; the fresh salt tang of the sea-breeze and the sight of the silent ships fuelling amidst the deep unrest of the dark oceans all seemed far away in a distant past, swiftly superseded by a hideous present.

We managed to find spaces to sling the hammocks with which we had been provided and turned in with heavy hearts. It was late and most men were already asleep. All the same, it seemed that we were the best clothed and shod, and that was our good fortune. Some of my neighbours looked to be peculiar customers and, although events proved that their looks did them scant justice, I kept my clothes in my hammock that night and viewed the future with deep distrust as I watched the long shadows swing across the square of the hatch. Certainly the path of my destiny had taken an unfortunate turn and, whether or not it had stemmed from attempting to balance my front stud on my tongue so many years previously, I was in no mood to assert myself in that or any other manner!

〜〜〜〜

VII

THE *CHARLOTTE SCHLIEMANN*

The light of the next morning softened the prospect a little, although it was bad enough in all conscience. Hammocks were slung all around in varying directions at different heights. They covered the entire area of the 'tween-deck except for a small space on the after end of the starboard side, where there were a few tables and benches for meals. There was no other furniture of any sort. The normal vertical ladder led up to the main-deck and down to the lower hold and, next to it, was an additional wooden one, enabling two men to ascend or descend at the same time. On a bench on the main-deck at the head of the ladder, with their backs to a bulkhead, sat two guards, armed with revolvers and with hand grenades stuck in their belts.

There were lavatories out on the fore-deck at the break of the foc's'le head, and we could wash in cold water on the open fore-deck. At meal times food was passed down in buckets slung on ropes by a detail who went aft to the galley under guard. Contrary to statements purporting to have come from survivors of the trip which have already been published, the food was extremely good, albeit somewhat short in quantity on occasions. Breakfast was sometimes *paté de foie gras* with black bread and *ersatz* coffee: dinner was usually wholesome and filling and there was generally plenty of it, but breakfast and tea were strictly rationed, and it was necessary to eat one's fill at dinner.

We were the only ship's company which was present in force. Apart from a few men from the American tanker *Stanvac Calcutta* (which had fought the *Stier* very gallantly soon after she had started raiding) who, badly injured, had been retained in the raider's hospital so long that they had become separated from their shipmates, all our other fellow prisoners had come from vessels which had been sunk by the *Michel*. We, from the *Dalhousie*, certainly could not complain about the behaviour of the *Stier*. She had appeared on the horizon and fired a shot across our bows. If we had chosen to run and to bring ourselves under her superior fire-power, that was hardly her affair. She had taken us aboard and treated us reasonably enough and, in a state of hostilities, she had acted well within all the accepted rules of war.

Captain Helmuth von Ruckteschell, in the *Michel*, had acted very differently, subsequently being arraigned before a War Crimes tribunal to be sentenced to a period of imprisonment. His technique was to steal up on a ship, either in a squall or in the darkness of night, and then to rake her without warning with his heavy armament whilst, at the same time, sweeping her decks with machine guns at almost point-blank range. If men were left to drown or die in the water, that was not his concern. We had a man named Goodridge aboard, who had been the chief engineer of the *Arabistan*, a coal-burner which had been wantonly attacked at night and sunk. A motor torpedo-boat appeared at the scene of the sinking, using a search-light. This picked him up on a raft and, seeing his uniform, a German officer called out:- *"Are you the captain?" "No"* he replied, *"but will you pick up this badly wounded man who is with me?" "You'll do"* was the response and, despite his pleas, he was taken aboard and the badly wounded man on the raft was left, with all the others, to die amidst the sea. There was a little Arab who may have come from that ship but, if so, he was the only other one.

There were some Norwegians aboard, who kept themselves in a tight little clique; a couple of American ships' survivors and various others from a variety of British vessels. The biggest contingent came from the old Union Castle liner *Gloucester Castle* which had been attacked at night without warning, her decks being machine-gunned unmercifully at point-blank range. Of her deck officers, only Pargiter, her senior second, survived. She had had passengers, mainly women and children, but of these only four were picked up, one being a little boy with smashed legs. There was the master of the British tanker *Patella*, Capt. Barber, who had himself been wounded when his ship was sunk and had been separated from all his crew save only three who were badly injured. There were men with amputated legs, men with ghastly scars and men with hands and fingers smashed and twisted almost out of recognition. A few of the ships had fought back, but none had had the luck of the *Stephen Hopkins* which held the inestimable advantage over all the victims of the *Michel*, in that her raider did not hold the ace card of surprise in her hand.

Some men had had to jump into the sea as they stood. Leslie Broomfield, the third Engineer of the *Gloucester Castle*, who was having a bath at the time of the attack, was picked up naked and was now clad only in a suit made out of German canvas. Many were pitifully clothed. Worst of all was the number of men who were not there at all.

The day after we came aboard the ship got under way. She was, we learned, the *Charlotte Schliemann*, formerly the Norwegian *Sir Karl Knudsen*, and it was said that she was bound for Batavia where we should be landed and installed in a German prisoner-of-war camp under German auspices: the buildings, which had been pre-fabricated, having already been sent out from Germany. At all events, this was the story which the Germans had initiated before we came aboard. The meeting with the *Stier* was the last in a series of rendez-vous which she had made with the raiders; her surplus fuel oil was finished and it was evident that there was nothing to detain her.

Exercise was allowed on the fore-deck during daylight hours but, like all tankers, this consisted of a mass of pipes and valves. Two ladders leading from the fore-deck to the centre-castle had been removed and the gaps railed in, whilst only one ladder, amidships, connected with the foc's'le head. A flying bridge connected the foc's'le head to the centre-castle and there was a guard at each end of it.

Before long it became evident that we were dipping down into the West Winds, probably to steer a great circle course to avoid meeting any other shipping. The weather soon became very chilly indeed and some men became undeniably cold. The Germans did what they could, providing straw for the men in the lower hold to supplement their bedding, and issuing a tot of rum all round on the coldest nights. I doubt if the *Charlotte Schliemann* was ever intended to act as a prison ship but, here again, the Germans made the bad conditions as tolerable as they could be in any tanker deep down in the Southern Ocean. The hatch covers, a few of which had previously been removed by day to provide light down below, were now perpetually in place and battened down owing to the worsening weather, and the lower hold, in particular, became very gloomy.

There were very few navigating officers amongst the prisoners. There were Llewellyn, myself and Brown from the *Dalhousie*, Pargiter, Capt Christiansen from the Norwegian tanker *Aramis*, with Hansen, his first mate, Leif Reistad who had been second and Willi Berg who had been third mate but spoke no English. There was Capt. Barber (who had been appointed 'leader' and spokesman for us), Knudsen, a chief mate and also the third mate of one of the American tankers. Few men had ever been in those latitudes before. Besides myself, only the American third mate had been in deep-water sail, and that mainly in the fair weather San Francisco-Honolulu sugar trade, while Reistad had spent six months cruising in summer time in a small training ship, the *Sorlandet*, with so many boys as crew that they were almost falling over each other. I was the only one who had been down there in big sailing ships running down their easting.

Many men, both in the 'tween deck and lower hold, had started complaining bitterly. It was, they felt, impossible to be under worse conditions; they were cold, ill-clad, short of food and the weather was, they thought, appalling. I had little faith in the pre-fabricated camp in Java which the Germans had apparently stated was our destination, as it seemed to me that their country had more important things to think about than sending pre-fabricated camps around the world in time of war, especially to areas of the cheapest labour. Consequently I warned these complainants that this might prove to be nothing and that their position would probably prove to be a good deal worse after they had left the ship and that, in any case, sea conditions could be infinitely worse than those they were undergoing. Many of them, I know, regarded me cynically and unbelievingly when I told them that I used to come down here from choice when we were not only cold, but perpetually wet as, when loaded, our decks on which we worked were often a maelstrom of several hundred tons of ice-cold water: that we spent hours aloft fighting threshing, storm-filled canvas which tore our finger nails on hands suppurating from salt-water cuts; that we were exposed to the snow, ice and sleet, and that all the while we were working really hard, often after whole watches below had been lost: often weary after losing endless sleep and with eyes held open, as it seemed, only by their encrusting of salt spray. It was true that it was a voluntary effort, whereas this, infinitely less uncomfortable, was involuntary. They were dry: they had all night in: they were neither aloft nor getting wet, and their food was better than in a sailing ship. I was not thanked for these strictures, but their attitudes showed how far awry was their sense of proportion. Perhaps I was lucky, in that the sailing ships had taught me a sense of perspective at sea. Their experiences at sea had been too easy.

Sometimes I walked on the deck with Capt. Barber, sometimes with Pargiter and often with Capt. Christiansen. They were all men who shared with me a sheer exultation in the west winds; in the glorious, long sweep of the grey seas of the Southern Ocean: the grace and grandeur of the wheeling flight of the wandering albatross overhead and in the constant delight of the hordes of pintado and small petrel which swooped and dived on the quarters. The very splendour of the clean and blue sky, spattered with rolling cumuli, served to lighten our load as, although in ballast, the odd swell ran over the foredeck to be smashed into cascades of foam, glistening in the sunlight, while we jumped clear on to the tank tops. There were, too, grey days of storm and heavy, sweeping sprays and seas when exercise was impossible, but these were the minority, and they, too, provided a scene of sheer inspiration. I had always regarded the seas of the Roaring Forties to be amongst the most moving sights in the world, whether in sail or steam, and their illusion of majesty was so strong that they lost little through being seen under our

27. The CHARLOTTE SCHLIEMANN as the Norwegian SIR KARL KNUDSEN in her peace time colours.

dreary circumstances. They are immutable, for all time, in their splendid grandeur. There is nothing mean or sordid about them, for they possess a virility of purpose which is unique amongst all the seas of the world.

As we steamed into these desolate waters, our minds became much exercised with all matters concerning an escape from our present and future lot, and a return to a more certain mastery of our fates. It was clear that our only hope lay in capturing the ship fairly soon and making for either Fremantle, in Western Australia, or for some South African port. Such an operation would need to be carried out before we hauled up out of the Westerlies to approach an Axis sphere of influence. Several times we were were ordered to write letters, as a meeting was said to be expected with a blockade-runner bound home from the Far East for Europe, but each time it proved that we missed the other ship if, indeed, she was ever there to miss. The act of letter-writing certainly did give a general boost to morale, but it also achieved what was probably its planned effect, namely: to postpone or to weaken confidence in any escape scheme which might be brewing. It was already apparent that the prisoners' worst enemies were certain of their own fellows, some of whom, whether 'fellow travellers' or not, had certainly made themselves altogether too friendly and confidential with some of the guards.

Partly because of this, and partly because of the leakage of information which is inevitable when a secret is shared by too many, especially in a confined space, it had become plain that any attempt to take the ship must be confined to a small body of trustworthy persons, possessed of a certain resolution of spirit and tenacity of purpose and of a requisite physical fitness. It was plain to all those involved that, once seized, the ship must be navigated. Being large and fit, and also a navigating officer, I was constantly embroiled in such schemes. Navigating officers were in short supply despite the names I have listed. Capt. Barber made it plain that he did not want to have anything to do with capturing the ship. Llewellyn was not considered, both on account of age and his slow reactions, nor was Brown, who was considered to be too nervous and of insuffient physique. The three Norwegian mates were placed in the same category and, in any case, their English was very poor. The American mate was a possible candidate but seemed to be unwilling to co-operate with the British. Maynard, the third mate of the same ship, was in bad odour with his fellows, as I shall relate.

Moreover, as the Norwegians had formed their own clique, so had the Americans. Despite efforts to break down these barriers, they were not successful, and the prisoners lacked that homogeneity and common purpose which would have been desirable. Thus, there were only three navigators involved: Capt. Christiansen, Pargiter and myself. It was astonishing how many men, on being approached, did not want to involve themselves. Every band of plotters was faced with the problem of what to do with their non-participating colleagues if they should prove successful, because no-one was under any illusions that they would promptly demand better conditions for themselves. The problem of where to confine the Germans was bad enough — we thought the centre-castle on balance, though it might have come down to a tank or two — but, although the other Allied prisoners would have to remain where they were, at all events for purposes of sleeping, there is no doubt that they would have been an embarrassment.

Few of us subscribed at the time to the theories of Craggs, the stocky, fire-breathing Tyneside second engineer of the *Dalhousie*, who took the view that we should not only keep the others where they were, but post guards over them and allow them no exercise. He felt that their gratitude to him and his fellows in any cutting out party would be more than enough to compensate for the additional discomfort which he would impose on them, partly in order to avoid any trouble from them and partly because, as he argued from the particular to the general, some of them had been too pusillanimous to accept the invitation to join the attempt to take the ship and, therefore, deserved no fruits of its success!

My own opinion was that, whatever the correct solution to this particular aspect of the problem, it was one which could wait and that the first essential was to take the ship. Any attempt would need to be made at night when the guard was relieved. There were four men in each guard roster, two of whom sat on the bench at the head of the hold ladders, as previously mentioned, and, after dark, one was at the entrance to the foc's'le head on the port side (the starboard entrance was sealed up) and the fourth was at the junction of the flying bridge and the centre-castle. On the master's deck, below the bridge, a machine gun was trained on the fore-deck, but whether it was a dummy or not we did not know and we had no means of finding out. It was known that the four-inch gun on the after end of the boat deck was a wooden dummy, but we had no idea what other precautions, if any, the Germans had prepared for such an eventuality as a break-out, once we had crossed the fore-deck.

Certainly we saw nothing to give rise to any suspicion of possible traps by day. The men who went aft to fetch the food saw nothing, nor did those who went to the second mate for medical attention in the mornings in a cabin on the after end of the midship deck. When I heard his name — Karl-Heinz Sperling — I invented an ailment and went along last of all because he, too, had been in the Finnish sailing ships running out to Australia before the war and, although we had not met, we knew each other's names and had common friends of diverse nationalities. He, I think, found the *Charlotte Schliemann* quite as loathsome as we did, and we talked long of the windjammers. He had been second mate in the 4-masted barque *Kommodore Johnsen* in the Baltic at the beginning of the war and wished that he was still there instead of in this slum of a ship. I did not go to him again for some time, as I had seen all that I thought that I should be likely to see, but had learnt nothing useful to an escape.

All the plotting parties in which I was involved were certain of one thing. Once we had overpowered the three guards under the foc's'le head, preferably during a dark night in poor weather and with no moon, three men would change into their uniforms and await the arrival of their reliefs, who would also be overpowered, all unsuspecting, in the comparative privacy of the main deck area under the foc's'le head. These three men would then march aft along the catwalk in the guise of the guard going off watch. When challenged by the guard on the centre-castle we should throw him overboard quickly, as being quieter and quicker than trying to subdue him in the open. As soon as this was done the bridge, radio room and machine gun below it were to be taken, together with the captain. We should have the revolvers and hand grenades taken from the six guards. Other men, then safe to come along the catwalk, would join in the taking of the rest of the ship and help to wipe up all pockets of resistance. Silence and speed were essential up to this point.

Observation from the lavatories at night had shown that all this part of the plan was quite possible once we had overpowered the first set of guards and, although we thought there might be a state of siege before the poop and engine room were taken, we thought it unlikely on the whole and that, on balance, we should be in better case to take the poop than the German crew there would be to take back the centre-castle.

We did not believe the story which the Germans had circulated to the effect that the bows were dynamited and would be blown up at any attempt at insurrection. If it were true, the loss of the bow would not be so great a loss to a tanker as to an ordinary dry-cargo ship, although it would be an embarrassment to navigation, especially in the big seas of the Westerlies, but the death and carnage to the men in the lower hold, most of whom would not have been privy to any such attempt, would be frightful to contemplate. Nevertheless, the story was highly unlikely, but I did feel very strongly — a feeling which was shared by the majority — that any attempt *must* be successful, particularly at the outset, and that any failure at that stage would undoubtedly result in a few hand grenades being lobbed down on the sleeping men below who were packed together almost like sardines, besides, in all probability, some indiscriminate revolver shooting. This was almost a certainty as one or two of the guards were young hot-heads and, before we had made up the complement, one had, in excitement, thrown a grenade down the hold, though fortunately it failed to explode.

Sperling, the tanker's second mate, did tell me both on arrival and after the war that he was thankful we had not taken the ship and that, as the Germans had no effective means of stopping us other than by bluff, they had been on tenter-hooks all the voyage. I do not believe that they realized that they and their ship had been saved by, literally, six inches of space. The whole problem, and the one which we never did overcome, was how to overpower the two guards at the top of the ladders. They did not always sit there in day time. During their periods of absence I, for one, carried out various experiments relating to the possibility of knocking them out.

It was necessary to knock both unconscious simultaneously and it was manifest, and unanimously agreed, that this must be done from the ladders. Not only was I possibly as fit and powerful as any prisoner, but I was certainly the tallest and possessed of the longest reach, but it was extremely doubtful if I could even reach the jaw of one of the guards, let alone knock him out. The more reasonable members of the various parties of plotters appreciated that this would not do, especially as the other man, whomsoever he might be, would have an even more difficult assignment on size alone. Many of our number, notably our two wireless operators who were soft and lethargic young men, thought it was an easy matter to knock a man out, having seen the act performed so easily, so often and with such aplomb, by many a Hollywood film actor on the cinema screens. Even the tough little engineer, Craggs, although he would have been a tower of strength in any rising on level terms, had to admit that he himself was too small to deal with the ladder problem but, like many others, he did not appreciate that although a man may be knocked out with a modicum of resolution, especially when sitting with a steel bulkhead immediately behind his head, it was not so easy as it seemed. In any case, any attempt to do so from a ladder below the intended victim's own level, whilst holding on with one hand, increased the problem beyond all measure, apart from the fact that, if a connection could be made at all, it would be at the very extent of one's reach and with no residual power to the punch. To knock out one guard under such conditions would have been a miracle: to knock out two simultaneously was beyond all credibility. Only two men were allowed up out of the hold at any one time at night (in order to go to the lavatory) and if, therefore, they were not immediately successful with their first blows, this spearhead of attack would inevitably be thrown back down the ladders and all attempt at escape might as well be given up for ever.

The Norwegian, Capt. Christiansen, was well aware that some of his own compatriots would be of very little use in any such enterprise so, with one or two of them, allied himself with Pargiter, myself, Craggs and one or two others. One of our chief difficulties was to prevent attempts being made by other parties which would be doomed to failure and which would preclude any further attempts being made, as the Germans would then be bound to strengthen their precautions. A few men in the lower hold were privy to what was going on, but only very few. We had little enough privacy, but they had none. On days of no exercise, it was difficult to speak with them, and it was clear that many would not support such an attempt, fearing the consequences of failure. Many were old. They were a mixed lot, including many of the *Gloucester Castle's* catering staff and the stewards and so on from other ships. Some were too friendly with the guards. It was not clear who might be trusted and who not. It was hard enough to know which of our own number to approach, but harder still to assess them. For instance, before we met the *Stier*, I would have recommended my gun-layer who had given every indication of being a first-class man. His craven conduct under fire will have been noted. If being a prisoner had no other advantage, it did demonstrate how many excellent men decline in crisis or adversity, and how many others, often thought unlikely ones, outshine their fellows in similar circumstances. At this period, such observations had been relatively limited, but the principles were already suspected. (Indeed, who can say which of his friends, in the ultimate extremity, might not resort to cannibalism? History demonstrates that the most unlikely people have done so — people who, in their normal lives, would have been revolted at the very mention of the subject.)

We were unable to procure for ourselves any sort of weapon or life-preserver with which to help with this ladder problem, nor was one party able to secure pepper, wherewith to blind the two guards for a few precious instants of time, in order that they might get clear of the ladders and closer to them. On the main deck level were berthed all the coloured men from the various crews, chiefly lascars and Chinese, together with all the sick and injured. Operations would have to be kept clear of the latter, as a matter of common humanity.

We considered trying to hook the guards and then jerking them back into the lower hold, but this, too, had several disadvantages, both in difficulty of operation, the time lag in securing their uniforms and, above all, probable injury or fatality to the men below, upon whom they would fall from a great height. Day after day we debated the problem, striding over the pipes on deck with the thunder and crash of the seas about us and the whine of the wind above; standing in groups on the 'tween deck, or sitting on our hammocks, continually racking our brains to discover a solution, and all the while the *Charlotte Schliemann* rolled on her way. The ship was held very lightly, almost by a thread, but oh! how strong was that thread!

We no longer knew our position, but were certain that time was getting short and that, if anything was to be done, it had to be done soon. For a time we had lost the albatross and petrels, so I knew that we were south of latitude fifty. Now that they were appearing once more, it was evident that we were starting to come north again. I was held to be something of a Jeremiah, having really been responsible for the abandonment of the double-knockout theory which, although I knew it to be quite impossible (as, indeed, did the more responsible of my colleagues), possibly came ill from one who, in virtue of age, size and physique, might reasonably have been expected to participate in the deed. Actually, the only people who believed in the possibility of the scheme were those who were physically unsuited to attempt it themselves!

The Germans were doing everything that they knew to keep us happy. A sing-song concert was arranged in the lower hold every Saturday evening — a completely international event. The officers craned over the rails of the 'tween deck hatchway to watch and the coloured men were, so to speak, in the gallery round the main-deck hatchway. Anybody who could do any sort of turn was encouraged to do so and it was astonishing how much talent there proved to be. The master-of-ceremonies was Leonard Lawes, the head waiter of the *Gloucester Castle*, who hailed from Edgware in Middlesex and who was well-liked. Being possessed of inexhaustible wit and repartee, he was the obvious candidate for the job. Often the German ship's officers would come to watch. Poor wretches! Enemy or no enemy, they were as bored with their condition as we were with ours, since they had been at sea for a very long time, often only giving the engines a daily kick for weeks on end between rendez-vous with the raiders, and they had no stomach for being floating gaolers.

They were all merchant seamen in peace-time and, in my own experience, these had been shown to be very free from the taint of Nazism. The incident of the Germans in the bar in Aruba (p. 39) will be remembered. One of our guards, who was a little younger than myself, had met me before the war when we were both in sail. He told me once that they were all sure that Germany would lose the war, but that she would fight to the last ditch because, as I must understand, one could still see black men in the Rhineland: offspring of the French colonial troops of occupation after the previous World War. The Germans, he said, could not risk another treaty like Versailles, as extermination was better. So the Goebbels propaganda had sowed itself in those who were not true believers.

Gradually, as time went on and no other solution was found, it became apparent that, if the ship was to be taken, it would only as a result of a massed, surprise attack, in which the centre-castle must be scaled from the fore-deck and the flying bridge rushed, whilst the forward guards must be overpowered simultaneously. Such an operation would certainly involve a casualty list, but that was a calculated risk and we argued, with great truth as subsequent events proved, that the alternative of complete inaction would inevitably lead to a large death roll, as it could not be expected that several years of captivity in the Far East would not take their toll. It was true that the victims of a sudden rush would be most likely to be the younger and more fit members, who would obviously be in the van, whereas the probability was that those who would die in a prison camp would be more likely to be the older and more infirm. It was not as if one could say to any section:- *"Look here! You're probably going to die anyway, so you might just as well die in one way as another. If lucky, you won't die at all, nor be a prisoner."* Much depended on whether or not that machine gun was a real one or a dummy, and also on how much heart the Germans displayed. Certainly the main tide of their own war had not yet turned, although the Russian front was clearly not what had been anticipated, yet some of us felt that the very circumstances of the *Charlotte Schliemann's* voyage had demoralised her men. These things might work in our favour, but we could not count on them.

It was not a satisfactory scheme by any means. Some of us favoured it simply because there seemed to be no alternative and because it offered a sporting chance. However, there were by now so many nationalistic cliques: so many men whom we could not trust, and there were so many older men who were often barely consulted, being unable to lend sufficient weight to the operation, while, regrettably, many of the younger ones objected, clearly seeing themselves as potential sacrifices for the older and more infirm. (This, of course, has been the function of armed forces throughout history but .... merchant sailors are civilians!!) In short, there was so much argument and so much distrust that the scheme could never get off the ground. I often wondered, long afterwards, whether we could have taken the ship. Had it not been for that six inches of space we could not reach from the ladders, while holding on with one hand, I am certain we could have done so easily. It was a strange situation, as the Germans honestly believed that we *could* take the ship while the prisoners were convinced that they *could not*, and it was all the more strange that the prisoners were right as the Germans knew not wherein lay their strength!

As to the mass rush proposal, I certainly favoured it at the time and, in the same circumstances, I believe I would vote for it again. However, with the benefit of hindsight, I am now not so sure. Had the prisoners in that ship subsequently been subject to the rate of mortality common to prisoners in the Far East, then the mass rush would probably have been the lesser evil. In the event, which we could not then foresee, their losses were well below the average in Japan itself. I cannot speak for those who remained in Singapore. The rights and wrongs of the matter are now past history. Some of us thought our fellows over-pusillanimous at the time and, doubtless, they regarded us as being potential dangers to their own safety. The issue tended to create two camps, each mistrusting the other. This was a bad thing.

So we rolled on and on. It was cold and, in the lower hold, uncomfortable as the accumulated sweat off the cold deckheads and shell-plating swished about the deck. A man could not sub-consciously brace himself in a hammock as he could in a bunk when the ship rolled, and we were grossly overcrowded. Most men used to turn out to wash on the fore-deck in the mornings, though it was a chilly enough undertaking, and there were days when the weather was too bad for such ablutions. Capt. Barber, who had been the youngest master in one of our foremost shipping companies, Shell-Mex, was a man who made a fetish of physical culture and always stripped right off to take a cold sluice, after which he went through a routine of physical jerks. He had a body like a Greek god and was supremely fit. Obviously a man of drive in his career, it also transpired that he was extremely happily married and madly anxious to see the child which should by then have arrived to grace his home. I looked to him as a potential leader, because it would save complications if a captain were to set himself in authority, and he appeared to be the obvious man. When approached, however, as already noted, he declined any part in such proposals and was quite useless to us in any capacity, although our nominal spokesman, but of his ultimate collapse I shall speak in Chapter Nine.

I suspect that the Norwegians had started the 'clique' system aboard. The Americans had virtually taken possession of one area of the 'tween deck and seldom stirred out of it. The British split up, rather in bands of similar personality and character than of rank. These cliques were by no means indivisible, but they were oppressive and unnecessary, although smaller ones became absolutely essential at a later stage of our existence. One disadvantage was that they led to a spirit of nationalism which was out of place at a time when there should have been a common pooling of ideas and material good-will. There was no ill-feeling, as such, but we were prone to speak of the 'Yanks' or the 'Norwegians' (they seemed to escape the opprobrious term of 'Square-heads', commonly used by seamen) and we were 'Limeys' to the Americans. Strangely enough, very few of them knew why an Englishman was called a 'Limey', as the British sailing ships had long sailed into the mists of time, and with them their custom of issuing lime-juice daily, after the tenth day out, as an anti-scorbutic. So the custom died but the word lived on!

Once again, I found my Swedish adequate to talk with the Norwegians well enough but, with the exception of Capt. Christiansen (who alone spoke excellent English) and Kjöstvedt, the electrician, they always talked very primly and seriously, as though at a formal tea party. I made it my business to talk to everybody, largely to assess each man with a view to the escape plans. The Americans had their own animosities. I suspect that the third mate of (I think) the *Stanvac Calcutta* had no certificate, though an older man. He had ignored the presence of the *Stier* when first sighted, enabling her to enter a rain squall and come close up on his ship to open fire at point-blank range. Because her captain and radio officer were killed by the first salvo, there had been no 'QQQ-QQQ-QQQ' signal sent out. She fought back gallantly, being hit forty times, and, even if he could forget the men who were lost, he had constantly before him the frightful injuries of some of his shipmates. Nor, at the outset, did his fellow officers spare his feelings on this score. The British, if a hotch-potch of nationalities by descent down the centuries, were relatively homogeneous at that time (even if this is no longer the case in their country now torn by racial tensions). I never felt that the Americans, so many of whom were immigrants of relatively recent origin, had entirely divested themselves of the loyalties of their forebears and they did not seem to speak with any common voice.

Llewellyn took his lot philosophically enough. Not only was he lacking in initiative and drive, but was what is normally termed a 'bromide', being excessively dull, while Brown, our third mate, was prone to wring his hands and bemoan our present and future fate. The *Dalhousie's* new chief engineer, Taylor, who was a son-in-law of the previous one whose fibres had been so shattered by the U-boat wolf-pack, was a very pleasant man but, with a physical defect arising, I think, from polio, was obviously a non-starter in an escape. I thus orientated myself towards Pargiter and our alliance with one another was the only one to stand up to all tests and to remain unbroken until the cessation of hostilities even though, as events will prove, it came under great strain towards the end. I believe that Craggs, who paired with our third engineer, Henry, another Tynesider, would also have lasted to the end had they not been forcibly separated during the latter part of the war. The implications of this will become more obvious in due course.

I think that Pargiter and I were thrown together in the first instance, not only by a simple process of elimination amongst the other deck officers, but because we both spoke the same language, had the same sort of background (which was not generally shared) and both came from the south of England (in which we were in a very small minority) and because we shared the same sort of taste in literature and kindred subjects, that placed us in an even smaller minority! Indeed, on such subjects, we had either to talk to each other or to no-one! It is very doubtful if we should have found much common ground in peace-time.

For his part, he was a sociable fellow, enjoying liner life, besides the procession of gins and the passing pageant of passengers and small talk: the dancing, the games and, in fact, all that side of life which I had come to regard as wholly artificial. He had, perhaps, an unfortunate manner, being prone to look down his nose superciliously, particularly at his inferiors, when speaking, and this was enhanced by his very manner of speech. He was not popular with everyone on that account, being distinctly unpopular with the lower deck, but he nevertheless had many qualities, as time was to show. I, on the other hand, regarded passengers with sheer loathing (however nice the same people might be ashore!), and disliked the whole life of a passenger liner which was the very antithesis of my own love, the deep-sea sailing ships of which I have already written sufficient for readers to appreciate that their life offered diametrically different rewards to the passenger liners.

However, we were neither in a liner nor in a windjammer, but in that tanker, and thereafter we had more in common with each other than either had with anyone else around us, and we both had sufficient sense to realize it. One might suppose that, in all those days, following in long succession, we might have come near to boredom and found little to speak about but, although it may have been true of some men — and we had no books or other recreation — it was certainly never true of Pargiter and myself. For so long as we were down in the realms of the wandering albatross and after we had turned north into the South-east trade, and until the chances of escape, if they had ever existed, had slipped behind us, we were hard pressed to make the days long enough, discussing and debating all possible means of capturing the tanker and all the implications of such an enterprise: sounding other men, convening small conferences, experimenting and observing the conduct and habits of the guards.

Then, as the end of the voyage approached, we discussed the various methods which we must employ in any eventuality which might arise in a study of what we came to term 'Good Gefangenism'. (*Gefangen* is the German word for 'prisoner').

Because it had already become evident that there was a pronounced tendency, growing almost daily, for each clique to act for itself rather than for the common good, we decided which were the essential prerequisites to any sort of tolerability in any camp ashore, and determined that we should either possess or control these things. The most important aspect, in our estimation, was fresh air, and we were resolved that we must, at all costs, be near to, or able to control, windows in either trains or camps, and that we should never allow ourselves to be parted, even if we had to separate occasionally for our mutual benefit. We decided what we must do: what we must avoid; what precautions we must take, and when initiative would be the most necessary in every situation which we could conceive. There might be occasions when we *must* stick together like limpets, and others when it would be provident to separate temporarily. All this, and more, virtually amounted to a compendium of *gefangen* practice, if not set on paper. It was, for instance, plain to us that, when entering a barrack, there would be no time to stand and ponder which were the best beds or bunks. We must know before we ever entered it, or even set eyes on it, and for this reason considered every permutation of shape and layout that we could envisage. In the event, although we followed our precepts to the letter and did all that we intended, we did so in a set of conditions which we had never imagined for a single instant! Nevertheless, the principles which we had enunciated held good. We became quite dizzy in all these discussions and once, when considering a hypothetical train journey through Java, we found ourselves in the absurd situation of deciding who should carry our gear and who should get the tickets!

As the *Charlotte Schliemann* hauled out of the southern latitudes to run almost due north towards Sunda Strait, conditions below became more tolerable, but this was only a momentary relief because, despite the hatch being now opened up and in spite of a big wind-sail rigged down it from the fore-stay, the atmosphere soon became intolerably hot. In this case the 'tween deck was probably the worst area, as the unpleasant odour of sweating flesh was all around us and also came wafting upwards from the lower hold.

One day the guard who had been in sail brought along one of the seaman to show me a model which he had made of the *Killoran*, one of the Finnish barques. The man had been serving under von Ruckteschell when he sank her in the raider *Widder*. The barque had been caught in the South Atlantic under all sail, bound from Buenos Aires towards Las Palmas with a cargo of grain and sugar — a veritable ghost from the past. There was no ceremony about the *Widder*: the barque was sunk and the ghost was laid for ever. I suppose it was not a bad model, such as it was, and the German meant well enough in bringing his friend along to show it to me, knowing that I had more than a passing interest in such vessels.

Perhaps he did not appreciate how well I had known that *Killoran*, how I had trodden her decks in the Thames: the first of a long succession of square-rigged ships and how she was therefore the more firmly engraved in my memory; how I had seen her moored peacefully to the pine trees in her home port in the Åland Islands; how I had watched her swaying her stately way down Channel and shifting into her anchorage in South Australia to load grain for the Cape Horn passage. He could not know how the very mention of her name took me down again to the stormy seas of the Southern Ocean, which we had just left, to a memory of the whole glory of arching canvas and towering masts as the ship crashed through a glitter of flying spray and a smother of frothing foam. Proud memories of the splendid days in sail welled up within me and turned to bitterness, for this lad had not made the model of this ship I had known because he loved or admired her but because he, in his small way, had assisted in her destruction, sending her to the bottom of the sea. I never spoke at all, but just turned away.

Afterwards I felt a boor because, war or no war, the events of the day had reached far beyond these two German boys. They were both merchant seamen, under no illusions about Nazism and, we had learnt, were on one side of what represented a clear dividing line amongst the tanker's crew, most of whom shared their views and corresponded, roughly, to British R.N.R. men, whilst the others, who might be equated to the R.N.V.R, had never previously been out of Germany in their lives and had therefore had no opportunity of judging the fallacies of their doctrines for themselves. It was these who so irritated their ship-mates almost beyond endurance by their perpetual repetition of Goebbels' cant.

As we proceeded, the Germans produced a new hatch tarpaulin which was spread over the hatch by night and kept in readiness to be hauled in place by day. It was painted with the Union Jack and we took some encouragement from this because it was a great mistake: no British ship being marked in this manner, and we knew that the vessel would be suspect at once if she were to be sighted by any Allied aircraft. Men spoke glibly about the ships, usually capital ships, which they hoped might rescue us. The general optimism on this score was such, and the faith in the British navy so great, that the majority began to believe that we must inevitably be intercepted: the only doubt lying in whether we should be wiped out in any such operation. Indeed, some men had declined to consider any attempt to take the tanker for this reason. I had thought, throughout, that the chance of interception was extremely remote, since the *Charlotte Schliemann* was only a very small fish in the world's seas so far as the Navy were concerned at that time and, should such a ship appear, it would be by luck rather than good judgement. In the unlikely event of meeting a British or Australian warship, I thought it almost certain that the Germans would surrender at once, since they had neither the armament nor the requisite speed to escape. Predictably, we saw nothing and, in due course, raised the smoking head of Krakatoa, the volcano which dominates the way through Sunda Strait.

As we came up to Achin Head at the northern tip of Java, a small land bird fluttered over us, terrified, as it evaded successive swoops by a pursuing hawk. The sun was very low in the western sky, turning the green Javanese jungle to a near gold as it dipped towards the horizon and Krakatoa loomed dark and bare against the western sea-line. As all the prisoners crowded on deck to watch this uneven contest they came, for once, into one accord with the Germans, whether on guard or on the bridge, and with the two lady passengers and the two boys from the Castle liner as they stood on the master's deck. One and all, we had hardened our hearts against the predatory hawk and gave our entire sympathies to the little bird. Once or twice it alighted under a portion of the rigging and, in the extremity of its fear for its pursuer, seemed to have little or no fear of humans, although no-one could catch it. Several times it flew up and was blown down to leeward, clear of the ship, when we feared that it was lost, but invariably it managed to elude its hunter and to regain the comparative sanctuary of the vessel, although each time its strength was obviously a little less and it was tiring quickly.

Loudly and vociferously the prisoners urged that the hawk be shot, pointing at the machine gun. The German officers appeared to be a little strained by the situation, but they did nothing. Then night fell with that startling suddenness so common in the Tropics, before the drama had played itself out. As we paced the decks — for the previous ruling that we must be below before dark had been relaxed in the face of the insufferable heat — we posed the question:- *"Was the machine-gun a dummy after all?"* What greater deterrent to the taking of the ship, and what better excuse for demonstrating it, could there have been than firing it, even if we were too close to Axis waters to do so now? Were it a dummy, how easily could we have taken the ship by a concerted rush!

We never did know the truth about that gun, and some of us never ceased to wonder. However, some years after the war was over, I learnt from Sperling, the second mate who was then master of a merchant ship, that it was NOT a dummy!

Even on receipt of that intelligence, I still thought that we should have succeeded, because the gun was not normally manned. It was my view that the first men to scale the centre-castle would have been out of its sights before it could be brought to bear and, the centre-castle guard having been disposed of, it could have been taken from the rear. However, whatever the result, the whole question by then ranked as a problematical 'might have been'.

It was not until we were past Anjer, the departure point of the old tea-clippers, that we learnt that our orders (if, indeed, there had ever been any) had been changed and that we were to go to Singapore. On many, I believe, this news made very little impression, as it seemed to them to be all the same whether we went there or to Batavia, since they could see little advantage in the one place over the other. To those who had steadfastly believed in the pre-fabricated prisoner-of-war camp it was a shattering blow. To those of us who had doubted its existence it marked a significant change, in that the mask of truth was being stripped away. The majority of our fellows, alive only by the grace of God and by no means by the grace of the captain of the *Michel*, had no illusions about the Germans. In von Ruckteschell they had undoubtedly seen one of the worst and they had no thought of condonation or forgiveness. In the light of their experiences, there was no reason why they should have had. I thought back to my pre-war German friends: to the excellent behaviour of the U-boat commander who had sunk the *Cheyenne* and even to the *Stier*, in which we had been treated well enough. Even if this trip in the *Charlotte Schliemann* had been such that the more naïve of our number regarded it as a 'Hell-ship voyage', that was because she was totally unsuited for the carriage of prisoners and not from any lack of effort by the Germans to ameliorate our conditions so far as they were able within the limited means at their disposal, and also because these men's lives had been too sheltered to broaden their sense of perspective. Certainly there had been tales of letters and blockade runners, which were probably mythical but, for men living on such thin ice as these Germans, such minor excesses might surely be excused.

I had already seen some of the horror of the war, both in convoys and air raids ashore, but the fact is that a total war was being fought on both sides and, within my own observation, the Germans had behaved well enough when there had been any opportunity to do so. Those who became what were known as 'war criminals' were surely the exceptions, and many of these were acting under orders. (This was the great

142

weakness of so many of those trials of the vanquished by the victors.) At that time the Germans were of course, as always, the first enemy: the most powerful partner in the Axis conjunction, but in our circumstances we regarded them in a slightly different light because, although they were responsible for our present lot, we regarded them as being infinitely preferable to their partners in crime — the Japanese.

We were heading for realms which were wholly under the control of the yellow men, and no race had ever maintained so strict a colour bar as the Teutons. Any man in the tanker with a suspicion of colour in his blood had been berthed on the main-deck with the Lascars, Arabs and Chinese. Filipinos were joined with them, not without reason, but one man who would have passed for white, yet who had a trace of Filipino ancestry, was made to join them. But now the German prisoner-of-war camp in Batavia had vanished as if a forgotten dream, and our fate loomed ominously in the balance. Surely, we thought, the Germans would never hand us over to the Japanese, if only on principles of colour? Nevertheless the future hung so much the more heavily and uncertainly upon us.

VIII

SAUERKRAUT TO RICE

Early one morning, before the dawn, we were awoken to the long unfamiliar sound of the cable running out and we felt the ship, silent and still, bring up to her anchor. It was many months since the *Charlotte Schliemann* had broken out of Las Palmas to service the raiders and her men had been constantly at sea, without friendly harbours available to them and unremittingly on the qui vive. Whatever our views about coming into port, theirs must have been one of intense relief and expectation.

When we came on deck it was to find the Horsburgh lighthouse, to the south of Singapore, quite close on the starboard beam and bathed in the yellow light of the early sun. We feasted our eyes on the dark green of the tropical vegetation. I knew from past experience of long voyages in sail how greatly this colour affects a man when his ship first makes a landfall after many weeks or months at sea. It is a colour which is never seen in the deep sea in its entirety: there may be the odd emerald flash of breaking water about the bows: there may be some green effect in the sky at times of concurrent sun and squall, and there is seldom any green about the paint-work of a ship. A man is not aware that he has missed it until he sees it again, and then he gazes long, deeply and with a heart almost overflowing with the sheer joy of it, although he knows not why.

Few steamer men were suited to long periods at sea. They had little experience of them in their normal runs: they were temperamentally unfitted for them and, as a rule, were not possessed of that self-sufficiency which is a pre-requisite to such passages. Not many of our men were of the stamp who could make long voyages with equanimity. They were not of the breed from which expeditions are recruited. Few of them had discovered any strength in this sphere and many had discovered their weaknesses although, had they but known it, the *Charlotte Schliemann* was no sort of trial at all. They thought that they had been too cold, too hot, too badly fed, too uncomfortable and too

145

miserable, and they longed to get ashore. Arguments about 'frying pans and fires' had touched them all too lightly and they had judged their conditions purely by their own reactions, which were not born of any true standards of comparison. So they gazed with unutterable longing at that tropic green as the ship hove up again and proceeded towards Singapore.

Some of us took a more jaundiced view of the events of the day. Perhaps we had rather more reserve, perhaps our hopes were not set quite so high, and perhaps we had some premonition of reality. Many of our Chinese lived in Singapore and stood, grouped along the rails, laughing and chattering excitedly, like a crowd of children on an outing. Others, who had never seen the East before, drunk in the beauty and superficial glamour of the scene: there were the junks with their matting sails and three masts raking different ways; the bright sun catching the islands in deep shadows and contrasting with the blue of the water until violent squalls drove across the azure sky with a hiss of torrential rain on the surface of the sea, to send them running for shelter, only to emerge again into that splendid silver light which the sun provides after a squall has passed by.

Others of us found it sad to see all the ships wearing the Japanese ensign, the red ball on a white field, with never a British ship to be seen. Singapore had been captured for nearly a year. The minefields did not appear to have been altered since the days of British sovereignty, but these things meant little to most of the excited rabble on deck. An outside observer might almost have considered that this was a cruise ship coming into port to savour the delights of the shore, so great was the chatter and so happy the demeanour of so many of our fellows.

We brought up close to another German ship: a fine modern freighter which, it was understood, was topping off a cargo loaded in Japan before running home in an attempt to beat the blockade back to Europe. We thought she was probably the *Regensburg*. The Japanese issued strict instructions to the Germans. There was to be no shore leave allowed to anyone except the captain, as it was still not safe ashore and an early curfew was in force, whilst Japanese soldiers were bound to walk the streets in parties of not less than three for their own safety, as elements of the Chinese population were striking terror into their hearts. Not long before, as we learnt subsequently from a Sikh policeman, a party of Chinese had broken into a prisoner-of-war camp, murdered the guards on duty, and departed again. Nor were our Germans to visit or communicate with the other German ship, which seemed to be an oasis in a sea of yellow faces and grinning mouths studded with golden teeth. This last instruction seemed to be wholly unnecessary and uncalled for, but Japanese guards were placed aboard to enforce the regulations and

146

anything else which they should deem to come within their province.

This was our first view of the Japanese soldiery; one private being stationed at each side of the forward end of the centre-castle, where they stood alongside the German guard who made them look all the more ridiculous in contrast. They were squat, small men, clad in a green uniform with a green cap to match. This latter was almost like a schoolboy's except that it had a flat top of considerably less diameter than its base, with built up sides. It had a peak, and the yellow star of the Japanese army on its front. The whole effect was sloppy: a feature which was inherent in both the uniform and the individuals, and few Japanese seemed able to handle a rifle as though it belonged to them. Their faces seemed to verge on the absurd, particularly when an outsize mouth, even for a Japanese, contained more then the average quota of gold fillings whilst, as often as not, the whole was surmounted by an enormous pair of horn-rimmed spectacles.

It is true that these guards took little notice of us, except to fix us with a curious stare at intervals, but it was clear that their relations with the Germans were strained almost to breaking point very quickly. There was no doubt that the latter, who had been so long at sea on so disagreeable a voyage, might have expected something better on arrival at a supposedly allied port and they were extremely disappointed. They did surreptitiously signal the other ship and I am not sure whether the master visited her or not but, apart from a few bags of potatoes which came aboard, there was little to relieve the monotony of the preceding weeks. Even the green vegetation, which had proved such a delight to both captors and captives but a few hours earlier, was already becoming abhorrent, being so near and yet so far.

The Germans obviously hated the Japanese: hated their regulations, their shoddiness, their over-bearing attitude and hated, above all, their very yellowness. All this, and the latter count in particular, was plain enough to the Japanese guards, who received short shrift aboard and who made no secret of their detestation of the Germans who so obviously despised them. It is hard to say which side started these feelings of mutual dislike in Singapore, though it was probably the Japanese, who made the opening gambits which ordered the nature of the play, and subsequent observations in their own country left no doubt that the feeling was inherent in them. The Germans quickly reciprocated their resentment — were *they* not the master race? Even if they did not all subscribe to the Nazi creed, this theory of belonging to the master race was a satisfactory and convenient one which, when added to a traditional feeling of Teutonic superiority to any coloured man, left little margin for doubt in their minds.

The Japanese, on the other hand, were drunk with their triumphs.

Like all upstart races, the wine of victory had gone to their heads and their nationalism, so long restrained, was running riot. They could not realise that the ship of their conquest had neither draft nor stability: that it was merely encrusted with a thin veneer of Western invention and teaching; that they had merely skimmed over the surface of the sea of success, and that neither their character nor their industry, their knowledge nor their philosophy, would serve to keep them afloat. Nevertheless they were, in the mass, an ignorant people who absorbed without question the propaganda which was fed to them and thus, when their editors and radio announcers told them that they were fighting for the Greater East Asia Co-prosperity Sphere (whatever they may have understood by that!); that they must eliminate the 'white blood-suckers', and that the yellow man must sweep back the white men whence he came, they believed it all. How should a nation of coolies question such things? It was not a matter of Axis versus Allies to the Japanese, but of the destruction of the white, or Western, races in the East, and the Germans were no exception.

On the whole, the prospect of Singapore, as seen from the Roads, looked much the same as it had done in peace-time. Traces of the scorched earth policy could be seen, but the prolific vegetation provided a good camouflage for it, and it was not until we went alongside the oil wharves at Pulo Bukham and Pula Sambo later, to gravity-load such little oil as was left in the tanks, that we saw at close quarters any of the damage that had been done. It was at one of these places that we found on guard a Sikh policeman who had transferred his allegiance to the Japanese. He was extremely nervous about speaking to us, and the difficulty was increased by the the fact that very few of the white men could speak Hindustani. Brown, having served in the Anchor Line, was probably the most fluent and was pushed forward, but he was almost as nervous as the policeman! However, we finally got them talking together with adequate safeguards, but we learnt very little of real interest, except about the trouble ashore, as already mentioned. He had anecdotes, this man of little loyalty, about the fall of Singapore. There was, for instance, his tale of how a Ghurka regiment was drawn up on the parade ground and ordered to surrender its *kukris* (knives), the Japanese not realizing that a Ghurka may not draw his *kukri* without drawing blood.

The situation became tense with machine guns being trained on the ranks before it was resolved by each man pricking his own hand. We learnt little of encouragement, but this man could not tell us much, since his world was not much wider than ours.

After several days we were told that all the deck and engine room ratings were to go ashore and that a Japanese officer would be coming to see them in a short time, but that all the officers, catering staff, coloured men and the sick were to be taken on to Japan as German prisoners. It was not only clear that the others were being handed over to the Japanese, but it was also apparent that the selection was based on those who, as a group, might most reasonably be expected to be the most physically fit. Some men blenched at the prospect, though mainly due to that fear of the unknown which attended any prisoner whenever he changed his circumstances — a sensation which is known to many a man who makes a change in the fullness of his freedom. Others, on the contrary, felt that they could not get ashore too quickly. I hope for their sakes (for I have seen few of them since) that their imaginations remained as obtuse for the rest of the war, because only this can have mitigated their lot.

The D.E.M.S. (naval) gunners from the *Dalhousie* were amongst the foremost who wished to go ashore. I had little enough time for the gunlayer who had deserted his gun, but the others seemed to be good enough fellows. I would not willingly have seen any man go ashore to come under the aegis of the Japanese at Singapore, but there was no help for the others. The gunners had not been specifically mentioned as belonging to either group and I had to talk long and hard to them to prevent them from lining up with the rest. Even if we all became prisoners of the Japanese in Japan, I argued, that at least would not be almost on the Equator, and conditions could hardly be worse than I imagined them to be ashore. Nor did I know the whole truth then: the tragedy of the Burma Road, where our bos'n and so many others died. Perhaps many of the men who lined up that day perished in that endeavour. I do not know, though I learnt after the war that some of our sailors were drafted to the Japanese Navy and spent most of their captivity clearing the wrecks in the harbour and approaches which, taken all in all, was a relatively good job.

At all events, the gunners agreed to stay with rather bad grace, giving the impression that they only did so as a favour to myself! It was sometimes convenient for a D.E.M.S. gunner to be classified as a deck-hand and I knew that this was not such an occasion. They stayed, and they were not questioned. What would have been their fate had they gone ashore with the rest, no-one can say, but the fact remains that, when the war was over, they were all still alive and in relatively good shape.

In due course, a Japanese officer arrived and came down on the fore-deck with several soldiers and a few of the Germans. He spoke reasonable English in a high falsetto and, looking like a character from a comic opera, told the proscribed men that they were to go ashore where they would work and that, so long as they worked well, they would be treated well. I think that there were one or two specious and unlikely promises, but it was hard for the rest of us, who had been segregated on to the other side of the deck, to hear exactly what was said and, when he had finished, the men were marshalled straight over the side into a waiting barge. We waved them "Good-bye" with sorrow as they were towed into the land. There was something final about their departure: final, perhaps, for them, and of a nature which opened up a whole field of utter insecurity for those of us who remained aboard.

We had only been in Singapore for five days when we sailed on a lovely blue afternoon on what was, we felt, to be the last lap of our journey — we knew not whither. Certainly the ship was bound towards Yokohama, but it did not follow that this was to be our ultimate destination. As we passed the Raffles light, a string of Japanese merchantmen passed up the channel in convoy, whilst we went on our way alone, almost as though the ship was an outcast. Indeed, I suspect that, to the Japanese, she was no less, for they sent her on her way, towards the China Sea, without escort or convoy. There was a rumour that we were to put into Borneo, but it came to nothing. There were those who hoped that the ship would be torpedoed, but the idea that any submarine would be able to pick up so many people was ludicrous and such a thing would have done us more harm than good.

Peacefully and very slowly (for the ship's bottom was by now very foul), we passed on our way until, having only seen two fast Japanese merchantmen far away on the horizon since we made our departure, we came on deck before breakfast one morning to see one of the more memorable of the world's landfalls fine away on the bow. There was a clear blue sky, light on the horizon where it was slightly hazy, but becoming a clearer and deeper blue as it approached the zenith. There was little swell and a slight sea, with the tanker pitching very slowly. The rising sun was still very low on the eastern horizon and everything promised a day of sheer glory. There, apparently unconnected with the sea or with the still invisible land over the horizon, the classic, snow-capped peak of Fujiyama stood, as it seemed, suspended in the sky, tinged with pink on a back-cloth of blue. The effect was so surprising that we at first believed it to be a mirage, but then appreciated that the sun reflecting on the snow threw it into relief before the rest of the mountain was visible to the eye. Veritably we were seeing the Land of the Rising Sun and it was a lovely sight, however little we may have wanted to see it. As we steamed on, we could gradually make out the symmetrical sides of the mountain stretching, as it seemed, down to the sea and then, almost imperceptibly, the coast lands rose into view whilst the summit of Mount Fuji turned an immaculate white in the autumn sky.

Passing through the narrows and into Tokyo Bay, we soon shut out the broad Pacific and were encompassed by the land of Japan. Fair and green it was to look upon, scintillating in the sun as the *Charlotte Schliemann* swung round to bring a signal station on the starboard beam almost astern and the sacred mountain fine on the starboard bow, whilst we saw two four-masted barques — two of the four Japanese school-ships which were restricted to sheltered waters by the war — performing manoeuvres on the other bow. They, too, were fair to behold as they gleamed in all the height of their faerie whiteness all the way from their lofty trucks to their waterlines: their hulls painted white and their square sails in full sunlight with the odd shadows on the fore-and-aft canvas accentuating the beauty of the effect. As I watched, one luffed up into the wind and went away on the other tack, in full shadow now, as smartly as anyone could wish. Sailing a big four-master in the placid waters of Tokyo Bay seemed rather like yachting on London's Serpentine, but the sight of any square-rigger was rare enough in all conscience and the mass of swelling canvas, arching from its cordage, sent my memory far away to other days in other seas.

I gazed with a bitter nostalgia until they were shut out from my view astern, whereupon I joined my fellows who were gazing ahead at Yokohama with, in the foreground, quite a bustle of shipping inside the breakwaters. In a matter of minutes our tanker had passed inside, and she was soon anchored with the other vessels there, most of which sported an imitation, dummy gun right aft, like the *Charlotte Schliemann*.

We lay there in the sun, peacefully enough, now much closer to the mountain which seemed to exercise so great a spell over everybody and everything within its environment. The school-ships still tacked up and down, sometimes shining in the sunlight, sometimes in silhouette in the shadow: sometimes clewing up the odd sail or two and then re-setting them as they exercised in their drill. I could only see their hulls over the breakwater very occasionally, but this was small loss because, like most school-ships, their decks were too cluttered with deck erections and their hulls too pierced with ports to match the merchantmen. Nevertheless, the sight was as nectar to me, and to me alone, as I watched them for most of the days until they both suddenly clewed up all sail at once, demonstrating their huge crews, and swung to their anchors with yards bare.

We were still faced with the ever-present problem of what was going to happen to us because, whatever it was to be, it was clear that we could not remain much longer in the tanker. However, we were not long left in doubt, so far as the immediate future was concerned. I was again ensconced, watching the school-ships, when it was announced that we were to leave the ship and, before long, a craft which we took for a cattle barge came alongside (though we subsequently realized it was not when we had had more experience of Japanese barges!) All those left in the lower hold, including my gunners, a large catering force from the *Gloucester Castle* and various others, together with the coloured men and the sick, were taken off and towed away into a basin which lay behind various other anchored ships, so we soon lost sight of them.

The barge was soon back and it was our turn. Although the life we had led in that tanker which had been our prison had not been such as to engender any pride in person, no-one had yet thrown their previous standards to the winds, and we all felt that our progress off Yokohama, herded like cattle into a wooden barge, was extremely *infra dignitate*. The short trip was not without interest because, as we passed into the basin, we saw that we were about to pass a vessel wearing the Swastika ensign and this, we knew, was the raider *Thor*, which had possibly earned herself more fame than any of the other surface raiders.

Although little more than three thousand tons, this little vessel, another erstwhile banana ship like the *Steir* and the famous *Wolf* and *Moewe* of the previous war, had traded under the name of *Santa Cruz* in peace-time, and was one of the only two of the German raiders to make two cruises during Hitler's war. In spite of being so small a ship, she was obviously well commanded and built of stern material, because it was she who had not only sunk one British armed merchant cruiser, the *Voltaire*, in fair combat but had, on separate occasions, fought two others, the *Alcantara* and *Carnarvon Castle*, until they had abandoned their actions, while she remained at sea.

She looked smart enough, very light in her paint-work and with a black funnel sporting two white bands, but we had little enough time to observe her as we were fast passing up the basin to go alongside the ship astern of her which we quickly recognized as the old P. & O. liner *Nankin* which had been transferred to the Australian ensign, under which she had been sailing when she had been captured and brought into Yokohama by the *Thor* as a prize of war. The Germans had renamed her *Leuthen*, but to us she was always the *Nankin*.

This was the first occasion on which Pargiter and I had the opportunity of putting our theories of 'good gefangenism' to the test. We had had to be prepared for all eventualities, from being thrust into some enormous barrack room in which each man must fend for himself, to being put into cubicles or cabins of from one person upwards. It was obvious to us that, if life was to be in any way tolerable, we must exercise some sort of control over the choice of our immediate companions for what promised to be a long sojourn in any accommodation where we berthed in any number over two. This called for the exercise of a certain tact and diplomacy. It was difficult to approach a man and say, in

152

effect:- *"Look here, we two intend to berth together, but if there is a berth for three we would like you to join in with us. If not, you can fend for yourself."* It was so much the harder to say to another:- *"Pargiter and I intend to team up together and, if there should be three berths, we have asked so-and-so to join us, but if there should be four berths, we would like you to join us too."* One could hardly add:- *"If not, you can make what arrangements you like, after it is clear that we shall not want you!"*

Naturally, any such approach could be tempered to some degree, but the situation would be clear enough. Alternatively, it was, we felt, intolerable to do nothing and to leave them to make their own arrangements to such a degree that they would not wish to join with us, even if it were possible, or to find two persons whom we regarded as undesirable joining us. It must be said that we had already formed a very strong impression that we did not wish to be in too close contact with certain of our fellows if it could possibly be avoided!

We had found that few of our companions were exercising much initiative about determining their own conditions. I think that, by now, most regarded their lives as being completely predestined, and thus immutable, as they made no effort to turn its course or to soften its impact. We both determined, therefore, to be quite ruthless and to ask three particular men to join with us, and to trust to our own discretion and initiative to cast out whomsoever we should regard as an extraneous member in the event. Immediate personal relationships, in the time to come, could make or mar our well-being.

This scheme worked more or less according to plan, the three men of our choice all being engineers from the Union Castle liner. Like us, they all came from the south of England and we considered that they shared much the same values as we did and to have more in common in normal life. It was, in any case, apparent that the clique system which had already developed was based to a large extent on locality; the Glaswegians tending to come together, as did those from Merseyside and the North-east coast. Nor did we consider those whose personalities had already demonstrated their owners' abrasiveness.

We were soon hustled up an accommodation ladder aboard the *Nankin*, along one deck, down to another, down a ladder on to the fore well-deck and then down a companionway where, on each side of the square of No. 2 hatch, were a number of cabins which, it seemed, were our quarters. I imagine that they were the native crews' accommodation when the ship had been trading in the old days, but they represented good quarters to a prisoner-of-war. Each cabin had four steel framework bunks, in two sets of two, with a couple of benches and a small folding table. The five of us had managed to stay together and it was our intention to dismiss Fox from the party in this set of conditions but, unfortunately, Broomfield, acting very much in accordance with his very nice nature, saw that we were too many and, excusing himself, silently faded away to take his chance elsewhere before we could do anything about it. Pargiter and I were sorry about this and subsequently made the position abundantly clear to him, lest he should act in the same way in any subsequent transfer.

It is always very hard to judge a man's true character. For normal purposes a good deal can be judged from the set and look of his eyes, from his general bearing and demeanour and from his habits. Few men display their true selves to the world in their accustomed way of life and always act to a greater or lesser degree as if they were of that sort which they would wish themselves to be. It is only when the chips are down that the true man emerges, and we felt that the chips *would* soon be down. I had learnt more about men in the square-rigged sailing ships than I ever did in steam for, in virtue of their long voyages and their utter isolation for so long at a time, coupled with their conditions and recurring emergencies all far removed from a normal way of life, they had demanded a standard of physical and spiritual self-sufficiency which generally brought out the best or the worst in a man. In a totally different way, this life as a prisoner represented a complete departure from each man's normal existence and, to most of the men, it was the first time in their lives that they were to be tested. Our problem was to identify the sheep from the goats.

The vast majority, whose seafaring had been confined to relatively comfortable motor-ships or steamers on mainly fair weather voyages, still believed that they had touched the nadir of discomfort in the *Charlotte Schliemann* down in the Westerlies, but the knowledge that that voyage must only be a transient stage in their captivity had buoyed them up, even in the midst of their misery, to hope for some future improvement. I, and one or two other prophets of doom, with our relative values in somewhat better perspective, suffered the usual fate of prophets and our warnings went unheeded. Thus, with very few exceptions, everybody had retained their customary standards. The *status quo* was enhanced on our arrival aboard the *Nankin* by the segregation of the coloured crews from the whites, the former being berthed on the other side of a bulkhead by No. 1 hatch, and the officers' cabins being grouped together.

Our chosen colleagues had been selected with the utmost care only after a long period of elimination. We had excluded the Americans from consideration because they were obviously determined to remain together. Broomfield was a fairly senior man and apparently well balanced in his outlook: a cheerful, pleasant fellow who, if he lacked that determination which makes a leader, promised to be a good colleague. Chadwick was the engineer next in seniority to Broomfield and was a fairly large, open-faced individual with a well-developed sense of humour and a certain panache which led us to believe that he might not be lacking in initiative. Fox, the fifth member, was a much smaller fellow whom I had never really seen properly, because almost his entire physiognomy was concealed behind a luxuriant growth of black beard. He had, it is true, rather small, ferrety eyes, but they often displayed a lightning twinkle and he had a certain reserve about him which might have sprung from several causes. It was our uncertainty whether this reserve was caused by strength or weakness which led us to place him after the other two in order of precedence. On the other hand, this reserve, often carried to the point of brusqueness, had one inestimable advantage, because the greatest danger of such close contact with one's fellow creatures lay in too great a familiarity which, if it did not lead to contempt, might well have led to something akin to loathing.

We were not unduly perturbed at our situation. There was a modicum of privacy in our cabins, which was a more than welcome change, and we were free to visit each other or not as we pleased. The weather was perfect and we had the run of the fore well-deck, where a deck erection containing lavatories and wash-places was situated. The food was adequate in quantity and quality, if somewhat dull, but those of us who relished sauerkraut had no complaint. We were left much to our own devices, our only official contact with the Germans being through Capt. Barber, our spokesman, who saw the prison officer every day. We had little enough to do, so set about discovering as much about our surroundings and likely fate as possible. The former was not difficult, because the Germans found their lot even less to their liking than we did.

Those of them who had transferred from the tanker had been at sea for a very long time, living a life which must have been no little strain because, however much risk the war may have held for Allied ships, the German vessels were no less than outlaws in all the length and breadth of the wide oceans, and they had known it only too well. They had looked forward to coming ashore and to a good spell in port; they had put the unhappy experience of Singapore behind them and, however they may have regarded themselves as the master-race, Japan had traditionally represented a sort of Mecca among the ports of the world to seamen of all countries and now it was also, for them, an allied country where they expected to be made welcome. Not only was that nation still virtually untouched by the vicissitudes of war but, on the contrary, it was still riding on the crest of a wave of high conquest, arrogant in its success and apparently rich beyond its reasonable dreams or expectations. Most goods were still in free supply and there were very few restrictions on peace-time living at that time.

On the other side of the world the Axis arms had been all victorious. The Allied armies had long been chased out of Europe and pushed back across the Channel, and now had been forced back along North Africa right into Egypt, while Allied shipping losses had been enormous. The United States, it is true, were in the war but, it was felt, that was forced upon them by the ignominy of Pearl Harbor and her Pacific losses. Certainly there was the small matter of the subjection of England still outstanding but, if the Japanese successes had been the more meteoric, the Nazi achievements had been no less substantial, and our Germans expected that their national heroics would deserve a mutual admiration.

The truth was that neither they nor the Japanese populace appreciated the fury of the cabinet in Tokyo with the Germans since, when believing themselves about to sign a mutual pact with Germany, Italy and Russia, Hitler had attacked the Soviets without consulting them in any way and, having done so, gave his assurances that it would all be over in a month or so. Now he had had to retract that optimistic prediction and Japan was left with this enormous and powerful neighbour at war with her ally. These things are now history, but they were not known to the average German or Japanese, let alone to the prisoners, at that time. Nevertheless, Germany had broken faith with Japan and official policy ensured that her nationals were made as little welcome as possible.

In blissful ignorance of the power politics involved, our Germans went ashore in happy anticipation, but it was not for several days that we discovered the truth or the depth of their disillusionment. Singly and in pairs, somewhat abashed, some of them came down to our flat to talk to whomsoever they could in the evenings. When we asked why they were not going ashore, the question was airily brushed aside in the first instance, with some such excuse as that they were taking it easy that particular evening for, they said, there was a limit to sustained enjoyment ashore.

Soon, however, they could conceal the truth no longer as their hatred of the Japanese became deep-rooted and implacable. They were, it is true, allowed ashore in their uniforms, although even this concession had been made to the German naval services only a week or so before our arrival, but this availed them little. They were bound to go ashore in twos and threes, but never singly, and they were not allowed to eat in any restaurant used by the Japanese, but only in one or two in the whole of Tokyo and Yokohama which were for the benefit of foreigners. These were very expensive. They were not allowed on any public conveyances: neither train, taxi nor even rickshaws, excepting only the captains and the German consul, and they found themselves humiliated and restricted at every turn. If they were walking along a pavement when a Japanese

28. *The NANKIN, re-named LEUTHEN after capture, was built in 1912 and is here seen off Gravesend in the Thames.*

soldier, albeit a one-star (most junior) private was approaching in the opposite direction, there was no question of passing in a normal and courteous fashion, but the Germans were obliged to step off into the gutter. Wherever they were, they were ostracized, and the Japanese edged away from them as if they harboured plague or some other contagious disease. Nor was this the worst of it, for they were constantly stopped by the *Kempetai* (the military police), who took multifarious particulars of each of them, severally, on immense forms. This might occur six or eight times in an evening and, as there were often a group of them together, (the operation being invariably accompanied by every form of arrogant suspicion, with a practically insuperable language barrier), it took up a large portion of their time ashore, quite apart from the indignity which was entailed by these interminable public examinations.

In all this, the Germans found a certain sympathy with us. We were bored by our own company to varying degrees and they were bored with theirs', while we shared a mutual dislike and distrust of the Japanese. In consequence, there sprang up a certain fraternization, although it was more restrained by some of us than by others. It was a fairly useful contact, because it provided a limited means of improving our knowledge of our circumstances. We learnt, for instance, that the *Nankin* was serving as a sort of hotel, or hostel, for all the Germans in Yokohama, apart from those in the few German ships which were in commission. The consul lived aboard with certain civilian families, besides our guards and various other Germans who were in the area either by accident or design. Those to whom we spoke evidently had no

157

certain knowledge of our impending fate, but they did give us the rather depressing news that there was a gang of British and American prisoners working in the docks quite close to us, and that they constituted the crews of ships previously captured by the *Michel* and *Stier* in the South Atlantic, which had been sent out to Japan in another German prison ship, the *Doggerbank* (the British *Speybank* before capture). These men were apparently working under the Japanese and were being treated very badly — a fact which enraged the Germans against the Japanese still further. It also served to depress our morale, particularly as a number of the prisoners concerned had served in the same ships as some of our party who had been held back due to injuries received in their own actions. It was hardly to be supposed that we were to be treated any differently.

Our depression was alleviated in some sort by a very remarkable discovery. We were still left very much to our own devices, apart from the evening social visits by the Germans. We were free to do what we liked on our flat around No. 2 hatch and we could use the fore-deck as we pleased. Still we had never been searched, and there was never any question of a muster or a check on our numbers. Indeed, no record of our names or anything else had ever been made. There were the odd guards posted, but they seldom came down the companionway and they interfered with us so little that they might have been wax-works. Certainly there was nowhere else for us to go as no-one aboard, whether captor or captive, had any inclination to sample the Japanese shore, and the Germans obviously regarded their guard duties as being little more than a farce.

One day a few hatch covers were removed in our full view, after which a Japanese went down the hold to inspect. Whilst we had seen the odd Japanese on the quay, this was the first who had presented himself at close quarters to us and, like most of his compatriots, he represented a faithful reproduction of the average Allied cartoon with his mouthful of teeth; black, close-cropped hair, broad and flattened features and ill-fitting clothes. Most civilians, other than the labouring coolies, wore a green suit and cap which was similar in form to the army uniform. We soon stopped looking at him when the hatch was exposed to view and our eyes nearly popped out of our heads because there, within feet of us, were hundreds of tons of Australian tinned foods in cases: the cargo that the *Nankin* was carrying when she was captured by the *Thor*. The Japanese soon completed his inspection, the hatch covers were replaced and we were left to consider and to scheme.

The cabin arrangement had naturally accentuated the clique system which had previously started amongst the prisoners in the tanker, and there was no longer any question of acting in a body for the common good. Whilst this was regrettable in one sense, it would have been folly to have involved all our number in any scheme, even if the cliques had not existed, because there was no doubt whatever that we harboured amongst our number several who put themselves before their fellows and who, taking their fraternization with the Germans to extremes, would not have hesitated to attempt to curry favour for themselves by exposing any subversive acts by their own people. This is a harsh statement, but time was to prove that a very small minority of our fellow prisoners were, in reality, our worst enemies, either for this sort of reason or due to their own selfishness and stupidity.

Our cabin had no doubt whatever about the action to be taken. We had been fed adequately, but the only pleasure derived from our meals lay in the fact that they represented a break in the monotony of the day. They had never been such as to satisfy the epicure. We were convinced that the majority of the prisoners were not possessed of sufficient spirit to steal from the hold, but that there were others who certainly were, and who would do so. It seemed to us that, although any theft would be a comparatively easy operation, it would be fatal to all parties if there should be a succession of raids. We therefore approached a party of engineers from the *Dalhousie* who shared a cabin, headed by the redoubtable Craggs, whom I knew would not be backward in any such enterprise, and the eight of us decided that we would make a large-scale raid on the hold and lay in a good store of food for ourselves and for distribution to a number of other trustworthy men, in order to keep the number of incursions, and thus the risk, to a minimum.

The greatest problem was not so much the attainment of the food, but its subsequent concealment, because it was not only essential that our *caches* should not be discovered, but also that whatever we distributed to others should be equally well concealed. Once eaten, empty tins could be filled with water and dropped through the outboard ports into the dock. Cases could be broken up and treated the same way, the tides being relied upon to scatter the evidence. Although we had never been subject to searches, we felt that this had been due either to the folly or the oversight of the Germans and that, as they must take such an action sooner or later, we could hardly expect them to view the exploit with acclamation. In fact, the results of discovery might be serious. Pargiter or I, (I forget which of us) then had a brainwave. I think we both had our minds trained ready to deal with all eventualities by then, and we decided to use the cisterns of the lavatory tanks, which we considered would represent a hiding place which would be equally safe from both the Germans and our fellow prisoners. In the event the Germans never looked, and our less trustworthy compatriots never guessed the secret.

The raid went very well. Four of us did the job: one man going down

29. *The raider* THOR *in her peace time role as the* SANTA CRUZ.

the hold, two taking the food to the nearest of our two cabins, and one watching the companionway against the chance arrival of a guard. The operation was carried out in semi-gloom and every sound aboard caused consternation, but we were undisturbed and made a good haul of tinned meats of various sorts, tinned fruits, butter and cheese. It was extraordinary to find such variety in so small an area. Once the hatch was re-covered, we distributed the goods between our cabins and waited until morning, as the sound of breaking cases would have disturbed the still of the night beyond all reason. We stole whole cases because it would have been fatal to have left pilfered ones in the square of the hatch and that would also have involved the noise of breaking them. From then onwards we lived very well indeed in the *Nankin* and, as a full stomach imparts a sense of well-being, life took on a rosier hue.

The early mornings were glorious. Fujiyama, its snowline descending a little further down its slopes with each night, was tinged with an ethereal pink by the rising sun. The *Thor*, lying ahead of us, was storing for another cruise and by day we watched her or lay and basked in the sun whilst discussing the latest rumours — and they were legion — until the next break came for a meal, when we stuffed ourselves, probably eating far better than the Germans further aft or anyone else in Yokohama! As to the war, we had no idea what was happening and there really might not have been one going on at all.

Pargiter had been to see the doctor in the German accommodation about some minor ill one day and, seeing a copy of the *Oxford Book of Verse* there, had surreptitiously and very properly annexed it, quickly slipping it into his clothing. This was a splendid acquisition! It represented our *only* book and we guarded it jealously for almost three

160

years, at the end of which we both knew much of it by heart. Mental recreation represented our greatest void and this was a gold-mine.

There were minor vexations. Certain things were in very short supply, notably combs. I had had the forethought to slip quite a large one into my pocket before abandoning the *Dalhousie* and, being the best amongst us, it was generally used for hair-cutting purposes, usually by Leif Reistad, the Norwegian second mate, who acted as 'barber'. One day, after cutting several heads, he decided to wash it but, although his intention was good, the result was disastrous because he used almost boiling water for the purpose and that was the end of my comb so far as its original function was concerned! In retrospect, it is difficult to conjure up the wrath which this engendered within me, although I do not think I said much. There was no point, but its loss was a source of regret and irritation for many moons. Many years later, when staying with Reistad at his home on the island of Hidra, I found that he had no recollection of the incident!

After a few days, when it was apparent to all that the food was there for the taking, others began to pluck up courage by groups, and we ourselves were equally exercised to see if we could not improve on our already lengthened menu. Consequently there was soon almost a state of queueing to get down the hatch, and we felt that stocks should be kept to a minimum when the game was being played so indiscriminately. Then came the day when the hatches were lifted again by the Germans and we felt that investigation would follow within minutes, but no-one noticed anything wrong and a quantity of the food was unloaded and taken round to the *Thor*.

Discovery would have followed sooner or later, but events moved too fast. The raids had always had a spice of danger about them, being carried out at one or two o'clock in the morning at first but, as they became more general, had tended to get earlier and earlier in order to avoid having to queue to go down. There had been near escapes: there was the occasion when some fool dropped a hatch cover down into the hold with a clatter that should have awakened the dead, let alone the somnolent guard: once a guard actually did come down in the middle of an operation (for some cabins failed to keep a watch on the companionway), but everyone kept as still as statues and, in the gloom, he saw nothing and shambled up on deck again: there was the time when the man in the hold moved a heavy case in such a manner that he could neither move it nor free himself from the position in which he had jammed himself, but the whole thing was too easy and it seemed impossible to get caught. However, one splendid autumn morning we were told that we were to go ashore in the afternoon, and we guessed that the real turning point in our lives had arrived. In this, we were correct.

It was plain, as we had expected, that we were to be handed over to the Japanese. I am convinced that the Germans were all genuinely sorry about this, not only because of their own loathing of the yellow men which had been accentuated by the treatment which they, themselves, had been receiving at their hands, but because it went very much against the grain with them to hand white men over to a coloured race in this manner. Further, these particular Germans were either professional seamen, or men who had been long out of their own country, and they had few illusions about the war or about us, knowing that we were, in fact, no worse than they were, whatever their propaganda ministry might declaim to the contrary. They were not men who had become fermented in the Nazi doctrines of bestiality, but who was actually responsible for deciding our fate I do not know. Without doubt we were something of an embarrassment and certainly of no possible use to the Germans in Yokohama, and I dare say that a batch of healthy prisoners represented a useful credit item which could be used in barter to assist the depreciated mark to pay for dock dues, stores and other services rendered to them by the Japanese.

The word had gone forth that we were to be handed over to the Japanese Navy which, according to the scanty information available to us, was to be preferred to the army. The navy certainly took the cream of the men into its own service and had the better reputation. We were scheduled to leave, I think, at about three o'clock in the afternoon, and we prepared for our departure accordingly. We made sure that our stocks of food were well concealed and that neither we nor anybody else was attempting to take any with them. It was as well that we did so.

We had no idea whither we were going, nor into what sort of condition. Pargiter and I went over our rules for *gefangenism* and ensured that Broomfield and our two cabin-mates knew their part. I had managed to construct some sort of haversack for my few possessions, and the weather was cool enough to wear my heavy bridge coat without undue discomfort. I was always very sorry for men like Broomfield who had been picked up naked out of the water and who possessed absolutely nothing at this time, apart from the canvas suit the Germans had given him. It is a very bad thing for a man's self-respect to possess no material item in a materialistic society, unless he should be under some voluntary, religious vow of poverty. My diary was now assuming quite large proportions. It had been continued without a break from the day of our capture and I had entered everything that had happened to us, collectively and severally, in its pages, together with a full account of our conditions, of the Germans and of anything, like the shipping we had seen, which could possibly be of interest afterwards. I had managed to scrounge a small supply of paper and to bind it into the semblance of a

162

book, and this I stowed very carefully, next to my person, prior to disembarking, being well aware that it would not be a popular document if discovered by our enemies.

We hung about the fore-deck in a state of nervous tension, rather quiet and subdued in that aura of uncertainty. There had been something solid about the German ships; something familiar to us about the bustle and hurry of the harbour, and some *je ne sais quoi* about the beauty of Mount Fuji, reaching up into the perfect cerulean of the sky. (We could not know of the trail of filth which littered the pilgrim's path all the way to its summit!)

Moreover latterly, uncertainty apart, we had been living in a manner which would have been envied by the many millions who, in those days, never had the opportunity to take a relaxed holiday in the sun. Indeed, our recent sybaritic existence made the greater contrast with all that followed.

The passing of three o'clock, and the subsequent and interminable passage of time during which nothing happened, did little to mitigate the general unease. Finally, with something of a clatter, a detachment of Japanese marines marched round the end of a warehouse at the end of the basin and formed up on the quay alongside the ship. Some nondescript-looking characters dressed in what supposedly passed for uniforms were lining up opposite to them and, after a good deal of mutual shuffling and re-forming, the two bodies of men were ready, so we were paraded down to the quay and formed up in two lines. Pargiter and I were next to each other, having determined that this was essential because, if we got into parallel positions in different ranks, there was always the chance that the two files might branch off in different directions or into different barracks at some time.

As soon as we were formed up, we were searched. This was the first time that this had happened to any of us and I often reflected on how stupid the Germans would have looked before the Japanese had we been discovered to have all sorts of things which are not normally allowed to prisoners because, for aught they knew, each one of us might be bristling with revolvers, cameras, tins of food or prison breaking implements! (It will be remembered that, when the chief steward of the *Dalhousie* made his ill-considered departure from the *Tannenfels*, he was still in possession of a camera and a revolver.) The search was carried out by the nondescript-looking men who, it transpired, were customs officers and who proved to be inordinately slow about the whole proceeding and not in the least thorough. Certainly they never discovered my diary nor, so far as I am aware, anything else.

By now the sun had shifted to beat full down on the quay and to change our position from one of relative coolness to one of insufferable heat in the windless hollow between the ship and the warehouse. Although we were standing at ease, it was very uncomfortable and, although divesting myself of my bridge coat, I still sweltered until the operation was finally finished. There was something faintly ridiculous about prisoners being examined by Customs on arrival on an enemy shore, and we found ourselves wondering whether we should be charged on anything which might be subject to duty! I felt sure that no other nation in the world could behave in such an extraordinary fashion!

At last, under the aegis of a revolting little man who was an interpreter, and guarded by the marines, we marched off, casting a last look back at the German ships as we lost them to sight at the end of a warehouse. (We had not seen the *Charlotte Schliemann* since the day we left her.*) The Germans had caught us in the first instance and had landed us in this predicament. Some men, from the ships which had been sunk without mercy by von Ruckteschell in the *Michel*, harboured bitter memories, but the rest of us, to a greater or lesser degree, deplored our departure from the German vessels which represented at worst a frying pan from which we marched into an unknown fire. We never ceased to regret our exodus from Yokohama docks in the months that followed.

We might have viewed the matter rather differently had we been able to prophesy the course of future events there for, although it could not occur to us, our departure had hidden advantages. We were not to learn until after the war how close was that Nemesis which was to bring those ships to their predestined doom.

Most people either remember, or have read about, the notorious tanker *Altmark*, a ship very similar to the *Charlotte Schliemann*, and of the stirring manner in which she was boarded by men of the British destroyer *Cossack* in Jössing Fjord, how she was held up at cutlass point, and how her prisoners, originally taken by the pocket-battleship *Graf Spee*, were re-captured and brought back to Britain. Her subsequent fate is less well-known. After that incident, so glorious to the British and so chastening to the Germans, her name was changed to *Uckermark* and she was sent to sea to supply the cruisers *Scharnhorst* and *Gneisenau*, only escaping by a hair's breadth when H.M.S. *Rodney* appeared over the horizon to engage the latter vessel. She had been in St. Nazaire at the time of the famous Allied air raids there in 1942 and, later in the year, had sailed in an attempt to beat the blockade to store the raiders, but had been beaten back by aircraft. This was in August, at about the time that the *Dalhousie* had been sunk, but she tried again in September and got through, supplying the *Michel* at sea before running up to Batavia and Singapore to load rubber and oil for Yokohama,

---

* The *Charlotte Schliemann* was ultimately sunk on 14 February, 1944, by H.M.S. *Relentless* to the south and east of Mauritius, when acting as a submarine supply ship.

where she arrived soon after we left the *Nankin*.

To have the *Uckermark* and the famous *Thor* in port together was a signal for German jollification and propaganda. The tanker was moored alongside the *Thor*, which was lying just ahead of the *Leuthen (Nankin)*, on one side of the basin. The Germans gave a luncheon party in celebration — a fine affair to which many Japanese newspaper reporters were invited together with a number of V.I.P.s, in order that they might propagate the idea of German naval might! All was going well and according to plan when, soon after the luncheon was over and the guests were on deck, there was an explosion aboard the *Uckermark* which was followed, within a very short time, by a much larger one accompanied by a gigantic sheet of flame rising from the hapless tanker. In an instant, so suddenly that it was almost breath-taking, both ships were well afire, part of the *Uckermark's* bridge and much of the raider's superstructure having already vanished.

Not only were both vessels well ablaze, but it was apparent that both were going to sink. Men leapt over the side in near panic, jumping into the basin in an effort to swim across the dock to the opposite quay, believing that the warehouses along the quay on the same side as the ships must surely join the conflagration in a matter of moments. So they did, but as these men swam, a wall of flaming oil spread across the surface of the water to engulf and envelop them and, as they died in the water, the *Nankin* was caught up in the conflagration. All that was left after eight hours of uncontrollable flames were three German ships and one Japanese wholly gutted and destroyed, besides much damage ashore to warehouses. So ended the Germans' day of jubilation and glory, but there is little doubt that we, the prisoners, were well away from such an affair, not only on grounds of personal safety, but because suspicion might well have been fastened on us in some manner. As it was, a chance spark from a workman's welding torch aboard the *Uckermark* was presumed to have caused the whole disaster.

None of this we could foresee as we marched along the streets of Yokohama. We knew that we were going to a station, but that was all. We must have presented an extraordinary spectacle, of all colours, sizes and creeds, and we were glad enough when the twilight, and finally the darkness, came down to hide the greater part of the crowds on the pavements who greeted us with obvious cat-calls, derisive laughter and, occasionally, with spittle. They, too, seemed to be a heterogeneous lot, but the Japanese certainly have more features universally in common with each other than any white race. All, for example, had black hair: the men's close-cropped and the women's long and made up on the top of their heads: all had brown eyes, in contradistinction to the multiplicity of hair styles and hair and eye colours of the Western peoples. All had flat, wide faces with the epicanthic fold, and almost all their mouths seemed to be overflowing with teeth, many of which were gold or studded with gold fillings. Many were dressed in green patrol jackets, knickerbockers and puttees with a green cap of the sort already mentioned, others were in native dress and rather more colourful, the men in kimonos whilst mothers, and even school-children, appeared with babies and younger children slung on their backs in *nennekos*. None seemed to be properly shod by our standards, all wearing either rubber-soled, cloth-sided shoes or bootees — the *jika-taki*, or else *geta*: the wooden sandals raised from the ground by wooden bars. Both of these forms of foot-gear tended to have the big toe split from the body of the other toes, rather like the thumb in fingerless gloves.

The crowd had lined the route to see us pass. All were curious and stood leering without any inhibitions, whilst many of them appeared to be definitely hostile. Once a young Jap addressed a prisoner in English, asking whence he came, but an officer shouted at him; a guard struck at him with a rifle butt and he melted back into the throng. Prisoners parading the streets of Japan were good propaganda for the populace to absorb, but not if they were known to be German prisoners!

So we walked in silence, four abreast. Talking was forbidden. Our rear was brought up by the wounded: a bearer party carrying the men with amputated legs on stretchers. After we had proceeded quite a long way, and because we had stood for so long on the quay, some of the older men were approaching exhaustion. We were told to halt and to sit down. Few of us relished sitting in the road but it was clear that there was no option in the matter, and we sat. There was one exception. Craggs, the tough little second engineer from the *Dalhousie*, remained standing. Knowing him, I suspect that he did this rather out of conceit to show his fellows that he, at least, was not tired than from any material distaste of the road surface, because he seldom missed any opportunity to demonstrate his toughness. He was small in stature, but certainly fitter and stronger than the majority of the men.

Then an officer noticed him. The marines had just been relieved by a detachment of soldiery and this army officer, whose presence we had hardly realized, drew his sword and rushed at Craggs, hitting him as hard as he could across the head with the flat of it. As he approached from behind him, I doubt if Craggs even knew what had happened, but he sat down exceedingly precipitately, his dignity gone to the winds. A few civilian bystanders tittered but otherwise there was silence — a silence of the sort which makes itself felt as every man occupied himself with his own thoughts. Nor were they pleasant ones, in any sense. Nor had the fact that the army had relieved the marines been lost on us. We were not the Navy's prisoners after all; it had merely escorted us out of the dock area, which was presumably its province. The attack which we had just witnessed presented food for much conjecture and dark forebodings, for it was evidently a representation, or foretaste, of things to come.

Nor was it pleasant to see one's colleague being publicly humiliated in such a manner. Not only were we totally unprepared for this sort of thing, but the contrast with our recent conditions made the crime seem so much the greater. However badly the *Michel* may have behaved in her attacks at sea, no-one could deny that our treatment by the Germans had been more than fair ever since our capture. Perhaps we had not always been comfortable down in the West Winds, but we had never felt otherwise than that they had done the best they could for us within the limited means at their disposal and we had certainly suffered a minimum of interference at their hands until this final act of atrocity — the handing of their white prisoners over to a semi-barbarous yellow race.

This sword blow on Craggs' head, then, was of much wider moment than the ringing headache which it must have caused him. It was a precursor of a stern discipline to be imposed on us by a people who were only half-civilized (as will become progessively apparent): it opened up a vista of fear for the future — a future which extended almost as far as the imagination could stretch. Soon the rest was over and, singularly unrefreshed, we marched on through the night.

In due course we reached a railway station where we were marshalled into a large waiting room and sat down in parallel seats, almost as though in school. This analogy, which occurred to some of us, was extraordinarily near the mark as it turned out. Soldiery, with fixed bayonets, stood around the room: the officer stood near the door and the interpreter took over. He was a disgusting little man with his Japanese features so exaggerated that he seemed so grotesque as to be a caricature of his own people. As he removed his cap, we saw that his hair grew down to his brow to almost touch his eyebrows, giving him a wholly simian appearance. We were to know him only too well in the months which followed. His name was Fujimoto and he had spent a portion of his early youth as a lift-boy in San Francisco. Whether he was ill-treated by the Californians or, as appeared to be more likely, he was filled with envy at their way of life, we never knew, but it is certain that he loathed the white races with every fibre of his being, and we later discovered that he was cunning almost beyond belief. He spoke in the lowest form of American slang with amazing facility, and he had no conception of the meaning of the word 'honour'.

Most of this we discovered later. That memorable evening at Yokohama station he exhibited few of these traits. He gave vent to his inherent megalomania and sadism, and enjoyed himself thoroughly.

First he delivered himself of an oration, couched in the metaphor of the New York Bowery, to the effect that we were now Nipponese prisoners (it was a part of their nationalism that we were called upon to refer to the country as Nippon, and to the people as Nipponese, throughout our sojourn), and that we must learn quickly to do as we were told. If we did this, he stated with blind inaccuracy, we should be treated well. If not — well, it was not quite clear what happened if not, but evidently good treatment was not to be expected. He then made a survey of our ranks.

Capt. Barber, who had been appointed our spokesman by the Germans, attempted to speak, but was told that he was only a merchant captain and no longer a leader, for he was a civilian. (This was true, to some degree, since the Merchant Services did not rank as fighting services.) I, and others, had repeatedly advised our D.E.M.S. gunners to conceal their rating in the hope that, for the very reason that we were not fighting men, we should either be placed in a civilian internment camp or, at worst, in a special merchant seamen's camp, as in Germany, which should certainly be no worse than an ordinary prisoner-of-war camp. If we achieved this, and the gunners kept quiet about their real position, they could share our conditions and, at all events, they stood to lose nothing by adopting this course even if, in the end, they gained nothing. Apart from one or two Americans, the gunners from the *Dalhousie* were the only men to whom this applied, but as soon as Fujimoto asked if there were any naval men present, they spoke up with alacrity, forgetting all these arguments in the glory of the moment, for now they could declare themselves superior to the humble, civilian merchantmen — even the captains. They saw their high moment and they seized it, lest it be lost.

It became apparent later that we were to be treated in every way as regular prisoners-of-war, and in this case it might have been reasonable for the captains and officers to have been recognised as such, but Japan was not a reasonable country and had not signed the Hague Convention on the subject. Thus my advice, though it could have done no harm, could not have done any good. After a short cross-questioning a new leader was appointed in the form of Jackson, my gunlayer: the man who had run from his gun in the grip of his cowardice, the man who had so quivered with fear in the lifeboat as to be incapable of plying his oar. Now, under the apparent protection of our yellow enemies, he appeared to be as bold as brass. This was all part of our humiliation and doubtless carefully planned in order to create discord within our ranks.

Next, we must learn essential Japanese — I beg their pardon, 'Nippon-go'. We must *bango*, or number off, in that language. There were still a number of men who did not realise the seriousness of their situation and who appeared to think that all this was some mild form of joke. There

168

were those who, being quite unaccustomed to using their brains at all, were quite incapable of absorbing either the Japanese numbering system or the individual words. It is simple enough, in all conscience, the first ten digits being:- One, *itchi*: two, *ne*: three, *san*: four, *se*: five, *go*: six, *roko*: seven, *sichi*: eight, *hachi*: nine, *ku (kukyu)* and ten, *ju*.

Once these ten digits are learned, anyone can count up to ninety-nine immediately, because eleven is *ju-itchi* (ten-one), twelve, *ju-ne* (ten-two) and so on until twenty which is *ne-ju* (two-ten) and twenty-one is *ne-ju-itchi* (two-ten-one). All the numbers are based on this system. *Haiku* is a hundred and is simply superimposed on the tens and units, a hundred and one being *haiku-itchi* and three hundred and fifty-six *san-haiku-go-ju-roko*. *Sen*, a thousand, follows the same principle.

At this stage we were not informed of the refinements by which *gohan* (pronounced 'yon') can be substituted for *se* (four), providing that the word *nanna* was substituted for *sichi* (seven), so that *gohan* and *nanna* were always used in combination, or *se* and *sichi*, but that the two pairs were never mixed.

Those of us who were accustomed to use our brains could count fluently within a matter of minutes, but several of the catering staffs and one or two of the gunners, together with a couple of Norwegians and some of the lascars who could not undertand English at all, let alone Fujimoto's interpretation of it, suffered blows with rifle butts, kicks and slapped faces before they had mastered the art. It was all very degrading and, by ten o'clock, we were all pretty tired. The situation was tense and a great strain. I am sure that all of us who are still alive have crystal-clear memories of that waiting room and of our introduction to the Japanese, but it is, perhaps, one of the kindest traits of human memory that the poignancy of acute discomfort, anguish or pain seldom remains for long in a man's recollection without being dulled (as few can recall the blinding pain of toothache after the tooth is removed), and thus none of us today can conjure up the stark awfulness of that evening precisely, even if we should wish to do so. I can still see the uncloaked fear in the eyes of some of the men, and I can still see the pleasure they evinced at the announcement that we were to have some food, as they were hungry and they believed that it signified some temporary relaxation.

They were wrong, neither for the first nor last time. Several men were detailed to distribute small wooden boxes which contained rice and a small side portion of vegetable. The rice was packed well down, but each grain was separate. There were no spoons, but only chop-sticks. Fujimoto exulted in his delight. We must eat our rice and we must use our chop-sticks. No man might use his fingers. He demonstrated how it should be done and, in a twinkling, his portion was gone. To some of his audience it was like a conjuring trick. Now we could see who was adaptable and who was not, for it is absurd for any man to say that he cannot eat with chop-sticks. It may be that he will not eat with elegance, if such a word can be applied to such a mode of eating at any time (but many did not bring elegance to bear on a knife and fork, anyway!), yet very little manipulation should enable him to hold his sticks in such wise that he can transfer the food from its receptacle into his mouth. If necessary, he can shorten the distance between the two to an almost irreducible minimum.

Some men were momentarily perplexed by the fact that their chop-sticks required separating. In a public place they are split down the middle, but not completely, to show that they have not been used before yet, although this was explained, a minority of men were still in difficulties. Either they failed to pick the food out of their boxes, or they dropped it on the floor. The Japanese became furious and indulged in an orgy of face-slapping, taunts and various measures of physical force. All this did little except to fluster the men concerned. We were still enjoined to silence and relaxation seemed very far away.

Most of us had eaten our rice fairly quickly, but others struggled on and I doubt if they would ever have finished at all if their dilemma had not been brought to an end by the arrival of the train. Gratefully, we left the waiting room to be herded into two carriages of the type which has a corridor down the middle with sets of four seats, two and two facing each other, on each side. Our party had managed to keep together and we found that talking in undertones was practicable, though none of us had anything very constructive or cheering to say after that evening. All the blinds in the compartments had to be drawn, and it was soon apparent that any attempts to look behind them were viewed in the worst possible light by our guards.

Some people can sleep in trains, whilst others find it very difficult. I think that an easy mind must be a prerequisite but, although most of us were tired, few slept much during the night. At that time we had not come to view the Germans in the light in which we afterwards did — as the Europeans who had handed us over to a race which they themselves despised, and with good reason. It was of no use to think of our homes in Britain or America, as that led to a sickening nostalgia which benefited no-one, but we all remembered the comparative peace of the Yokohama docks so few hours before: the placid water and the clear sun with the complete freedom within our section of the ship. Even the swastika, — and I hope I shall not be misunderstood when I say this, since it is but a comment in comparative values — even the swastika ensign, I repeat, had fluttered as a symbol of protection. The fried egg flag of Japan: the red sun on its white field, and the yellow star of the Japanese army: these stood for all that was evil in our eyes, and it was an

170

evil which was personified in the repellent little Fujimoto.

Our morale, so far as the crew of the *Dalhousie* was concerned, had been lowered by our arrival in the *Stier* because we had become prisoners suddenly in all the midst of a summer sea, but we had retained our standards. The entry into the *Charlotte Schliemann* had been a shock, all the ruder in the gloom with the uncertainty and the unexpected squalor which suddenly confronted us, appearing at first sight so much worse than it really was, but few of us had lost anything thereby. Morale, in general, had ebbed as we had come up into the tropics when our hopes of rescue or of taking the ship had receded, whilst the departure of the deck and engine-room ratings at Singapore had not improved the case. Still, standards had been maintained so far as they were possible and those who were wavering had been fortified by the life in the *Nankin* which, in our condition of captivity, had definitely improved our lot and, despite the proximity of the Land of the Rising Sun and all that it portended, puffed by the triumphs of its conquests, the standards of morale had risen in a startling fashion. It must be remembered that, by then, most of us were very well fed!

Now I could look around me. Some men showed blank despair: others appeared tense while a few were were frankly frightened. For myself, as previously recorded, I had long regarded the only tolerable philosophy in war, whether in air raids ashore, in convoys harried by wolf-packs, under dive bomber attack, or elsewhere, to be blind belief in the predestination of one's fate, which could only be deflected very slightly from its course by one's own efforts. It saved a great deal of worry and heart-burning and eliminated any sense of fear to a large degree, once one had reconciled oneself to the hand of destiny. It was very evident that such a philosophy would pay dividends in the life before us and I, for one, snatched at some little sleep. It was light when I awoke and managed to obtain an oblique view through a badly drawn blind, once glimpsing the sea and once a pagoda standing among some trees in a vista of paddy fields and distant hills. Then a soldier, suspicious, adjusted it and I saw no more. We rumbled on through the sunlight outside in a gloom which was only matched by our view of the future.

IX

CHIKKŌ CAMP

The morning was already well advanced when we finally arrived at a fairly large station and were shepherded out onto a square outside it, where we were told to sit down. On this occasion everyone sat without demur in the middle of an area which was bounded by our guards, and on the perimeter of which a heterogeneous crowd of Japanese had gathered. They were obviously somewhat hostile in their attitude to us; some spitting and others throwing stones. The guards expostulated at the stone throwing, but in so mild a manner that it was obvious that they did not expect anyone to take any notice. Fortunately our distance from the crowd was too great for the spitting activities to find any mark and there must have been a dearth of stones in the region, as they did not amount to much.

Personally I found one of the most irritating aspects of the situation to be that we had not the remotest idea where we were. Our surroundings, combined with the size of the railway station, led me to suppose that we were in one of the larger towns of the country but, as most of us had only the most cursory knowledge of the distances and relative geography of Japan, and had no idea whether we had been travelling north or south or across to the west coast during the train journey, we might really have been anywhere on the main island of Honshu. Certainly we could see a number of posters and signs, but all were written in Japanese characters and gave us no clue to the locality whatever.

After an interminable wait under the close and eager scrutiny of the chattering bystanders, we were formed up and again started to march through the streets. The general strain of the preceding evening, followed by the long, almost sleepless train journey, had not left the main body of men in any state to observe its surroundings with much interest. We must have seemed a motley collection. A few officers, like myself, had retained their uniforms in good order, while others, like Broomfield, were in very different case and wearing canvas suits. Others were clad in an assortment of garments. The craven gunner, Jackson, was our appointed leader and that situation was not to the liking of anybody. Although our little party of five remained intact, the white, black, brown and yellow men had all become mixed up *en route*. The Germans had been punctilious to the last degree in the maintenance of rank and racial segregation, but it was obvious that the Japanese were to be equally punctilious in its destruction.

The lower ranks evidently found it embarrassing whilst the lascars, too, exhibited a sense of uneasiness in rubbing shoulders on equal terms with men whom they were accustomed to address as *Sahib*. No-one could tell what the Chinese seamen thought, but I believe that they feared the Japanese more than any of the others, and that this over-riding fear banished any other considerations from their minds.

Occasionally we passed over small, hump-backed bridges leading over canals filled with barges. We were fast becoming inured to being stared at, and the area into which we were passing was becoming progressively poorer and more squalid. We were aware of the proximity of docks, having heard the odd ship's whistle and having seen a signal station and the truck of the odd mast, when we were suddenly wheeled off the road into a cinder-covered area bounded by a wooden fence, where we were lined up and stood at ease. I forget how long we stood, but it was a very long time. The two women and two boys from the Union Castle liner, who had been separated from us in the German ships, were standing slightly apart, at one end. The women made some effort to wave to those officers whom they remembered.

Whilst we were in Japan we often had to stand and wait. Whether this was initiated by the inherent unpunctuality of the Japanese or by a sadistic fore-knowledge of the effects of long waiting on morale, we had no means of telling but, as time went on, we became quite expert at standing without any effort or impatience. At this point in our career we had not conditioned ourselves to it, and we found it both tiring and irritating.

During the course of this particular hiatus we were subjected to certain drill and to a further insight into the Japanese language. We had to *bango* (number) *ad nauseam*, until even the most block-headed of our number could make some sort of a show at it and we had to learn, in particular, three other words. These were those for 'Attention' (*kyotski*), 'Stand at ease' (*yasumé*) and that word which proved to be the very life-blood of the military caste — almost, indeed, of the whole nation — the word *Kiri*. This means 'Salute'. If one is male and wearing a hat, it involves a hand salute; if bare-headed or a woman, it calls for a bow. No rows of debutantes, practising for their presentation to their sovereign, could have been drilled so assiduously in the art of the curtsey as we were in the art of the bow that afternoon. It was neither as easy as we supposed nor apparently possible to salute properly by the standards of

174

Japan. At the time we considered that our task-masters were being unduly strict and trying to humiliate us still further but, although this may have been true to some extent, it was not until some weeks had elapsed that we realized that this matter of *kiri* was far more important to them than any mere fetish and, by our subsequent observation, it is easy to understand that those first efforts by some of our members, particularly the lascars, Chinese and some of the older men, left a great deal to be desired. Besides, many of us could only bring ourselves to bow to the Japanese with the utmost reluctance. At intervals during that afternoon we were made to march, turn and form up to re-number — all these operations being ordered in Japanese.

We remembered that, less than eighteen hours previously, we had been told that we were only civilians, yet here we were, drilling to the commands of a strange tongue. It is unlikely that many people have ever seen Lascar or Chinese seamen being drilled. The result is almost grotesque, as the effect is diametrically removed from anything which is intended! I believe that they are quite incapable of marching in step or of bringing any military precision to their movements. Of course, some Indian regiments have been without peer, but these men were not of that sort. Few white merchant seamen are much better. Only one or two of us had been in school O.T.C.s, naturally enough. I had gone to sea older than most, who do so too early to participate in such activity. The majority of the men had never been drilled before in their lives. A large proportion of them were members of ships' galleys, stewards, waiters or others of catering staffs who are seldom, at the best of times, the smartest of men. The pick of the crews, the seamen and the engine-room gangs, had been taken ashore at Singapore. In addition to these disadvantages, our party, taken in sum, was something of a rabble and insufficiently homogeneous to work together. It could hardly have been more mixed had it been recruited from the Tower of Babel and, in retrospect, I can hardly blame the Japanese for waxing impatient over our performance if, indeed, it was necessary to drill us at all. That is quite another matter.

Once, during all this, we saw a party of white prisoners passing on the other side of the fence, and took some cheer unto ourselves from their presence. Finally there came a stir and, as several Japanese officers arrived, we were stood to attention and made to *kiri*. This was not performed satisfactorily, and once again had to be repeated times without number.

After this, the officers marched up and down our ranks, almost as though they were inspecting an O.T.C. or some regiment on an occasion of formal militarism. The interpreter then stood below a small wooden platform which had been placed in front of us and announced that we were going to be addressed by Colonel Murata, who was our commander.

Murata thereupon mounted the platform. He was older than any Japanese officer we had seen before, very stiff, very straight and obviously brimming over with his own sense of dignity. He carried this off in some measure, being very much better turned out than most army officers. His uniform looked as though it was tailored and not, as was more often the case, as though it was a second-hand 'reach-me-down' being worn by its third or fourth owner*. He had a short, clipped, grizzled moustache and, like his clothes, his sword also looked as though it belonged to him and was not worn by some accidental oversight. He spoke in pure Japanese in a rather high-pitched voice with excellent carrying power. His oration continued on for very long periods without a break during which we had not the slightest idea what he was talking about. In fact, his long speech made not the slightest impact on his audience which became progessively more bored.

At intervals, when the colonel did pause for an instant, Fujimoto seized the opportunity to do a little interpreting, but seven or eight minutes of Murata's unbroken Japanese was generally watered down to a couple of brief sentences in the broad American idiom which the interpreter employed. The colonel apparently saw nothing incongruous in this and continued with enormous staying power until we were almost at our last gasp, when the speech suddenly came to an end. We never did know what it was really about, because Fujimoto's translations would not have filled a half-sheet of octavo paper and simply amounted to such statements as:- *"You are now under the command of the Nipponese army. You must obey the Nipponese army"* — a statement which followed almost ten minutes of impassioned address by Murata. *"If you do what you are told, you will be treated well"*, which followed an even longer monologue, and there were a few other remarks in the same vein. In our circumstances, they smacked of the platitude and made no impression at all.

After Colonel Murata and his aides had left the cinder patch, we were formed up and marched away. In the constant manoeuvring on the parade ground (for so it was termed), Pargiter and I had managed to keep together, with our colleagues fairly close to us, but it had proved to be impossible to keep at the end of one rank or the other, although we had planned to keep up in the front. In the event, we had finished up somewhere about the middle and, as there was no indication of which end would ultimately prove to be the van, our position was fairly reasonable in the circumstances. We were slightly agog, as we were

---

* This was often the case. The pay of Japanese service officers was usually too low to permit the purchase of tailored uniforms.

176

obviously reaching our final barrack at long last, when all our precepts of 'good gefangenism' must be remembered and put into lightning operation. Although we were tired, our mental processes were quite clear and we were prepared, as we imagined, for any possible barrack layout. We had in our minds' eyes the desirable features — window control, a modicum of privacy and so on, together with all those features of position which were undesirable and to be avoided.

Soon we were halted outside a wooden building. It would be more correct to say that there were two buildings, separated by an alleyway, with steps leading up to them from the road. They were situated on the corner of a street so squalid that no house agent could have found anything flattering to say about it, and they did not inspire confidence from without.

Japanese soldiers appeared. Again we were called upon to *kiri* and to *bango* and, despite our recent coaching, it was all a failure and we had to repeat the manoeuvres over and over again until, finally, we were released and told to enter the camp. Although I do not believe that the Japanese intended it, the leading men started to march in maintaining their files. As the column proceeded down the open alleyway between the two buildings, we passed, on the left, a guard room (where we had to *kiri* yet again) and then another small room which later proved to be a cobbler's shop, while on the right was a another closed door which later turned out to be the bath-house. Beyond were three doors on each side, opposite each other. The men in front were still pressing on, they knew not whither, when it became apparent that we were to occupy the first two barracks on the left, entered by the first two of the left hand doors: the British in the first of them, the Americans in the second. By this time Pargiter and I were fortunately close to our door and, by dint of a little judicious shoving, were soon inside.

On looking back, I think that we both kept our heads very well, because nothing could have been further removed from anything we had envisaged yet, so far as it was possible, we did succeed in applying our principles to this unexpected condition.

The room, as we afterwards discovered, was thirty-two feet long. There were two tables, each about fourteen feet long, running down the middle with wooden benches on each side of them and there was a low square, trough-shaped object at the two ends of the room, under the ends of the tables, which proved to be *hibachi*, or charcoal braziers. There was a narrow space on each side of the benches, the whole central portion of the room occupying some nine feet of width. On the two sides were three tiers of wide shelves seven or eight feet in depth, running the entire length of the barrack. The lowest was, perhaps, six inches off the floor; the next five feet and the topmost about nine and a half feet high.

Thus there was about four and a half feet of headroom, nett, between them. Spread along these shelves were a series of *tatami* — yellow rush sleeping mats measuring about six by three feet with black ends where a piece of cloth acted as a hem. These were to be our mattresses! Along the walls, about eighteen inches above each sleeping bay, was a narrow shelf running the entire length of the room. There were windows at the ends, level with the middle tiers and extending into the top and bottom ones.

At intervals of about five feet along the outside of the sleeping bays were thick, vertical wooden stanchions which were equipped with footholds to ascend to the upper tiers. The roof reached a peak over the tables, and it sloped down to a height of three or four feet above the top bays, at the sides. Everything was of wood except the mats and the floor, which was of concrete.

All this we saw in the twinkling of an eye. The idea of lying in rows on shelves was as novel as it was repugnant to us, and it had certainly never occurred to us when considering all the possible eventualities aboard the *Charlotte Schliemann*. It was obvious that, of the large windows at each end of the room, those on the alleyway end allowed little air, besides being, by their very position, a great deal more public. Quickly, we went to the other end of the barrack whilst the others crowded about the door in bewildered amazement. This was typical, this indecision. The lower shelves we dismissed as being too low and airless, and it was easy to see that they would be constantly blocked and obstructed by passers-by. The top shelves, although they provided more head-room, were dismissed as being too high and we felt that they would be hot in summer, besides being awkward to reach. We therefore tossed such little gear as we possessed next to the end window on the middle shelf (which really controlled it) and our three engineer friends from the Castle ship took the three mats inside us. Then we turned to see how the others were getting on. A few had realized what we were doing and, following our example, had staked out their places, Brown having joined with Robertson, a junior engineer from another ship, but few men had teamed up together. That was the most extraordinary thing for, although cliques had been formed previously, they had generally had no sort of basis and, despite the general state of ennui which we had experienced, few men had bothered really to get to know each other. This was particularly true of the British.

It used to be a joke of the 'chestnut' variety that Englishmen needed to be introduced before they would talk together, but it certainly seemed, now, as though those were some of the many true words spoken in jest, for most of those who had come to act together, or who teamed up subsequently, did so simply because it was a necessity in that camp for two or more men to join forces for their mutual welfare. Such

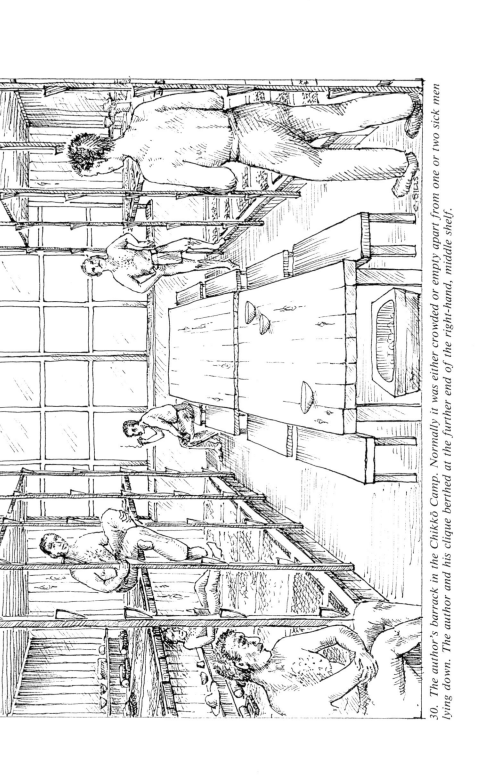

30. *The author's barrack in the Chikkō Camp. Normally it was either crowded or empty apart from one or two sick men lying down. The author and his clique berthed at the further end of the right-hand, middle shelf.*

friendships as occurred were generally formed by the merest chance. Craggs and his fellow Geordie and immediate junior, Henry, had joined forces very early on, with common interests and, apart from Pargiter and myself, they were the only couple in all our detachment who maintained their alliance throughout our captivity. (Actually, Henry was transferred to a camp by Lake Biwa just before the end of the war, but his relationship with Craggs had stood the strain.)

Faleide, the Norwegian radio operator, was always very antagonistic towards our barrack. He had been in a Norwegian ship in the Bay of Bengal in the preceding April when a strong Japanese naval force under Vice-Admiral Jisaburo Ozawa appeared and did great damage to the Allied shipping there. His ship was sunk and the men had been machine-gunned both in the water and in the boats, but the survivors of one boat had managed to get ashore on the coast of Madras, somewhat to the north of the city of that name. They gathered from the natives that the Japanese had landed and taken the city of Madras — a completely unfounded rumour based on the fact that a Japanese seaplane had landed on a nearby beach — but, acting on this, they decided to trek right across southern India to Bombay. This they proceeded to do, suffering many privations and passing through wide regions where they saw no white men at all and where, in the occasional villages, the natives gathered round them as though they were visitors from another planet. Apart from being white, they looked the part of ship-wrecked mariners and extraordinarily out of place in that jungle. Faleide had a complete photographic record of the journey, which was quite an epic, but the most remarkable feature of his tale concerned one village where a white man drove past at a time when they were in want of everything, looked over his shoulder at them in evident curiosity as he slowed his car and then .... drove on without stopping. Presumably there was no-one to introduce this lone Englishman to the castaways, who were in a sorry state by the time they reached Bombay, having walked barefoot for much of the way. No doubt this incident accounted for his attitude to us.

In the meantime there was a good deal of confusion and jostling round the door and in the alleyway. Most men were quite unable to comprehend the nature of the accommodation. Fujimoto's authoritative tones could be heard in conjunction with various American voices which were strange to us. Bewildered British voices added to the cacophony, ranging through the various accents peculiar to the bigger rivers of their native land: from the Glaswegian spoken on the banks of the Clyde, the harsh Geordie of Tyneside and a preponderance of Merseyside, to the Cockney of London River with the odd broad Yorkshire and a little West Country thrown in, as it were, for leavening. All this gave a sufficiently odd effect without the high, incessant chatter in Hindustani and the various dialects of Chinese which were all wafted in from the alleyway, together with Arabic, Norwegian and various other languages which scarcely made themselves heard at all. Even Fujimoto evidently felt that interpretation in this situation was impossible.

When the various white men were sorted out in some sort of order, a problem presented itself. What was to happen to the Lascars and Chinese? Neither barrack wished to have them, nor did they wish to berth with either the Americans or the British. Nor did they wish to berth together, but the question of their wishes scarcely arose, as they did not enter into the question. Fujimoto did not seem to care providing that the whole complement, whatever the colour, was quartered within the two designated barracks and, after a good deal of discussion, it was decided that the Lascars should occupy the top shelves in our barrack, and the Chinese a similar position in the other one. This led to a good deal more milling about, as all those who had pitched their camp on the top shelves had to move down and thus found themselves, for the most part, in undesirable places. There was no help for that.

Partly because of this, and partly because the vast majority had been too amazed to act with any premeditated thought, the various members of the two barracks found themselves berthed in any sort of order. A captain might be next to a galley boy although, on the whole, each man had somebody of more or less his own class or status on at least one side of him. Because we knew not what else to do, each man sat on his mat and the effect, as we looked around, was extremely odd, to say the least. Jackson, our 'leader', had, of course, accumulated a collection of hangers-on — waiters and others — who probably regarded him as a useful man to know. I knew well enough that he would not suit even the Japanese for very long!

That men are not born equal is a fact which should be obvious from its constant repetition in the history of mankind (however some may preach to the contrary), and the effects become most pronounced as the general standard of living falls. This was as applicable to the British contingent in our barrack as to any other body of men, but enhanced by the fact that they were such a very assorted bunch.

Very few Merchant Service* engineers or wireless operators would have been officers under naval aegis. Deck officers, who joined the R.N.R.‡ found their metiér in equivalent positions, but there was usually

---

* I use 'Merchant Service' (or 'Mercantile Marine') in preference to the term 'Merchant Navy', which only became prevalent in the Second World War, against all tradition.

‡ Royal Naval Reserve, at that time consisting of men who had been in the Merchant Service. The Royal Naval Volunteer Reserve (R.N.V.R.), since integrated with the R.N.R., had been in jobs ashore, rather like the Territorial Army.

a wide gulf between the deck and the other officers in a great variety of ships and the age-old feud between the bridge and the engine room was no mere myth. It was not necessarily a matter of birth or background, but in a whole outlook and way of life and, often enough, they lived in quite different parts of the ship. Many engineers were very good fellows, but in few ships at that date did they eat in the saloon with the deck officers, usually having their own mess-room. There is, in any case, a wide spectrum of types to be found among deck officers. Thus, from a purely social point of view, it was no great cause for concern that we had become split up, but the final results I shall analyse, as they became manifest. On the other hand, with such a great variation in types, classes, and outlooks as were arrayed on the shelves, few of whom had ever been subject to any strict discipline or even knew the meaning of 'self-discipline', it was clear that there was no hope of pulling together as a team unless led by the example of a small junta.

Soon after we were all settled, an American introduced himself. He was Sanders, a Chief Petty Officer in the American Navy, who, it seemed, had already been placed in charge of the camp by the Japanese army and, if somewhat bombastic in his manner, was evidently a man of a good deal of character, the effect being accentuated by two enormous handle-bar moustaches. The only other barrack occupied on our arrival was the one opposite to ours, which consisted of American marines and Naval personnel who had been taken prisoners in the Marianas, mainly on Guam, though there were also a New Zealander from Wake Island and a few men from the Carolines. I was very impressed with these fellows, who maintained a very good style, not only on our arrival but throughout the entire period of our incarceration. They were a comparatively small group, numbering less than sixty men, who must have been pretty tired of their own company already, as they had been prisoners for very much longer than we had, yet they made no advances to us but rather waited for us to address them. This was not motivated by the fact that we, in our barrack, were 'Limeys', because they did not invade the American barrack either, as one might have expected, but let everybody shake themselves down in good order. I admired them for this self-restraint.

From them we learned that the camp was in the Chikkō district of Osaka and was the No. 1 camp in the area. Most men had frankly never heard of the place, while some of us knew it as a large port, opposite Kobe, near the head of the Inland Sea. I doubt if any of us realized at that time that it was the fourth or fifth largest city in the world in terms of population.* Whether Tokyo or Osaka was the fourth largest was a

* Based on the last pre-war census figures, New York and London contained seven or eight million people (depending on the determined boundaries); Berlin some four

matter of dispute, owing to the vagaries of the Japanese census, but Osaka was then a growing town with probably over two and three-quarter million inhabitants. As time elapsed, we were to learn a good deal about the place.

In due course, food was served: each man having been issued with two china bowls and a spoon. This latter was gratifying, as we had not expected spoons after the affair at Yokohama station the previous evening although, of course, most of us had equipped ourselves with cutlery from the *Nankin*. The food arrived in a series of wooden buckets, half containing a rather watery vegetable soup, and half what we described, rather arbitrarily, as 'rice'. This was before we became connoisseurs of that commodity. Actually we were served with unpolished rice and barley in equal proportions.

The manner of taking our meals had yet to be determined, as the tables would not accommodate us all at one sitting. Certain of us felt that it was of paramount importance, for reasons of individual and collective morale, to maintain a proper sense of style and ordinary standards as far as it was possible and that, for this reason alone, we should endeavour to eat at the tables.

Sanders, the American, recommended that each man eat on his sleeping mat. A few of us did sit round the table, but the majority remained on their shelves and, in due course, it was found that it was only practicable to serve meals quickly if everyone except the servers kept off the floor. Thenceforth everyone ate on the shelves. Unadorned rice seemed to be a very poor sort of meal to many of the men who, depressed by the retrograde turn in their fortunes, decided to eat nothing. Others of us, determined to reject nothing that came our way and to keep our physical condition as high as possible, ate all the more. After the meal, we went out to wash our bowls in a wash-place of whose existence we were told and, at the same time, to explore the confines of the camp, such as they were.

I have already described the entrance alleyway. At its end was the perimeter fence, with the alleyway branching in both directions. That to the left turned left again round the left-hand barracks and up to the rear of the guard-house (passing our window), and that to the right went behind the third (empty) barrack on the right, and led to an area which, at that end, contained the *benjos*, beyond which were the urinals and, beyond them again, was the wash-place. The word *benjo* is of course Japanese, but there is no equivalent word in English since, fortunately,

---

millions and Tokyo and Osaka about two and a half millions each. Probably Osaka had rather more since the floating population made an accurate count extremely difficult. In the intervening years some cities have expanded enormously and the population league table has altered radically.

we know nothing so crude as the system which this term defines. It fulfils the function of a lavatory, but this word is in no sense a translation.

This Japanese lavatorial device is one of the most loathsome features of the country, which was almost devoid of any sewage system. It cannot be denied that sewage pipes would present serious problems in this earthquake area, but I do not believe that this alone accounts for the mediaevalism of the system. Our *benjos* were quite typical except that there were rather a lot in a row, which made them all the more offensive. They consisted of a long, semi-sunken concrete trough*, rectangular in shape and about three and a half feet wide.

This was planked on top and divided transversely into cubicles, each with a door. Every cubicle had a rectangular hole cut in the middle of its floor and across this one had to squat for the relief of nature. Once a week a horse-drawn wooden cart, built up like a big box with lids in the top, came round the streets. Every *benjo* had a removable trap on the top at the outside of the building (which is why they must always abut an external wall) and the *benjo* coolie — he who had charge of the cart — ran a couple of planks, which were part of his equipment, from the ground to the top of the cart, to form a ramp. He then bailed out the whole horrid affair into two buckets which he carried up the ramp on a yoke and emptied into the cart, and so continued, *benjo* after revolting *benjo*, until his cart was full and the stench, particularly in the hot weather, almost unendurable. Once loaded, he drove slowly through streets which might not have experienced the purgatory of the emptying that day, as if to give them their share of the aroma, until he was well clear of the town and away in the paddy fields or in farmlands, for this was the nitrate, or manure, of the country.

As a *benjo* became somewhat old, and especially in the summer, it became inhabited by all sorts of creeping and crawling life, large and small, which are best left undescribed. A spell of constipation would sometimes have been a blessing though, unfortunately, the reverse case was more commonly the lot of many of the prisoners. Nor was the stench confined to the days when they were emptied and, as the barracks on the opposite side of the alleyway to ours also opened on this part of the camp, there were times when it was not practicable to open their windows. I always regarded one of the most fortunate aspects of our position in the camp to be the fact that, quite unwittingly, Pargiter and I had chosen a location as far away from the *benjos* as it was possible to be.

Beyond the *benjos*, which lay along one corner of the camp, were the

* Often, as at the Osaka Shosen shipyard (*q.v.*) they were unlined trenches dug in the ground, never emptied, but the structure being moved and the trenches filled in after a period.

urinals which fed into the same sort of system, and then a long area with a series of taps over sinks with, occasionally, short draining boards. This section ended at the back of the bathroom, and led into an alleyway which connected at right-angles to the entrance alleyway, close to the guard-room. This alleyway contained in its length the camp boiler on one side and a small room which housed Sanders on the left, next to a Japanese store-room. The guards slept behind the guard-room. This, then, was the geography of the camp when we arrived and for the greater part of our stay. It will be noted that, apart from visits to the lavatorial area, the only practical place for a man to be was on his mat.

We wondered where the cooking was done. It transpired that there was another camp in the next street, known as the 'English camp' (to distinguish it from ours, which was the 'American camp') in which all the food was prepared and to which a detail had to go before meals with buckets to get them filled, and then bring them back with the rice and soup. These were fitted with wooden lids to keep their contents warm.

Such was the camp. That first evening each man was issued with a couple of blankets and a pillow. The latter was simply a small cylindrical bag filled with rice husks, and sewn up at the end. In our explorations we had discovered that it was better not to pass the guard-room when going round to the wash-place, as this was very prone to lead to trouble. It took a long time before it became automatic to *kiri*, and it had been explained quite clearly that we must salute every member of the Japanese army, whether a general or the humblest private. Thus the passing of the guard-room demanded a very special salute, and how often we either forgot, saluted when we had no cap or bowed when we had one on! Many of us detested saluting the Japanese at any time, but to be called back to do it again and again, bowing up and down whilst, as often as not, holding a couple of empty rice bowls, made a man feel utterly ridiculous, besides which he was quite likely to have his face slapped for his pains.

I remember that first night vividly. Most of us were tired and all slept soundly, but we awoke very stiff and sore on our hard beds, although it was not long before we never noticed them. I, for one, had often slept on the hatch of a ship for preference (especially in the tropics when one's bunk was invaded by bed-bugs!), so could hardly complain that this was a hardship!

We had arrived in the camp on a Friday. The next day the Americans from Guam were out working all day, but on the Sunday, when they had their rest day in the camp, we were marched down to the parade ground and drilled in Japanese again. It was not amusing.

We had not had any other exercise since our arrival, and were surprised that the Guam Americans constantly reiterated that the food was insufficient. We still had a number of men who would have none of the rice, and there were plenty of others who did not eat much. Pargiter and I, with a few others, ate as much as we could get inside us and actually quite enjoyed it. In fact, I learned to like rice in those first few days. Capt. Barber was amongst those who would not eat it. This was one of the first instances when the sheep became separated from the goats, because it was perfectly plain that there was no alternative to eating rice if one was to stay alive.

Nevertheless, there was always plenty left in our two barracks that first week-end, and we noticed that the Americans opposite were always pleased enough to finish it, although I should place on record that they never came hanging round for it but waited until it was offered. Both breakfast and supper consisted of vegetable soup and a mixture of rice and barley every day: lunch was non-existent and only provided when one went out to work (which soon became every day except Sunday). It then comprised a ball of hard-packed rice and a small loaf of bread or, sometimes, three small rolls, which were packed in a paper bag. Initially soya beans were issued in place of soup on Sunday mornings and were regarded as the great delicacy of the week, being an article of currency so long as they appeared. Camp food held no allure and we thought of the lavatory tanks in the *Nankin* in which we had left such a fine store of Australian food.

First thing every morning, after being called, we had to get up and dress to be ready for *Tenko*, or 'muster', at six o'clock. This caused a good deal of trouble at first, because each prisoner had to have his blankets made up neatly and his berth tidy, and to be sat cross-legged, facing outwards, on the end of his sleeping mat. This was really intended to be the Yoga lotus position, which few men could achieve, but the legs were crossed with knees well down and the back straight, the hands being placed between the feet. The room leader, in our case Jackson, had to receive the duty officer, his sergeant and the odd guard, often accompanied by the interpreter, and to reel off a piece of patter in Japanese to the effect that all were present and correct in the barrack, and to report any who were sick and unable to call out their number. First, of course, he saluted. Then the rest of us were ordered to *kiri*, which implied that we must bow from the forced position in which we were already sitting. Indeed, a man with a big frame who was not used to it found this position difficult to sustain for any length of time.

Then we were required to number off, starting along a lower shelf, along the one above it and then the top one, after which the shelves were taken in the same order on the opposite side of the room. As each man had to keep himself rigid, without *any* movement during this operation, it was not always easy for the first men on each row to know when their turn had come because, if a man on the lower shelf was sick, his number would not necessarily be the same as during the previous muster. Any hesitation or error in numbering always led to more or less trouble, and the whole affair took place again in the evening.

The next barrack had chosen Knudsen, the mate of an American tanker, to be their room leader, not being in the unfortunate position of having had any such creature as Jackson foisted upon them. Capt. Christiansen, as a Norwegian, was at an obvious disadvantage in any choice of this sort, although he did speak English very well, because he was thought to have a rather haughty and arrogant bearing, particularly towards the Japanese, which was not felt to be suitable in a room leader. He was, however, made the leader of our working party soon afterwards, which was very satisfactory to both Pargiter and myself as we both got on with him very well indeed, whilst we considered Capt. Barber to be a broken reed — an opinion which proved to be tragically correct.

Our two barracks were paraded in the street three or four mornings after our arrival. After the Guam Americans had gone off in various directions to the different stevedoring firms for which they worked, we were each issued with a tin disc bearing our camp number, which we were enjoined to wear at all times, and we then departed for a destination unknown, which proved to be a shipyard, and which was the place of our toil for twelve months. This was a matter in which, like so many, we had no choice, but it will be described in the next chapter.

Many of us, both severally and collectively, and representing the merchant service officers, protested on numerous occasions that we should not work. I doubt if our representations ever got beyond Fujimoto, the interpreter, and his successors, although Pargiter, Craggs, Henry and I only joined in this movement with our tongues in our cheeks because, whilst whole-heartedly supporting the cause as a matter of principle, we knew that we were better off working than moping about with nothing to do and nowhere to go in that dismal camp which had no facilities for recreation and which caught none of the glorious Japanese sun. Going out to work not only provided a modicum of healthy exercise, but also a change of scene which was a far greater boon than most of our colleagues realized.

In due course one more of the barracks was filled. The new arrivals were Americans, chiefly conscript soldiers who had been captured in Bataan or on Corregidor, in the Philippines. These men had had a bad time after capture and before their arrival in Japan and were in very bad physical shape when they arrived. Many of them had contracted dysentery before they ever embarked and nearly all looked ill. Some of them were exceptionally good fellows but many — all too many — were of the worst possible types to be found in their country. Some were real hill-billies from the Middle West. Many of these men were filthy in their habits, devoid of any apparent marks of civilized behaviour and wholly without honour or honesty, even among their own fellows. Their bearing was all the more striking in contrast with the original incumbents of the camp who were the best type of American servicemen and who never dropped their standards throughout the hostilities.

These new arrivals passed through a dreadful few months. The weather was by then extremely cold and they should remember it with evil memory: those, that is, who are left of them. Potentially they were a tough lot, at all events in spirit, and this was subsequently turned into unfortunate channels, but their bodies were too weakened and nearly half of them died in that first winter. Dysentery took a certain toll, but their greatest enemy was what we knew only as 'electric feet'. It was caused in the first instance, I believe, by vitamin deficiencies, but it took an extremely unpleasant form. At first the toes seemed to suffer a permanent condition rather like 'pins and needles', but to an infinitely worse degree, so that it was agony to lie still and a man simply had to walk about. Then it was worse. The condition gradually spread up the foot. The toes putrefied and had to be amputated. This was soon followed by other amputations as the disease spread but, before it reached the top of the legs, the victims were mercifully dead. When a man reached the amputation stage he was taken up to the Stadium, which passed for a hospital.

No man was taken to the Stadium until he was really bad, and relatively few ever returned to their camps. I never saw the inside of it (for which I remain thankful), but there were lurid tales concerning the place. It was, in fact, the area beneath the seats of a sports stadium; crude, gloomy and difficult to keep clean. An Englishman, a Dr. Jackson, who was taken prisoner, I think, at Hong Kong, actually ran the place as prisoner-in-charge, but was very much hampered by the Japanese who were nominally responsible. Dr. Jackson had the reputation of a saint and enjoyed the complete confidence of every prisoner of every nationality in every camp in the area. He became an almost legendary figure and it was universally believed that, if he could not cure a man, the case was hopeless. Probably no man ever had a succession of more difficult or more frustrating cases to treat; few men have had more dreadful or demoralising conditions in which to work, and few medical men can ever have inspired their patients with greater hope and uplift to their morale. No words can do justice to that man's work, and no praise of it should be held too lightly. If few patients emerged from that Hell of a Stadium, it was usually because they were not sent there until there was no hope for them. Some of the allied medical orderlies who worked for him did not inspire the same confidence. It was felt, for instance, that if they were going to remove the gold fillings from the teeth of the dead for such future profit as they evidently hoped, they might at least have waited until the deceased were cold.

Because the patients did not work they were kept on the minimum rationing scale, and no sort of recreation for mind or body existed there. Men from other camps might be seen in that Stadium but, in that first winter when the mortality in all the camps was exceedingly high (probably around 30 – 33% overall), it was a case of the survival of the fittest to a large degree. The winter helped to eliminate the weak without any mercy and, usually little more than animated bags of bones, few sick men could cheer or bequeath any hope to each other.

The Japanese regarded the normal camps as working camps and they were not prepared to carry any unproductive individuals. They accepted that there must be a small camp detail to maintain the camp services — the cooking, cleaning, and so on — but there could be no support for sick men. A man had to be very ill indeed, or physically incapacitated, before he could stay off work. After a time they ordained that not more than a certain percentage of the whole camp would be allowed to be on the sick roster (I think that 1% was the figure and anyone who is familiar with normal office or factory absentee rates will appreciate that this was an abnormally low target under healthy living conditions) and it was a condition of sickness that it must carry a high temperature. In the first instance the decision rested with our own medical orderlies: members of the camp detail who were following their former calling in the American navy, and with an American Army doctor to determine which men might stay in. As time progressed, the regulations became harsher and it became incumbent on these men, who found themselves in a truly invidious position, to enforce them rigidly because, did they not do so, the Japanese would arbitrarily drive out the surplus, often accompanied by a beating for good measure, without any consideration for the relative conditions of the sick.

The permanently maimed were the exceptions. These were the few men who had had legs amputated or who were in similar case and who, although not actually ill, were not potential workers. They were left in the camp initially, and not then moved to the Stadium. It was only for those who were beyond the normal crude treatment of the camp and it was only when a man reached that stage that he was moved up there. (Not that Dr. Jackson had anything more with which to work!) The mortality rates at the Stadium must have been quite phenomenally high, but this was no reflection on the ministrations of Jackson. Rather should one say that every single recovery was his triumph. Later on the permanently incapacitated *were* taken to the Stadium. Einar Ulgren, the Norwegian carpenter who had lost a leg, also had syphilis, and this probably doomed him, for he died soon afterwards. But a Chinaman, who had also had a leg taken off, recovered well, and one can imagine how dreadful life in that charnel house must have been for him.

In the earliest days it was almost impossible to extract even the most elementary first-aid supplies from our warders and when, after a long and bitter struggle, they finally produced such items as lint, sticking plaster and iodine, they were in cases labelled:- **'AMERICAN RED CROSS SUPPLIES — TOKYO EARTHQUAKE RELIEF.'** Now the Tokyo earthquake had taken place in 1923, twenty years previously! This brought out one of the inherent traits in the Japanese character: that of hoarding, which became more and more manifest to us as time went on.

As soon as the merchant seamen went out to work, they all discovered that they did like rice after all. Appetites were recovered at once: every grain of our ration was eaten and most people could have done with more. As the bowls were filled at meal times, the majority of men sat on the edge of their bays and stared down greedily at those who were serving it out, in order to be sure that it was being done fairly. This was typical of the lack of co-operation and general mistrust which constantly pervaded this assorted body of men. In order to ensure equality, a standard bowl was filled from the rice buckets with a wooden paddle and then inverted into the individual bowls which were ranged along the table, in rows. Anything left in the bucket at the end was added to these bowls with the wooden paddle as equitably as possible. When serving the soup, it was essential to keep the bucket well stirred to ensure that such vegetable matter as it might contain was distributed to everyone. It was no easy job to satisfy some of the men, but it was almost always done and the volunteers who undertook this thankless task gave a very good account of themselves, day after day.

Capt. Barber, however, did not overcome his repugnance to rice and continued to subsist purely on the soup, which was not much better than warm water. Buckets of edible seaweed were produced at intervals and, in the early days, very frequently. I really enjoyed this and ate a good deal of it, but was amongst a small minority. Green tea also appeared although I have no recollection of its frequency because I, personally, had never drunk tea, either black or green, and saw no reason to change my habits in these circumstances. (Nor did I ever drink it thereafter. To me, it was merely spoiling good water: I have never been impressed by the internal appearance of a broken tea-pot spout, quite apart from having a suspicion that the various flavours attributed to different leaves might equally be due to the sweat on the feet of the local coolies who tread the leaves!) While we watched, Barber got thinner and thinner; his magnificently developed torso wasting away to skin and bone and, as he declined, his morale dwindled with his physique. He took the uncompromising view that, if the Japanese were to win the war, we were doomed to more or less perpetual slavery and that if, on the other hand, the Allies should win, we should all be put to the sword. There was, therefore, no hope in life. This was not a point of view peculiar to himself but, being by then in the worst physical condition of any man in the barrack, he dwelt on it more and more until it became an obsession only equalled by his insensate belief that he could not eat rice.

I think many men deplored his attitude. A few of us also took exception to it. It was true that all were now on the same plane, mixed up together and, as it were, in the same boat, but a few of us took the view that such conditions stemmed from the Japanese and that, whilst the officers should not behave gregariously, they should maintain good relations and endeavour to maintain and to set as good an example as possible. This attitude was confined to a relatively few, since it has already been stated that many men who rank as officers in the merchant service are only such by sufferance. Those of us who did feel that way thought that Barber was setting the worst possible example and, almost from the first day, we had urged him to pull himself together, reminding him that he was not only the senior man (the only captain) in the barrack, but that it was not so long since he had been telling us all of his longings to get home to his wife and to the child which he had never seen. He owed it to them to show more spirit. We asked him what would be the effect on the young boy on the shelf opposite seeing a captain so losing his grip on his morale. We reminded him that he had been very successful in his career and that we were amazed that anyone who had exhibited such a joy of living as he had in the *Charlotte Schliemann*, with his fetish of physical culture, could have collapsed so quickly. If ever the tag *Mens sana in corpore sano* was disproved, it was in his case.

Certainly some of us had been disappointed by the lack of resolution he had displayed over any schemes to escape and take that tanker but, taking his mania for physical fitness into account, coupled with his (then) determination to see his wife and baby, I had regarded him as a man who would survive a set of unpleasant conditions far better than anyone else amongst our number. His was an outstanding example of how one can misjudge the essential fibre of a man and indeed, as events proved, the conditions under which we lived progressively sought out the primitive in the men around us, and demonstrated who were really the men of iron and who the men of straw. In each case, they were often the last whom one would have expected at the outset. We railed, we pleaded, we cajoled, but it made no difference. Some of the Guam Americans

191

very decently smuggled him in some tinned tangerines they had stolen, but this made no difference either. He had taken unto himself a death-wish, much as the old greaser in the *Raranga*, as I related earlier in this book.

Capt. Barber's conception of the future was by no means unique, but it was a silly one upon which to dwell. *'Sufficient unto the day is the evil thereof'* should surely have been the motto of those who viewed the ultimate future with such mistrust. Most of us thought that an Allied victory was assured sooner or later, although we conceded that it might be long delayed. We did not suppose that we should be put to the sword but, at that time, we found it very hard to conceive what our position would be in the event of an invasion of Japan, which we presumed to be the culmination of the war. It was not until a little later, when we had learnt more of the national character, that we realized that nothing would happen to us because the Japanese are incapable of improvisation and would have no idea what do with themselves, let alone with us, when they no longer had the initiative: a forecast which proved to be remarkably accurate.

Barber became weaker and weaker until he could no longer support himself in an upright position. To all intents and purposes he was on hunger-strike, though we did not think that that was his motive. Finally, he was removed to the Stadium where, after an interval, he died. Plenty of men died at that time, though very few of the ex-German prisoners, but Capt. Barber was unique in all our experience since there was nothing wrong with him whatever. At least, he had no physical ailment. A post-mortem was carried out and confirmed this. He had simply lost the will to live and, when I was called upon to see his widow (by then with a nice little girl) after the war, it was not an easy interview, since I did not feel that the truth would have been palatable. The example of his deplorable philosophy did no good to the men around him — men who might have expected a better lead from their erstwhile spokesman and 'leader' — and it was as well that few other men of authority gave way to such defeatism.

On the whole, morale was reasonably high. We had got over our initial shock at our environment and were shaking down very well. The Japanese we thought a lamentable lot, but even they varied a good deal. Our guard was changed every week or fortnight, and our fortunes rose or fell according to the temper of the different sergeants and camp commanders who were also changed at intervals. The majority of the prisoners had by now learnt to *kiri* and *bango* sufficiently well to appease the Japanese on routine occasions and, although there were constant incidents, they were generally confined to individuals. We were left alone most of the time that we were in the barracks and I continued writing my diary, still having a sufficiency of paper, while Pargiter had started one some time previously. I believe that a few other men were doing the same thing but, not long after our arrival, word reached us that an Englishman in the other camp had been found to have a fully-written account of the sinking of the *Lisbon Maru*.

That camp consisted of men who had been taken in Hong Kong, most of them being in the Royal Scots. They were being shipped over to Japan in very cramped conditions down the hold of a ship named the *Lisbon Maru* when she was torpedoed. As soon as this happened, the Japanese battened the hatches down on them and, as the vessel settled down in her death throes, set about saving themselves. The prisoners did succeed in breaking out and a number of them managed to get ashore to some small islands, while others were picked up by fishing boats or junks, but the death roll was enormous and it ranked amongst the more unpleasant incidents of the war. Those who had escaped were rounded up and were now in the 'English' camp.

The discovery of this written account drove the Japanese into a frenzy. It was made clear in both camps that diaries of any sort were anathema to them and that no-one might keep them, under direst penalties. We knew our gaolers well enough to know that this was no idle threat and a good deal of paper was surreptitiously thrown into the boiler during the next few days. I believe that all were voluntarily destroyed except three: Pargiter's, mine and that of MacAvoy, the second engineer of the *Gloucester Castle*. Although we did not advertise the keeping of these journals to our fellows, there was so little privacy that their existence must have been pretty evident and, if it was never voiced aloud, there was obviously a certain amount of resentment about them as they were thought to be prejudicial to the common safety. Perhaps they were. I felt that in our somewhat empty thraldom it was essential to sustain some objective, and I had determined that mine would be to maintain full accounts of all the events which impinged directly or indirectly on our lives, as I had done under the Germans, although at that time I had little idea of the ingenuity which it was going to entail.

At this time there was still a certain amount of doubt about the attitude to be adopted to and by ships' officers. Most men still continued to address us as 'Sir' or 'Mr.', and to the lascars we were still *'Sahib'*. It was important to retain our entity, as we had not, as a group, despaired of establishing our position with the Japanese but, when living and working cheek by jowl with our men, it would have been churlish to have insisted on such forms. Pargiter and I felt that the officers' own example was the straight-forward solution to the problem but, unfortunately, due to the variety of men and types under this heading, we hardly expected this view to be universally shared or to be put into effect. In this, too, we proved to be correct, regrettable as it may be to record.

There was a test case fairly early on. Jackson was our appointed leader and it was, of course, essential that his authority should be maintained for the sake of the common discipline, whether we liked it or not. He was unequal to the task and had become surrounded by sycophants — stewards, waiters and the like from another ship — who were somewhat 'bolshie' in their outlook and definitely anti-officer on principle.

Jackson was a weak character, as I knew too well, and he knew that I knew it. Pargiter and I, due to our seniority, self-sufficiency and obvious teamwork, which was more highly developed than in any other group, and to keeping ourselves very much to ourselves (backed to a large degree by our three colleagues) probably appeared to be a potential power group, although we had not, in fact, any designs in that direction. Further, our determination to maintain our diaries demonstrated that we were not to be over-ridden too lightly. (In fact, and on account of the diaries, we were at pains *not* to appear in the public eye at all so far as the Japanese were concerned.)

I was probably as well clothed as any man there. All the *Dalhousie's* ship's company had entered captivity well clad. Not only was I in my best (and fairly new) uniform which was still relatively smart, but the fresh gold braid probably enhanced my appearance of affluence. I also had a bridge coat in equally good condition. Some men were very badly clad and the weather was becoming very cold. Snow was beginning to lie on the surrounding hills and the wind was bitter. Broomfield, of our party, was still in his German canvas suit and Capt. Christiansen, the Norwegian with whom I was particularly friendly, was in much the same case. I had repeatedly offered to lend my bridge coat to these two, as I also wore a good cable-stitched jersey, but Christiansen, in his pride, would never accept it, though Broomfield had occasionally worn it. It was, however, only marginally useful, as it was scarcely practicable or desirable to wear it in the camp. In any case, being the largest man in our group, there were very few men who could wear this coat without becoming lost in it. Christiansen and Broomfield were two of the very few who could.

One evening I entered the barrack from the rear of the camp. Jackson's henchman nudged him and, rather diffidently but with such show of bravado as he could command, he said that he wished to speak to me. I think he hoped that I would walk over to him and thus avoid undue publicity or sheer confrontation, but I remained by the door. He might have been better advised to have approached some of us for advice in his administration rather than to have listened to the men who surrounded him and made the ammunition for him to fire, but he had not been able to bring himself to do this. On the contrary, he now suggested that it was wrong of me to keep so much clothing when so many men were badly clad and said that he had decided — (there was much nudging of him at this point) — that I should give up my bridge coat to Horsley. Now Horsley was a very diminutive deck-boy (the deck-boys not having been included in the Singapore party) and a nice lad, but so small that I could almost have lost him in one of the pockets of the coat, which he would scarcely have been able to lift! The coat was far longer than he was tall! He was a lad whom Jackson, who had demonstrated tendencies in this direction, evidently thought to be a 'pretty' lad, if that be the appropriate adjective.

The whole barrack was instantly silent and intent. Jackson was not a popular leader with the bulk of the men and this was the first occasion on which he had tried to exert his supposed authority. The atmosphere was electric and even the Lascars sensed that something was afoot and craned over the top shelf. I looked him up and down until he went red in the face, wondering, I dare say, if I would throw his desertion of his gun at him. I decided against this, in the interests of common discipline. Moreover, although the situation was unexpected, I realized at once that I had every advantage over him: education, background, language (without the need to resort to expletives) and even physical presence, while, standing by the door, I was in the most prominent possible position and able to address the whole barrack when answering. I made it clear that the suggestion was absurd, and stated why, but was then forthright in my comments both on his own and his cronies' ideas and behaviour. I had hardly started before his neighbours, fawning on him and egging him on so short a while before, were edging into the shadows at the back of their bays, leaving him alone at the front. Nor did I leave it at that, but verbally castigated both him and his fellows on issues extending far beyond the subject in hand to such a degree that they were all quelled for ever, for they never attempted to interfere with anyone, nor to impose their will, again.

When I had finally finished with him, there was some mild applause, but few of the audience realized the real stakes in the play. Llewellyn, perhaps with some premonition of his future, came up to me afterwards and, to my surprise, applauded what I had said. I was surprised because he was clearly astonished that I had acted as I had. It was obvious that he would not have done so in similar circumstances, and he was by no means the only one who applauded but made it clear that they would not be prepared to stand up for themselves (which meant 'ourselves'). This my coterie found to be depressing. It was not a matter of me and my coat: it went far beyond that. This was a test, somewhat clumsily staged, probably with the ultimate aim of forcing the destruction of the diaries (for which, I grant, they would have had some case), and in the same movement of destroying the officer status amongst us. The latter objective was not to be tolerated at a time when we were still endeavouring to establish that status in an attempt to be transferred to the officers' camp which we knew to exist at Zent Suji, or to another one elsewhere. Although neither motive was breathed aloud, the former was wholly unacceptable to me, and few men appreciated that any retreat which I might have made from my position would have established a precedent for a most undesirable autocracy.

In any case, if half a dozen of us had stripped naked and distributed our garments to others, it would have been the merest drop in the ocean of need where the general shortage of clothing was concerned. The Japanese had made no issue whatever, and there was a feeling that there would be none while there was no general want. No-one had a change of anything, which made washing one's clothes a great problem. The greater the general want, the sooner an issue was likely to be made.

This affair did quite a lot of good, as it cleared the air and established individual positions. Any man who allows a retrogression in his standards must automatically suffer a corresponding lowering of his morale, and morale is infectious. There was no desire by any officer to set himself in a superior position to those around him, but to relinquish his caste would be retrograde and, in the long run, a bad influence on everybody, quite apart from the matter of whether officers should be in a working camp at all. I had sailed in ships' foc's'les and knew my men, as did plenty of my colleagues, but any example or lead in morale which might be given would be made so much the harder by any pretence at resignation. It would simply have led to a general loss of self-respect and, if activated by a small group of the less pleasant elements, would automatically have increased their very undesirable influence.

It is one of the best features of the average Englishman that he will so often sing in adversity. Our history cites examples without number, for it is a feature which, if not unique to the British, is more marked in them than in any other race: even in the Americans who are, in reality, a very heterogeneous collection of races. In consequence, a number of our men went about the camp whistling and singing. This was possibly to maintain their spirits as there was little enough to sing about and, remembering the concerts in the tanker, a few sing-songs were arranged in our barrack at the week-ends.

At first, the Japanese came and watched, open-mouthed. Then they became angry. When a man was found singing in the camp he was prone to be slapped in the face or clubbed with a rifle butt. Sing-songs were forbidden. Finally Sanders was instructed to issue an edict that no man must whistle or sing. Those who did received short shrift. They sometimes endured long spells of standing to rigid attention in front of the guard room, being slapped by every Jap who passed, or other, more refined, forms of punishment. One might have supposed that the Japanese would have been pleased to see the morale of the camp so high, but this was not the case although the ruling was born of an innate lack of understanding of the Western mind. To them it was the greatest conceivable disgrace to be taken prisoner and most of them still honestly believed that no member of his own race would allow himself to be taken alive, but would first perform *hara-kiri* or kill himself by other means (as so many actually did.)

The Americans in the camp who had come from the Philippines had experienced terrible conditions in the ship which brought them to Japan, but in that vessel were some Japanese who had been taken by the Americans during the fighting, and who had then been re-taken on the surrender. The treatment meted out to these unfortunates was so dreadful that the Americans, for all their suffering, might almost have been on a pleasure cruise in contrast! The mind boggles when imagining the fate reserved for these Japanese who allowed themselves to be captured on their arrival back in their homeland.

Thus there was a complete dissimilarity of viewpoint on the whole question of prisoners between the Japanese and the Western races. To them, we must feel utterly disgraced: we must be degraded beyond words and we must surely wish ourselves dead. Feeling as they did, I could never understand why they took prisoners at all, as it was a condition which they evidently did not comprehend. It could not have been wholly for propaganda purposes, since prisoners attract resources of men and materials. They themselves are not a race which is given to promiscuous singing at the best of times, and it was incomprehensible to them that we, who should be in a perpetual state of abject contrition to our family gods (!) and to our ancestors for our defection in prolonging our lives so dishonourably, with the loss (as they saw it) of all our self-respect, should still sing. That we could (and did) worried them terribly: not because we did sing, but because they could not understand how we could bring ourselves to do so and thus, in order to restore their own peace of mind, they stopped all singing!*

If this was the worst that they did, their record would not be so bad. They were bad enemies but, in all the circumstances, it was an undeniable and fundamental truth that the prisoners' worst enemies were often their own fellows, and this will become increasingly apparent in this narrative.

---

* Readers may object that the prisoners sang in the film of *The Bridge on the River Kwai*. I thought this an excellent production, though this aspect did not ring true from our experience. Whether the prisoners depicted in that film were allowed to sing, or whether it is an essential that a modern film simply must have music, I cannot say!

When we first arrived in Osaka, we worked six days a week and were free on Sundays. Apart from the Philippine Americans' barrack, most men in the two camps were pretty fit. Food was barely adequate, but had not deteriorated to the degrees which we experienced later on. When in the camp there was nothing to do except to sleep, talk or wash such clothes as we had. Certainly Pargiter and I had the *Oxford Book of Verse*, but there was no other book of any sort. On Sundays, as there was no work, there was no lunch, and the consequence was that this day hung very heavily on the minds of a number of men. Sunday had originally been retained as a rest day on religious grounds but, when the Japanese soon realized that it entailed no form of religious observance whatever, they proposed to make it a working day. On this Sanders and Sergeant-Major Mathieson, (a very good man who was in charge of the English camp and who maintained his authority and the discipline of his men in an exemplary fashion throughout, despite a very tough element within his Royal Scots), successfully convinced the Japanese that white men were not used to this sort of diet and simply could not work entire weeks at a stretch without a break to regain their energy.

The alternative to this day was work and only the least intelligent could not foresee that our lot would deteriorate considerably before the close of play. There had been little effort made to dislodge the Japanese from any position as yet, nor had that country really begun to feel the pinch, while the Allies were still grouping as a prelude to the great offensives against Germany. It should have been sufficiently evident that such little advantages as we had should be held at all costs.

Jackson and his clique, however, found the ennui of Sundays more than they could stand, having no reserves of self-sufficiency. Somehow a ball had come into their possession, or been manufactured, and they desired to seek permission to go to the parade ground in order to play football. (This compulsion to kick a ball about was then another inherently British trait.) On learning of this, our patience gave out and led us to break our customary silence. We reasoned, implored and finally stormed at the very idea of such folly. As the whole point of our rest day was that we had not the energy to work, *"How then"*, we asked, *"could we have the energy to play football?"* Sanders, very rightly, refused to represent their case when they approached him, so they seethed and plotted.

Fujimoto sometimes came into the barracks late in the evenings, assuming friendliness, to chat with anyone who would talk with him. There were always some who would do so, chiefly at the other end of the barrack near Jackson and his followers, and on these occasions we went in deadly fear of careless talk, thinking of our diaries. He heard about this football scheme and, with seeming grace, said that he would see what he could do. In due course he returned and said that they might have their game, in the meantime encouraging some of the less intelligent members of the English camp to join them. When Sunday came all those who wished were allowed to go. They were a very small minority, almost all British, but they enjoyed themselves and returned ebullient with their success.

The next Sunday the performance was repeated. The following week we all had to go, whether we wanted to or not and, when most of us stood around declining to play in attitudes of feigned fatigue, we were given a gratuitous drilling for over an hour. Thereafter the question of Sunday rest was a lost cause and we progressively went on our working details more and more on this day until any thought of a rest day was a lost memory. I dare say that those footballers came to rue their action as much as the rest of us as the months wore on, but their regret will not bring back those older men who might have lived had they been able to snatch the occasional day of rest, when the energy which they expended at work was exceeded by any strength they may have derived from their meagre rations. Knowing what occurred in a given set of circumstances, no man can say precisely what would have occurred had those circumstances been different, but there can be little doubt that in due course this particular folly contributed in large measure to the deaths of the *Dalhousie's* chief mate, Mr. Llewellyn: of Tony Serafin, her Italian saloon steward, and of a number of other men who come to my mind. That act of insensate selfishness over football was but one example of how men could act to the detriment of their fellows, and I have not the slightest doubt that Jackson and his friends should carry a number of such deaths on their consciences for the rest of their lives.

X

OSAKA SHOSEN KAISHA

When the merchant seamen first fell out to go to work it was with very mixed feelings. Whilst the officers resented working at all, everyone was again experiencing the now familiar presentiments which arise when approaching a new unknown but, on the other hand, the effect of the limitations of the camp was being felt already and, in one sense, we were all pleased to think that we were going to have a change. Most of the Americans were working on stevedoring details and we supposed that we should do the same sort of thing. The information that we were all to go to one firm surprised us, as we were about a hundred and twenty strong, whilst most of the American details consisted of about a dozen men, or twenty at the most.

We were told that we must have a *honcho*, or foreman, and Capt. Christiansen was chosen for this post. Then, after the usual *kiri* and *bango* drill, we were moved off down the street in which the camp was situated and, for the first time, were enabled to see the extent of this narrow, squalid thoroughfare, whilst hordes of small boys with close-cropped and often scrofulous hair ran beside us. To the right, we could see that there was a large, multi-storied warehouse towering over the low, wooden buildings which clustered along their miserable streets, but at the end of the road we turned to the right and the prospect became a little better. The dwellings had come to an end and we were passing along a relatively open dock area. Over a small hump-backed bridge we went: over a canal which led to the basin on one side of which was the large warehouse — one of the two very large ones in the town owned by the great *Daibatsu* family of Sumitomo — and there was a reasonably large ship alongside it. Further out was the harbour with a variety of craft at buoys or at anchor and beyond them a long, low breakwater. Towards the horizon was a small island and, further away still, what appeared to be a cape or peninsula which we supposed (wrongly) bounded the ocean. We stared hard and long in that direction.

So we passed on along the harbour and dock basins with more warehouses on the right and various industrial premises lying along the left-hand side of the road, including what was evidently a distillery or brewery. The prospect behind this dock area was reasonably open, but we could see that the city itself, beyond, was densely packed with houses and that there was a huge network of barge canals covering the area. Soon we passed over another bridge to open out another basin in which lay a couple of hospital ships, looking very gay in their white paint. There was all the colour of the coolies in their blue tunics with their companies' logos in white or red Japanese characters on their backs, and their white breeches, as they loped along with loaded baskets on the ends of their yokes. There were the distinctive barges crowding the canals and basins with the high-pooped Japanese coastal craft, each with a boat slung over her stern, an auxiliary motor and a large fore-and-aft sail on one mast. Far away, to the left, we could see the clear outline of the hills and it was evident that Osaka and its environs lay in a semi-circular basin, bounded by the high ground and the bay.

A little beyond the basin containing the hospital ships, we turned left, evidently keeping inside the warehouse line of a river which ran into the harbour at that point. On each side the ground was now often waste but then, on the banks of the river, we passed a shipyard: its gantries towering above the surrounding terrain, and opposite to it lay the odd timber yard. We met few pedestrians or others on the road until we came to a cluster of houses where the people came pouring out into the street to watch our passing, as the sight of marching prisoners was still a novel one to them. Again we turned sharp right over a railway and then sharp right again, so that we were heading back in the same direction from which we had just come, but on the other side of the railway. Thus it was evident that our route was considerably elongated by this detour in order to cross the last bridge. After a march of about three miles from the camp we entered the shipyard which we had seen already, and were formed up outside an office at the end of the works drive.

We had two of the camp guards with the party together with a couple of Japanese civilians from the yard, who broke off and joined a small knot of their countrymen who were standing a little to one side. These were the foremen. Once more we had to *kiri* and *bango*, but without the fanatical fervour which characterized these manoeuvres in the camp. (Since some men wore hats and saluted, while others were bare-headed and bowed, the effect was bizarre, to say the least, in either case!) Soon a small, elderly man came out from the office and stood before us wearing formal tails and pin-striped trousers. Western dress seldom becomes Eastern peoples who always look more elegant in their native garb, but tails on a Japanese bring him a little too close to the natural history books. This little man was not amongst these, but he looked as though he had been dressed up for a joke, and he wore the long finger nail on the little finger, which protrudes nearly an inch beyond the finger-tip and is the mark of every educated and cultured Japanese. (We learnt that the object was to scrape the wax from the ear!)

He proceeded to address us in excellent English but in the high falsetto which always seemed to be pitched the higher when a Japanese was speaking in English. He was, he said, the President of the Osaka Shosen Shipyard where we were to work. We should be treated well and would be divided into different groups within the organization. He said that he sympathised with us and was sorry to see us there, but that ours was one of the fortunes of war, and concluded with the revelation that we should each be issued with a cap. He said little that was superfluous and I believe that he meant what he said. We seldom set eyes on him again, but it seemed that he was genuine in his rather unorthodox views in that community, and we never had the slightest ground to complain of any treatment which was meted out to us by his organization, with the possible exception of the actions of one foreman, as will be related.

While he had been speaking, we had been joined by one of the largest Japanese that we ever saw. Not only was his whole body much bigger than most of his countrymen, but it seemed to get larger in its proportions as it got higher, his shoulders being broad and ponderous, whilst his head was so large that it seemed to be too heavy for his broad shoulders, and it differed from the normal physiognomy of the land which tends to an extreme width of flat face across the eyes and at the top of the cheek-bone, because he had wide, pendulous jowls. He was the general manager of the yard, but we always referred to him as ''Frankenstein'' (whose monster we thought he resembled) or as Boris Karloff. He was invariably very affable to the prisoners, frequently proffering cigarettes, which were as gold to those who smoked them, and he often attempted to speak to us. These conversational attempts were invariably abortive as we never succeeded in understanding him or in making him understand us, either by signs or words. He never despaired of trying, though each attempt ended by him shaking his head and smiling sadly at us. It was a great pity, because it was clear that he was often trying to explain the latest war news which was strictly denied to us by the army.

After being issued with a green cap similar to that worn by the majority of Japanese, but with the Osaka Shosen logo on the front in white, Pargiter and I realized that this was a moment for a display of 'good gefangenism', for we were about to be split up into our working parties. Partly by good judgement and partly by luck (since we had no idea how large each party was to be), the five of us formed the nucleus of one, with the addition of Mackavoy and a couple of other engineer officers. Each Japanese *honcho* (foreman) led off his party and we found ourselves in the charge of a cheerful, broadly-built little man with the widest of faces in a sea of wide faces. His name, he made us understand, was Hirada (pronounced 'Hilada') and it transpired that he was a Korean who was settled in Japan.

Leading us over the maze of wires before the slipways, he steered us to the far corner of the yard where it was evident that the hot bending was carried on and where a number of deep forges were burning under forced draught. The benders seemed to be quite well disposed and smiled and nodded at us, but an immense crowd of other people gathered round to stare at us. No-one appeared to be at all hostile but rather intensely curious and, as every other squad received the same sort of welcome, we were agreeably surprised after the reception we had received in the streets of Yokohama and outside Osaka station. Later on we had no illusions that the President and Frankenstein had paved our way for us.

The benders were soon chattering excitedly together — they were nearly all Koreans — whereupon a number of students who were evidently employed in the yard pushed themselves forward and, as there was no common language, we had to use signs, because conversation was obviously expected of us. Our first purpose was to explain to the crowd that we had been taken prisoners by the Germans and not by the Japanese, in order to deflate any crowing spirits which might be present. I doubt if they ever did understand the point that we were trying to explain and have a horrible suspicion that in the end they believed that we were Germans who had been captured by the Japanese! Finally a student appeared with a board and a piece of chalk, with which he wrote his opening gambit:- *"I am a Christian."*

Although this was something of a *non sequitur*, supposing that he understood English, we answered him in that language, but without any discernible effect, so we wrote an answer on the board, but this was equally incomprehensible to him. Later we came across a number of Japanese who understood English and could write it with great facility, although they would seldom trust themselves to speak it, but this fellow was presumably of the variety which had learnt stock phrases out of a book, rather of the order of *"The gardener of my aunt has an umbrella"* and that this was the extent of his knowledge, as any further dicta which he wrote added no more to mutual understanding than the first.

Our job was to ensure that the bending fires always had sufficient coal. It was typical of the land that the coal heap should be situated in the corner of the yard diametrically opposite to that in which it was used, and we were provided with short poles and wicker baskets with which to carry it. The idea was that two men should carry the pole on their shoulders, one at each end, with the basket slung in the middle. To the Japanese, this was the easy way of doing it, because their usual method was to have one man in the middle of the pole (or yoke) and a basket at each end. The bearer would proceed at a long lope with his knees slightly bent. Somewhat irrationally, we always termed such a yoke a 'yo-ho' pole. There were some coolies in the yard who carried immensely heavy loads of pig iron to the foundry by this means and they were paid what ranked as very high wages by the comparative standards of the land. We were told that the strain of the job was such that they sometimes fell dead in the middle of a carry, but we never had any evidence of this.

Although our method was relatively easy, we found it awkward. It was only tolerable if the two men were of almost the same height, which was seldom the case, and it was made the more irritating by the necessity to walk in step over the wires and general clutter of the yard, and also by the fact that the baskets held so little that we had to make innumerable journeys to accomplish very little. We used to take it in turns to load (with shovels) or to carry, whilst the others lay in the sun while they were waiting, or stood by the warm fires, according to the season of the year. No-one appeared to worry how much or how little work we did so long as the fires were kept supplied. Our guards used to walk round occasionally but, as they seldom had any idea of what any individual prisoner was supposed to be doing, we found ourselves free to walk round the shipyard and explore almost at will, providing that we maintained a certain circumspection.

I think it was Fox who, when wandering about, discovered an old, broken-down wheelbarrow on a scrap dump one day fairly soon after we had started work at the yard. Apart from Pargiter and myself, our party were all engineers who had that barrow repaired and working in a very short time and, by using it instead of the baskets, we were enabled to bring round enough coal to last the fires for the day in about half an hour. It involved a slightly longer traverse but, as this necessitated passing the open cook-house, over which presided some rather slow-witted women, we were sometimes able to snatch a few pieces of root ginger or pickled radish which the Japanese used as a side dish for their rice and which, if they did not serve to fill our bellies, at least provided a change of taste.

All the Japanese were tremendously impressed by our activities and, one day, we arrived at the yard to split into our parties to find a vast array of shining new, red wheelbarrows in rows, ranged all the way up the works yard. Certainly we had never seen (nor ever did see, elsewhere) a wheelbarrow used any more than we had seen a baby in a pram, but they must have known about them, witness the wreck of the one Fox had found. However, these new ones were distributed to the various

Japanese carrying parties, who were all as pleased as punch with them.

They caused us unmitigated hilarity because, although a few were put to quite sensible uses, the majority were allocated for the transportation of long, heavy baulks of timber or for vast and cumbersome steel plates. In both cases the operation was fraught with tremendous difficulty, a large number of men staggering along beside each barrow in an endeavour to retain the load without letting it fall off and, in order that the handles might be used, such loads were always unbalanced. Each journey involved a number of crashes and as often as not the whole affair would collapse, usually bringing down a number of the Japs with it. As they all wore thin canvas covered *jika-taki**, the absentee rate soared after steel plates and baulks of timber landed on their toes and feet!

The use of wheelbarrows for such loads would only have been suitable for a slap-stick music hall turn, and in the event not only required far more men than the original method, but took something like ten times as long! No-one seemed to realize that the use of a barrow for coal and for steel plates was not the same thing, and there were those who seemed to regard our success as some sort of conjuring trick! In all this, it was observed that the one party who might have derived much benefit from a few wheelbarrows — the pig iron coolies — was about the only one not to receive any!

It turned out that we had made ourselves too comfortable by the introduction of the barrow and, when it became apparent that we had almost nothing to do, we were initiated into the art of bending with sixteen and eighteen pound sledge-hammers. The engineers were already quite proficient at this, but Pargiter and I soon learnt to swing our hammers accurately and in time — when we wanted to. Work was still not very arduous as we were constantly waiting for frames or other pieces of steel to heat before they could be bent to a template on the slabs, with pegs stuck in holes to hold the steel, and in this we probably had the best detail in the yard because we had plenty of rest periods and warmth in the very cold winter. The men in the foundry also had warmth, but were in a much more unpleasant environment. There were one or two unfortunate occasions when we struck the hand of a Japanese or Korean instead of the swage which he was holding at the end of a stiff wire. Such instances really were accidental, since we had nothing against these men at all but, although it must cause excruciating agony to be struck by an eighteen-pound sledge at the end of its swing, they always seemed to take it in relatively good part, even if their hand was put out of action for days, while their countrymen always found these incidents

---

* High-backed plimsolls with the big toe split from the others.

206

31. *Wheel-barrows at Osaka Shosen Shipyard were put to such absurd uses that they might have been part of a music hall turn.*

inordinately amusing and rocked about with laughter.

Occasionally we would break a hammer shaft. At first this happened by accident, but in due course we discovered how to do it on purpose but as though by accident, and Fox became so really expert at this that there came a glorious period when all bending in the yard was held up for nearly ten days until fresh supplies of shafts could be obtained! Hirada, who got the blame, was somewhat annoyed about this, but to the other Koreans and Japanese in the gang our reputation was much enhanced by this episode.

The shipyard was one of the easiest details ever worked by our camp, but it had the great disadvantage that it offered little to steal for our benefit, and many of the men were very cold in the winter months when a bitter wind swept the country and when snow was by no means uncommon. Cold can be a very demoralizing element. The worst jobs were probably those of the cold benders and the drillers, who were right out in the open, holding ice-cold sheets of steel into the machines. One of these squads had the only *honcho* who was generally unpleasant in his manner, but they dealt with him very effectively. An engineer in the party had a perfect understanding of the mechanics of the bending press and was able to adjust the speed of its operation. One day, when the gang was holding the outside edge of a plate as it was slowly bent into shape, the prisoners all stood back a little at a pre-arranged signal and the plate, which was rising very slowly with the pressure as it was bent, suddenly shot up with a speed that caught the *honcho* unawares and dealt him such a blow beneath his chin that it broke his jaw. The prisoners could hardly have seemed more sympathetic but, by the time that anyone had arrived, the machine had been re-adjusted and the whole affair ranked as a complete mystery to our employers. After the *honcho* had returned to work, the trick was accomplished on two other occasions, on one of which he was knocked out and on the other he received a nasty blow. After this it was felt that the long arm of coincidence would be stretched to breaking point if it was always the Japanese member of the gang who was hurt, but never the prisoners, so it was not repeated any more. The *honcho*, now a more chastened man, was by then more reasonable.

Some men worked in the foundry, some at drilling, at carrying timber and at various other jobs, but in each the tempo was much the same except in the case of those who were rivetting. There were a number of engineers in this party, who became obsessed with the idea of doing as much as they possibly could and who openly boasted of their increasing daily output: an attitude which the rest of us despised and vehemently derided. Certainly our best efforts would hardly have improved the output of the yard which was run on the most inefficient lines. When we had first arrived we were staggered to see no apparent advance in the ships on the stocks, which were either small cargo vessels of about 3,000 tons or submarine chasers, but later we learnt that the drawing office, which had been situated in a large wooden shed, had been burnt to the ground a few days before we had started, and that all the available plans of the vessels had been destroyed! This caused weeks of delay.

In due course, a ship was ready for launching and tremendous preparations were made. A canopied rostrum was erected for distinguished visitors and all work stopped whilst the employees lined the slips and gantries to watch her run down the ways. Frankenstein was rushing about and exuding self-importance whilst all the final arrangements for the launching were completed. Even the prisoners were allowed to stand at a distance to watch. Finally all was ready. It was high water and the President came and took up his stand on the rostrum with various Japanese of presumably high status. The ship was named; a bottle broke on her bow and .... nothing happened! The cheering stopped abruptly and the silence was such that it seemed that the hordes of assembled Japanese were trying to make the ship launch herself by sheer will-power. If so, they failed lamentably. I admired Frankenstein at this moment because he exhibited none of the usual Japanese characteristics of resigned despair in untoward circumstances, and none of us could think of anything which he might have tried and which he did not attempt. Men ran wires to winches and heaved on them: more and more heated tallow was spread over the already greased slipway, and checks were made to see that all the chocks were knocked out, but it was all to no avail and the distinguished company had to go home with the hull still on its keel-blocks. The ship was finally launched, somewhat surreptitiously, the following week!

That ship was built under an evil star. One day we were down on the quay where she was fitting out when the whistle went for the *ku-ké* (a short tea break). A workman aboard lit a cigarette and strolled over to lean against the rail along her after well-deck. These rails and their stanchions simply consisted of angle-irons spot-welded to each other and to the deck — a method unknown to any self-respecting shipbuilder. There was a crash as the whole length of rail went over the side under his weight, together with the miserable workman himself, who was mangled to death between the mass of steel and the quay-side. We found this incident highly diverting as many of us had sufficient technical knowledge of ship-building to derive great encouragement from such shoddy workmanship, and we were not likely to lose any sleep over the death of the hapless Japanese workman. The standards of construction and of craftmanship were quite appalling and, after that ship had completed a short maiden voyage, she had to come back for a long spell at the fitting out basin to be put right in almost every particular. Our drilling gang was able to perform a lot of minor sabotage by drilling holes in the wrong places, but all that they could do by intent was only a drop in the ocean of unintentional errors by the Japanese gangs in this respect.

When we had made our first appearance at the shipyard we were regarded with a good deal more curiosity than we felt our position warranted and, although we met with no hostility, it was a week or two before the workmen became really amiable. It was only then that we slowly began to learn that they had read such lurid tales of the British and Americans in their press that they really believed us to be little better than wild beasts (as their papers stated): that we must be the perpetrators of the most foul atrocities; that we were prone to eat babies and, generally, behaved in all sorts of revolting ways. All this was probably very good propaganda for a simple people. There was only an infinitesimally small middle class, as we know it, in Japan; a very few powerful families who were the overlords and owners of all industry — the Mitsui, Mitsubishi, Sumitomo and other *Daibatsu* holding companies of almost infinite potential — but the rest of the teeming millions of the land were basically of the coolie class.

Not only did these masses swallow these stories without question, but the constant display of small groups of prisoners marching about in the streets of all the main cities of Japan must have seemed to the war-lords to be of excellent propaganda value to impress the people with the might and success of the nation's arms. Men like the President and Frankenstein knew better, for they could foresee the ultimate day of reckoning, and there is no doubt that it was due to them that we had so easy a reception and I am certain, from the inferences in his initial address to us, that the President knew that the war was nothing short of a national disaster. Unfortunately, the propaganda effect of the display of prisoners acted as a boomerang and recoiled on the heads of its authors, as it was not long before the civilians with whom we worked came to appreciate that we were really quite pleasant people, and it was progressively obvious, as intercourse became more free and comprehensible in the working parties, that they were paying increasing attention to what we said and beginning to feel that there was something wrong with the reports in their press. Moreover, their reaction to us was spreading up and down their streets, and to their friends.

The Japanese army never ceased to go to fantastic lengths to prevent us from receiving any sort of information regarding international affairs or from receiving newspapers of any kind, and this was particularly galling. We were expressly forbidden to secure or possess any newsprint, and all the Japanese and Koreans with whom we came in contact were under similar instructions that we must have no opportunity of obtaining news, either in print or by word of mouth, under the direst penalties.

Language difficulties were always rather acute at Osaka Shosen but, by dint of drawings, signs and odd words, it was possible to conduct some sort of arduous conversation. Hirada once gave us a description of conditions in a Japanese gaol — I think as a deterrent to trying to obtain newspapers — but it was so horrific that we presumed that we had completely misunderstood him. We still had not got the measure of the country and it was not until long afterwards that we remembered this description and realized that it was wholly accurate and that we *had* understood him perfectly!

There was one little Korean who was particularly well disposed, and he frequently took two or three of us whom he evidently trusted on to one side and drew maps with chalk on pieces of steel to explain the war news. Unfortunately he was never very clear about Europe, saying in effect that there was no news. We found it mutually impossible to identify each other's maps of this theatre, whilst his descriptions of naval actions around the Solomons were very hard to understand and left us bewildered. Capt. Christiansen who, as prisoners' *honcho*, had a roving commission often joined in these discussions, which were most frustrating, as we were so near to information and yet so far, yet it was nobody's fault. We found it hard to believe that there was really no news from Europe although, at that time, it was substantially true, and finally the Korean, who seemed to be more or less naturalized in Japan, despaired of making us understand and came to an arrangement to buy us a paper.

The Japanese army used to pay us once a month in the early days, according to rank, but all the merchant seamen only received the minimum rate of a private of ten *sen* a day, because we were civilians. It was the merest pittance and it was particularly irritating for a ship-master like Christiansen to receive less than the corporals and the sergeants in the camp. One or two men had supplemented this meagre income by selling watches, pens and other items for which there was a ready market amongst the civilians and, strange though it may seem, there were always those prepared to sell their bread to fellow prisoners, even on our short rations. We always found that there was a small number of Japanese who would procure small items for us. I had secured sufficient paper and pencils for my diaries by this means, and we were all starting to accumulate a few necessities. Later on, when various men had had their watches forcibly taken from them by the guards in the camp, I sold mine for 240 *yen* — a fabulous sum to a prisoner — rather than suffer its loss without recompense. Some of this money I used to buy bread, but the rest was carefully hoarded and extremely useful over the months, being earmarked for necessities rather than luxuries.

The average coolie lived in such very poor circumstances that a gift of clothing was sufficient for our Korean to cover the risk of buying us a paper for a very considerable time, and it was much to his credit that he never abused his position by trying to blackmail us either by the extortion of additional payment or by cutting down the period of the contract. The problem was to obtain clothing at all, as we simply had none to spare and anything coming from us would, in any case, have made him a marked man. However, by dint of a certain amount of domestic barter within the camp, we secured some of the surplus clothing of the lascars, who seemed (unaccountably) to have limitless wardrobes, and this was far more suitable and equally welcome to our contact.

It may seem surprising that the Japanese continued to print newspapers in English all through the war. There were at least three, to my knowledge: *The Tokio Nichi-Nichi* which we had seen once or twice in Yokohama, *The Nippon Times* and the *Osaka Mainichi*. I believe that there were at least a couple of others. It was some time before we discovered why the publication of these papers was continued when England and anything English brought down such anathemas, as it seemed to us to be extraordinary to publish news in our language when there were only Japanese to buy it. The reason was that it is possible to compress a great deal more into a given space in Roman letters than in Hirakana or Katakana (the Japanese characters) and thus, in the interests of economy, the papers continued and were read by what must have been quite a measurable public who could at least read in English, and we did occasionally see them in the possession of Japanese about the streets. I was very seldom without a daily paper, except on Sundays so long as that day was one of rest, until the end of the war, but I was one of the very few who had this advantage, as most men never saw one at all throughout their captivity. I never ceased to marvel that, in a country rife with suspicion and informers, these papers should always be produced by coolies who knew not one word of English!

We usually had the *Osaka Mainichi* which we found to be the best for our purposes and, after a rather shaky start, the little man brought it in every day. To start with Capt. Christiansen was his contact, as he was more free to roam than anyone else, though sometimes Pargiter or I received it from him. The whole affair had to be carried out under conditions of the utmost secrecy, because the results of exposure would have been more than serious for either party, and few of the men in our own bending party were even aware of the existence of the paper. However much it went against the grain to withhold the news from our own colleagues, who craved it as much as they craved their food, we knew that the risk was far too great and, after due deliberation, we decided that the circulation must be extremely limited and that those who were not on it should know nothing about it. If anything which we read was to be repeated, it was to be as 'something which a Jap had said', which made it little better than rumour, but we could not help that. It was a pity, but unavoidable. Capt. Christiansen had great confidence in his surviving engineer and he was shown the paper. Otherwise there was only Pargiter and myself, although Craggs became included later on. Thus it changed hands several times during the day, each transfer having to be above suspicion, and then it was surreptitiously destroyed.

On the anniversary of Pearl Harbor and on other high days of the country's calendar, the paper would reproduce the original Imperial War Rescript of the Emperor which he issued on the outbreak of war when his envoys were still engaged in peace talks in Washington. Seldom in the history of mankind has it been exceeded for sheer effrontery, but it might pass unnoticed were it not for the fact that, in a country of Emperor worship, it carried immense weight with the people and every reminder of it provided a spur to the war effort. It ran as follows:-

IMPERIAL WAR RESCRIPT

We, by the grace of Heaven, Emperor of Japan, seated on the throne of a line unbroken for ages eternal, enjoin upon ye, Our loyal and brave subjects:

We hereby declare war on the United States of America and the British Empire. The men and officers of Our Army and Navy shall do their utmost in prosecuting the war. Our public servants of various departments shall perform diligently and faithfully their appointed tasks, and all other subjects of Ours shall pursue their respective duties; the entire nation with a united will shall mobilise their total strength so that nothing will miscarry in the attainment of Our war aims.

To ensure the stability of East Asia and to contribute to world peace is the far-sighted policy which was formulated by our Great illustrious Grandsire and Our Imperial Sire succeeding Him, and which we lay constantly to heart.

To cultivate friendship among nations and to enjoy prosperity in common with all nations has always been the guiding principle of Our Empire's foreign policy. It has been truly unavoidable and far from Our wishes that Our Empire has now been brought to cross swords with America and Britain.

More than four years have passed since China, failing to comprehend the true intention of Our Empire, and recklessly courting trouble, disturbed the peace of East Asia and compelled Our Empire to take up arms. Although there has been re-established the National Government of China, with which Japan has effected neighbourly intercourse and co-operation, the régime which has survived at Chungking, relying upon American and British protection, still continues its fratricidal opposition.

Eager for the realization of their immediate ambition to dominate the Orient, both America and Britain, giving support to the Chungking regime, have aggravated the disturbances in East Asia.

Moreover, these two powers, inducing other countries to follow suit, increased military preparations on all sides of Our Empire to challenge us. They have obstructed by every means our peaceful commerce, and finally resorted to a direct severance of economic relations, menacing gravely the existence of Our Empire.

Patiently have We waited and long have We endured in the hope that Our Government might retrieve the situation in peace, but Our adversaries, showing not the least spirit of conciliation, have unduly delayed a settlement; and, in the meantime, they have intensified the economic and political pressure to compel thereby Our Empire to submission.

This trend of affairs would, if left unchecked, not only nullify Our Empire's efforts of so many years for the sake of the stabilization of East Asia, but also endanger the very existence of Our nation. The situation being as it is, Our Empire for its existence and self-defence had no other recourse but to appeal to arms and to crush every obstacle in its path.

The hallowed spirits of Our Imperial ancestors guarding Us from above, We rely upon the loyalty and courage of Our subjects in Our confident expectation that the task bequeathed by Our Forefathers will be carried forward, and that the sources of evil will be speedily eradicated and an enduring peace immutably established in East Asia, preserving thereby the glory of Our Empire.

(Imperial Sign manual)

(Imperial Seal)

December 8th, the 16th year of Showa.

If anyone doubts the effrontery of that rescript, let him read the causes of the Far Eastern war in detail on the one hand, and remember on the other that the Great War is not dated by historians as starting in 1939, but in 1931, when the Japanese commenced their offensive against the Chinese in Manchuria, although they did not actually cross the Great Wall until 1933. That the meek and mild Hirohito, by then a puppet of a militaristic government, found himself bound to seal the Rescript was one of the sadder aspects of the era.

The news which we read did not amount to much and there was little, at that time, to the credit of the Allies, while there were absurd propaganda stories which were so futile as to make us disbelieve everything that the paper printed. There was, for example, the tale of the Japanese Zero fighter 'plane which was in combat with a number of American fighters somewhere in the Solomons region. Finally, after destroying all its superior force of antagonists except one, the Jap had exhausted its ammunition and found itself being chased round and round a clump of palm trees by the American aeroplane! The pilot was desperate until, bethinking himself of his food ration, he extracted a rice ball from its container and, turning in his seat, threw it back towards his pursuer. It hit the enemy's propeller, smashed it and sent the American crashing to the ground in a smoking ruin. *Banzai!* Apart from nonsense of this sort, there was generally a square devoted to the motto for the day: *"Exterminate the white blood-suckers"* or something equally opprobrious, but the news itself was so sparse that we derived little joy from it although, in the desperation of hope, we could seldom await the arrival of the next *Mainichi* with equanimity. It was not until the war was over that we realized that the factual news in these papers had been remarkably accurate, if sometimes belated.

As time went on, we started to take the paper back to the camp, as it was the only one seen by anyone at that period. We took it in turns to carry it and this was potentially the most dangerous part of the whole proceeding, as we were invariably searched on arrival. In the first instance these searches did not amount to much because, however well the stevedoring details might fare in their looting, it was sufficiently clear to all parties that there was little enough to steal in a shipyard, but new guards would search us meticulously at intervals, nevertheless.

There had been a clothes issue by the Army by this time, as a result of which we had all been given a rather stiff, green coat and trousers and a pair of heel-less white socks. My coat and trousers were rather small and uncomfortable for me, so I continued to wear my uniform, but I longed for a pair of boots or shoes. My own shoes were so thin by this time that I think I could have told the 'heads' from the 'tails' of a coin under my feet, and it was not long before I was actually walking on my bare soles. This would not have been so bad on tarred roads, but that long road to and from the shipyard was composed of multitudinous sharp pebbles, so that marching along it was worse than purgatory.

The winter views were glorious: the low light on the white snow crests of the surrounding hills; the silhouettes of the ships at the buoys standing hard against the evening sun with what we thought was the Wakayama Peninsula showing dark against a pink backcloth, and all the waters of the Gulf of Osaka shimmering gold and pink as the sun dipped behind the land. Often the wind was bitter, but it brought a clear, bright, silver light with it that seemed to infuse some sort of magic into all the surrounding squalor and to bring the peace of the snow-bound slopes a little closer to us. Both sea-line and sky-line sometimes seemed to come so close that we might reach out to touch them in that frigid weather. Then we would pass away from the distant views and back into our shabby street, sometimes to see a mad beggar who frequented the area. A Japanese beggar of his sort has to be seen, for he almost defies description. This one was tall, even for a European, and dirty beyond belief with long, matted hair which fell almost to his waist, and he was clothed in rags. He moved with an extraordinary, shambling gait, and the veriest glimpse of him would effectively shut out the memory of the scenic wonder we had just beheld (and which was, in spite of the Japanese, like so much of the beauty of their country).

The adult residents of the street soon took us for granted, and to some we were a source of mild curiosity. When we were forming up on summer mornings a number of mothers would sit on the edge of the low concrete wall between the camp and the first houses to gossip and watch with their babies slung on their backs in *nennekos* and, when the child became at all importunate, they would expose a breast and flip it back under one arm straight on target — a remarkable feat which astonished us when we first witnessed it. Nor was such beneficence confined to the babies, but toddlers and even older children seemed to be at liberty to feed off their mother so long as she was able to feed a child at all. Quite small girls used to stagger about the streets with younger brothers or sisters, often little smaller than themselves, slung on their backs and seemed to take it for granted. Never did we see a pram.

The small boys always ran alongside us as we marched back up the street in the evenings, as small boys will do in any country wherever a body of men are marching. Once one, somewhat overbold, dashed in amongst us to march too, but we were more or less in step as we approached the camp under the eagle eye of the sergeant of the guard, so he was knocked over and, quite unintentionally, considerably trampled upon before he could be extricated. This was obviously the purest accident as far as we were concerned, since even the most militant of us would not have taken out our feelings on so small a child, but it was some time before the citizens ceased muttering whenever we passed thereafter.

It was not long after this that one of the English camp details was returning home when a man suddenly dashed off the sidewalk and stabbed one of its members. He received a nasty wound, though it was not a dangerous one, and there was a great *furor* about it. The Japanese was caught and it appeared that the fact that he had just had a relative killed on one of the fighting fronts had driven him to take this frenzied revenge upon the first white man on whom he could lay his hands. We only heard the bare details of the affair through the food party, but both camps exploited the incident so far as it was possible to exploit anything. The Japanese army were, for once, exemplary in their conduct because, apart from catching the culprit and dealing with the guard in charge of the party by their own methods (though it was not clear how he could have done anything to prevent it!), they did take especial care of the wounded man and gave him quite exceptional care until he was recovered.

Once or twice we arrived at Osaka Shosen to find some sort of ceremony in progress with all the employees gathered together to listen to long speeches, at the conclusion of which they all bowed several times in the same direction. We were made to bow too, but as we never had the slightest idea whether we were supposed to be bowing towards the Emperor's palace, towards the rising sun or joining in obeisance to Buddha or to some lamented ancestors, the effect of our participation could only have been minimal. We used to find that this complete ignorance of what we were supposed to be doing was very irritating.

I started bringing the paper back into the camp and used my shoes as the place of concealment the first time, but I only did this once as I was lamed for days! As time went on and we were never caught, we became quite blasé about the operation, although there were some nasty moments. Finally Kjöstvedt, the Norwegian engineer, was caught with it and it was fortunate that he kept his head. He and Capt. Christiansen were at once removed for questioning and, I suspect, beating, in order to discover the source of the supply, but they stuck to their guns. Capt, Christiansen swore that he knew nothing of it whilst Kjöstvedt pretended that he could not speak English (which was not far removed from the truth!) which put their interrogators at a disadvantage as they had no means of direct interpretation, and it does not seem to have occurred to them to question Kjöstvedt through Christiansen! They were finally released, much to our surprise, as it was supposed that we should not see them again until the Japanese had learnt the truth by one means or another.

Nevertheless, we judged it better to stop bringing it into the camp after that, and Christiansen and Kjöstvedt made no effort to see it lest they were being watched. Thus only Pargiter and I saw it until we all thought it to be safe enough for the other two to read it again and, as there were a few encouraging items to report at that time, notably the extension of the Allied bombing offensives, the news was passed on verbally to one or two trusted individuals who were also told the source whence it came, but who were also given excellent reasons why they should not read it for themselves. It took some time to read the paper in those days, as it still had a few pages (though, as the war progressed, it deteriorated into one small sheet), and the only place where we could be safe to read it undisturbed was in the odiferous *benjo*: a lamentable necessity which had to be endured because these daily news readings were one of the few things to which we really looked forward, however depressed we might be after we had finished them. We were not cast down by any Allied reverses, as they had passed their nadir by then, but because there was nothing, in those days, to encourage us to see any end to our captivity.

We should have liked to have shown the paper to more of our friends, but we simply could not take the risk. Once or twice Faleide, the

Norwegian radio officer, saw it, but the Norwegians were a very tightly knit band and accepted everything that Capt. Christiansen told them without question and had, I imagine, a pretty shrewd idea of the source of the information, expecially after the incident when Kjöstvedt had been caught with the paper outside the camp. The whole community of prisoners was always seething with rumours of one sort or another which made it difficult to prove to most of those to whom we disseminated the war news that it had any more substance than most of the stories which were circulating and which were often fantastic in the lengths of their wishful thinking. We could not satisfy them without letting the cat out of the bag, although gradually more people were told the source in an effort to help their state of mind, but all these were carefully screened and confined to a small group of ships' officers. Only Craggs was allowed to see the paper itself, but Goodridge, the chief engineer of another vessel, was one of those aware of the source of the information. None, of course, knew from whom we obtained the paper. We had never approved of Goodridge's continual efforts to improve his work stint in the rivetting party, but we did consider him to be a responsible person though we thought that he might become flustered too easily if caught with the paper and that this was a real risk. There had been some narrow escapes from discovery at various times.

Jackson, the gunlayer, had long been ousted from the position of our barrack leader, since that situation had, predictably, not proved satisfactory to anyone — to us, to the Japanese nor, I suspect to himself — and Goodridge had been appointed in his place. Although this entailed little more than reporting to the Duty Officer at the two daily musters, he had acquitted himself perfectly well in that job.

We constantly used to change from one *benjo* to another in order to allay any suspicions which might arise from the length of time we spent in them. Once I went into one near the foundry to prospect and was amazed to find a woman coming in after me. Horror-struck that I had inadvertently entered a 'Ladies' (though it *did* contain a urinal), I was about to beat a hasty retreat when a coolie came in, so I stood my ground and pretended that I had entered for the usual purpose. To my astonishment, the woman came and stood beside me at the urinal, raised her skirts and, leaning back a little with her legs apart, put it to the same use as the coolie and myself, both of the Japanese taking this wholly for granted. It was only then that I discovered that there was no question of 'Ladies' and 'Gents' in the yard. It was an insignificant incident in itself, but served to demonstrate how little we knew of the customs of the land which would be a great disadvantage in any attempted escape or when doing anything outside our camp which was outside our stipulated routine.

218

Finally the inevitable disaster occurred. Goodridge was unable to resist the temptation to pass on the news we had given him — and it was a strong enough temptation in all conscience as it was unpleasant to feel that we could not tell our fellows the things they yearned to know. He had a strident voice with a clear, rather Northumbrian diction and, like a fool, started retailing all that he had to say while eating his lunch at the side of a timber stack. He never bothered to see if anyone was behind it. Capt. Christiansen was approaching and not only heard him loudly declaiming what he knew, quoting the *Osaka Mainichi* as its source, but he also saw that our guard for the week was on the other side of the stack, listening intently. This young man had already proved that he was one of the few who was more than competent in his mastery of the English language.

Fortunately, he did not take full advantage of the situation and the paper for the day was immediately destroyed. In one sense, it was lucky that Christiansen was there. We would have expected the guard to have taken Goodridge into custody immediately, when it would have been very hard for him not to have incriminated several of us under Japanese treatment. Precisely what did happen we never knew, but we never again saw the little Korean who bought us the paper and could only suppose that each coolie was searched on arrival the following morning. The others would not tell us exactly what had occurred, but it was stated that our contact had been shot. This may or may not have been the case but, whatever his fate, it was undoubtedly an unpleasant one. He had been a good friend to us and this was another example of how one's fellow prisoners could prove to be the worst of our enemies, and thereafter we never ceased to blame ourselves for being so soft-hearted as to pass the news out of our immediate circle.

The winter had passed away and given way to milder weather. We had had an issue of Japanese army boots and the clothing situation was a little easier. The snow-line receded on the hills until they stood out in their entirety against the cerulean of the sky in shades of green and purple. The water gleamed on the surface of the bay as we passed and, as that summer advanced, we divested ourselves of coats and shirts and enjoyed the heat of the sun. A new forced-draught furnace had been built by the bending fires, largely by our efforts, and had been covered in sand to preserve its heat. This sand served as an excellent oven in which to heat our rice balls in such tins as we managed to obtain, and we felt less hungry in the warm weather.

We still had some Sundays free in the barracks and were able to dispense with the two charcoal braziers which had been set at the end of each barrack and which were a mixed blessing. Gorgeous dragon-flies darted about the air in the shipyard, for we were never far from water, and we often took heart at seeing the sick and wounded being brought ashore from hospital ships at No. 2 pier, and were the more gratified on the occasions when we saw the hundreds of white caskets containing the ashes of the country's dead returning to join their ancestors at their family shrines. That was one item these ships carried. We also saw them discharging pig-iron, which was a gross abuse of international convention and when, much later, their papers made much of the sinking of one or two of these ships, we felt that there was no case to answer.

We had heard that, if a body of men marched over a bridge in perfect step, it was possible to set up such a set of vibrations that the bridge would collapse, and we frequently attempted to do this on such hump-backed bridges as we crossed. Either the theory is fallacious, as some of us always suspected, or we were singularly unsuccessful, as the bridges remained supremely unaffected! Nor did bad earthquakes have any deleterious effect on them, so we were in good company!

I had read that the Japanese were exceptional amongst Eastern peoples in their kindness to animals, but this scarcely accorded with our observation. Often we would come up to one of these hump-backed bridges during the winter to find a coolie with a horse-drawn *bodiki* attempting to cross it. A *bodiki* is a form of Japanese cart which has no sides and only three stout baulks of timber running longitudinally as a bottom, but they were often loaded beyond the reasonable capacity of a horse on the flat in ideal conditions. To cross these steep little bridges when they were slippery with ice and trodden snow, the horse's hooves slipping on the surface of the road and the animal beside itself with fear, called for a good deal of patience and coaxing. This was treatment which it never received: the driver usually yelling and beating the horse until both were in a frenzy and, not infrequently, the traces were broken or, alternatively, both horse and *bodiki* overturned.

Normally we marched in reasonable order and obeyed our guards as there was nothing to be gained by not doing so, but these were occasions when they could do nothing and when the prisoners, somewhat unusually, acted on impulse and in concert. Ranks were broken as we gathered round the *bodiki* and pushed both it and the horse over the bridge by brute force, but I never saw the drivers exhibit the least sign of gratitude for this assistance. On the contrary, they usually seemed rather resentful. We had one man, a past-master at dealing with horses, who could take the animal, restore it to a state of equanimity as if by magic, and coax it over the bridge with its load almost infallibly, but when this happened the rest of us had to impede the driver from taking any part in the operation. It never occurred to our guards or to the shipyard representatives who accompanied our marches that we were doing a good deed, as they were patently unable to understand our attitude of

220

fury over the treatment of the horses and merely contented themselves with fulminating at us for breaking the order of march.

The question of marching in step was a very vexed one amongst the shipyard party. It is much easier for a body of men to march in step and the army always wished us to do so. Our guard — for we only had one by then — usually found the effort to enforce it far beyond him and soon gave it up. The coloured men could not, or would not, co-operate in this and, as it was awkward for the rest of us to keep in step with so many members out of step, it made the bulk of the party rather angry, with men constantly treading on each other's heels, and we tried to make the Lascars and Chinese take up the rear, where they would not affect other people. By this time there was, in general, a great deal more fraternization between both ranks and between coloured men and whites, and most men preferred to talk to those next to him in the column than to walk in silence, but there was a wide difference of view about the degree to which this should be extended. Pargiter and I, probably at one end of the spectrum, made a point of never complaining about our lot or of bringing conversation to too personal a level, except when with our own clique, and we only spoke to the *serang* amongst the lascars. He was an excellent man and it was, perhaps, a significant effect of this, besides being a measure of our fellows, that we were the only two persons to whom he ever came for advice or for representation, and until the end we were the only two officers who continued to be addressed as *Sahib*. Nor was this actuated by any fear. To a lesser degree, the argument was true of the various members of the crews who, as they lost whatever respect they may have ever possessed for some of their officers, lost any additional boost to their morale which they might have attained from the example which they might have expected from them.

The effects of this were less tangible and not so immediately manifest, but were among the factors which led us to discern that some of our number were not 'playing the game' for our common good. We had few illusions about the ultimate effects of these defections, and we knew that things would get very much worse before the end of the war and that, the higher the standards that were maintained by every man, the more tolerable our common lot would be. The Japanese were the enemy and it was essential to preserve our strongest front, both for reasons of pride and for fostering a spirit which would induce all possible sabotage to their war effort. I remember how one officer queried our action and expostulated when two of us removed various parts from a steering engine for a new ship which was on the quay and threw them in the river. I despised him ever afterwards, but his attitude was all too common.

In addition to our boots, we had been issued with the canvas-sided, rubber-soled short boots of the country, which were infinitely more comfortable in hot weather. However, ours were not the common variety with split big toes. In my own case, the army boots issued to me were too narrow and, in consequence, I suffered from ingrowing toe-nails both then and for years afterwards. At intervals we had a bath in the bathroom, although this activity became less and less frequent as the boiler fuel situation became more acute.

The Japanese had no baths in their homes in the poorer areas, but they are a very clean people and there were communal bath places situated every few streets. These were quite unlike anything in Europe: the Finnish *sauna* being the nearest approach in my experience, although even it was far removed from the Japanese system. The principles applied in our camp. In a large room were three large, square, wooden baths which measured some four and a half or five feet square, each being equipped with taps and a plug. The first bath was filled with almost scalding water and the principle, rigidly enforced, was for each person to stand on the outside and wet himself all over by sluicing the water over his body either with his hands or with a tin, and then to soap himself. This water thus remains quite clean and free from soap. Then, with his body well soaped, he passes to the next bath and goes through the same procedure in reverse, rinsing all the soap off his body and finishing quite clean. The whole atmosphere is filled with steam from the almost scalding water which is only just endurable to the skin, and it is this steam which is reminiscent of the *sauna*. Being rinsed and clean, the man then enters the third bath, where he can sit or squat up to his neck and soak. It was strange at first, but it is a highly commendable manner in which to provide common bathing facilities for a large number of people as it is extremely hygienic and all the water in the baths remains clean throughout.

One evening, Sanders had looked in at our barrack and asked if there was anyone who could type. Pargiter and I both considered this for a brief instant, presuming that we could probably type as well as anyone, on the principle that 'to a sailor nothing is impossible' — a very useful dictum I frequently heard from the master of my first ship. Quite independently, we both decided against volunteering for any such job, because we were both determined not to mark ourselves out as exceptional in any way in the eyes of the Japanese, since we did not want to draw attention to ourselves for the greater safety of our precious diaries. It was likely that typing would put us in the position of obtaining information which would not otherwise come our way and which might provide a modicum of interest but, if so, we should obviously be subject to greater security checks, which was unthinkable. Alternatively, if the work was of no interest, there was no point in doing it. As we did not consult in coming to this mutual decision, we found some satisfaction in coming to the same conclusion for the same reasons.

Brown, however, did say that he could type. He and I had been thrown together in common cause aboard the *Dalhousie*, as already related, and we had got on well enough. He was, however, a man of rather poor physique who tended to mumble when he spoke, and whose attitude since capture had led me to think him somewhat pusillanimous. We had remained on perfectly friendly terms, although we saw little of each other and took rather a different view of life in the camp. He had no notion of what we termed 'good gefangenism': he disliked work at the shipyard intensely, not as a matter of principle so much as because he was in the least pleasant squad in the yard, and his rather rabbit-like physiognomy, which I had noticed when he first joined the *Dalhousie*, seemed to have become accentuated as a prisoner. He deprecated our situation but accepted it with a certain acquiescence and fatalism, making little effort to improve his lot. Pargiter and I found this a little maddening, although the final results of our respective philosophies may have had little enough to choose between them. He was not, for instance, a man to indulge in surreptitious sabotage.

At all events, he was installed in a small office near the boiler, complete with typewriter, and, initially, I found his new position very useful. He was making lists of the personnel in all the prison camps in the area and he thus came to learn of any major events or changes which took place within them and, by dint of a certain amount of cross-examination, I was enabled to transcribe an immense amount of this information into my diaries.

I learned, for instance, that ours was the headquarters camp of the *Chubugūn*, or central, command area, and that there were a large number of sub-camps within its jurisdiction, varying in strength from two hundred to about six hundred men. It seemed that our camp was unique in being under the direct control of the army. The system of the working camps was that the labour was hired out to civilian under-takings who undertook to employ a given number of prisoners for which they paid the army on a daily capitation basis. All these other camps were leased *en bloc* to some such firm, two or three being in steel works, one in a most unpleasant chrome mine, and others were in similar sorts of places.

As often as not, these camps were situated within the precincts of the works, which the prisoners never left at all, and they had no option but to work there in the jobs allocated to them, day after succeeding day. Life must have been incredibly drab under these conditions but, by way of compensation, they did not have the constant presence of the army to oppress them. It was becoming increasingly evident that there was a tremendous and widening gulf between the army and the civilians, who held the former in even greater loathing than we did. These camps were under the direct control of the civilian industrialists who, in turn, were responsible to the army for the maintenance and order of them. Certainly the odd guard was posted within the civilian camps, but all the military hierarchy was missing and, by all accounts, life was rather easier on that account because the majority of corporals and privates generally behaved well enough so long as they were not being prodded into activity by their superiors, which was continually the case in the Chikkō camp. On the other side of the scale, we derived certain benefits from being the headquarters camp as time went on, apart from which we had a greater variety of movement and change of scene as we moved about outside our camp on the various working parties and, of course, often had the benefit of the sun, which was seldom seen in a mine or a steel works.

The headquarters, which included both the English and American camps, also leased its prisoners out to civilian firms on a daily capitation basis, but there were a number of undertakings which had an interest in it and which were entitled to a minimum number of men each day. The army did not mind which men went to each firm although, so long as the shipyard was in being as a working detail, it did absorb the two merchant seamen's barracks. Apart from this one exception, men could fall out into the street and join any detail so far as the Japanese were concerned, providing that the total numbers were correct, and we thus attained more changes of environment than in the case of the majority of prisoners in Japan.

A stevedoring firm named *Sen Pakku* had the largest share in our camp, and there were Sundays when the entire working force went out under their aegis to discharge ships at the buoys, particularly just after the arrival of a convoy. We used to obtain excellent views of the shipping, together with a good idea of the cargoes being discharged into lighters or small coasters, and we felt that the quantity of shipping to be seen, which gradually declined, represented a very good yardstick of the success of the Allied sea offensive in the Far East. All this, together with details of the mortality in other camps, their composition and positions, the various rice and other rations and even the condition of the civilian Japanese, was all being laboriously entered in my diaries, and their retention became more and more of an obsession.

As time went on, it became harder and harder to extract any information from Brown and, in due course, he seldom volunteered a remark to anyone within the barrack, whilst even the most innocent questions were met with a startled mumble and, generally, a hasty retreat.

He had secured his companion, Robertson, a position in the camp detail as boiler-man, though this was a rather dubious advantage to him.

Whether Brown thought that he would inadvertently blurt out some information in conversation, or whatever the reason, he became more and more of a recluse in our midst and, in the fullness of time, he moved out of the barrack and slept apart with Sanders, the camp leader, who already had a small room adjacent to the store-room. I am sure he was happier away from us and, thenceforth, was only to be seen moving about the camp at rare intervals, almost as a wraith and more than ever like a rabbit. Many thought his attitude to be unfortunate, and it led to a belief that he was a creature of the Japanese, but I doubt if there was any substance in this except insofar that, because he was working directly for them and held them in some awe, he probably did his best not to run foul of them. It is much more likely that he had a shrewd suspicion that Pargiter and I were still maintaining our diaries and that, if they should ever be discovered and read, it would be abundantly apparent that much of the information in them could only have been obtained from him and that he would thus be treated as an accessory in their compilation. Of course, we found his silence perfectly maddening, since it cut back the information we were obtaining, but we appreciated that his actions in that respect were no different from our own restrictions on our fellows in the matter of the daily paper and, although more affected than anyone else by his change of attitude, probably appreciated his reasons more than the rest of the camp put together.

The camp detail was tending to get larger. There were three cobblers who made a very good job of keeping our boots in repair; a cook, a couple of medical orderlies, the boiler-man and one or two others. A position on the camp detail was much sought after by some men but, although they were subject to a great deal less supervision, the camp was pretty deserted both by prisoners and Japanese during the day and theirs was a deadly sort of existence with no variety attaching to it. These men could always be distinguished by their seedy, pallid countenances, which provided the greater contrast with the ruddy tan which most of us attained in the fresh wind or hot sun all day. Their outlook was, of necessity, narrower than that of their fellows who were prone to suspect them, with little enough justification, of obtaining perquisites for themselves and, in consequence, the men who provided our services came to be regarded as parasites. This was a pity, the more particularly since they never had any opportunity of stealing in the manner of those on the stevedoring details, but it was always open to them to go out to work if they wished, and some did, although there was no guarantee that they could return to the camp detail again once they had left it.

One evening a warehouse at Osaka Kō burnt down. This was a detail close to the camp which was worked exclusively by the Guam Americans at that time. Osaka Kō means 'Port of Osaka', but a certain stevedoring firm went by this name. Naturally, some suspicion fell on the prisoners who had left two or three hours previously, but nothing was ever discovered regarding the cause of the fire. I doubt if any of the Americans were responsible, but it was certain that, even in their very highly integrated party, no man could trust his fellows sufficiently to talk about any sabotage on that scale which he might undertake. Any such action had to be done privily for the private satisfaction of the individual for any disruption to the enemy war economy which he might cause thereby, however slight it might be. Only a very few men exercised themselves over this sort of thing.

A few days later a set of charts was discovered in a shack on the same premises. This was a small shed used by both the prisoners and the firm's coolies and was known as the *ku-ké* shack, being used during break periods. *Ku-ké* means 'rest period'. The discovery caused a great *furor* although, once again, nothing could be proved or brought home to anyone. Pargiter and I were the only two Englishmen who knew anything about these charts, the discovery of which flabbergasted the other prisoners almost as much as the Japanese.

Certain American marines had conceived the idea of an escape: an undertaking which presented problems incomparably greater than those which faced prisoners-of-war in European countries, such as Germany. Language was an impossible barrier, because no prisoner could hope to speak it fluently since it was not a mere matter of mastering grammar and vocabulary, but of the acquisition of a Japanese mind, which was impossible. This is because the mind of the people, and thus their language, is, as it were, back to front when compared with Occidental standards.

Moreover, our very size, shape and physiognomy made individual movement in a street a matter of public interest. Not only had few prisoners black hair, as every Japanese has, but it was not of the same coarse texture: the facial structure, the set of the eyes and mouth and nose were all quite different, and only few of us had brown eyes — a feature common to every Jap. Nor had we the epicanthic fold of the yellow races. For my own part, standing some six feet three, with brown hair and blue eyes, I had little hope of movement on land in that country, whilst any observant native would be likely to notice the half moons on our finger nails which are as rare in them as in all coloured peoples. I never heard of any prisoner escaping from the mainland of Japan, but two American officers who did break out of their camp were caught very quickly because, like the Piper of Hamelin, they were followed by hordes of children for the very reasons enumerated above.

These Americans had given a good deal of thought to escape before our arrival, and the advent of some navigating officers was a godsend to them. After a good deal of sounding and scrutiny, I was the man they approached, on grounds of physique, ability to navigate and because they discovered that I had a knowledge of sails, which were an integral part of their scheme. They had realized that, although an escape from the East coast might be easier in terms of sea-distance, the coasts of China or Korea offered little salvation and the idea of trying to reach Russia was not even considered. Even if anyone wished to take their chance of escaping to that country, it would be essential to start from the East coast of Hokkaido — the northern main island of Japan. In either case land travel was necessary to reach the requisite coast, of which no-one knew anything.

None of us had any illusions about the fact that success in any such enterprise must be assured. To be caught was unthinkable, as it was considered that execution would probably be by far the most merciful punishment which could be expected in such circumstances. Thus we could not travel by land. There was an aerodrome at Amagasaki, between Osaka and Kobe, but only one man in the camp was competent to fly an aeroplane — a New Zealander who had been shot down in the New Guinea area — but even if he were to be approached the difficulties and risks were insurmountable as we had no idea of the details of the security of the aerodrome, the aeroplanes, the fuel stores nor of anything else. The possibility was not worth considering, apart from being dependent entirely on one man. Thus only the sea was left and these men had reasoned, quite rightly, that the only possible hope lay therein. They had prospected very carefully and were certain that there were a number of small coasters with auxiliary sails which could be captured only a few minutes walk away.

The camp was not properly guarded: the fence leading round to the *benjos* was open at the top and could easily be scaled to give access to the street which lay behind it. There was no point in guarding it as it was presumed that there was nowhere a prisoner might go. These marines were aboard the coasters every day when stevedoring at Osaka Kō and were confident about this part of the scheme. All they had to to do was to sail her out of the harbour and, finally, into the open sea, but they had only the most rudimentary ideas about handling a vessel and no conception of navigation whatever. This was why I was approached. (There would not be sufficient fuel to cross the Pacific and it was clear that we should rely on sails sooner or later.) They were all very fine fellows, well disciplined, self-sufficient and possessed of a high degree of initiative and integrity. The smallest was over six feet one, and we were all powerfully built.

I found myself in a difficult position. Although no-one was more prepared to lend himself to an escape venture, I had already more or less brought the schemes to retake the *Charlotte Schliemann* by night to an abortive conclusion, and now was no more enamoured of this proposal. Had we been dealing with the Germans it might have been worth taking a chance, but we were all of one mind that any escape project where the Japanese were concerned should be almost one hundred per cent foolproof and that risk of detection or recapture must be negligible. It would be necessary to make any such attempt in mid-winter, when the nights were at their longest, and to carry the operation into effect immediately after evening muster. This would give us ten hours before our absence was discovered and, at the most, twelve hours before the loss of the coaster was noticed. It was not very long.

There would be six of us: four American marines, Pargiter and myself, though one or two others would have to be let into the secret so that they might move up their blankets and conceal the spaces on the sleeping bays during the night. First we should have to capture the vessel and overpower the crew, which usually consisted of a skipper, his wife and perhaps one other. These would have to be tied up and kept down below and, indeed, to be taken with us. Then we should have to leave the harbour and pass through the breakwaters. We had seen no evidence of any boom defence, examination or pilot boats there, but we had no idea whether movement of shipping was permitted at night.

Once clear, we should have to make for the Wakayama peninsula which I judged to be at least twenty-five miles away. This was a guess and based on eye observation, but as it looked to be low on the horizon and as the suffix *yama* means 'hill' or 'mountain', I felt that it might be even further. We had no knowledge of any minefields that might lie along the way nor, assuming that we got so far, what signal code would satisfy the inevitable examination vessel which I felt certain to be there, besides a possible boom defence. By this time it would be about two o'clock in the morning, which meant that we should be lucky to be thirty miles off the coast — for we assumed Wakayama to bound the deep sea — by the time that our defection was discovered, making perhaps seven knots, even if we had not been picked up by patrolling vessels or by aircraft in the interim. Then, again, we should have a long voyage before us and we knew that these craft only carried stores in very small quantities. This was the least of the problems, as the Americans were in a position to steal rice and soya beans at intervals and could hide enough for the passage adjacent to the quay, but it was one cogent reason for keeping the escape party small. There were other practical difficulties, one of the greatest being our ignorance of the channel from the harbour to the peninsula.

The marines fully appreciated the force of all these arguments and, to my utter astonishment, produced a full set of Japanese charts of the head of the Inland Sea (the Nakai), of Osaka Harbour and one or two others which were not needed, within a week. Although they showed us almost everything we wanted to know except the position of any booms or examination vessels, they were very bulky and it was unanimously decided that they were far too dangerous to keep in the camp so, being extremely necessary, they were hidden in the roof of the shack where they were ultimately discovered. The skipper of the coaster from which they were abstracted was doubtless too frightened of the consequences to himself to report their loss.

The information which they provided was most depressing, as reference to the map will show. The nearest way through the breakwaters was into and through the South harbour, only used by small vessels, which would probably be safer as there was likely to be less official security on that route, but there was very little water and we could not risk sitting on the mud until the dawn came. It was nearly two miles to the main entrance, which involved running along all the shipping in the harbour and then there was a run of twenty-nine miles to the Isumi Strait between the islands of Awaji and Tomogo off the Wakayama peninsula. Thus I had only been four miles out in my estimate, but the crux of the whole matter was that this proved *not* to be the departure point for the ocean passage, as we had supposed, since there was another twenty-six miles to the Kii Channel, which was about twelve miles wide between Hino Misaki and I Shima, which lay off the tip of Shikoku.

We were forced to abandon the scheme because, even assuming that we had no delay or hitch in the operation, the incidence of currents could hardly have put us in a better position than being more than six or seven miles between at least two points of land by daybreak when the hue and cry would be raised, and we never referred to it again. Later I came to work with these Americans, finding them to be real stalwarts, and I never ceased to regret the geography of our location, as no man could have had better comrades in such an exploit.

Camp life was deteriorating, although we saw less of Fujimoto. A young interpreter had come into the camp and was the only Japanese on the camp staff who ever did us any active good service, but his position was too lowly to ameliorate our conditions to any extent, as I am certain that he would have done had it lain within his power. The American and the English camps were looting on their stevedoring details to an increasing degree and, particularly after the discovery of the charts, the parties were being searched more thoroughly on their arrival back in the evenings. There had never been a general search within the barracks: our bays had remained sacrosanct and no-one had ever interfered with them. We had no reason to foresee any change. Then, one evening, this new interpreter let drop a warning that it was intended to search the entire

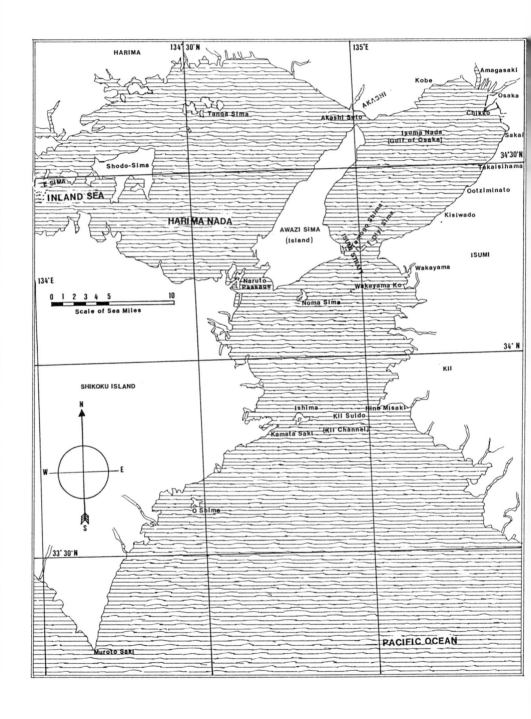

Map 1. From Osaka to the Pacific Ocean

camp the following day, which was a Sunday. This caused a certain panic. The Americans had quantities of beans, rice, sugar and other foodstuffs, together with cloth and various items. These were bad enough, but Pargiter, Mackavoy and I had our diaries to consider. There was little time to do much and there were few places in the camp in which to hide them. However, we did the best we could, mine being concealed in some loose timber stowed on top of the *benjos*, Pargiter's in a pile of coal intended for the boiler, and MacAvoy's, I believe, in some clothing hung up to dry between our barrrack and the perimeter fence.

On the Sunday the whole camp was paraded in the road whilst the building was searched, but our diaries survived and, although the Japanese made quite a good haul of loot, they only discovered a very small proportion of that concealed in the Americans' barracks. When we came in again, our barrack was clear. Nothing was found in it as we had nothing contraband (except the diaries) to conceal, but some of the Americans were in trouble, being taken to the guard room, beaten up and made to stand at strict attention until well into the night.

This incident was a shock and, as both Pargiter and I felt that the camp was no longer a safe repository, we removed our completed volumes — each volume being a relatively small, closely-written, contrived notebook — and buried them in the Shipyard until things had blown over and we had had a chance to evolve a plan for their preservation. Having done so, we were further embarrassed by the arrival of a gang of Korean conscript labour soon afterwards, part of which took over our job on the bending fires, while we were removed to a timber yard at the opposite end of the works, because our diaries were still buried near the furnace. However, we managed to recover them without exciting suspicion, but we decided that we might not be so lucky again and, as the camp was a certain base, concluded that it would be better to keep them there thenceforth, however great the difficulties might be. There had been no more 'shake-downs', but it was only common-sense to assume that there might be.

The lumber yard was quite easy work. It was pleasant and clean, and the weather was idyllic. Sometimes it rained in the evenings as we returned to the camp, but it was warm and quite refreshing. We were intrigued by the methods of some Japanese carpenters who were erecting new sheds near our working place. They were excellent craftsman and used the old saws of the biblical era, much as Christ must have used, which cut on the pulling stroke, and they used no nails in their construction, each piece being fitted and jointed into position. Their buildings possess a great elasticity, as we soon came to realize when the earthquake season commenced. There were a good many 'quakes in the late summer but, in that first year, no bad ones and, once we had got

231

over the initial shock, they quite fascinated us although later, when we had experienced some bad ones, we had different feelings about them.

The timber yard was an excellent place from which to view a minor earthquake: the water in an adjoining canal would undulate in a remarkable manner while the timber stacks seemed to be leaning in all directions at once and had something of the effect of a concertina, but they never came down. Over the river, where a good deal of heavy industry was situated, the tall factory chimneys bent and swayed in all their height but, although we did see one collapse, there never seemed to be much damage. At the first shudder, all the Japanese invariably ran into the open spaces and started kneeling and prostrating themselves, but resumed work again without comment as soon as the shocks were over. We had one rather more intense 'quake in the camp just as food was being served one evening (food went by the uncompromising Japanese word of *messi*), whereupon all the lascars in our barrack started peeling off the top bay in terror and rushing out of the door. Fear is infectious, and it was more by luck than good judgement that the whole camp was not infected with it. Their action caused a good deal of confusion, and it was certainly less pleasant being inside than outside a trembling building but, whilst our confidence was shaken at the time, it gave us a practical demonstration of the efficacy of the Japanese form of construction, so well adapted to this particular vagary of the country.

In due course another ship was ready for launching at the shipyard at a time when the national press, rather surprisingly, was giving some publicity to the mass production methods of the Kaiser shipbuilding yards in the United States. Nothing could have been further removed from the methods of this famous firm than the Osaka Shosen yard on the Shirinashi Kawa, where we worked, but a great show was arranged for this launching and Frankenstein made such preparations for ensuring better success than on the previous occasion that we were in some doubt whether the ship would not launch herself before the appointed day! She was a small freighter of, I should judge, some 2,800 tons dead-weight. When the time came, there was a vast concourse of people present and, again, all the workmen lined the slipway. As the vessel slid down the ways a gang of coolies dashed forward with a portion of the new keel which was laid on the blocks, while newspaper men filmed the scene. The ship entered the water: the check wires held her and, as lines were passed to a waiting tug, they were let go and cleared away while more of the new keel was rushed into position. A Buddhist priest, in full regalia, stepped forward and blessed it while the cameras still whirred on, taking a film showing how the production methods of the Japanese matched the Kaiser yards and, indeed, it must have looked very effective while the newly launched vessel was still visible in the background as she moved

232

over to the fitting out quay. I doubt if the press or the news films reported that, less than half an hour after the departure of the visitors, the new keel was taken up again and that the slipway was out of action for the next three months while it was renovated and repaired!

When we had been at the shipyard for nearly a year, and very soon after the disappearance of the Korean who had bought us the newspapers, we were formed up outside the office as usual in preparation for the march home. After some delay the President came out and made a short speech, saying that we should not be coming there any more: that we had performed our work very well and thanking us for all we had done. Certainly most of us had done no more than we had had to do, except the wicked riveters who had worked as though their very lives depended on it for as long as they had been on that job, but on the whole very little had been expected of us. We had realized that the detail had its disadvantages: the long walk there and back; the shortage of any desirable commodity to steal, and the fact that we were restricted to the same daily prospect, but we knew that we had been under the most sympathetic masters that we were likely to encounter. The merchant seamen never knew why they were withdrawn from the shipyard, though a few of us suspected that the paper had more than a little to do with it. To the others it was just one of those inexplicable affairs which were so irritating and which left them with a feeling of frustration and impotence.

XI

OSAKA KŌ

When the merchant seamen left the shipyard, they were thrown on to the open labour market. Some of the firms which had always drawn men from the camp had to take more, while a number of new details were started at the same time. Each party had to have its own *honcho* drawn from the ranks of the prisoners. This job was a thankless task, for such a man was not only more or less on his honour to obey the rules, but also responsible for seeing that his men did so as well. It was generally considered to be a good thing to stay on the same party, both in order to establish contacts and a certain *rapport* with the civilian workmen and also in order to be able to take advantage of all local opportunities which might present themselves. In consequence, the more popular details had a hard core of permanent members who tended to enforce the 'closed shop' principle, so that it was not easy to join these parties unless their numbers were unexpectedly raised for a day or two. The *honcho*, too, preferred to take men that he knew rather than those who might cause him trouble or embarrassment. Different parties were popular with different men: some preferred to go where the work was easiest; some where the firm supplemented their rice-ball lunch with additional food — usually rice — whilst others preferred to go where there was a chance of loot. Other details were universally unpopular.

To start with, we had to go where we could. Nakayama Seikko and Osaka Teikko were both steelworks which took a large quota at that time, the former being the more popular of the two because it provided an extra rice-ball, but both involved a long tram ride round to the Taisho area, which appealed to some men. Neither were hard work, but I found them a poor environment and preferred to work out of doors, particularly in view of the overcrowding in the barrack where sixty-five men occupied a room measuring 32 × 24 feet. As it was, some of the Lascars were sickening with consumption. Ships which carry Lascar crews were normally not allowed to carry them north of latitude 38° in the Eastern North Atlantic, so this was hardly the climate for them, permanently on the 35th parallel, and they had a very high mortality rate.

We had by this time managed to exchange them for the Chinese in the next barrack and, on balance, were better off because, although the Chinamen kept up an incessant chatter in their singularly unmelodious tongue, at least they were not in the constant state of mess and odd smells with all the myriad small tins and receptacles which surrounded the Lascars. Finally, both these minorities were put into an empty barrack by themselves, where they did not get on together, but it nevertheless made a lot more room for them and also in the two barracks which they evacuated.

There were two particularly bad working details and both involved handling timber. One was a small saw-mill, more or less opposite to Osaka Shosen, which was reached by a ferry. (See map.) It was a cramped and crowded place in which we had to heave and man-handle immensely heavy logs, sodden with water, out of the river and up a ramp. There was no winch and the job not only called for brute strength on a very slippery surface, but for a skill in which we were completely lacking, while the confined space made matters worse. The Japanese foreman was little better than a devil, often beating men unmercifully with a timber hook. Several suffered injury and bad strains on that detail which was a source of constant and bitter complaint until it was finally stopped.

The other was a party called Chubugūn which was a timber yard under the control, I believe, of the Japanese army. Going there involved a fairly long drive to high, open ground behind Amagasaki in charcoal-burning lorries which were almost the only type of motor transport in Japan during the war. The work consisted of long carries of timber from one stack to another, mainly for seasoning, and, as it was grassed and open, it should have been a pleasant job.

Unfortunately, most of the timber was so heavy that it was all a man could do to bear it on his shoulder, even with a thick pad, let alone to carry it for a quarter of a mile. He could not put it down for a rest, as he could never have raised it again single-handed and, in any case, he would have laid himself open to immediate attack. Nor could he saunter back, trying to recover himself from the effort, as he often needed to do when the weights made him feel physically ill. Sometimes two men made a carry, one at each end of a load which was piled up to the maximum limit that could be endured and, if one collapsed under it, both men were liable to be badly hurt as the heavy timbers took charge. The foreman evidently hated white men and used his timber hook without mercy on these occasions. Why the new seasoning stacks could not have been built

236

closer to the old ones we never fathomed. It was a dreadful party, often taking two or three lorry-loads of prisoners a day and, with very few exceptions, these were the men who could find nowhere else to go.

There was a gliding field on one side of this detail where parties of young Japanese made rather feeble efforts to learn the art. Large grasshoppers were rife there, and these the coolies used to toast and eat, while dragon-flies suffered the same fate. Small boys would catch them all through the vast connurbation and thread them on to strings whilst still alive, so that they would be behaving in a crazy fashion as the wretched insects flew round in their abortive attempts to escape. Then the boys would hawk them through the streets and sell them for some small pittance for toasting.

Sometimes a party from the 'English' camp went to Chubugūn with their *honcho*, an erstwhile policemen from Hong Kong, who used to catch some of the snakes which abounded there (he knew which were edible and which were not). He would skin and eat them with relish — an example which found a certain favour with some of our men who said that the meat was excellent and tasted like chicken, which it certainly resembled when cooked. Although I was well aware that tinned rattle-snake is on ready sale in the United States, I found the practice repellent and, in common with the majority, preferred to go without. Chubugūn timber yard only came to an end when the little Japanese *honcho*, after a great deal of trouble, finally over-reached himself and caused grave injury to several prisoners.

I had managed to join a stevedoring party situated close to the Umemachi basin, handling pig-iron, bales of rubber and innumerable empty steel drums. We had to cross the Aji Kawa ferry to get there and, one day, saw some Germans from a German ship in the harbour also waiting to cross. We smiled when we saw how the Japanese edged away from them as though they were lepers, and thought our secret thoughts!

Occasionally we had had an issue of a soft, white soya cake and, more rarely, of a thick brown soya butter, which was very salt. Once, when approaching the basin, we passed a booth selling what I took to be soya cake on the end of sticks. Waiting until the guard was absent during the lunch hour, I slipped off to buy some. The taste was indescribably horrible, but it was not until long afterwards that I realized it was raw whale blubber! For my part, I had had little opportunity to loot all this time, but one afternoon saw some fish being discharged and my eyes nearly popped out of my head when I noticed some large albacore amongst them. These are a species of the tunny family which I had known and caught in the deep-sea sailing ships before the war when they played ahead of the bows and which, although not such good eating as bonito (of the same family) represented the purest ambrosia to me then.

I determined to have one and, with another fellow, managed to remove two, which we took into the camp, each with one down a trouser leg. It was a highly unpleasant journey back, for it was winter-time and an albacore is a big fish weighing some sixty pounds and over three feet in length. I had tied mine to my belt, secured below its caudal fin. It was extremely difficult to walk upright, and I was more and more uncomfortable every second of the march. Somehow I survived the shake-down, possibly because the guards carrying it out were as cold as we were and, being that time of year, we were able to cook them in some sort over the charcoal braziers. The two fish made a real feast-dish which was shared out right through the two merchant seamen's barracks — the only occasion on which loot ever was so widely shared. (In fact, of course, there was no means of keeping them, since they would soon have advertised their presence by emitting a 'fishy' odour.)

The ground on which we worked, in common with a good deal of the Osaka water-front, had been reclaimed, and the land was being gradually advanced into the harbour. We were rolling fifty-gallon drums from a barge to a big stack of them one morning when the earth started to shake. Big fissures opened up in the ground as water came surging up through them, floating the drums about and destroying the stack, which came crashing down to join those already swirling about. We had no control over our legs, feeling as though we were drunk below our waists, and were all terrified that a fissure might open beneath us and swallow us up. In any case, since water covered the ground, we could not see where the existing fissures were. A sort of tidal wave ran into the harbour, throwing the vessels alongside the quay about, and everything we saw was shaking violently. Although it was all over quite quickly, we believed our last moments had come. Some of the fissures never closed up again.

Our rations in the camp had become very much reduced: the barley had long been a thing of the past and much of the residue was now polished rice and far less sustaining than the unpolished variety. The soup was seldom satisfying, except when it contained soya beans, although chrysanthemum roots, radish, bamboo or cabbage on the other days provided at least an illusion of sustenance. The bread ration was being reduced rapidly and was soon to be stopped altogether, so we found ourselves becoming more and more hungry. Pargiter and I were determined to get into more rewarding details where we might not only get some additional lunch but also have some scope for private loot. Sen Pakku was not satisfactory because, although one might handle the odd rice or sugar ship, there was no guarantee of returning to her and, after working such a cargo, one could be sure of a rigorous search on arrival outside the camp. All too often the cargoes were various ores, or pig-iron for the foundries, and once, in the worst of my own experience, a very old cargo of Chilean saltpetre which had set solid!

Quite by mistake, I was once drafted to Osaka Kō. This detail had a very bad name and was still worked by some of the Guam Americans who, in the first instance, had not been expected to work hard. They had observed the coolies carrying very heavy loads and, not wishing to be outdone or put to shame by any Jap, had very foolishly emulated them and shown what they could do. Thenceforth they were required to carry 120 kilogram bags of ore — some 264 pounds — with the coolies. Not only is this a heavy load for a man who is not used to it but, ores being particularly heavy materials, they were contained in stiff, straw sacks some two feet square, which sat very heavily on a man's shoulder and required to be loaded with great accuracy.

The party used to discharge barges into box cars and *bodikis* or into the warehouse, and indulged in general entrepôt stevedoring. It had the reputation of being the hardest working party in the two camps* but, because the returns were relatively high and it was virtually a 'closed shop', its members were in very poor odour with their fellows as it was believed that outsiders who tried to enlist in the detail were given short shrift. It is true that permanent membership was almost by invitation.

I only went there that day because my own party had unaccountably failed to work for some reason and, at first, I thought that I should never survive the day. The bags of ore — 'rock', as it was termed — seemed to bite right into my shoulder and my whole body was aching most painfully the next morning. Certainly there had been more to eat for lunch, but it had been a dreadful day, presided over by a large Japanese who appeared to be extremely intolerant of the strangers in his warehouse. The others, who had been drafted there with me, did all that they could to avoid the place the next morning, but I decided to take my chance, feeling that, if the regular men could do it, I could too. As the party was being increased from ten to fifteen men, I remained and, being asked to stay, seldom went anywhere else to work until late in the war, after the camp and surrounding district had been destroyed. Previously I had whiled away the dreary days of automaton motion by learning verses copied from the *Oxford Book* and soon found myself doing the same thing at Osaka Kō, whilst catching the heavy bags in mid-air and loping along with them as well as any coolie. We used hooks to handle them, and were really quite expert.

General merchandise passed through the warehouse and there were few bags or bales of whose contents we did not apprise ourselves, as we were all competent to extract almost everything out of any sort of container without detection. There was wine, 94% proof alcohol, dried

---

* Personally I thought the timber details to be the hardest.

239

sweet potatoes, rice, beans, clothing and, very occasionally, fruit. Also, the scaling of a retaining wall separating the next warehouse provided ingress to a large stack of tinned tangerines in cases which, oddly enough, was never moved throughout the war, except insofar as it diminished as a result of our depredations.

These things were the exceptions. Ores were our chief stock-in-trade, either in bags or in bulk: bauxite passed through by the barge-load and occasionally we had such undesirable cargoes to handle as graphite and plumbago. The only real reason that the party had a bad name was that it was highly organized and about the only body of prisoners working together in a party who pulled together for the common weal. The men on it were, of necessity, fairly powerful, but even the smallest man can achieve strength if he wishes, and two of our members who were of very small proportions were none the less able for that. The fact that most of us stood well over six feet created an illusion in the camp which grew into a myth.

The vast majority of men stole for themselves. They might share their plunder with their own clique in the camp but, because opportunities were relatively uncommon, there was little thought of concerted action, particularly on Sen Pakku, whence men would sometimes come in loaded with ridiculously large quantities of rice or sugar. This was excusable when working in a ship to which one might not return, but on the regular details it was mere folly. Wanton damage of bags infuriated the Japanese civilians, and the fact of a man getting caught not only got him into trouble, but reacted on the rest of his party for days and, at the same time, created more exacting shake-downs both of the parties and of the camp. Certainly we had learned ingenuity and, having obtained needles and thread from the coolies and cloth by stealth, we made bags for the concealment of rice, barley, sugar and other free-flowing items of that order. There were bags to fit the shoulders which, when filled tight, could not be distinguished from a man's frame by a searching Jap. Bags to fit under the crutch were less comfortable, but even the most vulgar guard seldom found them, and a wriggle at the appropriate moment was sufficient to put him off the scent. We had noticed that the guards always felt down the outsides of our arms and legs, but seldom the insides, and bags were made to fit against these portions of our anatomy accordingly.

A necessary piece of equipment was a short, thin length of hollow bamboo, cut square at one end and sharpened to a quill-like point at the other. There would be a hole in the trouser pocket. Then, perhaps even when a guard with fixed bayonet was standing within a couple of feet, a man who was stacking could lean nonchalantly against a stack of — say — sugar bags with his hands in his pockets whilst waiting for the next sack truck to come, but he would have the sharpened end of the bamboo in one hand and could unobtrusively slip it into the bag. The sugar would flow through it into the loot bag which was secured down the prisoner's leg until, when it felt reasonably full, the bamboo was withdrawn and, if done carefully, the hole closed itself and nothing whatever was spilt.

An army webbing belt, drawn tight over four or five tins of fruit, would effectively conceal them providing that a man kept his stomach well drawn in and, for a long time, all these and other methods worked very well. Gradually more and more men got caught, but the consequences were very uncertain. One day a man was discovered to have a bag containing, perhaps, eight pounds of sugar. The guard swore at him, gave him a bang on the head with it and — and this part was unique — returned it to him.

In the next party was a man who had been working sugar in the Sumitomo warehouse all day. The gang had been allowed to eat all that they wanted while on the job, provided that they took none away. This man had emptied out his pockets before leaving, but a few grains — no more — had been left accidentally. He was beaten up hard, there and then, both by face slapping and with a rifle butt. The rest of the party were dismissed, but he was left to the corporal of the guard who was working himself into a frenzy. As the following party arrived he was hauled into the guard-room which had sliding doors on metal runners, and there he was made to kneel with his knees just over the runner, holding a bucket of water straight out in front of him. This may not sound much. Forget the fact that the man had already been beaten up and that the runners were biting agonisingly into his shin, and let any reader try and hold a bucket of water straight out in front of him for five short minutes. He will find it five minutes too much. This man had to hold it out for over two hours, being beaten whenever he spilled a drop, until he finally passed out into unconsciousness.

Thus discovery was a lottery. The cases I have quoted were extremes, but the men concerned usually had to stand at strict attention in the guard-room — once or twice for the whole night — with spasmodic beatings. As loot bags became more common, more people were caught and we were liable to be made to strip in the street outside the camp. The first time that this happened the effect was grotesque, as the men who had loot were left standing naked, or nearly so, with bags securely tied to their persons! However, the prisoner who was prepared to steal was nothing if not resourceful, and bags were soon devised which could be divested with the clothes, and these were seldom found. Another trick was to take dirty clothes out of the camp to wash them on the job (at lunch time), and then to bring them in wet, with loot inside them, as the guards usually fought shy of searching these. Nevertheless, although a lot of stolen goods came into the camp, a great deal was found and each discovery tended to tighten up Japanese surveillance, however temporarily.

A good deal of the stolen material left the camp again on other details to be bartered with civilian Japanese for other desirable articles which we could not steal, such as cigarettes, or to be sold outright for cash. Barter was rife both within and without the camp and, by dint of our stevedoring proclivities, we gradually exercised an increasing influence on the *yami* (black market) values in the city. (I believe that the Kobe camp did the same thing.) Of course, not all prisoners were in a position to loot and many would seldom or never take the risk. Yet men working in steel works and the like were often acting as agents in the incessant barter that went on and, of course, took their 'commissions'.

Sometimes questions were asked, but it was our good fortune that the mental processes of the average Japanese worked very slowly. Once Venner, a member of an 'English' camp working party at Cemento — a cement works — was seen to produce, rather carelessly, a packet of cigarettes of a brand known as *Akatukis*, which were relatively expensive, whereas our own issues, when we had had them, had been *Kinchis*, the cheapest brand of all. Venner was a man who had recently shaved off a very striking fair beard and moustache, but he was well-known to all the Japanese at Cemento, where he had worked for about eighteen months, and they had come to respect his opinions and views.

A Jap observed the *akatukis* and asked where he had got them, as cigarettes were almost as gold in Osaka at that time. Surely, he asked, they were not an army issue. Venner had to think quickly. He could neither admit that they came off the 'Black Market', nor pretend that they were an army issue. *"Well"* he said, in the pidgin English-cum-Japanese which, with a measure of sign language and a little Hindustani, obtained as a sort of Esperanto wherever the prisoners were to be found; *"Do you remember that I had a beard until last week?"*.

"Yes" answered the Jap, who had been joined by one or two others.

Venner went on: *"You remember that I was not here one day last week? Well, I went to Sen Pakku that day, and a Japanese sailor bought my beard for two hundred and eighty akutakis."*

The Japs looked incredulous. *"You sold your beard?"* they echoed.

"Yes. That is how we get our rogos (cigarettes). *The Japanese men in the ships are always pleased to buy our hair. You see Thompson asoko* (over there)? *Well, you notice that he has just had his clipped short."* (Some men did do this.) *"He sold his hair on Sen Pakku the other day".* Then loudly, *"Hey, Thompson! How many cigarettes did you get for your hair?"*

"A hundred and fifty." called this man, taking his cue.

242

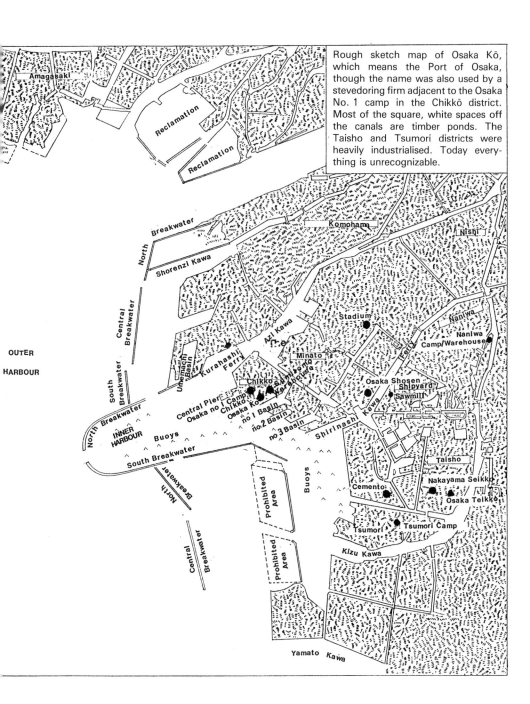

Rough sketch map of Osaka Kō, which means the Port of Osaka, though the name was also used by a stevedoring firm adjacent to the Osaka No. 1 camp in the Chikkō district. Most of the square, white spaces off the canals are timber ponds. The Taisho and Tsumori districts were heavily industrialised. Today everything is unrecognizable.

Map 2. Osaka Water-front.

The Japs were impressed. It was all so pat, but they still found it hard to believe, although they knew Venner and Thompson well and had always found them sound enough in the past. Venner saw that they were not wholly convinced, so pointed to another of his compatriots:-

"You see Harris," he said, *"His hair is getting pretty long. He is waiting for it to grow a bit more yet."* Then he shouted:- *"Harris, how many cigarettes to you expect to get for your hair?"*

"Not more than eighty akatukis. It's not very good hair" came the prompt response. Harris had gathered what was going on and, in any case, prisoners had developed an almost sixth sense. Here was corroborative evidence, and the Japs knew Harrisu (as they called him), too, but they had almost forgotten how to dream of so many cigarettes so, still stupefied, they almost whined:

"But why? Tell us why the Japanese men buy your hair."

"Why?" explained Venner with a face as straight as a die, *"Because before the war you used to import camel hair for paint brushes and things like that, but now there is a war, so you can't import any camels. Japanese men's hair is djoto nei,"* (no good) *"it is all stiff, but English and American men's hair is taksan djoto."* (Very good). *"Wakaru?"* (Do you understand?)

They felt his hair: they felt each other's, they felt the heads of the other Englishmen. It was true, there was no doubt of it. Theirs was stiff and coarse, ours was relatively fine.

"Ah, Sodeska!" (So that's it!) they muttered. They were wholly convinced and, so far as I know, they believe it to this day. Perhaps the finest touch was the implication that whole camels were imported for bristles, but that passed over them!*

At Osaka Kō a great deal more reason entered into the looting than in any other party, as we were very highly organised and we were only caught once, although on one occasion we managed to bring in one of our number without exciting suspicion when he was in such a state of drunkenness that he could not stand. He was, we said, *beoke* (sick) and he fortunately gave practical demonstration of this at the crucial moment! I had come into the camp with a bottle of wine inside the sleeve of each upper arm, four tins of tangerines at my waist, a bag of maize in my crutch, a bag of about five pounds of rice and another with as much soya beans down each thigh. It was difficult to *kiri* but, if required, I could have stripped in the street and dressed again without discovery, given a modicum of luck. This was something of an exceptional load for me, but there were a large number of men who habitually bought in far more than that, using their shoulders and backs as additional hiding

---

* Both parties fell prey to the common fallacy. Camel hair brushes are not made from the hair of camels but from that of Angora goats or, sometimes, of squirrels!

244

places. Neither I nor many of my party could do this, since our coats were generally too small and tight for us without being padded with loot. Almost everyone on the stevedoring parties had let long, triangular pieces of cloth into the legs of his trousers, ostensibly for comfort but actually to make them more capacious! Many men used to arrive back looking as though they were in an advanced state of pregnancy, and still they sometimes got through, though this was rather by luck than good judgement. It was a stupid practice which tended to redound on everybody else.

Yamamoto-san and Tor-san, the Japanese *honchos* at Osaka Kō, knew that they had a good gang and were loath to lose us. They gave us additional rice or beans for our lunch and often some dehydrated, sun-dried sweet potato, which was very filling, whilst we were generally allowed two bucketfuls of wine a day if there was any in the yard. (I considered this vitamin C sufficient reason, alone, for working on the detail.) We had no wish to prejudice these favours, but we wanted considerably more than we were given. It was clearly understood, particularly where wine and alcohol were concerned, that only the men detailed by Smith, our *honcho*, would do the job. The alcohol was generally mixed with tinned tangerines to make it palatable. We seldom stole from bags unless in a very small consignment, but took complete ones and shared them out at our convenience. One item which occasionally passed through was de-hydrated banana. It looked so disgusting that I did not at first realize what it was but, once the penny had dropped, I found it one of the better items of loot. Naturally, one had to be careful when eating de-hydrated foods and to be very circumspect. One idiot once ate a great deal of raw rice and was soon in excruciating agony as it swelled inside him to such a degree that there were fears that his stomach would, literally, burst.

Since so large a proportion of our work was concerned with the handling of ores, we always made a point of bringing our loot into the camp after we had been working bauxite, or something which had made us equally dirty, as this tended to make the search a great deal more perfunctory, partly because it did not occur to the guards that we would have anything to steal and partly because they did not care to soil their uniforms by being too thorough with us. On these occasions we not only brought in loot for ourselves and our own cliques, but wine, sugar and tangerines for the American doctor to give to the sick. (By this time a sick bay, as distinct from the Stadium, had been established within the camp). As we were the only detail to do this, we felt that this alone justified taking sufficient measures, if necessary, against other prisoners occasionally drafted into the party, to ensure that the practice might continue.

Not only did we become expert at carrying the bagged 'rock', but also at throwing it on to the shoulders of the carrier who, for his part, learned how to catch it in mid-air whilst spinning round on his heel, so that he landed the bag on his shoulders neatly with no feeling of shock. This was not done with the men who came to the party by accident and who were not used to it, as they might have been knocked flat by the heavy bags flying at them. These men were told that they would have the same treatment and facilities as everyone else, but that they must steal nothing. They must leave that to the men who knew the ropes, and they would have their share. They must co-operate in this and, if they did, they would be no worse off than anyone else.

All too often these men were only there for the odd day or so and they determined to disregard our warnings and to steal as much as they could for themselves, without thought for the damage they might do to the party as a whole. It was this which led to the belief that outsiders were given short shrift, as any man who did not obey our rules generally found himself lying on the ground with a badly ricked back. Once or twice it was accidental, but we knew the wrong way to throw a bag just as well as the right way, and had no compunction in putting this method into effect against anyone who acted in a prejudicial manner. It was one of the few instances in our existence when those prisoners who acted for themselves, with utter disregard for the common good, met with their just deserts.

For a long time I was the only Englishman in the party and, owing to its reputation, I think I was open to some suspicion in our barrack as a result. The detail suited me very well as I preferred not to work with those in my own barrack on the whole, since I considered that I saw quite enough of them as it was. There is much truth in the old adage that 'familiarity breeds contempt'. Pargiter and I thought it best for us to go to different working parties as far as possible and he normally went to Kurahashi, a stevedoring firm on a wharf at the mouth of the Aji Kawa. Not only did this double the opportunities for the common pot, but it provided for a broader common outlook in the camp and it was this, coupled with the fact that we made it a rule for quite a long time that we should not speak to each other for one day a week, which enabled us to stick together and not to break up like most of the cliques who could not bear such close association for so long a time.

Shortly after I joined Osaka Kō it transpired that Smith, the *honcho*, was getting a daily paper from an old coolie named Fuji, for which he paid some sort of price. Although this detail had far more *esprit de corps* than the merchant seamen ever had, the same rules which we had observed in the past had to apply, but Smith always passed it to me and to one other, and this was another reason which was sufficient to anchor

246

me to the party. We never took it into the camp except on days of very special news, but we had great difficulty in reading it as the premises only boasted one, utterly revolting *benjo*, so old and soggy that we were in constant fear lest the planks would give way and drop us in — a ghastly fate which actually befell a prisoner at another firm. Moreover, the waterside was continually being patrolled by both naval police and the *kempetai*, the latter being the military police who considered themselves to be lords of creation and who were held in awe by the army and the civilians alike, and we had to be exceptionally careful with our newspaper when these men were around.

We were able to work very well with the firm's coolies. They were quite a decent lot of fellows who shared the average civilian's loathing of the army. They were the victims of propaganda, who had exulted in their country's initial sweep of victory but, now that things were becoming more difficult, they were remembering the incidents in the early 1930s when the army had gained control of the country. They recalled the assassinations and the military uprisings, and were finding their lot harder and harder as the war progressed. It was the army that they cursed for the shortage of their food, of their cigarettes and for their poor clothes which were so thin as to be almost transparent, and it was to the army that they, too, were bound to *kiri*. Thus there was some sort of a common bond between the prisoners and the coolies in their mutual detestation of the Japanese military caste and, as the shortages created by the *senso* (war) turned against the country, that bond became closer. However, they had no idea of the seriousness of the military situation from the time that the United States took the offensive in the Solomons or even after the Battle of Midway until the bombing of their own cities actually started. We appreciated the turn of the tide, but the contraction of the Japanese sphere of influence was not wholly clear to us at the time. The news in the papers tended to be 'woolly'.

Oiwa was probably the strongest of the coolies. He had some sort of charge-hand status and once astounded us by a feat of prowess which none of us could match. When I had once seen a powerful Maori, loading a ship off Wanganui, shift a double dump of wool weighing about eight hundred pounds across a ship's hold and stow it, I believed that I had seen a demonstration of the very quintessence of strength. Oiwa was a well-built fellow of average (Japanese) height; very fit but in no way exceptional to look at, yet he took on his shoulders three of the 120-kilogram bags of ore — a total weight of some eight hundred pounds — balanced the one above the other, walked about twenty yards, stepped over some railway lines and ascended a narrow plank into a box car. Now eight hundred pounds is a tremendous weight for a man to carry with his back hollow and under the best conditions, but the measure of

Oiwa's effort was that he bent low to pass through the door and then straightened his back again before dropping the load on to the stack.

None of us could carry more than two of these bags, yet we had much greater staying power than any Japanese, even if we could not match the best of them in such isolated feats, and we could continue to carry normal loads long after they had knocked off for a rest. As we had to complete the work entailed by each railway shunt, however great or little it might be, there was no point in working slowly, which simply meant that we got back to camp later.

At about this time the movement of bulk ores at Osaka Kō increased considerably. The Japanese idea was that the material should be unloaded from a barge onto the quay by a winch and swinging derrick, and that it should be transported thence for about forty yards and up a ramp into a railway car, being carried in baskets on the end of yoke poles, which the prisoners always termed 'yo-ho' poles. Since these were not the same as the European yoke, but pole-like lengths of tapered oval cross-section, I shall refer to them as yo-ho poles. We were an adaptable party, but could never use these poles with ease and, the taller a man was, the more difficult it seemed to be, since any sort of success seemed to be based on attaining a form of lope which was foreign to us. Nor did we relish the prospect of developing a shoulder like that of Bai-san, one of the Japanese gang who worked with us. Small, swarthy and immensely cheerful with a sense of humour more highly developed than in most of his fellows, his right shoulder was deformed by a mountain of some sort of hard flesh or gristle which had been produced in a large lump as a result of long years under the yo-ho pole. Consequently we nick-named him 'Muscles', and there was nothing he liked better than for someone to grasp this lump and gasp admiringly!

Transporting iron ore by this method was by no means amusing and, remembering the lessons of the wheelbarrow at the shipyard, and with a large measure of co-operation from the civilian Japanese, long timbers were used to construct a ramp leading up to a platform which was slightly higher than the top of the largest railway truck which we normally worked — a twenty-tonner. This ramp was twenty-five or thirty feet long. We procured half a dozen sack trucks, or *detchies* as the Japanese called them, and seized on to them specially constructed boxes which held some three and a half hundredweights, with the lower end a flap on a hinge. This could be opened by releasing a hook which fitted over the lip of the upper end, and was attached to a wire made fast to the base of this flap. We then worked with four men discharging the barge or coaster, usually on cargo mats: one man, usually Cramer, who was small, on the winch; one on the cargo hook and bull-rope, and four men loading the box-*detchies* with shovels. Four men pulled these, one other

32. The method of loading ores into railway trucks introduced by the prisoners, who found it easier than using baskets on a yoke. The Japanese followed suit, but went back to their old way when the war was over. The 'Ku-ké' shack can be seen abutting the second warehouse in the background.

(usually myself) being stationed at the ramp with a stout stick wherewith to give them a good shove up it. Smith stood on the platform and released the hook when the box had been manoeuvred over the railway car. By this means we were enabled to load the cars in the shunt in far less time and with far less effort, often spending the rest of the afternoon stretched out in the sun.

Once more, the Japanese were immensely impressed and copying, as their race is so wont to do, built a similar system for themselves, since they were doing the same job at the next winch: both ramps being on the site of the previously burnt-out warehouse. Most of the summer it was splendidly hot and few of us wore more than a *fundoshi* — a sort of loin-cloth — all the day, but the Japs seldom stripped down when working and, as the whole success of the method depended on hauling the *detchies* at fairly high speed all the way, the older coolies, wearing enormous straw sun hats (which we had also procured), a cotton coat, white breeches and puttees, looked very comical doing this, as they found it hard to run after years of loping under the yo-ho poles. Nevertheless, they all admitted it was a better system and it was also adopted by a gang of young Koreans who worked the third winch, but, when I walked down there after the country had surrendered, I found the ramps deserted and the ores being loaded into the railway cars with yo-ho poles, in the old, old way!

Whilst on this job in the summer-time we consumed, literally, buckets of wine. It normally passed through in barrels and then back, much later, after being bottled. The foremen of all the stevedoring details knew very well that we could not do a decent day's work on the army rations in the camp, and always provided some sort of extra food. Some gave the ordinary workman's *bento* — a form of packed lunch consisting of rice with a small side dish of pickled *daicon* or something like that, all wrapped in a banana leaf. (*Daicon* were a huge form of radish, presumably attaining their size by the generous application of fertiliser in the form of the night-soil from the *benjos*.) Others, like Osaka Kō, varied their issue with the merchandise passing through their hands! In fact, we learnt, before a consignment of goods was dispatched, it was normally calculated how many times it would be handled *en route* and an extra case or bale added for each such transhipment. Thus, if sending sixty parcels, to be handled four times, it was necessary to send sixty-four to ensure that sixty arrived at the final destination. (Of course, an extra one *should* have been included for each handling by prisoners!) This was the common measure of honesty in the land.

They were always generous with the consignee's wine and gave us as much as they supposed we could drink. They supposed wrongly and had no conception of our capacity, but this caused us little worry as we had

250

discovered how to tap the casks without leaving any visible sign that they had been touched. In the summer we sweated it straight out of our systems, but in winter often had a certain amount of difficulty in sobering up the weaker-headed brethren before returning to camp. However, the potency of the wine was as nothing to the alcohol which used to arrive by the barge load, usually when a big four-masted German ship, which we believed to be the *Moselle*, was in harbour. She was one vessel which was never worked by Sen Pakku details, and we supposed that she traded between Osaka and Formosa or Indo-China, whence she brought the alcohol. Two square tins, each of about five gallons, were packed in a wooden case, and many the case and many the tin which we diverted to ourselves, as often as not sharing them with the coolies! It was raw stuff, but excellent if mixed with the tinned tangerines obtained from the adjacent warehouse!

We also worked a neighbouring goods platform handling more domestic shipments, and this also yielded small, but useful, finds, but it should not be thought that our lives were an orgy of looting. On the contrary, although its importance cannot be over-stressed, there was less and less as time went on, although the communal system which obtained at Osaka Kō generally ensured that we had something extra for lunch. Towards the end of the war we were glad enough to scrounge spilt maize, wherewith to make pop-corn, from the floors of box wagons. Ours was the one detail where we shared with each other and, having established a good system, it was enforced on anyone who entered the party, or else he suffered the ricked back mentioned previously: this being sufficient to keep him away thereafter.

In fine weather the prospect was splendid, the shipping, albeit steadily decreasing in volume, spread out fan-wise before us on the shimmering water which reflected the perfect azure sky of Japan and, after lunch, many of us would lie and glory in the perfection of the hot sun. This detail never quarrelled nor bore any rancour amongst themselves, but were all invariably cheerful, never giving way to the rather apathetic despair which was so prevalent in my own barrack. We took fair turns at the rough and the smooth, or did those jobs which each was best qualified to do, and every man pulled his weight. To the Japs I was always 'Hursto-san'*, and it was surprising how many of them, even in our circumstances, always gave us the suffix -*san*, meaning 'Mister'. The only exceptions were men like Legato who, on account of his invariably beaming countenance, was known by everyone as *Daikoku* — an ancient Japanese god. Somehow, the Japs could infallibly and unaccountably differentiate between our proper names and the odd nicknames.

---

* Japanese names end with a vowel and they seemed to be incapable of pronouncing one ending in a consonant without tacking on a vowel.

Occasionally, one or other of us would arrange to exchange parties with another man for a day or so, to obtain a temporary change of scene, but there was a lot to be said for remaining on one party, and I reaped the practical benefit of this on several occasions.

Once I had sinusitis so badly that I did not know where to put myself and was allowed one or two days in the camp but, because I had no temperature, the Japanese army could not conceive that I was in pain and I had to go out to work again. The doctors could do little for me until finally, somehow, somewhere, one of them, who had his own Ear, Nose and Throat clinic in New York, managed to get some Vitamin C to inject into me, and that did the trick. In the meantime I received every sympathy from the Japanese in the firm, frequently being urged to go and lie down in the *ku-ké* (or rest) shack. Later, I was one of those affected by an epidemic of mumps which swept the camp. As is known, this does not always affect the neck glands in men as it does in children, but takes a more unpleasant form. This was how it took me, but again the Japanese *honchos*, who knew me well enough, found me a job sitting down until I was better. Had I been a stranger to them I should probably have had to perform coolie work with, probably, wholly adverse effects on any possiblity of ever raising a family. Much the same occurred when many of us developed jaundice and were feeling rather low.

There were few means of sabotage open to us at Osaka Kō. One favourite amusement was to switch the labels on the loaded railway wagons before a shunt but, as we had no idea what the ideographs on them signified, we were in no position to judge the extent of our mischief, though it was pleasant to think that many of them arrived at the wrong destinations.

The average Japanese was quite incapable of performing the most elementary exercise in mental arithmetic, and could not calculate the number of cases in a stack of, say, eight wide by seven high by seven deep but, given an abacus, he could vie with any European on a calculating machine in quite abstruse calculations. (Micro-chips were not then invented!) One result of this was that they soon realized that we could do these calculations without batting an eyelid and they then usually deputed us to put the right number of bags or boxes into a railway car. We never knew whether the country was short of rolling stock, but many a short-loaded car was shunted out of Osaka Kō in those years!

Sometimes the Japs exhibited really incredible stupidity, and an example of this caused the only really unpleasant incident on that party. We never enjoyed handling the heavy bags of ore, especially when it involved negotiating ramps and bending through box-car doors. Often we would unload a car only to re-stow its contents into another one in the same string of wagons. This we considered to be both crazy and unnecessary. One morning we were told to discharge a car containing 180 bags on to the platform, so Smith asked how long they were going to stay there. He was told that 160 of them were going into the second car along from it, whereupon he asked if certain box-cars were restricted to certain routes. The *honcho* said that this was not the case. We then discharged 20 bags on to the platform and switched the wagon label with that of the car which was supposed to receive the 160 bags, having thus achieved the result with 20 carries instead of 340.

The Japanese foreman was furious. We tried to explain: we drew diagrams; we opened the car and counted the bags, but he could not be made to understand. Nor could any of the other Japs make head or tail of the manoeuvre: not even 'Old Pop', (as we called him), an ancient foreman who was more or less pensioned off but who sometimes showed glimmerings of reason. Tuji, Tor, Trudida (he who, when drunk, became so simian that we suspected his humanity), Oiwa, Yamamoto, Sumitomo, Tanaka, 'Muscles' and old Fuji: we appealed to them all, but each thought we had gone mad. They did their best, but the logic was beyond them. We had been told to take 180 bags from one car and to put 160 of them in another, but we had taken 20 from the first car and changed the labels. *"How could it be the same?"* they asked. Either we were mad or it was mutiny.

They sent to their office and the manager came, but he found it incomprehensible. The consigning clerk was baffled. A message was sent to the camp and a guard arrived. He could not understand the reasoning, so fell back on the infallible salve for all awkward occasions: he lined us up and slapped us, but we still stuck to our point. In desperation, the guard sent for a corporal who went through the same procedure until his arm was tired, when he sent for an interpreter. This was Hayeshi, who had once worked for General Motors in Hawaii and, after another long and unpleasant half hour, he understood and we were finally vindicated. I believe that the consigning clerk finally appreciated the principle involved, but neither Tor-san nor Yamamoto-san (the two *honchos*) ever did. To them the whole affair was some sort of black magic, and I am sure that they envisaged a spate of complaints from the receivers of those two cars! The incident did some good, however, as our word was taken on subsequent occasions, albeit with much dubious muttering and head-shakings!

As already mentioned, a gang of young Korean conscript labour had been drafted to the detail. The Japanese did not really want them and they were generally given the less pleasant jobs, which was our gain. Once we complained that the derrick we were using was unsafe, as its topping lift was badly stranded. At once we were moved to the other derrick where the Koreans were working and they were transferred to ours. We did not think that this was the correct approach to the problem and said so. This was brushed aside and, within a couple of hours, the loaded derrick came down, killing one Korean outright and seriously injuring two others. As far as we could determine, these Koreans were kept in a camp in very similar circumstances to ourselves.

Until then we had certainly worked very hard, but the advent of the Koreans slowed our tempo a little. Osaka Kō was not, perhaps, the richest working party: it did not provide the highest regular returns for the real entrepreneur, and it demanded the greatest effort. On the other hand it came in the first flight of the looting parties and, if only from a purely practical point of view, the constant toping of wine, in which it was almost unique, probably did more good than all the rice and beans in the land to the handful of men who worked there. It was, however, the detail *élite*. Moreover, so far as three of us were concerned, we read a paper every day. We not only had the best style, some of the strongest men and the greatest *esprit de corps* but, incidentally, some of the most intelligent inmates of the camp.

I never ceased to be astonished at the literary knowledge of these regular American service men. Most (though not all) of them came from California or the Down East States, but all were widely read and both competent and interested to talk intelligently on an immense range of subjects. None of the British details could begin to approach them in this. Smith had picked his men, and it is true that they represented not only the best in the camp but a section of the cream of the American fighting services. Only one other Englishman ever graduated to the detail permanently (Pargiter had had a spell there), and this was a young ship's writer from Glasgow, named Trocchi.

I only made contact with him again years later after he had retired from a successful career (which, incidentally, used to take him to Japan) and he had by then changed his name. For his part, he has, in particular, lurid memories of a hernia operation performed on him under Japanese aegis, but I suspect that, despite all that is said about Japanese prison camps, that detail may well have been the making of him and opened his eyes beyond horizons of which he had never dreamed. Not only did he learn a self-discipline and that pride bred of achievement, but he experienced a general style and mental stimulation which I doubt that he would ever have gained had he not been captured and arrived, if belatedly, in that detail. Moreover he developed a physique normally impossible aboard a passenger liner. Japan segregated the sheep from the goats. Certainly, many had no chance, but in retrospect the contrast between, for example, Capt. Barber, with all his potential advantage, and the youth Trocchi, who had joined the *Gloucester Castle* — his first ship — at the age of eighteen, gives food for thought when seen in perspective. As an aside, those men who were occasionally taken to a local Japanese dentist for treatment, spoke very highly of him.

There was no man there whom I would not welcome with open arms tomorrow. Smith, the *honcho*, a naval petty officer who was always good humoured but exercised complete authority with the lightest touch: Sewell Lufkin, with his love of music and the red-wood country whence he came: Boyle and Goebbels, two gigantic marines who had approached me about escape long before: the cheerful 'Daikoku' and Neale, who was so broad that he could pitch a bag with a man twice his size. 'Little Man' Cramer who drove the winch and who gave us such heart-aches when we could not restore him to sobriety: 'Squeegee' Herod, Burcher and Jones from Colorado who, after three years of captivity, still would not read *Ben Hur* when we finally received some books, because it was on the Codex. I am no papist, so perhaps failed to understand the fundamentals underlying this, but it did demonstrate the strength of his principles.

There were others, too: Pedigo, the Californian with a Cornish name who worked long with Lufkin and myself, there were Mojer and Schwab and the others. One and all, they maintained their sense of perspective, their sense of humour and their personal pride, and these were the greatest possessions a man could keep. Some American states are as foreign to each other as the European countries, and it was, for instance, incomprehensible to some how others could have played in football teams with blacks.* These things were discussed very rationally, but never with the slightest heat, as with so many points of potential disagreement within the camp.

When the camp was afflicted with a plague of rats from an adjoining rubbish dump soon after we had arrived, they not only ran over our faces at night and nibbled our toes, but infested both us and our blankets with fleas to such a degree that we were nearly demented with frustration. Finally a couple of cats were obtained somehow — I never knew how. Two mangy and scraggy animals they were, but lion-hearted, and many were the death-fights over our bodies during the next few weeks until the rats were a thing of the past. Then we were gradually able to rid ourselves of the fleas. The cats were retained to maintain the *status quo* but, as time went on, three hungry Middle-Westerners in the Philippine barrack eyed them greedily until, unable to contain themselves any longer, they killed one, skinned it and cooked it as best they

---

* In the present age, when equality of rights is preached so freely, such remarks may strike a discordant note in some quarters. Times have changed even if, however much legislation may have been passed, one can take a horse to water, but still cannot always make it drink!

could over a charcoal brazier, and then ate it. One of them was so ill that it was thought he would die and the other two fared little better. These were the men at the other end of the scale who knew no restraint.

Shake-downs continued both inside and outside the camp, but the rigour of the operations suffered sudden and unpredictable changes. Generally the guards were evidently instructed to look for some specified item, and they never seemed to see anything else. The fact that many of us openly wore straw sun-hats, which were manifestly obtained outside the camp, was tacitly accepted, as were a number of other things. Our party was only caught with loot once, but that was one of the lucky days when nothing much happened. Pargiter was caught once, and had a trying time in the guard-room.

By this time another building, into which the 'English' camp moved, had been erected next to ours, and the boundary fence on that side was removed. Each section retained its autonomy and the working parties were never mixed. This change created fresh diary problems. Mackavoy, we knew, had lost his when he had hidden them prior to a rumoured camp shake-down, for they had not been there when he went to retrieve them. As nothing was heard of it, we supposed that a prisoner had accidentally happened on them and consigned them to the boiler. Mackavoy was not a popular man, being truculent and unpleasant to all and sundry, apparently in some effort to assert himself. For his part, he said little about his loss. There was no point and no proof, but Pargiter and I had no illusions that many of our own people thought these diaries far too dangerous to be kept, and that they must be as well hidden from them as from the Japanese. Had some of our fellows known that I also read an English-printed paper every day, I should doubtless have played the principal part in an *auto-da-fé!*

I had hidden my diaries in almost every conceivable place in the camp at one time or another, sometimes even strapping them to my person and marching out with them on shake-down days, only to bring them in again afterwards, in the belief that the guards would have had enough searching for one day to bother much about searching us. Pargiter, who had used the trick successfully on returning from working parties with loot, once hung his up inside some wet trousers he had washed. Only Mackavoy and I saw him do it, yet he never saw them again. Mackavoy was jealous of Pargiter for a number of reasons unconnected with camp life and we believed that he had wished for diaries (which he had lost, as recorded) in order to present the best story to their company on their return home, whilst to deprive Pargiter of his would be a master stroke. Perhaps we misjudged him.

Circumstantial evidence can be dangerous but, at all events, Pargiter's diaries were gone and we never knew the truth of their fate. Certainly the

Japs never had them. Both he and I had always appreciated that we should be lucky to get them out of the country, but it was clearly understood between us that, if one succeeded and the other failed, each would have equal access to the surviving manuscript.

Mine was now voluminous, so I placed it in a 'panic' bag which consisted of a haversack containing my private papers, my pocket book, a small amount of English money, my family photographs and a few necessaries, including a spare pair of socks, a toothbrush and small items I should need in case of a sudden evacuation of the camp. We removed a batten from the wall flanking Pargiter's *tatami* (he was at the end of the bay) and hung the whole thing from a nail between the plaster of the outer and inner wooden skins of the building before replacing the batten. It could be removed again easily enough, but represented an invisible, secret drawer. Only my current volume was kept aside. I included my family's photographs as I found that viewing them created too great a nostalgia and tended to upset such victory of mind over circumstance as I had achieved. Pargiter also had a small panic bag which, no longer being so dangerous on search days, could be stowed on the shelf in the open. The Chikkō camp was right in the centre of an obvious target area and was bound to be bombed sooner or later.

In such an event we might both be out at work or, alternatively, we might both be bombed too. Such eventualities we were neither able to predict nor could we legislate for them, but **it was solemnly agreed between us that, if either of us was in the barrack when the camp was bombed, that man would bring out both panic bags with him.** This agreement is stressed, for reasons which will become apparent. We knew by this time that the Japanese could not cope with crises and would not know what to do when they occurred. The bombing of the camp would constitute a crisis, and the likelihood of any shakedown then would be more than remote. Pargiter was devoid of any fear in such matters and one of the most accomplished 'looters' in the camp. More than this, we could hardly do.

The amalgamation with the 'English' camp made us appreciate how superior many of their details were to ours, as some of their stevedoring parties were veritable '*El Dorados*'. After one shakedown when the Japs made a very good haul which, we began to suspect, was their chief reason for these operations, they were not so much infuriated by the fact that they had found such large quantities of loot as by the fact that one man had concealed under his sleeping bay more sugar than Colonel Murata received for his ration in five years! — an item of intelligence which the prisoners received with supreme indifference, although it was a most gratifying sidelight on our activities!

In retrospect, I think that one of the most peculiar features of the

257

camp to an outside observer would have been the vast gulf between the feeding standards of those who looted or who entered into black market activities and those who could not, or would not, do so. Loot was seldom distributed outside a man's immediate clique and those things which required cooking presented problems when the charcoal braziers were not burning. I sometimes passed food to two of my gunners from the *Dalhousie* who worked in a foundry and occasionally to Llewellyn who had the misfortune to be berthed next to Mackavoy but, on the whole, very little such distribution was made: the bulk of the very considerable surpluses being directed out to the black market of Osaka for the greater well-being of the chief looters. Many people in the non-looting details — the steelworks, cement works, and so on — took a commission on such transactions.

Pargiter and I used the black market to obtain paper, pencils, cloth and other items we needed, but did not enter into this activity to any great extent and generally tried to bring in loot in fairly large quantities occasionally rather than a little often, on the basis that, if one was caught, it did not matter how much one was carrying and, the fewer carries, the less the risk of discovery. On the face of it, it was all very bad style, but the *esprit de corps* of Osaka Kō was utterly lacking in our barrack on the one hand and, on the other, it is the basis of every commercial system that he who takes the biggest risk expects the biggest dividend. It may be that our commercial methods do not bear close investigation, but at least the prisoners in Japan were no worse in their principles, which merely seemed to be the more stark as the hunger line was approached. Had our barracks been more homogeneous and better disciplined to act for the common good, it is possible that the situation might have been different, though I incline to doubt it. Much of the black market centred round cigarettes but, as I smoked a pipe and disliked cigarettes, I stopped smoking altogether, since no suitable pipe tobacco was available.

The mortality rate had decreased, but there were still those who died. An old Italian named Serafin, long since naturalized in Britain, who had been the saloon steward in the *Dalhousie*, had constantly appealed to the Japs that he was an Italian: an ally of theirs. It was disloyal to the country of his adoption and was always met with the question of what he was doing in a British ship. All the same, he was old and, when he was shaken for muster one morning, he was dead. Nor was he the only one, though his was surely the most peaceful of the deaths amongst us. Slowly, inexorably, the numbers increased. On the face of it we were a fine, bronzed, strong and healthy group of men, often with added muscle and heavier than before capture, but all this was only on the surface. A man had no resistance; when he got sick he wasted away very rapidly, almost while one watched, with no reserves to call upon, and sometimes it was incredible how swiftly a man might die. There was little help for these and nothing that anybody could do. They were lamented, but they had no memorial and no mourning, while the rest of us went on through the monotony of our days. We were not callous, but it did no good to dwell too long on these things. Those who recovered in time took long to restore their condition and were pitiable to behold, with their bones scarcely held together by their wasted flesh.

At Osaka Kō we sometimes worked graphite in very large paper bales which one could lift with one hand and which were so light that it was difficult to keep them on the sack trucks. They exuded a black dust which permeated everything and made the ground more slippery than a skating rink. For this we abandoned our *fundoshis* and worked naked. We could wash ourselves, but it was hard to remove the graphite from clothing. Sometimes we dived into the harbour. This was not allowed, but winked at so long as a close watch was kept for the *kempetai*, and on these occasions we were often able to collect mussels from the edge of the quay. Normally we washed with the coolies at a pump on the premises before returning to camp. There were times when the foremen caught us looting, which always caused a temporary coolness. They fulminated and threatened to report us to the army, but I doubt if they ever did, as they were too frightened of losing a good gang.

When a Japanese hospital ship was sunk at sea, the press made the most of it and her picture was splashed across the pages. She was a ship we knew well and was one I had seen discharging pig-iron at a wharf near a steel-works not so many months previously. We explained this to the coolies who were angry about it, but they nodded and talked amongst themselves. It was no way for a hospital ship to behave, they admitted. The tide was turning, slowly and almost imperceptibly. The Japanese no longer called *"Horio-na!"* (Prisoner eh!) at us in the streets, and often they asked for information about our countries. There were rumours that Prince Konoye, known to be a peace-maker, was about to become Prime Minister: the criminal Tojo was no longer the idol of a victorious country: the ships in the harbour were becoming fewer and fewer; taxation was insupportable and consumer goods were at a premium. Islands in the Pacific, the stepping stones to Japan, were falling to the Americans and, although their significance was not apparent to the coolies, from whom we concealed our jubilation, they were weary of the war. Neither they nor we knew that the oil situation of their country had demanded that the war should be finished within six months of the Pearl Harbor attack and that, having failed in this, their cause was, in effect, lost from that time, nor were either of us aware of the continual strife between the elder statesmen and the army, which was only known after the hostilities were over.

The earthquake season had come round again and we had several shakes. One, said to equal in intensity the great Tokyo 'quake of 1923, started when I was standing outside the *ku-ké* shack. I glanced up to see a vast crack in an adjoining warehouse opening and shutting all up and down its height, with a rhythm steadily increasing in tempo. Somehow, with splaying feet, I managed to reach a barge and jump in and, whenever possible, I made for a barge in every earthquake thereafter. This was a bad one, though Osaka did not have the worst of it, the seismic centre being near Kyoto, but it caused immense damage elsewhere. On this occasion I found myself ship-wrecked as a great tidal wave swept in over the breakwaters of the artificial harbour and, lifting my craft, deposited it right over the quay to crash on to the sea-wall, sending me flying. Further along this sea-wall, which bounded the reclaimed land from the harbour, had cracked badly in several places and there were, in consequence, bad floods all over the Chikkō area. Disasters of this sort affected us little except insofar as they raised our morale. However well we might mix with the civilians, they were still the Japanese, and the enemy. If the people allowed themselves to be ruled by their army, that was hardly our fault and we were devoid of any pity for them.

XII

REDEMPTION THEME

One of the worst features of our confinement was the almost total absence of any sense of humour. Not only did so many prisoners lose theirs, but few Japanese gave any indication that they had ever possessed such a thing, and it is certain that they had no sense of the ridiculous. Perhaps the best example of this occurred after the sea-wall had been cracked by the earthquake and the town had become tidal for some three-quarters of a mile inland, flooding the raised camp to a depth of about a foot, so that the lower bays were uninhabitable.* Muster was carried out normally, all the men in each barrack being crowded on to the two upper bays. The duty officer duly arrived clad, as usual, in his cap, uniform tunic, duty sash and with his sword slung from his belt. Below this he wore nothing but a loin cloth, but neither from his manner nor from the attitude of his entourage would one have supposed that there was anything unusual about him!

Nor did the Japanese find anything humorous when this duty officer, in the darkness, stepped into a hole, nearly five feet deep, which had not been filled in after the new 'English' camp had been built, and became totally immersed. Dignity was the key-note of the military caste and it was never abandoned. We suffered, as head-quarters camp, from a constant change of camp commanders who, oddly enough, were usually young lieutenants who had seen no active service, and who were anxious to obtain promotion by a display of excessive zeal which generally took the form of making the lives of the prisoners even less tolerable than usual. Lieut. Tanaka, on the other hand, had seen service and had distinguished himself in the Philippine operations, but he was a sadist before a soldier, though I am not sure that we did not prefer him to a flabby, bespectacled young man who spent much of his time delivering us long lectures through his interpreter on the evils of masturbation.

---

* The effect of a flood above the level of the *benjos* may be imagined. That area of the camp was highly unpleasant.

261

Perhaps he judged others by himself! Certainly the only effect of his strictures was to earn himself the sobriquet of 'The Masturbator'.

Once a new officer joined the camp staff. He was very much smarter than most; spoke tolerable English and had, so we learned, undergone a long period of training in Germany. He behaved in a perfectly rational way, treating us reasonably and taking a certain cognisance of complaints, never being guilty of 'hazing' the prisoners. This was a most welcome change until one evening, when taking muster, he suddenly lost his temper for no apparent reason and hit a man hard across the head with his long torch. This was a bad enough thing to do, if unexceptional, but we had never expected it of him. After this he realized that he had lost face: that the veneer of civilizing influence which he had achieved had been laid bare, and from that day onwards he behaved little better than a wild beast, always standing on the top of the camp steps when he was on duty to club the men with his sword when they fell out to work in the mornings. This one man typified the veneer of the nation whose whole outlook and attitude was so very different from ours. That veneer of civilization was woefully thin.*

Sometimes a captain, in finding fault with a lieutenant, would slap his face and, on such occasions, it seemed to be an established national trait that the aggressor would work himself into such a state of frenzy that he was no longer in control of his actions. Often, I doubt not, it started even higher than a captain but, wherever it began, the chain of events could be followed right down the scale, through sergeants, corporals and privates, each being well slapped, until it reached some of us. Revenge was taken for granted but, because it could not be vented on a superior, the next most inferior person bore each victim's brunt until a number of prisoners were receiving their share in the guard-room on one pretext or another. The fact that the guard changed every week entailed constant repetition and re-establishment of minor points of order.

One of the 'English' details once performed a fine piece of sabotage. There was a series of goods lines which ran all round the Chikkō waterfront, serving the wharfingers. Beyond the No. 2 Basin were some points reducing the system to a single line over a bridge, with a short siding which contained a stop-piece, instead of a buffer. The party working there removed the stop-piece, managed to manipulate the points

---

* I use the word in its popular sense. Undoubtedly many individuals in all nations, whether savage, barbarous or more advanced, have achieved a high standard of civilization: that is, of refinement and enlightenment. Whether any one nation or people has ever, in the whole course of known history, really been civilized is very doubtful. If so, it was probably long before the Christian era in such centres as Ugarit. Knowledge and technology are not to be equated with civilization, which is a matter of human nature. The latter part of the twentieth century has seen a world-wide decline in civilizing influences.

at the last moment and awaited developments.

The affair went off splendidly. The engine came puffing up at its best speed, drawing a lot of wagons behind it. It was diverted: there was a screaming of brakes, a gargantuan splash and the engine was lying in the shallow water at the head of the basin, almost completely submerged, while some cars were derailed and upset. The driver was injured to some degree, but the fireman escaped completely. There was great jubilation about this: the line was blocked; we knew of no other engine on the system and we saw little likelihood of movement for days, which meant the virtual paralysis of Osaka Kō and many other firms. In the event, this was only true to a limited extent because the Japanese salved the engine and put things right very much more quickly than we had expected, which was disappointing, but it nevertheless had a useful 'nuisance' value. Naturally, there were a good many questions asked but, once again, nothing could be proved.

The most intelligent men were often those with the lowest morale, and the converse was also the case. There were some soldiers in the 'English' camp who made little secret of their disappointment when the war was over, for they were stevedoring, they were stealing, and they had a bare sufficiency of food and cigarettes. Their lives were completely controlled; they had no sense of responsibility for anything which they might do, and they had no occasion to think except when it suited them. All this they found eminently satisfying and an improvement on the army! It was the men who were accustomed to use their brains and to think who experienced the greatest void.

Pargiter and I had been fortunate in our *Oxford Book* and I had learned literally thousands of lines from it. During the last year we reaped what was, to many of us, the greatest reward of being the Headquarters camp, as we suddenly found ourselves in possession of a large and well-stocked library of books, most of them chosen with skill and ranging from the classics to modern fiction, yet covering almost every sphere of human activity.

This had been sent by the American Red Cross, though I have no doubt that the books had long been hoarded by the Japanese before they were finally issued. Many of our lives became transformed on their arrival and I, for my part, always made a practice of making a précis of every book I read, as a form of mental exercise. Previously I had designed dream-yachts, houses and all manner of things to occupy my mind: an occupation which had the additional advantage of making both my fellows and the Japanese accustomed to seeing me with paper and pencil, and thus detracted from undue suspicion about the writing of diaries. On the whole, the Americans were far better about amusing themselves in this sort of fashion than the English in the camp.

When the two camps amalgamated into one complex, there was very little fraternization and the lack of inclination to visit, or to seek out new friends, seemed to be mutual. This apathy about social intercourse with his fellow creatures was, to me, one of the oddest features of the average man. He was not wholly apathetic however, as I discovered, on the occasions when it fell to me to make any issue in our barrack, that the call: *"Next prisoner"* was sufficient to make blood boil. To say *"Next, please"* or *"Next man"* caused no ill-feeling, but *"Next prisoner"*, well! — the results had to be seen to be believed, and showed that mentality rather unfairly attributed to the ostrich!

Pargiter and I had found one or two kindred spirits amongst the Englishmen. There was Reg. Castleton, a very nice fellow indeed who had spent years before the war in various Butterfield and Swires offices in both China and Japan and who had not allowed the situation to alter his outlook in any way. He knew much about the public figures in Japan and was of inestimable value in assessing the worth of the domestic news which I read in the papers. I was deeply shocked when he died shortly after repatriation and only a few days before he was to attend my wedding. We enjoyed his company, together with that of his colleague Bignall, who worked with Courtaulds in peace-time and whose appearance rather belied his toughness. These two had paired off in their camp for much the same reasons as Pargiter and I had done in the first instance.

Sometimes we saw Venner, whose beard story at Cemento had won him immortal fame (actually, he had shaved off his beard as a result of a bet, which he lost!), and occasionally a small band of British and American service officers. These men had had very bad luck because, apart from the doctors who had something to do, they were virtually confined to their room year in and year out, as there was nowhere else for them to go. They had few people with whom to talk, having taken care not to lend themselves to promiscuous fraternization, and they did not work. Thus their lives and prospects were bounded within the narrowest limits and, because they did not work, they were, in theory, on the minimum rice ration. Actually, the food rations were always distributed equally amongst everybody.

These officers were extremely unfortunate not to have been placed in an officers' camp, where they could have mixed with men in their own predicament. In our camp they found themselves very much the odd men out, but they maintained their standards, their rank and their pride, and this was their salvation, as pride in himself was ever a man's most important asset in all that time. Once he had lost his self-respect he had virtually lost his soul and he was beyond help or hope.

Many men, notably those with little or no imagination, accepted their altered condition of life with complete equanimity of spirit. Some, who had never used their bodies in hard physical exertion and who had never experienced any adverse conditions previously, suddenly found themselves for the first time in their lives. Increased in their physical and spiritual stature, they finally came away with their whole pattern of life in a better perspective than they had ever known before. Of the men whose morale had remained high throughout, there were none who had not had to adapt their philosophy to some degree and, where there was a void to be filled in their accustomed mental exercises, they had had to find something or other to occupy themselves to that end. Some had failed in this and spent long hours delivering wearisome monologues to their fellows on their conditions (which were no worse than anyone else's), but most of these turned their minds into one channel and one only — the contemplation of imaginary food.

This was a sterile recreation which seemed to occupy hours of thought and discussion, compiling perfect menus and opening up vast vistas of roast beef, steaks, desserts and of endless tables groaning with viands. Broomfield and Chadwick became obsessed with this topic, although discussing it in a very civilized fashion, but it had the effect of accentuating the meagreness of the diet on which we were subsisting and making them the more miserable, thus lowering their morale and, in all probability, their very resistance all the more. It always struck me as odd that so many men seemed to be more anxious to provide themselves with tastes than with solid foods, and they were more concerned to obtain packets of red pepper, curry powder and like condiments than additional bulk.

We had been in camp for a year before we were allowed to send the barest form-postcard home, and it was nearly two years after my capture that my family were aware of my whereabouts. When we were finally told that we might write short letters of so many words, it was clear that, in order to be sent at all, they must contain no matter to which the Japanese might take exception. One man, an American who was badly infected with food dreams, wrote in his letter a request that he be sent a variety of essences, ranging from sarsaparilla to lemon, which he might eat with his rice! Not only did this demonstrate how sadly awry was his sense of perspective, but it caused *all* our letters be thrown into the boiler and it was long before another opportunity of writing home was given to us.

It was sometimes very hard to differentiate between cause and effect. There were a number of vitamin deficiency conditions which were very prevalent in the camp, and these caused some men acute discomfort. There were instances of beri-beri, when the knees became swollen and so spongy that if a finger was pressed into the skin the hole would remain, and when a man's teeth became loose. I had seen this before in sailing ships, but the most common complaints consisted of the tongue becoming extremely tender and almost raw, or else a completely raw condition of the scrotum. In the former case it was agony to take any food or liquid at all (which tended to make matters worse) and, in the latter, colloquially known as 'strawberry balls', the slightest movement caused the most excruciating agony, especially in its advanced stages.

The one empty barrack, which abutted on the alleyway to the *benjos*, was used as a store-room by the Japanese, the bulk of its contents being Red Cross food parcels, but it was very seldom that there was ever an issue. There was no evidence that our gaolers took them for themselves to any extent: it was simply their national instinct for hoarding, and we were well aware that there was a whole warehouse full of these parcels at Kobe — parcels which were finally bombed and destroyed as they stood after being stored for many moons. We had little enough of these parcels in all conscience and, on the very, very rare occasions when there was an issue, the parcel usually had to be divided between anything from two to ten men, which was totally unsatisfactory. Seldom though we saw these things I believe that we, as Headquarters camp, were better off than some of the subsidiary camps.

Those who dispatched the parcels could have had little idea of the worth of the smallest item of all — a minute folding tin-opener which had evidently been designed to save weight. These fitted into the peaks of our caps perfectly and were invaluable for opening tins of tangerines and other eatables on our details quickly and easily, and a tremendous improvement on cumbersome methods with a hook or old nail. The Japs never tumbled to the great potential of these little gadgets.

It only required a very little milk powder from a parcel to put a man's tongue back to normal, and this showed how fine is the hair-line between sufficiency and insufficiency of essential food-stuffs. It was significant that most of the men who suffered from these pellagra complaints were those who dwelt on the food topic to the exclusion of everything else. Broomfield and Chadwick were the only two on the end of our bay who were contaminated with this conversational disease and they were the only two of us to experience pellagric conditions, from which they suffered greatly. It is true that those whose morale dropped to so low a level that they thought exclusively about food were seldom of the calibre to loot to any extent (though some did), although, in general, the food which we looted was pure bulk and provided little of those vitamins which we needed, so that it could not be argued that the fruits of looting would avoid pellagra to any extent — they merely served to reduce the pangs of an empty belly. In any case, rice and beans were little use to us in the camp in the summer when we had no charcoal braziers whereon to cook them. Thus more loot was brought back in the winter.

In effect, therefore, we were probably all in very much the same case. Some, in virtue of their very metabolism or of their condition, had more or less resistance than others. It was simply a matter of spirit which tipped the balance and I am sure that the sufferings from pellagra were brought about for no better reasons than those which caused Capt. Barber to die in the early days, when he believed that he could not eat rice and that life held no further prospect to which he might look forward.

Our rations had only changed in that they had deteriorated in quality and quantity, but there was no change in the daily menu. Breakfast was still rice and soup: supper soup and rice. At the outset there had been enough soya beans to serve them instead of soup on Sunday mornings. They were relatively tasty and became a common form of currency, but in due course the ration became too small and Sunday, too, became a soup day. Sometimes there were odd additional issues which became rarer and rarer with the endless succession of the days. There was the odd piece of pink, boiled squid which was so tough that it had to be chewed by the hour: there was sea-weed and soya butter, very occasionally sugar in minute quantity, or salt and, on very high days, a small piece of fish or a thin slice of meat. Meat was what was craved most of all, but this was almost tasteless and hard to identify. It was believed to be goat. Not only did it stimulate some sort of memory of what we termed 'proper food', but when we awoke on the mornings following the issue we invariably realized that we were still in possession of our virility — a fact which we should not otherwise have known. Here again, was that narrow border-line between too little and enough. I have often been asked whether homo-sexuality was not rife in the camp and, as we had several stewards whose very gait proclaimed their tendencies, it might reasonably have been presumed to have been so. I believe that there was absolutely none, though this was probably due to the deficiencies in the diet rather than to the morals and lack of perversion of the inmates. Nevertheless, the Japanese were filled with wonderment when two Americans developed gonorrhea — apparently contracted, as I learnt, from the complaisant wife of a coaster skipper!

The food had other physical effects. Men who normally slept the night through found themselves hard put to reach the urinals as the fat round their kidneys became dissipated. (I have never returned to real normality in this respect.) Although many men were apparently in better condition than ever before and able to perform feats of strength which they would never have considered prior to capture, they had, as I have remarked, no reserves whatever. When a man became sick, particularly with dysentery or diarrhoea, he was liable to lose an average of half a pound a day and, as no-one could afford to do this for long, it was imperative to preserve one's health by every means at one's disposal.

One of the worst spells arose in the hot summer weather when there was a complete dearth of salt in the town. Never until then had any of us appreciated how necessary salt is for the well-being of the body, and we felt as though we were wilting and growing old, as the old Asa gods when Thiasse-Volund abducted Iduna from the Grove of Brunnaker and deprived them of the golden apples which preserved their youth.

It would be futile to pretend that there was a single member of our community who did not sometimes hanker after more and better food and all the other necessities and luxuries of life of which we were deprived, but it was essential to subjugate all such thoughts — food, family, home and comfort — and to exclude them from the mind. The measure of the capability of a prisoner was his ability to do this, and those who failed were those who watched the daily rationing of the rice bowls with such patent avidity. Although it may seem strange in retrospect, Pargiter and I found that we could remain completely unmoved while Broomfield and Chadwick indulged in their gourmet imagination alongside us.

There were other things to occupy our minds. Fleas and rats had been eliminated and kept at bay by the surviving cat until the rubbish dump, on which the rats bred, was cleared away to make room for the new 'English' camp. Bed-bugs and body lice were rampant, and much of our spare time was spent in waging incessant warfare against these pests, the lice being insufferable in winter. Every evening in the cooler weather we had to examine the seams of our clothes and, with our finger nails, press the life from their white bodies, so swollen with our blood that they exploded with a pop. Loin cloths were the order of the day in summer, and their opportunities for annoyance were more limited, but then the bed-bugs, living in wood, multiplied until we were demented. Even in the hottest weather it was cool enough at nights to warrant a blanket and, in any case, it was a rule of the camp that no-one must sleep uncovered. Any man who did so was liable to be clubbed in his sleep by a patrolling guard with his rifle-butt. This was actually done for our welfare, and most Japanese wore a thick woollen cummerbund, even in the summer.

It was both illuminating and disillusioning to observe how many of our number had resigned themselves to a state of recreative destitution, often losing their spirit in a welter of self-pity or, sometimes, finding an outlet by fermenting trouble. Such a man was Mackavoy, a truculent fellow at the best of times, who evidently felt himself to be insufficiently important to satisfy his sense of self-esteem and who actively manufactured quarrels in the confined barrack. He had been a big man but was by now physically weak and a mere ghost of his former self. He did not seem to appreciate these short-comings and on several occasions assaulted other prisoners. The Japanese would not tolerate fighting at any price and there was no doubt but that, apart from the immediate consequences, a man found fighting would be marked for attention thenceforth.

Once he picked a quarrel with me and aimed a blow at my head, catching me a glancing blow. Never had I had to resist temptation more strongly than then, so great was my inclination to treat him in the manner which he so richly deserved and which I, still fighting fit, could so easily have meted out to him. I thought of my diaries, the retention of which was now little short of an obsession, and of the dangers of personal surveillance attendant on thrashing Mackavoy, and did nothing. Otherwise I might have taken the chance of giving him a hiding which would have improved the atmosphere of the barrack beyond all measure, not only because the fellow was doing acute harm to its harmony, but because the very fact of his example, coming from one of the most senior men, had become an acute embarrassment to some of us.

Quite the worst men in the camp were among the group of Americans from the Philippines. Early in our confinement Sanders, with an American officer, had commanded silence in each barrack successively, while he presented Tressil for our inspection. We were all to look well on this man that we might always recognize him, never trust him, nor allow him to borrow or to touch our possessions, because he would steal anything and everything. We were not likely to forget him. Possessing the most criminal features which it has ever been my misfortune to behold, he was perpetually unclean — efforts to keep him washed being abysmally abortive — and he had, it transpired, spent most of his adult life in various gaols in the United States until he was conscripted into the army in which he was a lasting disgrace. Tressil was in no way abashed by this introduction: rather he appeared to feel honoured and he spent much of his captivity expiating his thieving proclivities when they were directed towards the Japanese. He was incorrigible, but incredibly tough.

Two other men in that barrack were the cause of the most deplorable affair which ever occurred. It was a continual source of fury that the Red Cross parcels in the camp were not issued. No-one who has not subsisted on a monotonous diet of rice can appreciate the craving which the contents of these parcels engendered, both for the delectation which they promised and for the beneficial effect which they would have on our condition — particularly where the sick were concerned. There was no good reason why they were not issued and I doubt if the Japanese ever realized their value to us. A people who sent tins of bamboo shoots for the relief of their own internees in California could hardly be expected to appreciate our point of view!

There were some who talked of stealing some of the parcels, but it was held, and rightly so, that such a move would be fatal and effectively preclude all hope of any further issue. For purposes of camp discipline, Sanders made it clear that no-one was to consider such a thing but, one night when visiting a *benjo*, an American from the Guam barrack found several of the parcels piled inside. He called Sanders and a watch was kept until two men were seen to collect them. They were Americans from the Philippine barrack; one being a small, mean, rat-faced man of very poor type, and the other a decent enough lad who had a weak character and who had come under the complete dominion of his confederate. The parcels were returned privily and all signs of entry obliterated.

Sanders had some very tough elements to control and, in consequence, a very difficult job, as there were few retributive measures open to him for the maintenance of discipline. In this case it was unanimously agreed that the two men had acted in a manner highly prejudicial to the good of the camp at large, but there was little that could be done without attracting the attention of the Japanese.

Each barrack normally performed its own chores: washing the food buckets, sweeping the floor, fetching the food and so forth on a weekly rota basis. Those two men were given this job in their barrack, together with various other cleaning jobs, and were put into Coventry until further notice. The punishment was much too mild to fit the crime, but no-one could think of a better one. Any form of corporal punishment went against the grain, especially under our conditions and, in any case, descended to the level of our captors. The rat-faced little man appreciated the position and, still retaining his hold on his weaker partner, they both refused to do any more fatigue duty after the first week. In effect, they were calling Sanders' bluff. It created a precedent of tremendous importance for, if they were to win the day, it would open the door to utter lawlessness and insubordination by the less desirable elements in our community and everyone would suffer. After consulting leading opinions in the camp, Sanders played his last card: he would, he said, report them to the Japanese with a full explanation if they did not do what they were told within two days.

When the two days had elapsed, they still refused, never believing that he would make good his threat. Nor did Sanders, or anyone else, wish that it should be carried into effect, but in this case it was imperative that the men recant. They were given two more days, but still they stood their ground, possibly believing the extension of time to be a sign of weakness. They should have been under no illusions: the position had been made abundantly clear to them and they were shunned by their fellows. As, later, the old Prime Minister of Japan, Admiral Kantaro Susuki, flouted the Potsdam Declaration and brought the atom bomb upon his country, so these two flouted the order of the camp, and Sanders had the unenviable job of handing them over to the Japanese army.

For some days we saw them as we passed the guard-room. Sometimes they were kneeling: sometimes they were tied up, sometimes they were being beaten up, sometimes they were holding out buckets of water for fantastic periods and they suffered other degradations. Usually they had dried or fresh blood on their faces; they looked worn beyond measure and they were evidently allowed the minimum of food and no sleep. (In general, there was no food for a man in the guard room.) We felt sick each time we passed them until, in due course, they disappeared.

The following Sunday we were paraded, or rather herded, into a small compound which had been created between the two camps. After the usual preliminaries the colonel arrived and proceeded to make one of his long, falsetto speeches. We had occasionally seen him since our first arrival on the parade ground; there had been the odd inspection by high ranking officers which had thrown the military establishment into a state of ferment for days beforehand and there had been the odd time when he had appeared in the road and had taken innumerable *kiris* whilst we had been marched up and down incessantly, but it was seldom that he delivered an oration. Now he made up for lost time. It was insufferably hot; we were crowded together and his high falsetto cut the air interminably. Hayeshi was a more conscientious interpreter than Fujimoto, so we did get a very fair idea of what it was all about. Largely repetitive, the speech consisted of a series of awful warnings concerning our fate if we disobeyed the commands of the Japanese army: the two men who had left being held up as examples. What had happened to them in the camp before they left was nothing. Now they were in a Japanese military prison where they would understand their folly. This we did not doubt for an instant, though I am sure that there was not a man amongst us who did not feel nauseated at the situation which the two had forced upon themselves. We often wondered whether anyone would ever see them again, but a prisoner lives for the present and they were soon forgotten.

There was a curious and unpleasant incident after this speech of the colonel's. While he was speaking two or three men, who were sick and were anxious to know what was going on, had dragged themselves to a window on the first floor of the new 'English' camp (it was a two-storied building) and from there had surveyed the proceedings. As soon as the colonel had left, the duty officer pointed at them and spoke to a couple of guards, who rushed upstairs, hauled the men off to the guard-room and beat them up. No explanation was given at the time and it was not until long afterwards that we learned that their crime was to have looked down on the colonel. No-one is allowed to look down on the Emperor of Japan and this, it seemed, was an extension of that principle.

Later Brown, in one of his rare moments of expansion, told me that he had been instructed to delete from the camp register the names of the two Americans who had been taken away, so we supposed that they were dead. We were hardly surprised.

It was not until nearly a week after the capitulation of Japan that we saw them again. A lorry arrived under guard and decanted five men who had every appearance of being living human skeletons. It was not for some little while that we recognized that two of them were the same couple of which I have written. There were also three who had originally come from other camps: a Dutchman, an American Air Force sergeant and one other. We marvelled that men could still live in such an appalling state of skin and bone, and our horror was only exceeeded by their story, which gradually unfolded. It is worth relating, for all its bestiality, because it demonstrates that the gulf between the Japanese and the Western viewpoint and systems is so wide that it can never be bridged in our generation, and serves as a potent reminder that we must never judge their treatment of prisoners-of-war by our own standards.

These men had been confined in the Sendai civil gaol somewhere in the Osaka region. Our two men were there for the reasons already stated, while the air force pilot had been involved in an explosion in a chrome ore mine where he had been working and had evidently experienced a temporary loss of memory. In that state he had been found walking down a road and, on the (false) assumption that he was trying to escape, the Japanese had confined him in that hell of Sendai for more than two years. Nor had the crimes of the other men merited the fate they received, for that gaol exceeded anything of which I have read in the barbarism of mediaeval Europe, and that is a large claim. It housed several thousand prisoners as far as they could judge: all the others being Japanese who were confined for varying terms, mainly for robbery or for political offences. Some were there for life, and there was no evidence that there was any remission for good conduct: remission came about solely from the reduction in their natural expectation of life brought about by the very nature of the place.

The cells were in rows and in tiers, each containing one man in solitary confinement on a floor area so small that he could barely lie stretched out. There was only a tiny window, high in the wall, and he had but one blanket against the rigours of the dreadfully cold winter. He must never speak and for the whole day must sit, squatting at attention in the lotus position, hour after hour, facing the door. The only break was for meals — if the two meagre rice-balls he received during the day could be honoured by such a description — and to use the *benjo*. So they sat for fourteen or fifteen hours a day, day after day, week after week, month after month. They were only allowed to wash once a week, and that was the only other time they ever left their cells.

Each door had a slit, sloping downwards from the outside as if to take a letter-box, at the eye-level of the warder or 'trusty' who patrolled the corridor and who could thus observe the inmate without being seen himself. If he saw that the man was not sitting in the correct attitude, or that his lips were moving, the prisoner was taken out and thrashed. There were three types of beating, involving different types of stick or split bamboos. If a man so far forgot himself as to be beaten too frequently, or otherwise gave additional offence, he was taken out and put in a punishment cell which measured about five feet long by three feet wide and four feet high. His arms were confined to a leather belt round his waist by iron bands and he could not move them while he was there — perhaps for days — for any purpose whatever, either for the relief of nature, to eat the minute rice ball which was passed through a hatch, or to drink from a bowl. He was in worse case than any animal and, in this state, he might still be hauled out and beaten.

The Dutchman had spent long in these punishment cells on numerous occasions. He seemed even thinner than a skeleton and the wasted flesh on his fore-arms was hideously discoloured by the scars left by the chafing of the bands. His survival was a miracle. He must have been more stiff-necked than any of his stiff-necked race. The air force pilot, in a strange voice, kept asking piteously if he was speaking all right. We assured him that he was. Poor fellow! He no longer had any faith in his ability to articulate after so long a silence.

These men said little, on the whole, but the fifth man was a Hungarian who had been thrown into that gaol on a charge of espionage before Japan had entered the war. He had become a 'trusty' and worked in the prison hospital, coming out in more reasonable condition, and it was he who gave us most of the story, although he himself remained something of an enigma. Europe has assimilated the horrors of Belsen and other atrocities, which were crimes against humanity but which were born of war. These five men achieved a similar, or worse, condition in a normal Japanese prison, and that is the difference between the hemispheres.

All this time we had seen groups of cadets and young soldiers practising bayonet drill against sacks. The rifles were held rigid and they leapt sideways towards their targets, uttering blood-curdling yells which seemed to be the most dangerous part of the operation. Civilians formed bucket chains and held fire drills. The buckets were quickly filled and passed from hand to hand along a human chain to the last person, who flung what was left in them at a hole in a target on a stand, about eight feet above the ground. We laughed at the ingenuous idea that this could do the slightest good in a town of wooden buildings which would burn like tinder, and failed to reconcile it with the statement, so often reiterated in the press, that enemy raiders would never defile the sacred sky. The Doolittle raid had made little impression and it was generally understood (wrongly) that the captured airmen had been decapitated, while the papers proclaimed that a similar fate would be accorded to any airman who attempted to cross the coast.

The *Jushin* knew the real state of play, but the mass of the people knew only that they were tired of this nonsense; that they resented the favoured conditions of the commonest *haiti* (soldier) and that they themselves were longing to see the end of the military caste which was pulling them to national suicide.* They had been on a minimum living standard of feeding before the war, and now it was much lower than that. Sugar, which would have cost just over two yen a *kan* on the non-existent *haikyu* (ration), fetched five hundred and thirty yen on the black market, and we did well out of this! The civilian rice ration was well below three hundred grams a day, though it should have been more according to the law. The rice was simply not there. Even though the truth about the loss of the islands and the Philippines was leaking out, it was much delayed in the press, nor were the enormous losses of the navy, amounting to its near extinction, made manifest, but the people had no confidence in their leaders. Their morale was ebbing rapidly and they only took heart from such news as the fate of the men of Iwojima who died to a man. This appealed to the latent nationalism of the humblest coolie, and led us to ponder on the ultimate invasion of their homeland.

Nevertheless, the fighting was still remote from us and the deadly monotony of the days was oppressive beyond imagination. There is no way of describing such monotony without becoming monotonous. The anecdotes I have related of triumph and disaster in our lives were spread over a very long period and were no more than flashes in the endless succession of days which was the greatest cross we had to bear, as we could see no end to them. We had not even seen the odd reconnaissance 'plane. Certainly the shipping was sparse and the condition of the country was deteriorating rapidly, but we felt that there was no minimum standard of life below which the Japanese would cease to exist. This awful monotony was, perhaps, the most powerful element sapping at the morale of the camp.

Then, one Sunday morning, during an alert, Pargiter suddenly became wildly excited. *"Look!"* he cried, leaning out of the window from his

---

* This book is not about Japanese politics, but it is well-known that the Japanese cabinet did not — and was not trusted to — speak with a single voice. This was because the Army and Navy ministers were not responsible to the Prime Minister, resulting in a complete lack of cohesion, particularly after the fall of General Hideki Tojo.

bay, and there, winging their way over the harbour towards Kobe, were several flights of the largest aeroplanes that we had ever seen — the Super-fortresses — grey against the rain clouds, and giving such an appearance of power that we suddenly felt that we had turned a corner.

Unfortunately, few of us saw them before they were hidden from view, but we all heard the dull rumble of their bombs a short time afterwards.

One night there was another air-raid alert and, soon afterwards, a 'plane flew over with a different note to its engines to anything we had heard before. It flew around for a long time and we were aware of flares being dropped. A few A.A. guns were fired in a desultory fashion, but there was nothing more. Then we read that on 10 March, 1945, Tokyo had suffered a bad air-raid by super-fortresses — the huge American bombers. It was only after the war that we learned the full horror of that night, of the fire-storm and how the wind turned the inferno into a pure hell, allowing no escape, to create one of the most terrible raids of all time.

Four nights later, on 14 March, 1945 came the real turning point in our lives. The sirens screamed soon after evening muster and Pargiter and I craned at our window. Soon we heard a dull, ever-increasing roar. Anti-aircraft flashes lit the sky and we were suddenly aware of aeroplanes thundering right overhead, very low, and then we heard the swish as their bombs were released to come screaming down to earth. Within minutes the whole sky was pink with the reflection of fires which, we judged, must commence about half a mile inland from our camp.

By this infernal light we could see the aircraft approaching three abreast in wave after wave, and they were coming in low — probably at little over 2,000 feet. The anti-aircraft guns were firing, but their fuses were set far too high and the huge super-forts, gleaming a silver tinged with pink, kept coming straight in from the head of the Inland Sea: the centre ones right over our heads, never wavering in their course, with their engines rising to a roaring reverberation of revenge as they shattered the erstwhile sacred sky, before they passed to loose their incendiaries to increase a conflagration of such proportions that we felt that the world had only known bonfires until that night.

As more and more super-forts swept in over the waterfront, first in hard silhouette against the crimson sky and then, as they closed on us, in a silver that seemed as a shining armour, it became evident that the bombs were being dropped further and further back into the town. We had no fear, and crowded into the window bays, scarcely hearing the cacophany of the powerful engines which might have been crashing out the chords of the Triumphal March in *Aida*, so great was the splendour of the sound and the scene to our ears and eyes, and so high the

33.

34. *B29s (Super-fortresses) dropping packed incendiary bombs over the 'sacred' land.*

exultation in our souls. This display of martial magnificence was the harbinger of our deliverance, and no herald was ever more welcome.

We did not see the incendiaries, but it seems that the lead 'planes dropped 70lb. canisters which were fused to explode 100 feet above the ground and to eject dozens of 2-foot canisters of napalm, and that those which followed used 6-lb. oil bombs which were ignited by the blazing napalm. Some 1,733 tons of bombs were dropped that night by 274 'planes. The anti-aircraft fire gradually diminished until, as the final waves of destruction swept in from the sea, only one gun was firing, away out in the harbour, perhaps from the German ship *Moselle** which was at the buoys. The raid at such low altitude was similar to that over Tokyo a few days before and a master stroke, as the Japs had to reset their fuses.

Over two hundred thousand Japanese were rendered homeless by that night of fire: there were some thirteen thousand casualties, nearly 134,750 houses destroyed, and thousands of people fled the city. Had the people been familiar with Wagner they might have found in all that scene and sound some parallel with the last scene of the *Götterdämmerung* as the destruction waxed to the accompaniment of the aerial orchestra until it seemed that the very sky was ablaze. Even did they sense the theme of redemption, for all their losses, and in this we had common ground. We felt that we must be somewhat tactful with the coolies the next morning, for the war had come too close to home, but we need not have worried. They were not disturbed: tired of the war, they bore us no resentment and simply regarded the whole affair as a welcome prelude to peace. If this was the price, so be it. Italy was long forgotten, Germany had collapsed and Berlin was besieged and of no more account, while the Pacific sphere of Axis dominion was contracting upon its centre. When they heard that 'Roosevelto' had died a week or so later they showed so little jubilation that we almost looked to see if the ensign on the naval signal station was at half-mast. Coolies or prisoners, we had seen a night of promise.

~~~~~~

---

* We never established whether this ship really was the *Moselle*, though it seems likely. She had been transferred to the Japanese in 1941 and renamed *Teizu Maru*. She was mined off Shimoneseki on 18 April 1945 — five weeks after this incident. The ship we used to see certainly had some Germans still aboard.

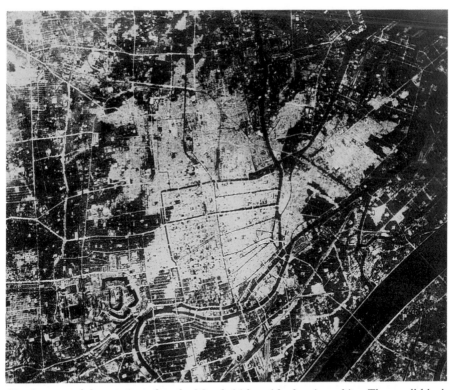

35. *An area of devastation after the March 14th. raid, showing white. The small black blobs are mainly scarred lathes and bigger ones bath boilers. The largest are corrugated iron shelters. The building surrounded by a moat above the top left-hand corner of the white area is Osaka Castle. (Actually a ferro-concrete facsmile of the original!)*

XIII

SAYONARA

Events moved rather more slowly than we had anticipated. There were no more air raids but, at least, there were usually reconnaissance 'planes to be seen on most days: sometimes, and increasingly often, there were two or three in the air together. These Super-fortresses usually flew at a great height, their silver ghost-like against the cerulean of Japan, seeming almost immobile over short periods when the only sign of their progression was the sharp, white vapour trails which lay behind them, marking their course in from the Pacific Ocean and from the islands far beyond our horizons. Puffs of anti-aircraft fire sometimes burst below them, but there were no Japanese 'planes going up to dispute their national sky with the enemy. The big Americans, hanging like silver crosses at the end of their vapour trails, hardly looked to be of this world at all, so high and ethereal did they seem.

The Japanese had an excellent and efficient system of air-raid warnings. There were wardens' huts at frequent intervals, each equipped with a radio which, as soon as the enemy aircraft was reported to be approaching the coast, gave a running commentary on their progress until they left again. We knew enough of the language by then to follow the gist of these broadcasts. The coolies used to laugh the next day when the press, in reporting the raid, would invariably state that the raiders were shot down over the sea, because they were obviously the masters of the sky when they were within our vision.

One day, groups of Super-fortresses came swooping in from the head of the Nakai between Osaka and Kobe, almost right over Amagasaki. The radio commentary had already indicated their course and, as Amagasaki aerodrome lay right in their path, every 'plane on the airfield was manned and sent up: some to cruise under the shadow of the hills; others to hedge-hop the waterside warehouses, but all to avoid the attention of the invading aircraft. We heard a few bombs being dropped in the direction of the aerodrome, but it was clear that most of their

279

striking power was being borne further inland.

The following night there was a very unpleasant incident. During muster the officer told one man from each barrack to go to the guard-room, where they were either beaten up or savagely caned. No-one knew the reason for this at the time, and it was not for some days that it was realized that each of the victims had numbered *ne-ju-ku* (twenty-nine) at the *tenko*, or muster. The Super-fortresses were known as the B29s, and the duty officer had apparently had a brother killed at Amagasaki in that raid — by the B29s. Hence his extraordinary action. A few days later the same officer sent more men to the guard-room for allegedly 'bad attitude' during *tenko*, Pargiter being amongst them and, with them, he received a severe caning — purely at this officer's whim.

The question of caning was a very vexed one, which only arose towards the end of our stay in the country. Men had had their faces slapped by all ranks of the Japanese army, down to the humblest private, with monotonous regularity during our confinement, often on the flimsiest pretexts and usually preceded by the shout *"Kurra!"*, which the Japanese express with great effect. It seemed to serve in almost any circumstances and had a tremendous width of meaning. I cannot translate it better than *Hey, You!*, although it was far stronger than this and we heard it constantly. Sanders and others constantly represented to the Japanese that, although face-slapping was doubtless common enough in Nippon, it was intensely humiliating to us and had this effect even when it was not intended. Finally someone was asked what punishment was used in our own countries and the answer, with full explanation, was 'caning'. No answer could have been more foolish.

Face slapping was irritating in the extreme, but it needed little understanding of our captors to appreciate that it was not the studied insult that it seemed: it was almost the Japanese 'way of life' so far as its own army was concerned. Caning, often with a split bamboo on a man's bare buttocks, was a far greater humiliation and, as the mentor seldom knew when to stop, infinitely more painful. (It is true that one or two men did receive ear damage from face/head slapping.) One American, also named Hurst, was treated to the cane when his backside was a mass of boils but, oddly, it had the effect of curing them! Nevertheless, the man who spoke so foolishly did the camp great disservice and it was as well that he gave his information so late that comparatively few of his fellows suffered from his teaching.

The First of June, 1945, was perhaps the most memorable day of all. The weather was perfect; a hot sun beating down from a cloudless sky which was marred only by the presence of a few predatory bromley kites as they hovered, vulture-like with their serrated wings, over the waterside. The harbour shimmered in the sun; Awaji Island stood in sharp purple outline in the distance, and there was all the colour of the East around us. I was a little depressed, finding that I could not read the strings of signal flags so far down the harbour as before, having become aware by this means over the past couple of years that my sight was slowly deteriorating. The air-raid siren had gone, but we thought little of that as the odd reconnaissance 'plane was now commonplace. I was standing by the *ku-ké* hut but, when someone shouted and pointed, I looked up and saw a scene of utter wonder. Normally, I detest aeroplanes, but there was something majestic about those huge, silvered Super-forts, shaped like slightly bent crosses, when they stood in relief against the deep blue sky. Now I saw more aeroplanes than I had ever seen at any one time before: all those grand, phantom-like 'planes, coming in from the sea in wave after wave on a front almost as broad as the bay itself. Although it may sound hard to believe, the sight was entrancingly beautiful: they looked so splendid and so utterly remote from war as they swept on, their very numbers granting them a grandeur which seemed to crown the glory of the scene, and I stood staring in sublime enchantment as the centre formations came in, right before me.

Suddenly my dreaming was shattered as the air filled with a screaming which steadily rose to a shrill crescendo and I realized that I was standing alone in my lunatic contemplation as my companions, with rather more realism, had already run for shelter. I started to run too, but had scarcely started before the all-embracing sound of the falling bombs induced me to throw myself on my face. Almost simultaneously a myriad of small incendiaries dropped all around me: one hit a stone and ricochetted under the legs of a horse which was standing in the shafts of a wine-laden *bodiki*, whereupon he took fright and fled, the barrels being thrown off and bursting open as he bolted. In that instant I saw two wisps of smoke rising from the camp, some fifty yards away between the go-downs, and at the same time I saw more and more of the stately phantoms sweeping in from the sea and that, worse still, I was lying by a stack of carboys of formaldehyde, so I jumped up and sprinted as fast as I could for the sea-wall against which a concrete shelter had been erected, and arrived there just as the next loads of bombs fell about me.

The next hour was incredible. After the second wave had passed everything was aflame: warehouses, stacks of produce, our camp, the barges and the coasters at the quay — indeed, almost everything we could see except the big re-inforced concrete Sumitomo warehouse was ablaze. Then I saw our *ku-ké* shack catch alight, so I dashed to it and grabbed a long loot bag full of walnuts which I had stolen earlier in the morning but, as I reached for my clothes which were already taking fire on the hook on which they hung, the roof collapsed in a flaming mass, and I only escaped from the inferno with a pair of shorts to add to the

36. *Three super-fortresses wing their way across the 'sacred' sky past Fujiyama — the sacred mountain — early in 1945. The ease with which they did so brought home to the teeming Japanese masses that the tide of fortune had turned. Claims in the papers that so many had been shot down over the sea as they returned were met with incredulity.*

fundoshi I was wearing.

After the third wave, when we emerged again only a few minutes later, many of the warehouses were already mere smouldering shells, so fast and so furious was the burning of Japan. Still the silver bombers swept in, the formations clear over the water until they became lost to view in the rising pall of smoke as they passed. They were bombing further inland by this time and we felt sufficiently safe to remain in the open, so I dashed towards the camp, which was well a-fire, to try to ensure the safety of my diaries, but my way was barred by a blazing wall of oil drums. By some incredibly fortunate chance Pargiter was confined to the camp that day with a badly sprained ankle and, as we had always worked in so well together, I had no fear that they would be lost. Our compact was clear and binding. Almost at that moment I saw the steady trickle of the camp detail and the sick staggering up the road. Pargiter, a man of no little resource, was hobbling amongst them, laden like a Kabuli camel with blankets, bags and everything he could carry.

Next time I saw the camp it was no more than a few courses of bricks

37. *Flying over the same area as in Pl.35 (vide Osaka Castle) in the June 1 raid, a super-fort flies on with No. 3 engine damaged (unusually) by A.A.fire. The black stains are leaking oil. Note some of the fire-power of these giant 'planes in the two turrets on top of the fuselage.*

around its base, where the walls had stood, and a fire-scarred boiler. There was no other sign that it had ever been a habitation. By then it was hard to assess the position. The wind was slightly off the land, and we could see the apparently endless arrays of 'planes afar off, and follow them until they disappeared into the solid smoke with a thundering roar, for all their height. There was an almost continuous belt of flame all along the waterfront from Amagasaki to Sakai and Taksaishihama, but there was nothing wherewith to fight such a conflagration. Oiwa alone: Oiwa the stalwart, dashed to and from the quay with buckets of water which he flung indefatigably on the scorching ruins about him, but he

38. *Super-fortresses leaving Guam for Japan.*

achieved nothing at all. One bucket against, as we learnt much later, 3,200 tons of bombs comprising well over a million six-pound incendiaries, mainly based on napalm! We rejoiced, pretended to help and gloried in the situation, whilst all the other Japs sat cross-legged and impassive, as if in silent reverie.

I admired them that day. Many knew that their homes were gone and everything that they possessed. The bargees and their families saw their barges, all that they had, destroyed before their eyes, but there was no complaint, no panic and no recrimination. It was as though they were stunned, and we knew that some of us had always been right in thinking that the Japanese had no power of improvisation in times of crisis. They had no idea what to do, so they squatted, crossed their legs and waited. (All their brilliant military and naval victories, incidentally, had been the result of meticulous planning and practice.)

The raid only lasted for a little over three-quarters of an hour, but it was eight hours before the funeral pyre of the waterfront subsided, and

284

we never did appreciate the full scale of the destruction during that day. After that raid, it became a weekly event for a large force of bombers to eliminate another section of the city each Friday morning until it was virtually flattened, almost as though for our entertainment.

We spent that night on the ground floor of the old 'English' camp, which had miraculously escaped total destruction. It was very crowded with men lying all over the floor wherever they could find a space. No-one had had any lunch and everybody was hungry, despite the frantic efforts of the cooks to improvise some sort of dish from burnt rice late in the night. I found Pargiter, who was better equipped than anybody, and we shared the walnuts and some sugar which I had also salved, passing some to our friends. Never, until then, did either of us realize the amount of nutrition in these nuts. He had brought out all his clothes — and he had accumulated a large wardrobe by prison standards — many of which he gave to me there and then.

Next day we were herded into a string of barges and towed over to another camp in the Tsumori district behind the south end of the harbour which was less affected by the bombing. This camp had been discovered by some of our fellows who had gone out on an official reconnaissance expedition, as the Japanese army had not the faintest idea what to do in the circumstances. This was a better camp than our old one, consisting of a number of long, parallel huts with only one sleeping bay over the floor, and had been abandoned some time before by a British contingent which, with various other camps in the area, had been evacuated to new and better surroundings around Lake Biwa. A few of our men had also been sent to these camps a month or so previously, including Henry, one of the *Dalhousie's* engineers. It was believed to presage that the Japanese were at last able to read the writing on the wall. Not only was there a tendency for camps to be moved out of target areas — one at Amagasaki had already been bombed with some casualties — but a fine new hospital had been built on the slopes behind Kobe to replace the notorious Stadium. This piece of window-dressing was also, unfortunately, bombed and utterly destroyed.

It was pouring with rain when we entered this Tsumori camp and the water was trickling down my bare knees. They tickled, so I slapped them automatically when someone, looking horrified, suddenly asked:- *"What's wrong with your knees?"* I looked down to see the skin invisible under a black crawling mass of a large species of flea! We discovered that some sort of shelters had been dug at the heads of the sleeping mats, under removable hatches, and that these had become full of water and provided a breeding ground for the fleas. It took a week to drain off all the water and to eliminate the survivors to reasonable proportions, but during that week life was well-nigh intolerable. If, as

39. (opposite). Japan burned splendidly. This aerial photograph was probably taken after the second wave had passed and is concentrated on the Chikkō district. It may be compared with the map of Osaka and its harbour on p. 243. In fact, the total north/south distance (for this is the orientation of the picture), from top to bottom, is almost precisely 5 miles. The dark patch on the top left is the Shin-yoda Kawa below which, inside the North breakwater, land is being reclaimed and, below it, is the Shorenji Kawa (Osaka was well supplied with rivers) and, below it, yet more land just reclaimed. All this is within the North Harbour.

Then we see the mouth of the Aji Kawa and, running almost north and south, the Umemachi Basin leading into the inner harbour. This was also reclaimed land (vide p. 238). Bombs from the third wave can be seen falling to its left. From this point onwards were many of the firms mainly worked by the Chikkō camp. The white rectangle below the mouth of the Aji is the central pier, behind which was the Custom House and Harbour Signal Station. Working down the waterfront, the space on the waterfront between it and the first of the three basins was occupied by another stevedoring company (who owned the tangerines!) and Osaka Kō Stevedoring Co. Right behind, concealed by smoke, the Chikkō Camp has already burnt in the general conflagration. Its footings can just be discerned, together with the semi-destroyed 'English' camp. The so-called 'parade ground' lay half way between the camp and the signal station. The immediate area of the camp is somewhat distorted by the angle of the photo, but the distance from the Central pier to No.1 basin was approximately a third of a mile.

In the middle of the quay of the first basin is the tall, concrete, Sumitomo warehouse, also concealed, but which survived that raid. No 2 basin was shallow and only used for coasters, but the third of the basins was where we had sometimes seen hospital ships discharging pig iron and, on the other side of No.3 Pier, is the Shirinashi Kawa, about half a mile up which lay the Osaka Shosen Kaisha Shipyard, with many timber yards and ponds opposite. This is all obscured by very black smoke, evidently from blazing fuel oil.

On the lower side of the Shirinashi Kawa is an industrial district, including Osaka Teikko and Nakayama Seikko steel-works, Cemento, etc. and the Tsumori camp to which we were moved temporarily. Almost everything within this picture, and well inland, was destroyed in the 1st. June raid. As stated, I had run to the sea wall at Osaka Kō after the first wave, and was probably dashing to the Ku-ké shack to save my walnuts and (unsuccessfully!) my clothes at the moment when this picture was taken! Immediately afterwards I realised the impossibility of reaching the camp which was wholly burnt by the time the third wave had passed over, apart from my way being blocked by blazing oil drums.

At the bottom of the picture, abutting the harbour, are more reclamation schemes, below the Kizu Kawa, on which were ship-building yards, though the water was shallow after about a mile from its mouth.

If I give this picture and its caption undue prominence, I do so because, even after the span of nearly half a century, it still gives me enormous pleasure. Standing virtually at the edge of the target area, on the waterfront, I could see the fires and dense columns of smoke almost as far as the eye could reach and far beyond the confines of this picture. All our working parties were destroyed, along with almost everything else but, above all, the sheer omnipotence of the super-fortresses coupled with the unbelievable devastation and (to us) the matchless splendour of the scene, put an implicit term on our captivity. If our camp was the first casualty, so be it.

286

40. *Bombs from the 2nd. wave raining down on the Chikkō district on 1 June, 1945. We are looking at the North Harbour (see map, p. 243) with the Umemachi basin in the lower centre and the Aji Kawa extending to the right under clouds of already increasing smoke. The ferry, where we sometimes saw Germans, is just under a quarter of a mile up the river from the Umemachi Basin, beneath the smoke. The Chikkō camp and Osaka Kō stevedoring Company are only just below the Central pier — the white rectangle at the bottom of the picture.*

was supposed, these spaces *were* originally shelters, they would have proved to be perfect baking ovens for their occupants.

Pargiter and I were still together, sharing all the carriage of his gear. When we had found a place on the sleeping bays, he commenced to unpack his things and to stow them away, and it was only then that I realized that he had not got my panic bag. My papers and my precious diaries simply were not there! It was unbelievable. I was quite overwhelmed and have never understood to this day how it could have come about. It had been a Heaven-sent piece of luck that he was in the camp on the *beoke* (sick) list that day: he and I had worked in longer and closer collaboration and union than any other two men in the camp and we had got on perfectly together. He was resourceful and did not panic, as was proved by the way that he had brought out such a variety of other things in very difficult circumstances, and our compact that our two panic bags took precedence over everything else was perfectly clear. He had shared his clothes willingly and voluntarily the previous day and behaved as he always had, yet he had simply left my diaries which had been my obsession and his common cause ever since he had lost his own. Had he not been in the camp that day (as was much more likely), they would have been burnt and it would have been by the hand of Fate, but .... he *was* in the camp, and it was nothing to do with the hand of Fate.

Of course the diaries have been mentioned previously, but to have given full coverage to the time I spent on them, to the risks involved, to all the matter which they contained (which would have been welcomed by many a museum) and to all the ingenuity which had been expended in the maintenance of their safety (by both of us) would have made boring and repetitive reading, but they had nevertheless transcended everything else in my life and had represented virtually my very *raison d'être* since being taken prisoner. It had been solemnly agreed that, in the event of only one of our diaries surviving, it would be typed out in duplicate — one copy for each of us.

Neither he nor I referred to the matter then, nor have either of us done so since in Japan, on the way home or subsequently in England. I have often been asked why I never did raise the topic with him, but there was no point, as the diaries were gone and, although I am by no means a violent man, I *had* to keep quiet about it. If I had said one single word, every particle of my pent-up feeling would have been unleashed and, if I did not actually kill him, I would most certainly have done him the most fearful damage. I knew that there was no middle way, for far too much time, thought, worry and cunning had gone into the structure and survival of those little books.

We still went out to work, going by barge over to Chikkō where we were employed in clearing up the debris. Once we were hauled into the harbour breakwater during a raid, to have the most remarkable grandstand view of several formations of Super-fortresses roaring in over the harbour from beyond Awaji Shima to bomb the Amagasaki aerodrome with high explosive before they sped on over the hills. We saw the bombs leave the 'planes and then explode into columns of smoke and flame on the ground. It was all too unreal in that summer sunshine.

Some men were clearing a bombed bottling plant and one evening, when their party returned to the barge, two of their number were unmistakably drunk. The officer in charge, dancing with rage, asked where they had got the drink, to be told that a Korean had given it to them. This seemed a sensible enough answer, as it avoided the admission of stealing and, since the waterfront was teeming with Koreans, this mythical one could never be identified. No-one could have foreseen the consequences of this answer, however, as the officer, glancing round, espied a Korean sitting innocuously on the sea wall. He drew his sword, rushed at the unfortunate man and, swinging at his head, knocked him off on to the other side of the wall. Whether he was killed or merely stunned, we never knew, but in either case we were sorry about it.

I came very much into the public eye at Tsumori. The water supply to the town was badly disrupted and there was none in the camp. Every day a gang of men had to parade with buckets and to take them to be filled at a factory yard rather less than a quarter of a mile away: the detail being performed by rota. The first time that I had to do this the party was under the control of an assertive and unpleasant Japanese medical orderly whom we all detested. His unpopularity was such that, when he had performed the incredible feat of leaving an operating table and scaling a ten-foot vertical partition whilst being operated on for hernia by the Japanese army doctor, he had received no sympathy from us for the torment which must have driven him to such extremity!

On this occasion he was particularly irritating. Only ten men were allowed to go into the factory yard at once. He signalled me on, re-counted, waved me back, changed his mind, and then waved me back a second time. Exasperated by this minor matter, yet probably giving vent to all that exasperation which had been pent up within me for so long whilst I was almost living for my diaries, besides being distinctly out of temper at their loss, I threw my buckets to the ground and gave my opinion of him, succinctly and gratuitously. Doubtless he understood not a word, but my meaning was none the less clear. The word *"Kurra!"* was shouted and the guards converged on me. I was fallen out on the opposite side of the road and marched back to camp where the sergeant of the guard took over and proceeded to beat me about the head until such time as the duty officer appeared.

On arrival he asked what I had done and, with surprising reasonable-ness, enquired why I had done it, saying that, if I would apologise to the medical orderly, I might go. I replied that I would not do so and that the medical orderly was not a fit person to be put in charge of anyone, never had been and never would be. This earned me further face slapping, after which I was put into a bare cell off the guard-room; my hands were tied behind my back with grass rope, my feet were tied together and it was indicated that I must stand upright without touching the wall.

All this I found highly distasteful. I had a vile headache as a result of the sergeant's efforts; the cell was intensely stuffy, I was extremely hungry and thirsty and was evidently being held incommunicado. However, I soon succeeded in loosening my wrists and, as the guard appeared to take little notice of me, managed to make my ankle lashing more tolerable and to arrange my wrists so that I could slip them in or out of the lashing without any apparent alteration having been effected, simply by dint of twisting one hand round. Even then, standing still is a recreation which palls very quickly and I was soon heartily sick of it. I started to lean against the back wall, but a guard saw me, shouted *"Kurra!"* and clubbed me with the butt of his rifle. After that I waited till the guard changed at midnight when, observing that the new watch had little more interest in keeping awake than I had, I decided to lie down and snatch some sleep, trusting to be able to wake at intervals to keep an eye on the guard who were, when all is said and done, within six feet of me, and resolving that if I was caught I would feign unconsciousness.

In the event I probably had about four hours broken sleep and might have snatched more if some premonition had not made me stand up and simulate intense tiredness, whilst I arranged my lashings to appear as though they had not been tampered with at all. It was as well that I did so because, at the first crack of dawn, I was haled before the duty officer who had the medical orderly with him. Believing, perhaps, that a night of standing with my hands tied might have broken my spirit, he once again stated that, if I would apologise, I might go. Once more, I refused and gave the same reason. He said that I would not have another chance, to which I replied that, if anyone was to do any apologising, it should be the medical orderly to me. On this I was led back to resume my former position.

An hour or two later a very remarkable thing happened. There was a commotion in the guard room, and then I saw Pargiter, who had brought my rice and soup and somehow persuaded the guard to give it to me. This was unprecedented. Not only did Pargiter run some risk to himself, but no-one in the position that I was in ever received any normal ration. Nor did he confine himself to my breakfast, but brought my other meals so long as I was in the cell, and this was an effort that was as unique as it was distinguished, and wholly out of accord with his recent failure over the diaries. Perhaps he realized that it was this very matter which had led me to rail at the orderly and landed me in my present predicament.

As the day advanced it became insupportably hot, and an air-raid took place not far off. I managed to attract the attention of the duty officer — a different one by then — to protest about being tied up behind a locked door in an air-raid, but could not make myself understood. However, an interpreter appeared in due course and it was agreed that I might be untied when an 'Alert' sounded and that my door should be unlocked. (I saw no merit in being roasted alive in the event of the camp being hit). After twenty-four hours of reflection, I was beginning to regret the whole affair because I could see no end to my situation, as matters of 'face' were involved on both sides, but I was as determined as the

Japanese that my face was not going to be lost. I had come to the conclusion that the presence of the medical orderly at dawn had demonstrated that a certain weight was being admitted to my contention, even if pride forbade any such admission, and I therefore resolved that some mutual face-saving formula must be evolved. The next night I dared sleep very little, as the guard were wakeful and talkative, and the following day was hotter than ever. By then I was very tired indeed, so I decided to stage a faint the next time that I heard the interpreter anywhere nearby.

The floor was hollow, and the effect was so tremendous that I feel it would have earned me a lasting place in any theatrical company. I had braced every muscle and let myself fall on my side with such force that I even startled myself with the result, as the acoustics of the floor were such that it sounded like an explosion. There was a moment of panic in the guard-room, and then everyone shouted *"Kurra!"* at the tops of their voices! I hoped that I looked pale, but suspected that I was sufficiently tired to have little colour in my face.

After a little while I opened my eyes and groaned a little. Peremptorily, I was ordered to stand, but immediately collapsed again. This time it was more difficult, being performed before an audience, but it evidently passed muster and, after much discussion, the interpreter and the duty officer (whom I knew was the army medical officer) were summoned. There was more confabulation, as a first result of which it was agreed that the small window in the wall might be opened but, as I still gave every indication of complete inability to stand (whilst taking a calculated risk that I might be beaten into either submission or unconsciousness), I was relieved when told that I might remain untied and might sit down, providing that I did not lie down. After a further night in the cell, which seemed relatively comfortable by contrast, I was released, as the Japanese had evidently lost interest in what had developed into a rather tame affair. There is no doubt that I was very lucky on the whole, but I returned to the barrack to find myself something of a hero because my original burst of ill-temper had been interpreted as a calculated act of defiance which, for obvious reasons, was almost without precedent. This was far from the truth, which only Pargiter could have known or guessed.

We still went out to work and Pargiter and I continued to steal for the common pot whenever it was possible, though opportunities were now rare. We could hardly do otherwise as it was still necessary to live and to act in concert either in groups or pairs but, despite nothing being said, the loss of the diaries had created some sort of an invisible barrier between us, besides leaving a void in my own activities, the more especially as our library had been destroyed in the fire. For his part,

Pargiter had never mentioned the incident not long before the fire when he had been caned in the guard-room, which I suspect affected him far more deeply than the mere physical aspect. When he had arrived back, able only to lie on his stomach, Broomfield, Chadwick, Fox and I had immediately commiserated with him, but been swiftly brushed off. We knew well enough what had happened, since it was not only obvious but the others involved made no secret of it. Yet, almost in parallel to the diaries on my side, it was for ever a closed subject on his, and I believed, and still believe, that he himself felt he had suffered a degradation beyond anything else which had occurred to him or to our immediate coterie. Neither I nor anybody else can make any judgement on the effects of this on him. As Byron wrote in *Napoleon's Farewell* (to France):- *"There are links that must break in the chain that has bound us ...."*

Years later, and only recently, a lady of much perspicacity who read the draft of this book advanced the theory that the diaries had been left in the burning camp because they would probably have recorded that occasion when Pargiter was taken to the guard-room and caned. Right or wrong, it is the only solution which has ever been advanced, and it had never occurred to me. The incident concerned was so small an item in so vast a compendium of information, which had occupied so much of our common thought for so long a time, that to allow it to be destroyed *in toto* seems to be out of all proportion, especially when any such passage could so easily have been expunged on request, but ..... Who knows? or will ever know?

I dare say that the most famous instance of the loss of a manuscript was when, Thomas Carlyle having lent a large portion of that of his *French Revolution* to John Stuart Mill, the maid inadvertently used it to light a fire, long before the days of carbon copies. Carlyle was at least able to re-research and re-write his *magnum opus*, but to re-constitute my diaries was manifestly impossible ....

In the meantime, our headquarters staff, appreciating their vulnerability in the middle of a foundry and industrial area, had commenced to build themselves a quiet new retreat in the foothills behind the city: a party of us going out there every day to assist in its preparation. This detail did not last for very long, but it was easily the pleasantest job which ever came my way, as it was situated in an environment far removed from the squalid dockside on a lovely wooded slope with butterflies fluttering amongst the camellias and rhododendron bushes and all the other flowers which we had missed for so long. It was a change, too, to see the bullocks, knee-deep in water, ploughing the rice paddies on the way. This was the real old Japan and the green fields, the vegetation and the increased altitude acted as a tonic, the more especially as we had a certain freedom there, often being dispatched to walk a mile or so across the country to a village school with no supervision whatever. Oddly enough, work under the direct aegis of the army was often of the lightest order.

There were certain disadvantages. Carrier-based 'planes were starting to sweep the skies, sometimes becoming involved with Japanese fighters, a few of which now sometimes ventured into their sacred sky. Whenever a 'plane was shot down, all the Japs would shout:- *"Banzai! Banzai!!"* ("Hurrah! Hurrah!!") and cheer wildly, only to moan *"Banzai-nei! Békoku-nei!"* ("Not Hurrah! Not an American!") only a few moments later. This was the invariable result of these encounters but although, like the ranks of Tuscany, we "could scarce forbear to cheer", no-one ever seemed to bear us the slightest ill-will. The most irritating part of the detail in the hills was the maddening regularity with which the American fighters strafed our train as we returned: the roof of our carriage being peppered and a Japanese passenger killed on one occasion.

Only once did we see an American aircraft brought down. This was as the result of anti-aircraft fire when several waves of Super-fortresses were approaching from the head of the Inland Sea. One received a lucky shell right in its belly and disintegrated in mid-air. We only saw one survivor whom we presumed to be the tail gunner. He was brought ashore near Osaka Kō, wet from his immersion in the harbour and with his eyes blind-folded. Poor fellow! It was a swift transition from eggs and flapjacks and all the luxury of the American service man.

This event was very isolated and the average Japanese, now laughing openly at the claims of the Japanese *kamikaze* suicide 'planes, was actually giving them a great deal less credit than was their due. Only seldom did we see defending aircraft challenge the Super-fortresses. On one such occasion it was a dull, cloudy day when there was little to see save the occasional glimpse of the big bombers, almost right overhead, but we heard the thudding of the cannon above us and twice Japanese fighters hurtled to the ground in flames, suddenly dropping from the cloud in which they may have hoped for safety.

Often, at this time, we were sent out to the Eastern suburbs to pull down rows of houses to make fire-breaks. This was one of the few jobs that we really enjoyed and into which we entered with a will. Not only did we take delight in the destruction of Japan which was involved for, after chopping through four or five uprights, it was usually possible to heave the whole house down in a crashing mass by hauling on a rope. This was an eminently satisfactory sensation, although I doubt if the depth of the fire-breaks was sufficient to do any good. When Japan burnt, it was like a bush fire with inflammatory sparks travelling along the wind to set alight everything in their path.

The question of whether the indiscriminate bombing of a town in total war is justified is not within the province of this book. There were nearly a quarter of a million homes destroyed by air raids on Osaka* representing, perhaps, a quarter of the population (quite apart from the many who lived afloat) but it must be remembered that it was an industrial city with a great deal of work sub-contracted. After the destruction of an area there was nothing in the vast areas of flatness, apart from ash and rubble, save the courses of bricks which were the foundations of the lath and plaster walls; the odd boilers of the communal baths and hundred and hundreds of lathes, which demonstrated that even the humblest homes were operating towards the war effort. For this reason alone, there was ample reason for their destruction. Because the bulk of the bombing was by incendiaries, the loss of life was relatively light as compared with the losses that would have occurred had high explosive bombs been used to a greater degree.

As the war progressed the shipping in the harbour came to a virtual standstill and the Sen Pakku detail was practically extinct, but we were now moved again: this time to a large re-inforced concrete warehouse on the edge of the Naniwa district. This stood alone, surrounded by some timber stacks which had miraculously been spared from the fires and by apparently limitless desolation. The building had a long, wide and comparatively low first storey, and it was here that we slept, four across the floor, right down its length. Pargiter and I again controlled a window and it was reasonably cool up there. We ate in one of the main storerooms which was empty on the ground level, but the *benjo*, home made and covered with corrugated iron, was the hottest and worst that we ever knew.

Most of Osaka, one of the most populous cities in the world, was a shambles with only a few landmarks left standing for final attention. Nor did these have long to wait, as the bombers soon started coming in for target practice with high explosive and we rejoiced when we saw the huge cranes at a ship-building yard on the Aji Kawa receive direct hits and topple into the water with gargantuan splashes. In that open ruin of an erstwhile metropolis the blast of an explosion was felt for immense distances, but our sleeping quarters provided a wonderful grandstand for viewing night attacks. There was the memorable occasion when a large Allied task force came right in and shelled the Wakayama Peninsula. We could hear the distant boom of their salvoes while, simultaneously, a bomber force ran in and bombed the airfield at

---

* Such are the quoted figures, which give Osaka as a whole as being 35% destroyed, but some 70% in the commercial and industrial area where we were. When the war was over we had a high view from the roof of the Naniwa camp, and the devastation appeared to be almost complete as far as we could see.

Amagasaki, detonating the ammunition dump in a delightful pyrotechnic display for our delight, after which carrier-borne fighters roared over the land with the dawn, to strafe the streets and tram-cars from little more than house-top level — had there been any houses!

When we went out to work the next morning we were slightly apprehensive because we thought that, whatever had gone before, the shelling of the land itself might have induced a more extreme reaction amongst the civilians. We were right in a sense, although it was quite the reverse of what we expected for, as soon as our guards sauntered off, the coolies came running up to us in a state of great excitement saying, in effect:- *"Did you hear that racket last night? Taksan Djoto"* (very good), *"A few more times like that and the Americans will come and land here, and then we shall have more food, more clothes and more tobacco!"* Thus was the civilian attitude to the situation summed up.*

The low-flying fighters were our greatest curse, because bodies of moving men were conspicuous enough in that skeleton city and, as all were clad in green uniforms — soldiers, civilians, prisoners, students and Korean labour contingents (though the students were sometimes in black) — all were equally vulnerable. There was little enough shelter for us against rockets and bullets where the buildings were literally razed to the earth and our only protection lay in the banks of the canals and the old earthquake fissures where they were conveniently situated.

The people seemed to be punch-drunk and made little effort to do anything for themselves except to salve odd pieces of corrugated iron to make themselves bare shelters. There was little enough they *could* do. Only when a horse was killed in an air raid was there any spontaneous action, and then the warm carcass would swiftly be transformed into a skeleton whose steaks were being borne off in a matter of moments. The

---

* What would have happened had the Atom bombs not been dropped and the Russians had not declared war on Japan almost simultaneously raises hypothetical questions. Certainly it was hoped to starve Japan into submission by blockade. The history of the great sieges throughout the ages demonstrates that this is a very long-drawn out process, even in a single town or city, such as Bonifacio or Leningrad. I believe the Japanese could have survived a state of siege (by sea) for an almost indefinite period, however low their food supply. It is inconceivable that the attitude of the coolies would have carried the day in the event of an Allied invasion. Latterly the *Kamikaze* and *Ohka* pilots were recruited by a form of voluntary compulsion and such compulsion might well have forced a large section of the population to emulate the defeated Japanese forces on Tarawa, Iwojima and other islands who either committed suicide *en masse* or launched themselves in final suicidal attacks rather than submit. It is not inconceivable that the same coolies, who so yearned for the American invasion, might have found themselves driven forward to repel it armed with staves! On the actual surrender a number of service officers did perform *hara-kiri* or take off on suicide missions. No doubt they placated the shades of their ancestors, but such men would have called the tune had an invasion been mounted and the teeming millions would have had no alternative leaders of their own with which to oppose them ....

prisoners were not behind-hand in this activity, nor was there ever the slightest objection when we cut steaks for ourselves: it was simply a question of 'First come, first served', and this was more than welcome in a time of great want, especially as almost all opportunity for loot had vanished in the various conflagrations. Of course, we had no fire on which to cook the meat, but the answer was to share it with some Japanese, who could usually arrange that somehow.

The harbour area was tidal for nearly three-quarters of a mile inland, and the railway tracks were slippery with green slime. Bodies still lay drunkenly across half-collapsed telephone wires and electric cables, as they had done since they had been blown there days before, as no-one bothered to remove them. The air was filled with the stench of exposed *benjos* and an increasing number of bromley kites began to darken the sky as they hovered in search of carrion, while the flies multiplied to such a degree, particularly in areas where there was burnt food, that one had to flail one's way through them. Their profusion made the myriads of insects in the old Watgun Road, in the Kidderpore Dock area of Calcutta, seem like a sterile area in contrast!

Worst of all was the question of water. There was no longer any in the town and a water barge was towed in from Kobe every day, whilst one or two tank cars arrived on the railway, but these were no more than a drop in an ocean of need. This was as much due to the effect of the big earthquake as to the bombing, but no-one was concerned with causes any more: the effects were all that mattered. All the camp water was drawn from a communal pump that produced a very brackish liquid which was transferred into a series of barrels and these were loaded onto a *bodiki*. We acted in place of the horse.

All this water had to be boiled before use and it tasted vile, while the flies were worse than a plague. Our eating spaces were blocked by mosquito netting and every reasonable precaution was taken, but there were too many of us and the flies could not be excluded. Buckets of rice were brought in with their lids on but, nevertheless, as a bowl was filled its contents became invisible under a black, crawling mass before it could be placed on a table. It was impossible to transfer a spoonful to the mouth without including a troop of the insects, and they settled on men's exposed flesh until they were simply taken for granted. All this, taken in conjunction with the matter of the water and the stench of rotting material in the heat of the summer, led us to expect an outbreak of cholera.

We felt that we must be on the last lap but, had we known it, the invasion of the islands was still far away. Llewellyn, the mate of the *Dalhousie*, had died before the Chikkō Camp had been destroyed. A man of limited imagination, he had tended to keep to himself and to take things as they came, although he several times told me that he regretted not taking the chance of remaining in the *Stier*. Once the Osaka Shosen detail had finished he found the work arduous, being a much older man. He never complained and was always cheerful when we spoke, but I had frequently found it necessary to give him tips and suggestions for his own welfare and, often enough, to furnish him with food or materials. However, he had managed to become a working party *honcho* which he found the lesser of the evils but, one day when the air raid alert was sounded, his party had to run some distance to a shelter and, in doing so, he had collapsed with a heart attack and expired. Others, too, had fallen by the way.

For my part I had been lucky and had had little wrong with me to affect my physical condition, but now I began to know the insides of the *benjos* too well and, as I lost control of my bowels, found myself starting that descent in health wherein a man lost some half a pound of weight a day, accompanied by the most acute discomfort and embarrassment, and which I had seen prove fatal in so many men previously.

During this period there was a pamphlet raid, some of which we succeeded in secreting and bringing back to the camp. They were written in Japanese, but we had a Chinaman amongst us who could read the language well enough, although he had some difficulty in translating it into English. His translation was in some disrepute, as he had often been asked to translate Japanese newspapers which had been picked up during our confinement, but his results had seldom found favour although, as history proved, this was through no fault of his but due to our consistent and unjustified disbelief in the Japanese news until very near the end of the war, because it did not accord with what we thought it ought to be!

We knew that a big bomb had been dropped on Hiroshima, but that was all. I still have the Japanese English-version newspapers relating to this event, and it is very interesting to note how piano were the first reports, because it was not for several days that they rose to a screaming crescendo of protest. Now the Chinaman excelled himself, translating the pamphlet to the extent that it was an exhortation to the people to evacuate the town and to rise against their wicked war-leaders to stop the war because, if they did not do so, an atomic bomb would be dropped on one or more of several named cities, including Osaka. The translator read the words 'atomic bomb' all right, but of course it meant little to us then since we had no more idea what an atomic bomb was any more than the Japanese, presuming it to be a slang term for some enormous 'block-buster' and felt perfectly safe, as there could be no point in dropping such a thing in the area of devastation which surrounded us. Such was the comfort of ignorance!

Smith and I were still seeing a paper, but not so regularly because we were not always at Osaka Kō and did not see Fuji every day. We knew that Russia had declared war on Japan, but would have known that without a paper, as the Japs were all talking about it, for it was an event which seemed to shake them more than anything else which had happened. Then, almost exactly three years after being taken prisoner, I was in a party clearing the bombed bottling plant, which was not a pleasant task as stacks of thousands of bottles had become fused together into solid masses in the heat of the flames. The Japs were very unsure of themselves that day, gave us little attention and were constantly chattering together, so we knew that something unusual was afoot. Gradually we learned that Emperor Hirohito was going to address the nation on the radio, which was an event without any precedent. In due course our *honcho* parked us, as it were, under a ruined wall, and soon not a Jap was to be seen as each and every man and woman clustered round one wireless receiver or another. After the broadcast they were very silent and we were told nothing, but marched back to camp. The rumour that the war was over was too tempting to believe.

Later we read the Emperor's speech. It was short, and he also issued the last war rescript, so far removed from the terms of the first at the time of the attack on Pearl Harbor that, for purposes of comparison, I reproduce it here. It ran as follows:-

"Three years and eight months have elapsed since We declared war on the United States and Britain, during which period Our loyal servicemen of the Army and Navy have fought valiantly, defying death on the plague infested fields and in the angry tropic seas, for which We are deeply gratified.

With the Soviet participation in the War and in consideration of various conditions, internal and external, We have come to realize that further continuation of the war would needlessly enhance calamities and that it would likely cause the collapse of the foundation of the existence of Our Empire, and so we are about to seek peace with the United States, Britain, the Soviet Union, and China in order to maintain Our glorious polity despite the burning spirit of the Imperial Army and Navy.

We deeply sympathise with the numerous loyal and valiant officers and men who have fallen on the battlefields or died of illness. Simultaneously We are convinced that the burning patriotism and loyalty of ye, servicemen, will shine forever as the *élite* of the nation.

Ye, servicemen! We command that ye leave intact the lasting foundation of Our State, fully comprehending Our wishes, maintaining solid unity, clarifying entry into and retirement from service, conquering a thousand difficulties and enduring the unendurable."

This was the version in the papers. In fact, the Emperor also spoke, *inter alia*, of '.... *a new and most cruel bomb, the power of which to do damage is indeed incalculable .... it would lead to the total extinction of human civilization ...."*. Poor Hirohito! The cost to him was not that he had to put his name to this face-saving rescript which never mentioned the word 'defeat' but that, being the mere figurehead of his military junta, he had been unable to issue it long before. There is ample evidence that, in essentials, he had long been of the same mind as our coolie friends.

When we returned to camp, we became certain that the news was substantially true. Two American army officers had been trussed up in front of the guard room for some time, and were believed to be awaiting execution. They had embarked on the most absurd method of escape ever conceived by man, having reckoned that, as the tide of war had turned and the Japan Sea must be full of allied ships, all they had to do was to make their way to the East coast, which was not far distant from their camp at Fukui, push off a log or boat, and that they would drift out to sea and soon be picked up. No kindergarten child was ever more ignorant of the action of tides, of the vastness of the sea or of the limits of the sea horizon at so low a level. It was the conception of insanity.

In the event, they had never got as far as the shore. They were ill prepared and had no provisions to take with them, being determined to live on roots and such raw vegetables as they might find on the way, travelling by night! One of them soon became prostrate with dysentery and so, being desperate, they travelled by day. The result was inevitable: they were followed by such scores of curious children that the interest of the police was excited and they were arrested. They were awaiting their certain retribution on the historic afternoon of the Emperor's speech, but when they were released and allowed to come amongst us we knew that something had happened, after which we remained in the camp for several days, during which no Allied 'planes appeared.

Still we were told nothing, and the camp was divided in its opinions whether it was peace or merely a truce, until some men from the Kobe camp appeared, having heard the real news from an internment camp close to them (which held, *inter alios*, the passengers from the Union Castle ship), and which possessed a secret radio. Then the truth was out and we knew that the war was over. We were then told that we should remain in the camp for fear of civilian demonstrations, but little effort was made to control us in any way. The guards by the guard-room sat in an embarrassed silence. We still gave them the *kiri* as it had become a habit, and it was now as difficult to remember not to do so as it had been to do so when we had first arrived! Actually there was no civilian demonstration, although there was some refusal to surrender by the army, but we saw none of that.

Miraculously, the flies vanished overnight. Why they did so, or where they went, we never knew. This was a help, but I knew that my own time was critical even now, for my bodily functions were still out of control and I could see myself wasting and felt that I was patently weakening, though a course of M. & B. tablets, astonishingly produced by an American doctor, stabilized me to a greater degree than many of the poor fellows who had suffered in like manner in the past.

We were told to paint "P.W." in white letters on the flat roof, and we commandeered a daylight signalling lamp from the signal station on the quay. A few of us wandered out of the camp though I, for my part, did not dare to stray too far from a *benjo*. One day a policeman came and solicited our help. It seemed that a Korean labour camp had herded most of the local police into their own gaol and had locked them in, and he begged us to use our influence to have them released! Magnanimously, we acceded to this request, and the law was soon at liberty again!

Many of us now slept on the flat roof, which was very pleasant and was reached by climbing out of a window and up a connecting sloping roof. Then, early one afternoon, as a bomber circled the town, we called it up with the lamp and received an answer. Next morning, at dawn, whilst we were still asleep, a Corsair fighter roared down on us out of the sunrise: there was a crash and a large parcel of magazines plummeted amongst the sleeping men. It ran in again and this time a large ham, tied to a handkerchief as a makeshift parachute, descended with a venom which struck terror into our hearts and we evacuated the roof in sheer panic. Fortunately no-one was hurt, but the ham was unrecognizable.

After that a wave of terror, infinitely worse than any war-time bombing, began. The Super-fortresses swept in on us, one at a time, some of them very low indeed. Previously we had admired them, but now they terrified us as we became the target. At such close quarters they lost all the ethereal quality we had admired when they were high in the blue skies. Now they looked quite different and we saw little escape. One after another, in steady procession, they ran in, opened their bomb doors and loosed their loads in the form of two fifty-gallon drums lashed together on the ends of totally inadequate parachutes. Most of these had no time to open, so low were the huge aircraft. We had no cover and the drums dropped at fantastic speed. Certainly each contained tinned foods — fruit juices, meats, butter, milk, chocolate, cigarettes, and all manner of eatables which we had missed and craved for so long, but the manner of their arrival was as awe-inspiring as it was terrifying. It was a wonderful gesture, if mistakenly applied, and we soon had enough good food to last for months, despite the enormous loss of drums which were either irretrievably smashed or which fell into the canals all around us, while one hit the camp building and carried away a huge chunk of masonry. All this bounty was accompanied by pamphlets urging us not to eat too much initially, though this advice seemed to be contradicted by

41. Flying very low indeed and opening their bomb doors to loose two 50-gallon drums of provisions at a time attached to a totally inadequate parachute, with no cover available, was infinitely more terrifying than their incendiary or H.E bombing, or even than the strafing of the streets by carrier-based fighters. Now, especially when seen from the front, the big bombers lost that ethereal appearance when they were high in the cerulean, and appeared wholly ominous. (98 feet long, they had a wing-span of 141 feet and 2,200 horse-power, being half as big again as a Flying Fortress.)

the profusion which fell from the sky and was completely ignored. Our capacities were certainly more limited than we expected, but we ate all we could hold and no-one suffered any ill effects. My own troubles ceased overnight.

Day after day we were bombed with food, yet more food, and with quantities of clothing and shoes, until we managed to divert the big aircraft to make the old, notorious stadium a dropping ground. Still the air was alive with all manner of fighters, each of whose pilots made his own private contribution, causing us to seek shelter under the timber stacks until they had disgorged their presents and started diverting themselves with feats of aerial aerobatics. The trouble was that our movements in seeking shelter were restricted, as there were so many canals and timber ponds in the immediate area. Fortunately, no-one was hurt in all this magnificent but highly dangerous generosity although at Kobe, where a similar performance took place, a couple of looting Japanese were telescoped by falling drums. The Japs were very much agog with all this profusion from the sky and our erstwhile masters had soon thrown all thought of 'face' to the winds and were begging outside the camp for all they could get.

302

42. *The Naniwa camp after the peace, with P.W. painted on the roof. At this time many of us slept up there. It was reached from a window and a piece of sloping roof in the shadow. The objects between the building and the road are the 'benjos'. (Naniwa was the old name for Osaka and presumably the original site of the town.)*

At this moment I found myself most unpopular. I said that, although I saw no reason why we should not now be repatriated, it seemed to me that the most important thing to be done was for the British and American forces to invade Russia whilst they were fully mobilised and in a position to do so and that, if it was not done then, the opportunity would be lost. The fact that we were allied with Russia was bizarre and purely because the common enemy, Germany, had attacked that country but that the alliance was a travesty of reason on every other count. I felt that Russia represented the greatest threat to the world at large, and said that, even if such action should delay our own departure, I hoped that it would be taken. Roosevelt, who had been so duped by Stalin, was now dead. Truman, so far as we were concerned, was an unknown quantity, as was Attlee who had apparently replaced Churchill. This point of view was received with universal condemnation and was repeated to many to whom I had never spoken. Later, I was gratified to find that Winston Churchill, no longer in power, was of the same view. As is well known, no action was taken against Russia, but the passage of the years, with all the events brought in their train, has convinced me that I was right and that failure to overthrow the Soviet régime at that time, when it was so easily possible, ranks as one of the major errors of history.

By the time that we had a whole warehouse stacked with good foods, an American army party came to collect us: flabby, pallid men who bore

303

43. The ashes of Osaka. Top right is No. 2 Pier with two of the three basins in Pl. 34 visible. The road crossing the bridge at the head of No.1 Basin is the one we used to reach the Osaka Shosen Shipyard. A little to the right (off the picture) is a turning to the left which had led to the Osaka No. 1 camp and its squalid street — by then mere memories. Note the sunken and water-logged barges and coasters, and the destruction down to the three courses of bricks. The shacks on the left foreground are corrugated iron, makeshift shelters. The traditional wooden buildings, together with the great canal network of the town, after being badly damaged by the bombing, virtually disappeared under the post-war re-development in re-inforced concrete with broad avenues.

stretchers with which to bear us, the tanned, fit prisoners, away! At the time, it seemed laughable. Indeed, we were free and we did laugh at the time, though it needed little reflection to see that it was not absurd. They had come too late, for the stretcher cases were no longer with us. They were dead: Barber, Llewellyn, old Serafin, the men with electric feet, the lascars who had wasted to die of consumption, the men who had succumbed to dysentery and so many others who never saw that day. There was still the recollection of the hideous death roll in the barrack of the Philippine army men of that first winter — a mortality rate which was by no means confined to our camp.

We were loaded into trucks and taken to Osaka station, some men throwing cigarettes to the crowds who grovelled in the streets in our wake as we passed. No marching this time, uncertain of an evil future, but a cheering, frenzied crowd of men who were already looking forward in their imaginations towards their homes in the further extremities of the world. Their yesterdays were forgotten together with such errors as the football and the men who had died and now, belatedly and at long last, they seemed as one happy family. Incongruously, we found Colonel Murata on the station square, standing stiff and erect and still with all his dignity, to take his last salute before we boarded the train for Tokyo.

No drawn blinds now: no enforced silence; no Fujimoto, but men sleeping easily in their seats until they woke with the dawn to find the blue Pacific shimmering to the eastward and the rising sun falling in golden splendour on a country which was glorious to behold, despite its memories. The great Buddha of Kamakura stared impassively as we passed, unaware of peace or war, and so we came to Tokyo to take more lorries through mile upon mile of destruction and on through flattened Yokohama which we had last seen in all the bustling importance of its commerce. Then, after some slight formalities, we had an American breakfast and drove up to the Atsugi airfield where Skymaster after four-engined Skymaster swooped in and touched down to disgorge squads of occupation troops. Still together, Pargiter and I, with a crowd of others, boarded one as it was turned round and, almost at once, we were in the air.

We were lucky. Ours had been a staff 'plane and we stretched out in utter relief in the comfort of its seats. Below, in Tsuruga Bay, the vast array of the grim, grey Allied Pacific task forces lay in their anchored ranks and, with a smother of bow wave, a battle-ship passed through the peaceful sea right beneath us, on her way to join the vast, victorious armada in all its spectacular strength and might. Fujiyama, still serene, faded in its immutable majesty. Was it *Sayonara* or 'Good-bye'? It is said that, if one sees its mountain top when leaving the country, one will return, but whether the rule held good for aeroplanes might be open to question. I hoped that it meant *Sayonara* (adieu) but not 'farewell', because Japan is a lovely country which I was sure I could enjoy mightily in happier circumstances.

As the 'plane winged its way southwards, the Japanese coastline passed below in patterns of sunlight and shade. After seeing the distant ruins of Osaka away to the right, we passed over the Inland Sea, and then saw the wreck of Hiroshima. There was little of the horror of it all apparent from the air and it looked no different from the ravages elsewhere. Along Kyushu, the countryside looked lovelier and lovelier, now free of the stench of the *benjo* carts: the often scrofulous heads of the small boys and the squalid dockland areas we had known so long. Finally Japan dropped below the horizon and we headed towards the Okinawas where we landed on a coral runway on an island where the scars of bloody battle were already being masked by the tropical vegetation.

We had three days of waiting there, in which we marvelled at the way the Americans were cutting through coral, while a typhoon took its course over the China Sea, and then there was a dreadful flight to the Philippines in a 'plane which was bare and had hurriedly been stripped down from operational duties and in which everybody except myself was made to sit in the bomb-rack. I had spoken up when the pilot asked if anyone could use the telephone, and was in the body of the aircraft, at least able to see out of it, though suffering all the draughts from the holes which formerly housed machine guns. As we circled over the airfield after take-off and were coming round to our course, I saw another 'plane which was taking off on the runway burst into flames. Only later did I learn that all aboard were lost and that their number included Brown. Such is the sad lottery of life.

In the meantime, our aircraft literally jolted on its way, suddenly dropping like a stone every so often in the air-pockets left in the wake of the typhoon, with all the sensation of leaving one's stomach a few hundred feet above! *En route,* we circled over Formosa, which appeared to be solid vegetation, in an unsuccessful attempt to locate a 'plane which had left before us but had failed to arrive, and later swooped down to inspect fishing boats at sea, only to arrive and circle Clark Field outside Manila in driving rain until we could land. Indeed, when we did, I thought that we had come down in the sea, so immense was the splash of water from the runway right over the aeroplane itself. Thence, after a short flight in a lighter aircraft, we came to a large camp of tents where we should await repatriation.

This camp was quite incredible to our eyes. The tents were comfortable enough with truckle beds, and it was pleasant to have fried eggs and flapjacks for breakfast and as much as we could eat. Two, four, six or eight eggs we might have, or any multiple of two, but never an odd number nor a single egg. Such a request was quite beyond the capacity of the United States army! In our tent were two elderly Lancastrians who became most excited when it was announced that Gracie Fields was to sing to the assembled company, but who became most affronted when Pargiter and I declined to listen to her, solely on the grounds that we did not think her worth listening to and that we thought she made a dreadful noise, though we did not want to give offence by giving our other reason. Notwithstanding, these two men took great offence that anyone should not want to hear 'Oor Gracie' and riled us by their protests. This led us to state that, if Gracie Fields had wished to sing to troops, she had had years of opportunity to do so, but was only now emerging when the war was over after taking refuge in America. The atmosphere in the tent was distinctly cool after that!

Often it rained and we were so anxious to leave and to get on our way that, when the *Empress of Australia* came in from Hong Kong with a

44. The EMPRESS OF AUSTRALIA — *here lying off Valetta.*

load of internees who had spent the war there in the Stanley camp, many of those aboard refused to go any further in such a floating oven. Pargiter and I, with several others, volunteered to take their places, being quite able to withstand any amount of heat in our desire to get home. In fact, an old ship built for the Northern Atlantic run, she was ill equipped for Eastern waters. We had no crystal ball. Had we waited, we could have been shipped to the West Coast of North America in a carrier, been transported by train across that continent and then brought across the North Atlantic, which we would have preferred. But we did not know what lay around the corner.

There was a stop at Singapore, where those who wished to remain in Australia or the Far East might disembark and where the Chinese wife of a British 'tommy' in Hong Kong, who had spent the war in internment, declined to go ashore. *"Where are you going?"* she was asked. *"Home,"* was her answer. *"And where is your home?"* "Rondon" (London) She replied. *"Where do you live in London?"* "Oh!" she said gaily, *"Near the station".* In their wisdom, the British authorities brought her to England!

There had been good and bad influences in the Chikkō camp but, as we talked in the saloons of this ship we realized that we had seen little of the social evils of confinement. Children played on the deck — poor, miserable little creatures born in captivity to whom no-one could define the names of many of their fathers. There were those who held in their pockets cheques and I.O.U.s for hundreds of pounds in exchange for the most trivial necessities of their camp which had been traded at rates for which the term 'unconscionable' would be a mild description and many of these must have been presented, as the first question which my bank manager asked me on my return was whether I had drawn any cheques of this nature. The air was filled with the retailed scandals of the years in that camp and I was glad to escape to the boat deck, where women were not allowed, to stew in the sun with a noble lord who had occupied himself over the past years in the role of camp cobbler, and we watched the procession of landmarks till we halted at Colombo, and then steamed over to Socotra, passed Perim and up the Red Sea and through the Canal into the Mediterranean.

Part of the Middlesex Regiment were aboard, and their senior officer had been at school with me*, so I was asked to join their mess. This was pleasant and avoided much of the unpleasant gossip. As we had approached Socotra, there had been much talk of the 'Green Flash', which is sometimes seen when the air has no humidity just as the sun sets. Rare at any time, it is more likely to be seen in, say, the Gobi desert and scarcely ever at sea. However, on this day the sea was like a mirror and wholly calm, while there was not the vestige of cloud in the sky. The subject, hitherto unknown to most of those aboard, spread right through the ship and, as the sun set, the rails were crowded with people waiting for the 'Green Flash'. It was incredible how many of them swore they had seen it, such is the power of suggestion!

So we passed Gibraltar and then, on the last lap, dropped the Birlings and ran up into the Irish Sea with a big sea and a long swell which sent the ship dancing and pitching, while throwing heavy swells all over herself. Most of our fellow passengers scuttled below, leaving Pargiter and myself almost alone on deck as we came home in the way we knew so well. We alone, in all our contingent, had kept together in all the time since the far off days in the *Charlotte Schliemann* and had stood by one another through thick and thin, which was a record of which none of our fellows could boast. For all that, our partnership had hung on the slender thread of convenience in the latter days, for the word 'diaries' had not been mentioned between us since that day of fire. No reader can assess the value of those books. Only he and I can do that, but even we cannot weigh the *contra* of their loss against the *pro* of three years of such mutual co-operation.

It was three and a half years since the *Dalhousie* had last left the

* Major-General Christopher M.M. Mann died in October 1989, rising to his rank through commanding troops, which was unique amongst ex-Japanese P.o.W. officers.

darkened coast of England with war materials for the Middle East. For the past three of them, her missing mooring ropes no longer needed, she had formed a playground for the creatures of the deep ocean. Her master, as I was soon to learn, had been repatriated from Germany, broken in health. Her mate had died in Osaka; her third mate had been killed on the Okinawa runway, the Steward was fathoms deep off Cape Finisterre and the Bo's'n died on the Burma Road. There were others, too, who never made their landfall on the coastwise lights of England again, for the game had been played too long.

~~~~~

EPILOGUE

Had my diaries not been burnt, my first charge on returning home would have been to type them out and to produce a very different book from this, for there was much statistical information within them which reached far beyond the life of our camp. This was impossible to reproduce in the event, but I did set down all that is contained in Chapters Six to Thirteen almost immediately and purely for my own benefit while it was fresh in my memory. I had kept diaries previously at sea, and thus simply maintained my own personal record.

In the 1950s I read a book about sailing ships in which the distortion and inaccuracy so maddened me that I decided to write one myself. I found this quite enjoyable and, in fact, wrote several in quick succession, after which I decided to try and publish the typescript covering my period as a prisoner-of-war. At that time I failed, since both my agents and a number of publishers rejected it on identical grounds, namely: that it was insufficiently jingoistic: that it contained 'neither a good death march nor a gas chamber' *(sic)* and that it was too controversial.

As to the first, it is absurd to pretend that all the Allies were 'goodies' and all the Axis 'baddies', because this was never the case. If the reading public must subsist purely on grisly sensation, they fail to grasp the perspective of the whole as, indeed, one famous book on the Burma Road detailed horrors without number although, when analysed, the period of the author's reminiscences only covered a relatively short period of his captivity. We were not told about the rest! The overall impression was quite different from the truth of the matter. Certainly I am the last to shrink from controversy, but it must be accepted that that word is often used in error when a statement is made which others do not wish to hear, whether it is true or not. At the time I was told that, had I submitted the script as soon as the war had finished, it would have been a best seller, but that times had changed. Now even more water has passed under the bridges and attitudes on many subjects have altered radically.

Certainly Japan and Germany, who lost the most during the war, soon became the envy of the world for their economies and their progress ..... Meanwhile, the Japanese have been engaged in an exercise of self-analyzing their national soul. It is nevertheless true that the essential human nature of mankind has not changed down the ages, despite the advances in technical intelligence. It can all happen again, and probably will do so. When the Russian President, Gorbachev, visited German cities in 1989 the emotional scenes of the welcoming crowds had a familiar ring, resembling the rallies and *Heil Hitlers* of the Nazi era. Apparent national changes are no more than a thin veneer. Peoples do not change, unless it be to advance out of primeval barbarism*.

It would be idle to pretend otherwise than that I, and the majority of those with me in Japan, were lucky, when our experiences are set against the lot of Japanese prisoners as a whole, although we were by no means unique. We were better off in Japan than were those in The Dutch East Indies (as they then were) or on mainland South-East Asia. The advantages of being a head-quarters camp probably outweighed its undoubted disadvantages and, for my own personal part, I was probably fortunate in my age, in being very fit at the outset and in being single, for those with wives or families generally found such separations to be an additional strain.

Moreover, I believe that my time in sail had tempered me to discomfort to a much greater degree than most of those with whom I found myself, for that life had entailed an inherent discipline. On the one hand, that background was of great benefit to me in coping with the various situations which arose, but on the other it probably made me the more intolerant of some of those who allowed themselves to slide down that slippery slope on which they lowered their standards and lost their morale. Only two of us in our barrack had had the advantage of being at a public school (or any other boarding school) but the others, as merchant seamen, had never experienced real discipline of any sort, least of all the catering staffs. A man in a regular fighting service is generally in better case in this respect, and there is no question that the merchant

---

* When, in 1990, a British Cabinet Minister in a published interview containing much good sense drew attention to the character and ambitions of Germany, he had to resign. It was said that 45 years had passed since the Second World War and that much had changed in Germany in that period. This was true, but was not to say that the Germans themselves have changed. Since Germany emerged from the status of minor states, it has launched three major wars — their assault on France culminating in the capitulation of Paris in 1871 and the two World Wars. It was not a matter of a mere 80 years. Their forebears, the Marcomanni, Vandals, Sarmatians, Alamanni and others left their conquests on the history books from 167 onwards for centuries. It will be surprising if France is not invaded by Germany once again — E.E.C. or no E.E.C. Nor can such comments by any means be confined to the Germans.

seamen, in particular, were disadvantaged individually and collectively in their lack of self-discipline, *esprit de corps* and their inability to work towards a common cause.

Nevertheless, I dare say that every man learnt to adjust his values as a result of his period in captivity, and to assess his fellows the better. This is not to say that such benefits which accrued were not vastly outweighed by the evils, nor that the whole period was not far too prolonged. Yet all experience teaches something, and much should have been learnt. Perhaps one of the most cogent object lessons was that, if we had too little to eat in Japan, we normally eat far more than we need! Again, one became far more aware of the true nature of many of one's fellows, which often became bared in odd ways which I have not described, emphasizing the façade with which most people cloak themselves in their normal lives. If I learnt nothing else, the conversations which I had, and which I overheard, amongst catering staffs, opened my eyes to much that went on behind the scenes in passenger liners and led to my resolve that I would *never* travel in a passenger liner manned by British stewards thereafter!

Now, many years later, the western world has 'advanced' in the sense that items which were then regarded as luxuries are now accepted as common-place. Television, then unknown, is watched by 98% of the British population (but not by me, so I may be prejudiced!), and, incredible as it might seem so few years ago, vast numbers actually sit at home by the hour and watch other people playing snooker!

Indeed, the tendency to watch other people doing things has increased. Television, computers and like technological advances all tend to create a nation of 'zombies' with a consequent reduction in individual self-sufficiency and even pride in jobs or hobbies. The proliferation of motor cars has destroyed much of the quality of both towns and country. Much else has deteriorated and it may be that in an age when so many preach 'unilateral disarmament', which flies in the face of all the lessons of history (however repugnant the thought of another war may be), not everyone will wish to accept all that is contained in this book. Inevitably, it contains some unpleasant incidents, but it is not such a 'horror' story of the period as some could have written. It is simply the unvarnished, unexaggerated truth set, to the best of my ability, in the context of the Japanese outlook.

At the request of Trocchi, who had worked with me at Osaka Kō and who was by then living abroad and was interested in a matter of a claim being made at that late hour against the Japanese*, I did contact one

---

* The Japanese forcibly operated on Trocchi for hernia in most unhygienic conditions and made a terrible mess of it, as a result of which he almost died. Transferred to the notorious Stadium, Dr. Jackson, who was furious when he saw what had been done,

association, which rejoices in the emotive title 'The Jap Labour Camp Survivors Association'. I had never joined any Prisoner of War organisation, since the only common factor amongst its members must lie in their varying experiences, about which they can indulge in mutual sympathy and boost the hatred which seems to dwell in their hearts like a canker. However, after a perfectly pleasant chat on the telephone with its secretary, I was sent much of their literature which detailed horrors and the like beyond measure. Sending a cheque to join, I did venture to suggest that overstating the case would probably not help their cause, as a result of which my cheque was returned since *"... the Committee ... feel that your appreciation of experiences with the Japanese who attacked and overran Greater South-East Asia is not in line with the aims of this Association"*!!!

Of course, everything which they said was true. There were prisoners who received unspeakable treatment: there were those who were used for surgical experiments; there were those who were tortured and those who were executed and many returned — if they returned at all — as broken men. This is all undeniable but, physically or mentally, many men who were never prisoners were equally broken by the war as, indeed, were many civilians. Prisoners were but one facet of the whole operation of the hostilities in which death, injury and horror were widespread.

Human nature being what it is, lurid accounts of captivity are the more popular. As stated above, objections to this book, years ago, were that it contained neither a 'good' death march, a gas chamber nor anything of that sort. People who delight in such accounts can rank little higher that those who perpetrate such deeds. Probably more literature has been produced on the *Titanic* disaster than all other passenger liner operations put together, thereby pandering to popular taste. Of course many camps were infinitely worse than ours, but there were a great number which were no better and no worse. It is a matter of keeping a sense of perspective and setting out both sides of the question, before those who can provide evidence are all dead.

I imagine that few of my fellow prisoners were truly musical, but the utter lack of opportunity to hear any music at all created a void, the loss of which was not immediately apparent. As to Japanese music, it is not melodious at all to western ears (if infinitely preferable to the various forms of so-called 'pop' music which have proliferated the air in the intervening years), though was sometimes played on a loud-speaker system at Osaka Shosen. Only on two occasions, when they rather

---

shouting out: *"Bloody Butchers! I'll report them to the League of Nations for this after the war!"*, undoubtedly saved his life. After being returned to camp, an American surgeon was finally allowed to operate and repair the massive damage which had been done, and Trocchi finally got back on his feet. In the circumstances he was lucky.

strangely played the *Horst Wessel Song*, did we realize how much it was missed.

I saw less of the Norwegians after the shipyard detail stopped since we never again worked on the same parties, but I maintained contact with them in the camp. They were constantly trying to get exchanged, on the grounds that Norway was not at war with Japan, and although they never succeeded in this they did occasionally think that they had grounds for hope. Once Reistad, a mild and pleasant fellow, offered to take a letter away with him and to post it for me. I doubted if he would be repatriated, but nevertheless wrote such a letter to my parents in the hope that he would succeed, and forgot all about it. Years later, he wrote to me and asked if my letter might be placed in his local museum with other prisoner-of-war ephemera. (I believe that our Norwegians were unique in their country in being incarcerated in Japan). Later he asked me to visit him and finally I did so, spending a most enjoyable time at his home on the island of Hidra, whence we made splendid expeditions to people in isolated areas on the mainland. Indeed, on arrival, I had found several Union Jacks flying (Reistad's being hoisted every day I was there!) and, when taken to the local museum at Rosväg, was met outside by its Director who rather embarrassingly sang a solo of *God Save the King* in my honour! (He could not understand a word of English, but had learnt every verse of it like a parrot!)

Subsequently, as I was conducted round his museum, he sang in Norwegian folk-songs relating to the various items on view. Had he spoken them, I might have understood. As it was, I understood nothing! I was also surprised to find myself being photographed and featured in the local paper. There was a grand re-union with those still there: Thoresen, Jensen, Kjöstvedt and some of the others, though Hansen, the mate (an older man) had died. Their ship, the *Aramis*, had hailed from Flekkefjord, and most of them still lived locally. Naturally I enquired for Capt. Christiansen with whom, after Pargiter, I was more friendly than with anyone else in the camp. He always excited my admiration, as he never yielded an inch in his standards. It seemed that he had started a salvage business but had taken to the bottle and died of drink. Thus one can never judge, for a more apparently self-disciplined man I had never met.

Reistad was not a fit man. He had had a bad fall down the hold of a ship before he was ever captured and had a plate in his head. Two years later he wrote to tell me that he was dying and to ask me to write a poem for his death, 'bringing in drink and horses'. What a request! and as if I was a poet!! I finally produced some verses which did at least scan (which is more than can be said for much modern poetry!) but, before dispatching them, showed them to a niece of his who lived close to my home and who had recently returned from an equally pleasant visit to Hidra when she had also enjoyed his hospitality. A charming woman who was a missionary with narrow views, she clearly felt that the whole thing was a waste of time, as her Uncle Leif would most assuredly go to Hell! I was appalled. If Leif Reistad was bound for Hell because he had sipped a single whisky each evening, God help the rest of us! Sadly, his cancer acted fast and he was dead while the poem was still in transit.

I have seen few of the others. One of my men, dropped off at Singapore, was nice enough to write to me after the war. He was then a policeman in Methil, and had spent his time under the Japanese Navy salving sunken ships in Singapore harbour and its environs. I gathered it might have been worse. Others I heard of only at second-hand.

After the war, Pargiter was chosen to represent his company in a Victory March and appealed to me for a bed in London — such things then being at a premium. I was able to help, but never saw him again. If he had failed to retrieve the diaries, I felt very strongly that I might at least have had an explanation .... It was like a blight on any future relationship. I know he went back in his passenger ships for as long as they lasted before the aeroplane ousted them from the seas, and learnt that, after one particular voyage, he had left his wife for one of the female passengers. A regrettably commonplace situation in these days, it was less so at that time and I was sorry to hear it, since I had heard so much of his first wife in those years when we were together.

I spent much time trying to track down Broomfield, and finally succeeded. For domestic reasons (his wife was ill) we did not meet for some time, and intended to foregather with Chadwick, whom he saw constantly. By the time we did meet, Chadwick had dropped dead of a heart attack. Broomfield had news of Fox and of Mackavoy who were both in Africa. The Atlantic separated me from most of the men with whom I had worked and established close contacts working at Osaka Kō. One of them, Martin Boyle, wrote a book in the 1960s but, by the time that I heard of it, it was long out of print. I finally obtained a copy, however, and found myself gasping! Perhaps he, too, had been told his script was insufficiently sensational and had amended it accordingly! Yet there were errors of fact and place, and neither he nor his own colleagues equated with my recollections, whilst the escape scheme (in which he was involved); the stolen Red Cross parcels, and much else were all omitted. I wondered whether he had really written it himself, despite the photograph, which was obviously him, on its back cover!*

For my own part, being unable to pass statutory sight tests on my return, I had to leave the sea, since no navigating officer could then

---

* *Yanks don't Cry*, by Martin Boyle, Bernard Geis Associates, 1963.

follow his calling with spectacles. For a short time I was looking after and loading Blue Funnel ships in London during which, in the presence of a marine superintendent, I happened to relate our looting exploits in Japan. It was a period when the 'black market' was still rife and when the London dockers were pilfering cargo to such a great extent that the leading companies were combining to form anti-pilferage squads of ex-policeman. I was promptly asked to take charge of the operation! I knew enough to appreciate that a looter could only be caught when he made a mistake and, since I was finding it harrowing to prepare a ship for sea only be left ashore, and also because I knew that turning down a job did not enhance one's standing, I then turned my back on ships and the sea professionally.

That decision was a great wrench at the time but, having watched the so-called advance of ships to vast barges of many hundred thousands of tons, soulless and ugly, dependent to a large degree on the micro-chip and often enough navigated by satellite, my regrets completely evaporated over the years, and I became thankful that I had no part in it.

My first loves, the merchant sailing ships, soon became extinct in all their forms; the passenger liners were driven from the seas by the ubiquitous aeroplane, and more and more vessels, under flags of convenience, are now often incompetently manned: dangers to themselves, to other ships, to the very environment and potentially to cities and towns, for the scaling up of size in vessels with lethal cargoes can do damage of sorts undreamed of by the ships of former generations. The structural weaknesses in vast super-tankers and VLCCs are well-known and their very draught and size precludes certain manoeuvering essentials. Container ships may have overcome dock labour problems but, apart from the fact that the bottom of the seas are now littered with containers, they have nothing of the allure of the ships of my youth, despite all their comfort and conditions. Indeed, whole crews in so many vessels must be changed at frequent intervals. At first, thinking back to the long voyages of the sailing ships, which were never monotonous whatever their disadvantages, it was easy to presume that the modern seamen lacked stamina, but investigation will show that the majority of modern deep-sea ships produce an ennui almost beyond comprehension to a landsman. This is all in the name of progress.

Yet, in the great ship-building boom, I found it astonishing that Japan should have achieved such pre-eminence, since the Osaka Shosen Kaisha yard in which we worked was little better than a music-hall turn. Why this was so I have no idea, since no-one disputes the worth of their great naval vessels, or many others, both during and before the war. Clearly, our observation of that yard was no criterion on which to judge the country's ship-building as a whole. It is often said that the Japanese are marvellous copiers, but poor innovators, yet this is no longer the case and, in the field of shipping alone, they have made remarkable advances, particularly in computer-controlled wind-assisted ships, and it may not be long before they are operating unmanned robot vessels in the deep sea. So they have led in other spheres of invention.

Certainly we had not suffered conditions in Japan comparable with the men on the Burma Road, nor had we experienced the horrors perpetrated by the front-line Japanese soldiery. We knew that we had received far better treatment in Japan than their own civilian prisoners and, indeed, as good as many of the ordinary civilians in certain respects. The innate savagery of the Japanese character had not been eradicated by machines, and on all this they should be judged, quietly and dispassionately, whilst taking a view of European history all down the ages.

As for the people, the mass of them are pleasant enough. Their leaders in the war, who set the tone and were their own country's worst enemies, were tried as war-criminals and many were executed or imprisoned. Was the country to be blamed because it still remained feudal in the midst of its steelworks: because its peoples had not changed their natures in four short generations, or because they retained the *bushido* beliefs and religions of many centuries? When we fight cannibals, do we hold war crimes tribunals on the reprobates who stew the captured sergeant-major in their pot before they are vanquished? Of course not. We send in missionaries, usually of different denominations, who thus confuse their minds and make them wear clothes which are unnatural to them! It may be said that the Japanese were not cannibals, though it is known that their forces in the Solomons and New Guinea *did* eat the flesh of Americans, Australian and even of their own dead. Granted that the majority present declined this food, but their 18th. Army Headquarters issued an order in December, 1944, permitting the eating of the flesh of Allied dead, but forbidding the flesh of Japanese.

There is hardly a country that cannot point to instances of anthropophagy in ultimate extremity, and there are well authenticated instances in both Russia and Germany in the Second World War. Nevertheless, these were surreptitious: the Japanese issued official memoranda on the subject* and, in so doing, set themselves on a quite different plane from the *ad hoc* instances which stain the records of other nations. Early in 1945 during the Aitape campaign in North-west New Guinea, an officer ordered a private to the cookhouse to be killed for the common pot. This man had other ideas for his future and escaped.‡

---

* To cite but one instance. Also see Mr. Justice Webb's *Report to the Commonwealth Government* quoted in *The Knights of Bushido* by Lord Russell of Liverpool.

‡ He surrendered to the 2/25th Australian battalion.

I doubt if such an instance can be discovered in the history of any other people.

We can find examples of cannibalism in practically every country's recent history and, when it occurs, it is commonly said, not without reason, that there was no alternative. When an aeroplane, bound for the hospital at Yellow Knife, crashed in the Canadian North-West Territory in 1972, an English nurse was killed and an Eskimo woman soon died of her injuries. The German-born pilot had two broken ankles and a smashed knee-cap: the only other survivor being an Eskimo boy who was the nephew of the Eskimo woman. They failed to snare any rabbits after exhausting their meagre supplies. The boy refused to eat either of the women and died. The pilot ate the nurse and survived. Who was the more civilized — the boy or the pilot? When those in the boats of the American whaler *Essex* (which had been sunk by a whale) resorted to cannibalism, they not only drew lots amongst the living, but the captain joined in the eating of his nephew. The Eskimo boy had higher standards. Nevertheless, two races cannot be judged by two examples and, in any case, no man, whoever he may be, can judge what he would do in similar circumstances (which have been common enough), when his mind is going 'fey', but it is surely a measure of the skin depth of ingrained principles.

Yet, the Allies tried the Japanese who had only the thinnest veneer of our beliefs! They should have been judged for what they were: they did not believe in becoming prisoners themselves; they had not signed the Hague Convention and, in a state of total war, they had no obligation to make or retain prisoners at all. Indeed, I often wondered why they did so, for prisoners are a drain on a country's resources.

As previously remarked, Japan was forced to open her frontiers against her will. Emperor Hidetada had closed them two hundred years previously, largely as a result of the activities of Jesuit missionaries who reached his country and abused the privileges accorded to them. It may be thought that he acted very wisely. Indeed, when Perry first arrived in Sagami Bay to demand that Japan open her ports to world trade, the then Emperor, Iesada, issued a rescript which contained the passage:-

'... Let none, so long as the sun illuminates the World, presume to sail to Japan — on pain of death."

Every effort has since been made to 'Westernise' the country. One may ask: *"To what end?"* On the one hand, it resulted in the attacks on Port Arthur and, later, on Pearl Harbor and all that stemmed from those actions, and on the other we now find that Japan has captured many of the Occidental markets! Then one must ask: *"What way of life* *has the West to offer Japan?''* Cities where people dare not go out at night lest they be 'mugged'? Drug-addiction on a massive scale? Declining moral values and the virtual beatification of homosexual perverts?* Or perhaps, as in the case of the United States, a society in which one person in eight is illiterate? As to example, the history of the Western peoples with their incessant wars, massacres, tortures, slavery and much else makes sorry reading since the earliest extant records. The West can offer a civilization which is surely doomed by over-population, by racial tensions, by pollution of its seas and by an imbalance of nature and climate brought about by insecticides and de-forestation, by sheer bureaucracy and by lowered ethical standards. I neglect the popular *canard* of the nuclear bomb, since I believe nuclear power, its by-product, to be one of the few hopes for the future, because fossil fuels are finite and may be exhausted relatively soon. Moreover, the leading Western nations pride themselves on their 'democracy' (which is another much mis-used term) despite the fact that the system only works when the vast majority of their people are democratically-minded, which is seldom the case.‡

It must be accepted that those who tempted Japan out of its seclusion in the nineteenth century could not foresee the evils of the twentieth but, taken all in all, it is little enough to offer. When Japan was forced to open her frontiers, it was in a state which must be equated with the time of the Norman conquest at best in England — centuries before the United States ever existed. If, in her advancement, the country had the benefit of modern technologies from the time that she entered the world of nations, she nevertheless proceeded at an astounding rate along that road which we rather naïvely term 'civilization'. Was she to be blamed if

---

* I am reminded of the late Sir John Colville's parody of John of Gaunt's dying speech in Shakespeare's *Richard II*:-
  "This Royal throne of Kings, this scepter'd isle,
  This muggers' playground, this half-closed shop,
  This Welfare State, this pickets' paradise,
  This fortress built to guard trade union power
  Against free enterprise and common sense,
  This pill-fed breed of men, this racial world,
  This garden city set in an oil-slicked sea
  Saved by permissiveness from any care
  For old discarded themes of right and wrong,
  This sparkling jewel of sociology,
  This blessed plot, this earth, this realm this Britain.''

‡ This is not to decry democracy. It is probably true that the more advanced nations have become too complex to be governed satisfactorily by any system. Universal suffrage, which is 'democratic', tends to be self-defeating when many of those who can vote are either illiterate, have no form of stake in their country, or understand few of the issues involved.

320

she had not advanced quite as far as the great powers in less t
century? Civilization is not a mere matter of technology and of s
(perhaps one of man's most real advances!), but of the mind. How ι....y
nations are truly civilized? It should be easy for an affluent society to
behave in a civilized manner but, the higher the standards of living that it
reaches, the greater is the drop in its moral values. The test comes when
the chips are down, and then it is found that all civilization is but a
veneer, so easily stripped away because, although human knowledge has
advanced beyond all measure, human nature has not advanced one whit!

Western peoples, with modern medicines, now keep old people alive
often against their will, their minds gone and their physical abilities
minimal. The Pelly Bay tribe of Eskimos used to drag the very old on to
the ice when they could no longer be supported in the community and
leave them there to freeze to death. This was done with the consent of
all. As was often said in the days of sail: *"Different ships, different long
splices"*. It is not for me to judge which is the right course, though I
sometimes wonder ....

Mediaeval man knew that life was a lottery. His history highlights the
perpetual ravages of plague in the Middle Ages; the massacres in war and
the tortures and executions carried out in the name of the Christian
religion, mainly by the Roman Catholic Church. This fact is overlooked
by his descendants. No-one can defend Genghiz Khan's razing of whole
cities to the ground and massacring their populations to the last child,
but the fact remains that, after the vast Mongol conquests, a traveller
might move through the length and breadth of those dominions in the
certainty of not being molested. Can the President of the United States,
or the Prime Minister of Great Britain, make such a claim today?

The Oriental mind bears no resemblance to that of its western
counterpart and, by Occidental standards, works backwards (which is
one of the several reasons why it is so hard to master the art of writing
Japanese.) Yet, when Commodore Perry made his second visit to
Yokohama and concluded the Treaty of Kanagawa in 1854, to all intents
and purposes the Japanese crossed their Rubicon, and there can be no
return for them, any more than those in an English city can return to
tribal life in forests which no longer exist. Yet the traditions of a people
take centuries to eradicate, as has been evidenced by the miseries brought
on so many African countries when they achieved their independence in
the years after the second World War.

How, for instance, can the Americans equate the virtual extermination
of the native Red Indians in their own land with the 'war crimes' of the
Japanese who were relatively less advanced towards 'civilized' ideas in
the twentieth century than the Americans in the preceding centuries?
What has Spain to say about the de-population of Mexico in her quest

for gold? Or of her treatment of the peoples of the Low Countries? If it be objected that such events were three or four centuries ago, that is but an instant in the cycle of history. The 'cultured' white men have depopulated vast areas of the world of its indigenous inhabitants, right through the Americas and across the Pacific, by conquest and by importing diseases when colonizing lands to which they had no title, ever since the time of Columbus. The War Crimes tribunals held to judge the Japanese represented one of the most extraordinary displays of double standards and hypocrisy in the whole history of mankind. The Japanese were forced to open up their country against their will and, having done so, were arraigned because they had not absorbed in less than a mere ninety years those standards which it had taken Occidental man a whole millennium to achieve!

What shall we say of Venice and Genoa, who both aided the Crusaders (at a price), while they were treating with the Tartar hordes and selling their myriad slaves to the Mohammedan armies of Egypt to become the Mamelukes? If this was in the 13th. Century, it was when Venice was at the height of its power and of its history, so commonly admired yet so constantly stained by its sordid perfidy and double-dealing. Indeed, in 1573, after Lepanto, 'La Serenissima' signed a peace treaty with the Porte whilst engaged in swearing allegiance to the Holy League, which led the 70-year old Pope to physically chase its ambassador out of the building! There was nothing new about the Japanese plenipotentiaries negotiating in Washington when the Pearl Harbor attack took place.

The Germans were a very different case. The ethics of the victors trying the vanquished is outside my scope but, so far as some of us who had been taken prisoners by them were concerned, *they* were the villains of the piece, for they *had* signed the Hague Convention, yet they handed us over to a race which had not done so and they could have had no illusions about our likely treatment. They knew, for example, the details of the Japanese Rape of Nankin in 1937 when a Japanese army ran amok and raped, tortured and slaughtered well over 200,000 people with other attendant atrocities. As for those who were captured by the Japanese, whatever their treatment, they did not suffer the fate of those vanquished by the Tartar Khans. The comparison is not so far-fetched. It was their ill-fortune in the lottery of life to be taken prisoner at all. That the Germans handed their prisoners over to an innately savage people was a different matter for, although our treatment was *relatively* mild in the event, it was outside German control and something for which they can take no credit.

Whether the War Crimes Tribunals really stemmed from a demand for revenge or for justice may be open to debate. To me, they echoed the vengeance of vendetta. No doubt those who conducted them congratulated themselves on their achievements yet, given that the trials in Germany of a supposedly cultured race took place, what greater punishment could there have been to the Japanese nation as a whole: what greater loss of collective 'face', what greater insult to that teeming people; than to impose peace terms whilst saying that their 'war-criminals' were not to be tried because it was clear that their standards had not reached that level when they could be judged — any more than the cannibal-kings of past centuries? In any case, there was little significance in a few judicial executions or judicial murders — call them what one will — in a country where political assassination had been the norm.

No one will deny the brilliance of the initial Japanese assaults, when their soldiery, often on bicycles and living off the land with, perhaps, a handful of rice, achieved lightning conquests unmatched in the history of the world. That the Americans, who bore the brunt of the Pacific war, finally defeated them largely due to sheer weight of metal and fire-power is well-known (albeit with one ship in their supply train whose sole function, thereby providing the contrast between the antagonists, was to manufacture 5,000 gallons of ice cream each *hour*!). How many people have paused to consider what would have happened had the Japanese — and not the Allies — invented the atom bomb? Who, then, would have been the war criminals? I suspect that that criminality would have been judged to stem from the age of European discovery: from the Treaty of Tordisillas* and the subsequent grab of Eastern territory by those nations who had no title to it. The cannons of the sixteenth and seventeenth century warships and East Indiamen were, in point of invincibility, the atom bombs of the twentieth. That guilt, if guilt it be, was shared initially by Spain and Portugal and later by the British, Dutch, French, Danes and others. I have already recorded the Japanese war objective — that of 'driving the white blood-suckers out of the Greater East Asia Co-prosperity Sphere' and that is what their war was all about, coupled with a certain aggrandisement based on the need to expand their over-crowded population.‡ When Japan was defeated, the

---

* In 1493 the infamous Pope Alexander VI issued two papal bulls, decreeing that all territory to the west of a line drawn from Pole to Pole 350 miles off the Cape Verde Islands should be Spanish, and all that to the east of it Portuguese. This extraordinary judgement was ratified between Spain and Portugal the following year as the Treaty of Tordesillas. It did not define the dividing line on the other side of the world, and, in any case, outraged all other maritime nations who determined to stake their claims. In fact, this treaty contributed to the ruination of Spain.

‡ The Tripartite Pact, signed by Germany, Italy and Japan in September 1940 gave predominance to Germany in Europe: Japanese hegemony in South-East Asia was recognised, and North Africa was to be ceded to Italy. Central Africa would be German and the South Seas Japanese, whilst Russia's sphere of influence in India and Iran was

objective of Asia for the Asians remained. Yet, such are the quirks of history, the Japanese were our allies in the First World War ....

The foregoing implies no defence of the Japanese. On the contrary, their vile and sadistic excesses in so many theatres of the war, usually with the tacit approval of their officers, are well-documented, if not germane to this book. It is because their behaviour, actuated by their very nature, fell so far short of all bounds of acceptable standards that I maintain that they should not — and indeed cannot — be judged by those standards which we have come to accept. We did not approve the practices of head-hunters but .... that was their way of life.

I do not wish to end this book with a mass of statistics, but will merely record that the Japanese held some 145,000 prisoners of all nationalities. Probably some 25 – 33% of these did not survive (12,443 British died in Japanese hands.). The Soviet Union suffered 13,600,000 military personnel dead and 7,720,000 civilians: startling figures when compared with Britain's 312,457 and the United States' 297,793 service men and merchant seamen killed. The casualty figures for Japan were 1,665,429 military personnel dead and 668,000 civilians killed in air raids on the home islands. To cite the comparable figures for all other combatants would be wearisome, if sometimes surprising (for instance, Yugo-Slavia suffered 305,000 military and 1,355,000 civilian dead) but in sum they add up to the conclusion that all the prisoners, in whatever theatre, represented a miniscule proportion of those who died (some 59,000,000), and an even smaller proportion of all those deployed in the world-wide struggle. However, in considering prisoners, one must exclude the Soviet Union, since the best estimates are that some *three million* Russians died or were killed *after being taken prisoner*. If the lot of the prisoners under Japanese aegis pales into utter insignificance before such a figure, it provides no absolution for that country, even if it does set matters in some sort of perspective. It must be remembered that two Blacks never made one White ..... The fact is that, apart from the Nazi extermination camps, the greatest horrors and atrocities of the Second World War never really registered with the mass of the people in — say — Great Britain and the United States and are virtually unknown to the

---

recognized. Japan should have waited until Russia was prepared to sign a Quadripartite pact. (Japan did sign a non-aggression pact with Russia in 1941, the Emperor having objected to the Tripartite Pact while Russia, whose intentions were assured by Germany but who had signed nothing, lay between the Axis partners.) In the event, Hitler's monumental blunder when he invaded Russia torpedoed the pact, and was something which the Japanese never forgave, as mentioned in Chapter 8, p. 156. Moreover, it led to the declaration of war by Russia on Japan three months after the defeat of Germany, which caused sheer, undisguised fear amongst the *civilian* population of the islands. In some sense they regarded the Americans and British as potential saviours from the situation in which they found themselves, but they had very different feelings about the Russians.

generations which have matured in the interim.

In considering the figures cited for Russia, it must be remembered that the numberless casualties of Stalin's inter-war purges exceeded the war losses for most countries put together and, by way of taking a further figure at random, that some twenty million people died of famine in Bengal in 1942 — slightly less than the number of people who died of Spanish 'flu in 1918/9. Some three-quarters of a million people probably perished in the Tangshan earthquake in 1976 and the world took little notice. Yet, if a hundred odd people are lost in a 'plane or train crash, or less than a dozen in a major pile-up on a motor-way, it becomes a source of national, and often international, concern. Yet, every day, far more people are killed in individual accidents and scarcely anyone thinks twice about them. Thus my plea that people should recognize the lottery of life and keep a sense of proportion in judging the events of the world, whether in war or peace. Torture, which appears to be ever more wide-spread, is a different matter and, if I have said previously that human nature does not change in the face of material progress, I may well be wrong in that it appears to be deteriorating rapidly, and not improving at all if one views the world as a whole. As has always been said, the sun rises in the East and sets in the West. When one looks at the declining standards of the West and the economic advances in Asia, it is probably more accurate today to state that the Sun rises in the East and is setting on the West .....

History treats of the rise and fall of civilizations, and it must surely be recognized that both Britain and the United States have passed their peaks to become effete and less dependant on themselves, whilst becoming increasingly litigious. Affluence and increasing standards of living erode the spirit and moral fibre of any nation and, for all its theoretical merits, democratic societies are subject to periodic socialist rule. It is strange that, although many of the proponents of the Socialist ideals are people of great intelligence, they can never appreciate that the system simply does not work and invariably debilitates a nation's economy.

I have read a number of books by other prisoners-of-war in the Japanese sphere. Almost all end on a note of self-pity, stressing how an ungrateful country did little for them on their return, although they had been subject to worse conditions than any of their countrymen at any time and, for those on, say, the Burma Road, this was probably very true even when it is difficult to equate many statements in their books with truth. (How, for example, could a young aircraftsman of twenty who admitted total ignorance of the Japanese, when just taken prisoner in Java and before contact with other prisoners, have asked a guard for a cigarette *in Japanese*?)

Nevertheless, true or false, the incidence of death, of fevers, dysentery, beri-beri, tropical ulcers and so on were far more prevalent there than in Japan. What was the country to do for them? The inference is that they should have had some payment. (Such gratuities as were paid were, admittedly, minimal.) For my part, I could pass sight tests before capture, and I could not do so afterwards, having to leave the sea in consequence. It was said that my eyes might have deteriorated anyway. That might or might not be true, though the long arm of coincidence should have spoken for itself. Moreover, I was left with other physical defects .....

These arguments, however, lead to a bottomless pit, for where does compensation begin and end? One man argued that the American hostages in Teheran were claiming $400 *per diem* while they were there. I do not know whether they got it, but it must be accepted that the peoples of the United States display, as a whole, a national lunacy, as evidenced at regular intervals by their Presidential elections and by the decisions of their Supreme Court which have opened the door to every form of depravity in their land. Litigation has reached absurd and idiotic levels and damages are paid for unbelievable reasons.* Regrettably, England tends to copy the U.S.A. within a few years. The matter of the Iranian hostages was long after the end of the war by which time attitudes had changed, in any case. I have already recorded that the Japanese did not understand the concept of being taken prisoner and, until almost the end of the war, never allowed themselves to be taken — witness the mass suicides on Tarawa and elsewhere. Nor did they comprehend how we could have so disgraced ourselves and our ancestors as to allow ourselves to be taken.‡ Thus, as stated above, it remained a mystery to me why they took prisoners at all and did not shoot them at once. It was quite within their character and nature to do so. What price compensation if they had acted thus? Whether the work accomplished by prisoners compensated for their keep, the logistics, administration, guards involved and so forth is, at best, a very moot point.

It may be said: *"How, then, could the Burma Railroad have been*

---

* For instance, a man stung by a wasp in a U.S. country club sued and received damages of $1.5 million. A man tried to commit suicide in New York by jumping in front of a subway train. The driver being very alert, he was not killed but merely injured. He then claimed and received $600,000 damages. So a man giving a party in his flat — part of a block — announced that he would walk from one end of the swimming pool to the other. Neither his wife nor any of the 15 guests tried to stop him. He drowned and his wife successfully sued the owners of the flats for high damages and won. There are innumerable such instances. How can anybody take such a nation seriously?

‡ Indeed, it was the Spartan ethic that one either returned home victorious or on one's shield — hence the famous inscription on the monument in the Pass of Thermopylae:-
"Tell them in Sparta, O thou who passeth by,
That here, obedient to her laws, we lie."

built?'' As an exercise in cruelty, it could scarcely be surpassed, but it was equally an exercise in incredible folly to set white men to do the job at all. It was not all done by white prisoners, but also by forced labour of various Asian nationalities who, although their treatment was no better, were more fitted to work in such jungle conditions, in virtue of being better attuned climatically and of their lower expectations of life. Similarly, in Japan, we were often working alongside Korean forced labour, of which there was also an almost inexhaustible supply.

Thus, had the Japanese liquidated all their prisoners, I do not believe that it would have had the slightest effect on their war effort. It would have been inexcusable, as was their behaviour anyway, but quite in keeping with their innate barbarism. When all is said and done, 145,000 Japanese prisoners in all was a mere drop in the ocean of the war's 59 million dead, many of whom died horribly.

There are other imponderables to be considered. The Pearl Harbor attack brought the United States into the war and was a crushing American defeat. They had ample and precise warnings of the attack, both from the British who had broken the Japanese naval code and from their own ambassador, yet they did nothing. Had they taken appropriate action and put themselves in a position to counter-attack the Japanese force, what then would the state of play have been in the ensuing months?* Who can say? This is not to deny that the defences of Singapore proved to be absurd in the event, and that much else was wrong with the Allied strategy, but it is irrefutable that, had the Americans heeded the advance warnings relating to the Pearl Harbor attack and been in a proper state of preparedness, the whole prisoner-of-war situation in the Far East would have taken a very different form, if it had ever even existed at all.

As to the dropping of the Atom bombs on Japan, about which there have been such divergent opinions, it seems to me that one must either fight a total war or no war at all. Part of the success of the Tatar *tumans* lay in their sheer ruthlessness. To fight a 'limited' war, whether in one age or another, is a certain recipe for disaster. Whilst accepting the side and long term effects of nuclear explosions, it makes little odds to individual victims if they are killed by that means, in such fire raids as Tokyo or Hamburg, in a blazing tanker or by any other method. I

---

* And what would it have been had Admiral Isoruku Yamamoto had his way? Although opposed to the war on the grounds that it could not be won, he co-operated in its execution and, in discussing the initial strike against Pearl Harbor, demanded troops to occupy the Hawaiian Islands in the same movement. This was over-ruled in cabinet: it being said that such troops could not be made available. Whether or not this was so, the failure to land occupying troops was a crashing Japanese mistake. The Japanese code being broken, Yamamoto was intercepted in a 'plane and shot down near Bougainville in April 1942.

believe the Hiroshima — the first — bomb was justified, for any invasion of Japan was still some 12 months away and it, alone, would probably have caused a far greater death toll. The rationale for dropping the second bomb on Nagasaki (which was in any case somewhat off target) is more debateable.

I confess to, and declare, a personal interest. Without doubt, another year of captivity would have been infinitely worse than the preceding years, even if we had been moved out to a country camp but, so far as I myself was concerned, having maintained my condition until the very end, in the very last days of hostilities I was visibly wasting with dysentery in that downward spiral which I had seen cause the death of so many. The Atom bombs brought about the end of the war and thus the food drops by the Americans, which cured me almost overnight. I am under no illusions that, had those bombs not been dropped, this book could never have been written ....

Elsewhere there were instances of prisoners being buried with only their heads above ground, and left in the hot sun to die. Recently, if not left to die, two school-boys were buried in this manner near the edge of the sea by their teachers 'to correct their thinking'. Soon afterwards, in 1990, a school-girl arrived at her school one second late. The quarter-ton sliding door was shut as she entered, crushing her skull. The headmaster defended the action. There was criticism, but no general outcry. In 1984 a sixteen year old boy was kicked to death by his teacher for using a hair-dryer. The veneer of civilization remains woefully thin since the essential character of the people has not changed.

Many surviving prisoners-of-war from the Far East may disapprove of much that is contained in this Epilogue. Their hearts contain such abiding and cankerous hatred, with good reason, that they can countenance no excuses. Yet how much better were they to take personal pride in having won through that particular lottery! For my part, I forgive nothing, but I believe that the content of this chapter is far more damning to the Japanese than all their accumulated hatred.

Finally, I have often been asked how the Japanese treated me/us. There is no short answer, and I usually counter the question by asking whether the answer is to be based on Japanese or on our own standards. If the first, then we were treated reasonably well. If the latter, then we were not.

This is probably the fairest comment, since it is manifestly impossible to relate two diametrically opposite sets of standards to one another and to discover any common factor.*

---

* *Long the Imperial Way* by Hanama Tasaki, published by Gollancz in 1951, is based on the author's three years service in China as a private. It is neither dramatic nor sensational, but it serves to set the Japanese army in a certain perspective which is not always appreciated.

GLOSSARY OF NAUTICAL WORDS AND TERMS

ABACK: — A ship is aback when caught with the wind on the forward (wrong) side of her sails.

BACKSPRING: — A mooring wire which leads in a forward direction from aft, or aft from forward.

BALLAST:- is carried low in the ship when she has no cargo in order to retain her stability. It might consist of rubble, sand, chalk or anything of little value. Today most ships carry water ballast in tanks.

BARQUE:- A sailing vessel of three or more masts, square-rigged except on the after mast, which is fore-and-aft rigged.

BARQUENTINE: A vessel of three or more masts, square-rigged on the fore and fore-and-aft on the others.

BOWSPRIT:- a spar extending in front of the bows, to which the head stays and headsails lead.

BROACH TO:- A ship can broach to in a big following sea when she will 'yaw' (deviate) each side of her course. A bad helmsman can let her fall off and lie across the trough of the seas, which can then crash aboard and do great damage. perhaps staving in the hatches, when she will sink like a stone.

CHAINS, the: A folding platform from which the hand-lead is operated outside the hull.

CLINOMETER: A dial which shows the angle of heel of a vessel.

CLOSE-HAULED:- A vessel is close-hauled when the direction of the wind prevents her making her course. She sails as close to the wind as the sails will allow.

DEADLIGHT, a: A metal plate secured inside the port-hole glass in bad weather.

DONKEYS' BREAKFASTS: Mattresses stuffed with straw.

FALL, a: A permament tackle used to hoist or lower lifeboats.

FORE-AND-AFT SAILS:- are those set from gaffs and booms (spars) broadly speaking on the longitudinal plane of the ship, though they can be hauled to to one side or the other.

GASKETS: Lines used to secure furled sails to their spars.

GRIPE, to: When the sail set to the wind is unbalanced and the ship is fighting to come head to wind.

GYBE, to: To change course bringing the wind from one quarter to the other in a fore-and-aft vessel, allowing the booms to pass from one side to the other.

HEAVE TO, to: In this context, to lie, virtually stopped, as comfortably as possible a point or so off the wind and sea.

JIGGER MAST; The fourth mast from forward.

KETCH: A two masted fore-and-aft sailing vessel with the foremast considerably taller than the mizzen.

LUFF, to: when close-hauled, to come too close to the wind so that the sails are shaking.

MAIN DECK:- Principal deck of a ship; generally that inside the bulwarks and from which the foc's'le head and poop rise, where they exist.

PARAVANES: Torpedo-shaped objects equipped with cutters streamed over each bow and connected by wires. Their object is to avoid and cut loose moored mines.

PITCH (of propellor): The distance that one revolution of the propellor would advance the ship if proceeding through a hypothetical solid substance. Clearly, this depends upon the curve of its blades.

POOPED, to be:- When running before the wind, if a following sea breaks clean over the poop (the after part of the ship). Consequences can be serious.

RUNNER:- Wire from a winch leading up and along a derrick, for the handling of cargo, etc.

SCHOONER:- A vessel of two or more masts in which each mast is essentially fore-and-aft (*q.v.*) rigged.

SERVE, to: The splices in the ends of standing rigging were normally 'wormed' with small stuff to make them level: 'parcelled' with burlap and then 'served' with spunyarn or marlin wound round and round the whole, to keep it watertight.

SPANKER:- a fore-and-aft sail set on the after-mast, usually leg-of-mutton shaped.

SQUARE-RIGGED (SQUARE-SAILS):- Sails set on yards which, although they can be 'braced' to different angles, are primarily square to the length of the ship.

STAY, TO: To pass from one tack to the other, head to wind.

TACK, a: The forward lower corner of a sail, or the rope leading from it.

TOPGALLANTSAILS: Set above the topsails (*q.v.*)

TOPSAILS:- Oddly, these are the bottom sails but one in a square-rigger. Normally split into two — upper and lower topsails.

'TWEEN DECK (Between deck):- A deck below the level of the main deck which not only has structural advantages, but enables some cargoes to be distributed to better advantage.

WARP, to: To heave the ship in one direction or another by means of wires or ropes.

WEAR SHIP, to: See footnote, p. 14

WHIPPING: A binding on the end of a rope to prevent it fraying.

YARD:- A spar from which a square-sail is set, moveable but broadly slung square to the line of the ship.

GLOSSARY OF JAPANESE WORDS

(Japanese words are generally spelt phonetically where used. There are varying opinions about the spelling of this language in Roman characters. The meanings are as they applied in the text.)

BANGO: To number off.

BANZAI: Hurrah! (Originally "Live forever".)

BÉKOKU: American

BENJO: The Japanese form of lavatory.

BENTO: A Japanese meal, sometimes in a permament box, sometimes wrapped in a banana leaf, consisting of cooked rice and a small side dish.

BEOKE: Sick, ill.

BODIKI:- Horse drawn vehicle, with no sides and generally with only about three longitudinal beams as a base for stowage. Usually used for carrying barrels and the like.

BUSHIDO:- Code of chivalric honour amongst the Military caste.

DAICON: A large form of radish, often pickled.

DETCHI: Sack truck.

DJOTO: Good.

ÉKOKU: British.

FUNDOSHI: A form of loin cloth consisting of a tape led round the waist. A piece of cloth is attached to the rear and led between the legs and passed over the tape in front, hanging loose.

GETA: Wooden sandals built on two cross pieces of wood which raise them. The big toe is usually separated from the others.

GO: Five.

GOHAN: Four (used with 'nanna' — pronounced 'yon'.).

HACHI: Eight.

HAIKU: A Hundred.

HAIKYU: Ration.

HAITI: Private soldier. (Pronounced 'Hay-ti.)

HARA KIRI: A ritual form of suicide, generally by disembowelling with a sword.

HIBACHI: Charcoal brazier.

HONCHO: Foreman.

HORIO: Prisoner.

ITCHI: One

JIKATAKI: Cloth, high-sided plimsolls, usually with the big toe separate.

JU: Ten.

JUSHIN: Elder statesmen.

KAMIKAZE: Originally meaning 'Divine Wind' to describe the typhoon which destroyed the invading fleet of 3500 Mongol ships in the reign of Kublai Khan, without touching the Japanese defenders, it came to be used of suicide missions.

KAN: A measure of weight.

KEMPETAI: Military Police.

KIRI: Bow, or salute.

KU: Nine.

KURRA: A word of disapprobation that is difficult to define. 'Hey' is too mild!

KYOTSKI: Stand at Attention. (Command)

MESSI: Food.

NAKAI: Inland Sea, the.

NANNA: Seven (with 'gohan').

NANNEKO: A sling-like garment in which Japanese females carry children on their backs.

NE: Two.

NEI: No, not.

OHKA: The word means 'Cherry blossom', but within the context of the text applies to a wooden glider with a pilot over a ton of T.N.T. which was towed into position and then propelled by three rockets on a kamikaze mission. Called by the Americans "Baka" (stupid), it was not a success. Ohkas appeared in 1945.

ROGO: Cigarette

ROKO: Six

SAN: Three.

-SAN (as suffix): Mister.

SAYONARA: Adieu.

SE: Four.

SEN: a) A thousand.
　　　 b) A small coin. 100 sen = 1 yen. 10 sen was rather less than 2.5d — old coinage.

SENSO: War.
SHIMA: Island
SICHI: Seven
SODESKA: So that's it.
TAKSAN: Very.
TATAMI:- Rush sleeping mat.
TENKO: Muster.
WAKARU?: Do you understand?
YAMA: Hill or mountain.
YAMI: Black market.
YASUME: Stand at ease.
YEN: The currency of Japan. At the rate of exchange in 1939, 1 yen approximated to 24d. (i.e. Old and proper coinage before it was debased by decimalisation.)
YON — see Gohan.